2nd Virginia Infantry

4th Edition

Dennis E. Frye

ISBN 0-930919-06-8

ACKNOWLEDGEMENTS

This study would not have been possible without the generous support and interest of several individuals.

Robert K. Krick of Fredericksburg eagerly shared his volumnious collection and his thorough expertise throughout the course of this project. Christopher Calkins of Petersburg National Battlefield translated my scribblings into the first-rate maps which appear in this volume. The esteemed Michael Musick of the National Archives proved once again that he is the Civil War researcher's best friend.

Several of my National Park Service friends deserve special recognition for their kind cooperation and support. Paul R. Lee, II of Harpers Ferry Park generously approved my leave requests and consequently provided me with the opportunity to research and write the manuscript. Harpers Ferry Park librarian Hilda Staubs saved me countless hours by obtaining the Second Virginia's muster rolls through inter-library loan. Woody Harrell and James Burgess of Manassas Battlefield patiently fielded my inquiries and helped me make sense out of the confusion of First Manassas and the hectic movements of Second Bull Run. The hospitality of David and Kathy Lilley made my visits to Fredericksburg comfortable and enjoyable.

Others who provided valuable assistance include Stuart E. Brown, Jr. of Berryville who willingly granted permission to reprint several rare photographs of individuals who served in the Second Virginia; Dr. James I. "Bud" Robertson, Jr. of Virginia Polytechnic Institute and State University, Blacksburg; Larry Allen, Sedalia, Missouri; Ron Sheetz, Harpers Ferry Center of the National Park Service; Jean Elliott of Shepherd College, Shepherdstown, West Virginia; Robert E. L. Krick, Hartwood, Virginia; Frank Silver, Berkeley County Courthouse, Martinsburg, West Virginia; and John E. Divine, Leesburg, Virginia.

Harold E. Howard of Lynchburg and Ben Ritter of Winchester merit a separate paragraph for their magnanimous contributions to this endeavor. Mr. Howard's patience, as well as his trust and confidence in me, made my first effort as an author a most rewarding and enjoyable experience. A thousand thank yous to Ben Ritter! Ben spent hundreds of hours searching through cemeteries, death records, and stacks of newspapers. Ben's countless discoveries are scattered throughout this book. Ben, your gracious assistance during the past year has been greatly appreciated.

Not enough laurels can be extended to my wife Susan. She has weathered microfilm readers, computer breakdowns, pages of proofs, and my selfish interests. Throughout it all, she has remained a close and cheerful supporter. Thank you, my dear, for being my best friend.

To all who contributed so generously to memorialize the Second Virginia, I am grateful.

February 14, 1984   Dennis E. Frye

CHAPTER I

INNOCENT SOLDIERS

"Nothing was serious yet; everything was like a joke."—
Pvt. Henry Kyd Douglas—Company B

Charles Town exploded with excitement. "Fall in!" echoed through the streets. Local militiamen assembled with alacrity. Officers barked harsh orders. The Jefferson Guards snapped to attention. The Botts Greys closed up ranks. Suspense enveloped the column. Anxiety permeated the air.

Spectators gathered along the street. Almost every family in the county had one or more representatives in the ranks. All sensed that this martial display represented no ordinary demonstration. Leather cartridge boxes, usually empty, were packed with live ammunition. Officers inspected weapons with grim resolve. Each springing rammer warned astute onlookers of the upcoming danger. As the column began its mid-afternoon advance, husbands, brothers, sons, and sweethearts exchanged parting glances with the crowd. All realized this was no ostentatious parade to the local barbecue. Such spectacles were reserved for holidays. April 18, 1861 was no holiday.

Couriers had arrived earlier that day with news of startling events transpiring in Richmond. The Old Dominion had determined to cast its fortunes with the fledgling Confederacy. Virginia would secede. A printed proclamation accompanied the secession announcement, urging military volunteers and the people generally to "rise and protect their honor, their property, and their rights, by seizing the national arsenals at Harpers Ferry."

Harpers Ferry. Capture of its valuable weapons and gun-manufacturing equipment was deemed essential by Southern authorities. Only the local militia could seize Harpers Ferry before the United States forwarded reinforcements to that position. The militia must move promptly and boldly. Not all agreed, however, that the militia must move at all.

Some questioned the legality of the venture to Harpers Ferry. Did Virginians have the right to seize a United States installation? Concerned militia officers called upon Colonel James Allen, commander of the force gathered at Charles Town, and expressed their reservations. Captain Lawson Botts, a noted Charles Town lawyer and a "decided and uncompromising opponent of secession doctrines," reminded Colonel Allen that Union sentiment reigned supreme in Charles Town and neighboring communities.

LOWER SHENANDOAH VALLEY:

ORIGIN of the SECOND VIRGINIA INFANTRY

B.&O. R.R.

POTOMAC RIVER

Maryland

Virginia

Hedgesville

Martinsburg

BERKELEY CO.

Shepherdstown

Duffields

FREDERICK CO.

JEFFERSON CO.

Harpers Ferry

PIKE

CREEK

Win. & Pot. R.R.

Charles Town

VALLEY

Winchester

CLARKE CO.

Berryville

OPEQUON

Millwood

SHENANDOAH RIVER

Blue Ridge Mountains

Others bombarded the colonel with similar reminders. Local newspapers had blasted secessionists as demagogues whose "madness ruled the hour." Citizens of Jefferson County had passed resolutions adamantly declaring that their "first and most earnest desire was to preserve and perpetuate the Union." Jefferson's two delegates to the Virginia Secession Convention had both supported the Unionist platform. Would not this attack on Harpers Ferry betray the local Union sentiment? Did it not represent an act of treason?

Such troublesome questions demanded careful deliberation. Colonel Allen corralled his officers, and after exhaustive discussion, Allen made his decision. The advance would continue. The militia would halt, however, at Halltown, a village four miles west of Harpers Ferry. Allen would move his force no further without receiving a direct order from a recognizable state authority. The colonel's compromise satisfied the Unionists, but it dashed all hopes for a rapid capture of Harpers Ferry.

Each passing hour produced a new rumor regarding the situation at Harpers Ferry. One report claimed the armory militia intended to safeguard the government's property. Another account expressed the resolve of the town's people to defend the stars and stripes. The most distressing story reported the arrival of Federal reinforcements. A fight for Harpers Ferry appeared imminent.

Despite the rumors and the anxiety they created, the march from Charles Town to Halltown proved uneventful. As promised, Colonel Allen halted his troops at Halltown and patiently awaited further instructions. During this lull, militia companies began pouring in from other quarters. The Clarke Rifles arrived about sundown after a bruising 17-mile jolt from Berryville in four-horse wagons. Another Clarke County organization, the Nelson Rifles, approached as the sun dipped below North Mountain. Nearly 300 volunteers had now rendezvoused at Halltown. Scouts reported additional support only hours away.

The Berryville boys enviously eyed their counterparts from Millwood during this delay at Halltown. Confidently expecting that they would "soon settle matters and be at home again," the men of the Clarke Rifles suffered greatly from growling stomachs as no provisions had been made for rations to be issued even for one day. In marked contrast, William Nelson had prepared his Millwood company for an extended campaign that included the comforts of home. "We took with us beds and bedding," Nelson recalled years after the war, and "all sorts of provisions and everything necessary for a pleasant encampment of a summer's holiday."

Dreams of a summer's holiday abruptly ended at about 8 p.m. Positive orders to seize Harpers Ferry had just been received and the terse "Fall in!" once again pierced the air. "Porte Crayon," the famed illustrator, witnessed the action: "Spurs jingled, sabres rattled, horses neighed, and the voices of officers were heard in every direction marshal-

3

ing their troops. The men, flattered with the idea of being foremost in the enterprise, sprung to arms and formed their column with alacrity . . . It was an awful opportunity for reflection."

The damp April air chilled the column as it crawled in silence toward its target. Few questioned the advance this time. The men were Virginians first, United States citizens second. Suddenly a resounding "Halt!" broke the stillness two miles from Harpers Ferry. The volunteers were being challenged. What should they do? Fire on a fellow American?

Officers reacted quickly. The command "load at will" was heard for the first time. "That sounded like business," recalled 16 year-old Tom Gold. The next few moments witnessed excitement that at times bordered on hysteria. Fear gripped some. One fellow in the Clarke Rifles dropped from the ranks, deadly sick. Another who had been trailing the column soon replaced him after exchanging his clothing with the frightened soul. Others snarled the loading of their weapons in the intense darkness. Balls went in before powder. Dropped percussion caps littered the ground. Loose bayonets fell off rifle muzzles.

All the excitement and flurry amounted to nothing, however, as the opposing sentries retired without incident. Twice more the advance would be challenged. Twice more the challengers would withdraw. Confidence abounded as the men pressed toward Harpers Ferry in "high spirits, with about as little realization of the consequences of our move as a regiment of children on stick horses."

Upon reaching Bolivar Heights, the advance halted and awaited additional reinforcements. One long mile separated the militia from Harpers Ferry. Then it happened. A sudden flash illuminated the gorge where the two rivers meet. A thunderous roar soon followed, reverberating from mountain to mountain. The flames grew increasingly brighter until "each rock and tree on the Loudon (sic) and Maryland Heights were distinctly visible." Lieutenant Roger Jones and his U.S. regulars had blown up the arsenals. The time was 10 p.m.

Three hours passed before Captain John Rowan and the Jefferson Guards led the volunteer infantry down High Street into Harpers Ferry. The move met no opposition, a situation which suited the militia just fine. William Nelson recalled that "no one felt any regret at the escape of Lieutenant Jones and his men." The flames that had consumed the arsenals had died into ashes. Only charred skeletons remained. Fifteen thousand arms had been destroyed, but not all was lost. Most of the armory buildings had been rescued from the torch by alert townspeople. The valuable weapons-producing machinery remained intact.

Harpers Ferry had been seized, the mission accomplished with no casualties, and the new revolution begun. The national standard was soon lowered from the armory flagstaff. In its place now floated the state flag of Virginia. There was cause for celebration. No one celebrated though. It had been a long, hard day. The men were too tired to contemplate the meaning of their action, too wearied to consider the terrible events which were soon to follow. Clouded minds and sore feet focused only on one thought—sleep.

Officers directed their exhausted soldiers inside the buildings of the armory. Dozens of tired bodies quickly stretched out between the rows of dormant machinery, enjoying at last a respite from the tension of the day. The Clarke Rifles bunked in the Catholic Church, still hungry and short on rations. Drums beating throughout the early-morning hours signaled the arrival of more troops. It was not a peaceful night. For the boys of Shenandoah's lower valley, the war had begun.

—2—

Not since the trauma of John Brown's Raid had Harpers Ferry witnessed such pandemonium.

Disorder and chaos characterized the first days of the military occupation. Individual companies preserved their independent organization and held company meetings as at home. Military arrangements were discussed, votes taken, resolutions passed, and no authority acknowledged "beyond the will of the majority of the company." Militia generals, strutting about in glittering uniforms and seeking the support of their men, offered whiskey to all comers as a display of their goodwill and courtesy. Sober warriors, when they could be found, stretched battle lines across the town's streets as alarm after alarm warned of the approaching enemy. False reports of Yankee invasion via the Baltimore and Ohio Railroad kept the troops in a "pleasant state of excitement." Soldiers stopped and boarded trains passing through, searching the cars to insure that no Yankees were "coming down into the Ferry to deliver themselves up." Few took the war seriously. Most discovered they were enjoying this "heyday of amateur soldiering."

Between false alarms, company meetings, and occasional drills, the volunteers concentrated on adjusting to life in the army. Procuring the conveniences of home ranked as the first order of business. Beds, bunks, and cook stoves soon replaced machinery as armory buildings gradually were converted into comfortable quarters. Black servants shortly arrived to polish boots and to tend to the washing and cooking. The servants' timely appearance relieved many of the men as "no one knew how to make a cake of bread or cook a piece of meat." Even a simple coffee-making demonstration by Bob Whittington of the Clarke Rifles attracted a large and curious audience.

The inconveniences of war were further reduced by visiting mothers and fathers who delivered "every imaginable delicacy" and fine suits of clothes. Each volunteer made himself as comfortable as possible, as if he

5

expected to remain at Harpers Ferry for the war. Those who could not adjust to the hardships of camp life simply returned home. Indeed, "these were the good, easy days."

Thomas Jonathan Jackson abruptly ended this festive worldliness. When Jackson arrived at Harpers Ferry on Monday, April 29, "things presented a most hopeless aspect." The colonel from the Virginia Military Institute quickly remedied the situation. Jackson disposed of the whiskey and deposed the "feather-bed and corn-stalk" militia generals. Companies were organized into regiments "greatly to the indignation" of the company members and with little heed "to the remonstrances of company meetings." William Nelson recalled that "few had a good word to throw at the new man." All quickly discovered, however, that their "notions of war were so completely revolutionized in a short time."

Part of the revolution included the organization of the Virginia troops into one brigade composed of five regiments. The lower valley regiment, officially designated the Second Virginia Volunteer Infantry, was mustered into the Confederate States service May 11-13, 1861, under the command of Colonel James W. Allen of Jefferson County. The regiments consisted of ten companies as follows:

Company	Pre-War Designation	Hometown	County	Captain
A	Jefferson Guards	Charles Town	Jefferson	John W. Rowan
B	Hamtramck Guards	Shepherdstown	Jefferson	Vincent M. Butler
C	Nelson Rifles	Millwood	Clarke	William N. Nelson
D	Berkeley Border Guards	Martinsburg	Berkeley	John Q.A. Nadenbousch
E	Hedgesville Blues	Hedgesville	Berkeley	Raleigh T. Colston
F	Winchester Riflemen	Winchester	Frederick	William L. Clark, Jr.
G	Botts Greys	Charles Town	Jefferson	Lawson Botts
H	Letcher Riflemen	Duffields	Jefferson	James H.L. Hunter
I	Clarke Rifles	Berryville	Clarke	Strother H. Bowen
K	Floyd Guards	Harpers Ferry	Jefferson	George W. Chambers

Colonel James Allen headed a well-educated and highly-disciplined group of commissioned officers, most of whom were superbly versed in the theory and practice of war. The influence of the Virginia Military Institute was most distinctive in the background of the regiment's high command. Colonel Allen and his second in command, Lieutenant Colonel Francis Lackland, were classmates at the Institute, both graduating with distinction in 1849. Major Lawson Botts and Captain Raleigh Colston had attended the Institute, but both had been compelled to return home before graduating due to death and illness in their respective families. Mexican War veterans also had the privilege of rank in the Second Virginia Infantry. Four of Allen's captains—John W. Rowan, Vincent Moore Butler, William N. Nelson, and George W. Chambers—had gained valuable experience in Mexico. Since the John Brown affair had "stirred up the Virginia people and aroused them to the fact that they should prepare for such emergencies," each of Allen's company commanders had drilled regularly and seriously for over a year.

Despite this regular practice of war, the Second Virginia Infantry in May, 1861, certainly represented **no** regiment of soldiers. One month in the army had not transformed farmers into warriors. Secession had not changed laborers into fighters. Marches and drills had not produced combat veterans from craftsmen. Devotion to Virginia and fervor for victory aside, merchants still scrambled to find responsible substitutes to operate their businesses; carpenters still yearned to complete their projects; and teachers still worried about sacrificing their students' education. **Civilians** they were, not soldiers. The Second Infantry was simply a collection of civilians.

Examination of the regiment's Compiled Service Records provides a rare glimpse into the civilian personality of the Second Virginia. It is hardly surprising that farmers and laborers comprise the largest occupational groups in the regiment. Taken together, farmers and laborers constitute more than one-third of the regiment's strength at the June 30, 1861 muster. Twenty-one percent of the Second's manpower—including Colonel Allen and Captains Nelson and Colston—farmed or owned farms in the fertile lower Shenandoah Valley.

A closer examination at the company level discloses additional revelations. Company G's rolls boast the highest number of farmers (33) while Company K's shows the greatest proportion of laborers. It is not surprising to find this large number of laborers in Company K—the Harpers Ferry organization—since the Federal armory at the Ferry employed many laborers on its payroll. Company D of Martinsburg has the most variety in its ranks (26 different occupational titles), but Company G of Charles Town receives the award for having the most **mosts:** most students (16); most clerks (11); most lawyers (6); most teachers (5); most physicians (4); and as previously stated, most farmers (33).

Several occupations listed in the Compiled Service Records capture the eye. Samuel Hudson of Company K enlisted as a "sailor." James L. Towner of Company B signed in as a "postmaster." Company I's Benjamin Thompson identified himself as an "overseer." Company F's William G. Burke joked that he was a "comedian." Addison Munsall of Company C dared to announce that he was a "Yankee school master." Francis Beverly Whiting of Company C declared, in his most distinguished voice, that he, of course, was a "gentleman;" and 16-year-old Philip Shearer, dumbfounded by his role in society, shrugged his shoulders and stated simply that he was a "boy."

Thus when Jackson formally organized the Second Virginia, he brought together ten well-armed, handsomely-uniformed, and sharply-drilled companies of citizen soldiers; but these citizens were not ready for war. Executing drill at the company level represented one skill. Performing maneuvers at the regimental level presented an entirely strange and unfamiliar situation. To be a regiment, Company B could no longer act simply as "Shepherdstown in martial display." To form a regiment, the Clarke Rifles could no longer squat and spring about like "a set of Commanches in a war dance in what was called the 'zove' drill." Pre-war company habits had to melt away. Molding ten distinct companies into one indivisible regiment was a new goal. Transforming civilians into soldiers was another.

Jackson wasted no time breaking the men into their new organization. Tom Gold remembered that his "days and nights were all full of work and unrest" as Jackson drilled his men "most industriously" 12 hours each day. With each passing week in May, the regiment gradually mastered complex manuevers and began jelling into a single unit. Soon only the plethora of colorful pre-war uniforms separated the Second Regiment into distinct parts. The dark blue regular army uniforms of Company A sharply contrasted with the gray and yellow cloth of Shepherdstown's Company B. The white belts and large brass buckles of the Winchester Riflemen alone distinguished Company F's dark green uniforms from the green gentle slopes of Bolivar Heights.

The men practiced and practiced and practiced; but perfection required time, as was evidenced by the following incident. One day in late May 1861, shortly after General Joseph E. Johnston had assumed command of the Harpers Ferry garrison, the Second Virginia passed by the general and his staff. Dr. Hunter McGuire, a Winchester native who had served in the Second for a short time, boldly proclaimed to Johnston: "If these men of the Second Virginia will not fight, you have no troops that will." General Johnston eyed the regiment, and obviously not impressed, snapped back: "I would not give a company of regulars for the whole regiment." Johnston reversed this opinion six weeks later on the field of First Manassas.

Outpost duty and marching added additional burdens to the Second Virginia's incessant drill schedule. During Jackson's first week of command at Harpers Ferry, he detached Companies A and I of the Second, ordering both into Maryland to protect Harpers Ferry from attack from the north. Company I positioned itself near the "schoolhouse on the Hagerstown Road" where old John Brown had stashed his pikes and weapons 18 months earlier. Company A did not fare as well, as it was ordered to ascend the rugged slopes of Maryland Heights. Here the company encamped under the most primitive conditions "without tents or cooking utensils" for over a week. Men had to carry their rations and water up the steep mountain paths and ingeniously cooked their meat on flat rocks and baked their dough by "wrapping it around the ramrods of the guns and holding it over the fires." All sorely missed the bunks and cook stoves in their quarters at the armory.

Jackson recalled his forces from Maryland in mid-May 1861, after Virginia authorities cautioned him that Confederate troops in Maryland might alienate a potential ally. After returning to Harpers Ferry, the reunited Second pounded out a march to Shepherdstown, then another to Williamsport, to guard fords across the Potomac River.

Disagreeable weather marked both of these ventures. On the road to Shepherdstown, the regiment suffered through a severe rain and hail shower that pelted and beat upon the men "as their bleeding faces and torn and soaked uniforms amply proved." Disgusted by Mother Nature's harsh welcome to soldiering, nine of the Second's newest recruits promptly deserted. Most like D. B. Conrad did not complain, however, because "for the first time in our lives, it looked and felt like war." When the Second Virginia arrived across from Williamsport on May 18 with no tents, and nearly 26 miles from comfortable quarters at Harpers Ferry, more bad weather greeted the regiment as the rain "fell pitilessly," making the stay here "quite unpleasant in the woods."

After observing the Williamsport area for more than two weeks without any contact with the enemy, the Second returned to Harpers Ferry and staked out at Camp Jackson on Bolivar Heights. On June 14, 1861, General Johnston evacuated Harpers Ferry, proclaiming the place "untenable." Nearby bridges across the Potomac were to be destroyed. As Johnston's army marched south towards Charles Town, the Second Virginia proceeded 12 miles north to Shepherdstown. Henry Kyd Douglas, a private in the ranks of Company B, the Shepherdstown company, vividly recalled torching the Shepherdstown bridge: "I was with the company that set fire to it, and when, in the glare of the burning timbers, I saw the glowing windows in my house on the hill beyond the river and knew my father was a stockholder in the property I was helping to destroy, I realized that war had begun."

As crackling bridge timbers sizzled and splashed into the Potomac, the Second Virginia faced south and proceeded to Bull Skin Creek, rejoining Johnston's encamped army four miles south of Charles Town. On June 16, 1861, the men bid farewell to Jefferson County and embarked on a two-week adventure with Jackson during which "he marched us back and forth every day, and at least half of every night." The regiment changed camps seven times in 17 days, bouncing from Martinsburg to Winchester and to points between. This incessant pounding so disturbed some prominent men of the lower valley that they complained Jackson was "unfit to command gentlemen and was killing up their sons by hard and useless marching." The men bore the shuffling well, however, and soon "were in perfect trim, and knew each other well and felt like soldiers."

Indeed, the men did know each other well. Two months of marching, drilling, and campfire chats had transformed a collection of strangers into a family of friends. Members of this new family—the Second Virginia Infantry—had discovered through countless conversations that George

Washington dominated the ranks as the regiment's most popular name. America's first hero shared his name with 44 of the muster rolls's surnames. Some had even learned that Company G's George Washington had been born in 1842 on the former president's 110th birthday. In addition to the Washington name, the regiment proudly claimed Lieutenant Richard Henry Lee of Company G. Word had spread that Lee was the grandson of the mover of the Declaration of Independence. The regiment's fraternity-like spirit also affected relative unknowns like Benjamin Boyd and John Yates Beall. No one realized, of course, that Boyd later would become famous as the father of Confederate spy Belle Boyd and that Beall would be hanged in 1865 after being sentenced by Federal authorities as a guerilla and spy.

Two months of war had revealed several anomalies in the regiment. The 6′3″ frame of Company I's William Hannum towered above all others in the Second Virginia. On the other hand, all others dwarfed the five-foot stature of Company E's James Blamer, the regiment's shortest member. Although 72.6% of the soldiers in the Second Infantry ranged between 18 and 30 years of age, Albert Moore and George Rutter proved notable exceptions. Moore, a boyish 15 year-old in Company A, enlisted as the regiment's youngest recruit. Company C's Rutter occupied the opposite end of the age scale, and at 53, he represented the regiment's most senior member.

The men knew each other well indeed. They knew also, after two months of false alarms, that the sounding of the long roll was nothing to be concerned about; but on July 2, 1861, the war suddenly "meant something more than drilling and dress parades." Union Major General Robert Patterson had ventured across the Potomac near Falling Waters. Jackson immediately advanced, noted Henry Kyd Douglas, "to get some practice." After halting at Hainesville to load weapons and to remove extra baggage, the Second Regiment formed in line of battle on Jackson's right to protect against a Federal flank attack. As the enemy approached, D. B. Conrad and his friends marveled in silence: "There, for the first time, we saw the long line of blue, with the United States flag in the center."

Although the Second Virginia saw no action and "can hardly be said to have smelt powder," the skirmish at Falling Waters proved memorable; for the first time the men had "heard the whiz of a musket ball and the shriek of a cannon shot." Tom Gold of Company I summarized succinctly the opinions of most regarding the Falling Waters affair: "The experience was helpful to all; it gave us some idea of what we should have to do, and braced our nerves for that which would surely come to pass."

Although the Second suffered no casualties at Falling Waters, Federal capture of the regiment's prized and cherished tents produced a harsh blow to the men's morale. The loss was severe for this reason—shortly after the eruption of the war, several of the lower valley counties had appropriated money to provide provisions for their troops. Folks on the homefront soon busied themselves manufacturing tents, knapsacks, wagons, and overcoats. The tents had arrived just prior to Patterson's demonstration into Virginia. When the long roll sounded announcing the approach of the invaders, the recently staked-down tents were "carefully taken down, rolled up neatly, and left to be captured." "Oh, how mad we were, when we heard them cheering in exulation over their capture!" steamed David Humphreys of Company G. "Many curses loud and deep we uttered at the failure of our general to have our belongings put out of harm's way." Humphreys and the rest of the Second soon learned, however, that General Jackson considered "a gum cloth, a blanket, a tooth-brush and forty rounds of cartridges as the full equipment for a gentleman soldier."

Following the episode at Falling Waters, the regiment retired to Darkesville, encamping there for four days before returning to Winchester on July 11. At Winchester the men made "wonderful preparations for battle," tearing down fences north of the town and awaiting eagerly the approach of General Patterson. The Second Virginia witnessed no action, though, except the squashing of a mutiny in General Johnston's army. No Yankees emerged on the horizon. No battle appeared imminent.

Scrambling officers and galloping horses signaled important news on the afternoon of July 18. The announcement stunned the ranks. Federal troops had attacked Confederate forces at Manassas Junction! The Southern defenders needed help! General Johnston's army must hurry and save the nation!

"Every man sprang to his place," bragged D. B. Conrad with patriotic ardor—every man, that is, but the ten who deserted the Second when the call to arms was sounded. Nothing explained why these men left the army at this juncture, but careful examination of the regiment's muster rolls reveals that the mass exodus embarrassed Company E the most. Eight of the ten guilty skedaddlers—including Lieutenants Aaron Myers and Cromwell Myers—deserted from Raleigh Colston's command.

Company E's ordeal proved the exception, however, as most in the Second responded with cheers to the urgent Southern appeal. Moments after "On to Manassas" resounded through the camps, a column was heading eastward for the Blue Ridge and Ashby's Gap. The Second Virginia "footed it fast and furious" on familiar roads through Frederick and Clarke Counties, but its fervent pace soon cooled when the regiment met the chilly and swift waters of the Shenandoah River at Berry's Ferry. As the men contemplated the chest-high current, the Thirty-third Virginia Infantry came up and splashed right into the water. "We were put to shame," sulked Tom Gold as he and his comrades stripped off trousers and began crossing the churning waters with muskets, clothing and ammunition held aloft. Only the men of Company C escaped the dip into the

Shenandoah, as Mr. Otway McCormick arrived with his own horses to ferry his Clarke County neighbors across the river. Wet bodies quickly dried as the column snaked its way up and over the Blue Ridge, reaching Paris and finally Piedmont on the night of the 18th.

Freight and cattle cars arrived at Piedmont at sunrise the next morning. In accordance with orders, the men of the Second Infantry ungraciously packed themselves into the empty cars "like so many pins and needles." Grumbling that such unflattering carriers represented no way to transport gentlemen, several enterprising eyes in Company G spied a coach a little superior to the others. The Botts Greys commandeered the car, and the Charles Town boys soon seated themselves snugly within. Shortly thereafter, Sandy Pendleton, then on General Johnston's staff, approached Company G's car. George Baylor recorded the scene: "[Pendleton] entered and ordered us to vacate, saying that was the officer's coach. The boys, saying they were as good as the officers, refused to vacate, and after some idle threats Pendleton disappeared, and the coach was retained."

On the morning of July 19, the cars began jolting toward Manassas Junction. As the engine belched smoke and the cars creaked along, the excitement was interrupted occasionally by ponderous thoughts — thoughts that crowded minds as men stared at each other in silence. Would my friend Isaac Glaize finally clash with the Yankees? Would my neighbor John Fryatt taste victory? My brother, Holmes Conrad — would he survive the fight? Would my cousin Peyton Harrison see his family and home again?. . . The answers lay ahead.

—3—

An ugly sight greeted the Second Virginia Infantry upon its arrival near Mitchell's Ford on Bull Run on the evening of July 19. Trees lopped and mangled by shot and perforated by minie balls gave evidence that the regiment's new post on the Confederate right was the scene of the action the previous day. Dark craters blasted into the short dry grass spotted the landscape. A line of fresh graves under the broken pine forest foreshadowed the days ahead. Such strong warnings dampened no one's enthusiasm, however, as all anxiously awaited their day with the Yankees.

The opportunity to "settle matters and return home" arrived on July 21, 1861. Jackson aroused his men before dawn that Sunday morning, first positioning them at Blackburn's Ford, then jockeying and hustling them four miles west to assist the hard-pressed Confederate left. At about 11:30 a.m., Jackson's brigade arrived on the summit behind the Widow Henry's House and deployed in line of battle. Colonel Allen was instructed to post his regiment on the left of the brigade in a position southeast of the Henry House and slightly in front of a pine thicket. The

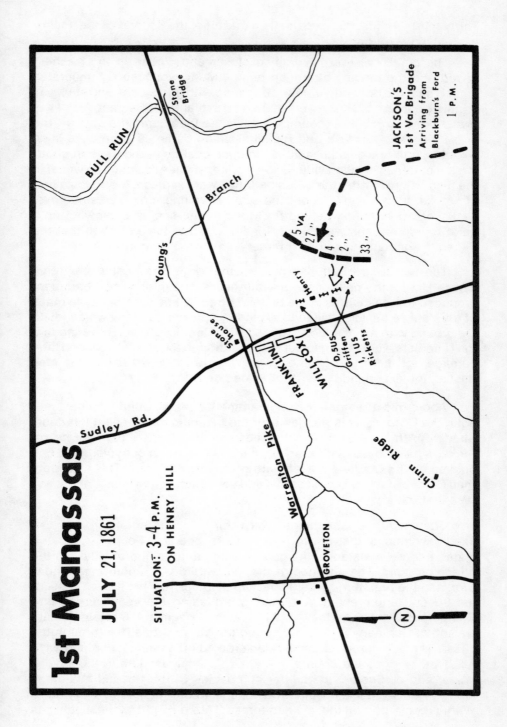

1st Manassas

JULY 21, 1861

SITUATION: 3-4 P.M. ON HENRY HILL

BULL RUN

Stone Bridge

JACKSON'S 1st Va. Brigade Arriving from Blackburn's Ford 1 P.M.

Branch

5 Va.
27 "
4 "
2 "
33 "

Young's

Henry

D, 5US Griffen
I, 1US Ricketts

Stone house

FRANKLIN

WILLCOX

Sudley Rd.

Warrenton Pike

Chinn Ridge

GROVETON

N

13

Thirty-third Virginia arranged itself on the left of the Second as the anchor of Jackson's left flank.

The crack of musketry inched closer and closer as the morning ended and the steamy afternoon began. Many wounded Confederates limped past the Second Virginia, struggling with gun stocks and sticks as primitive supports. Others were carried off in blankets, bleeding their lives away. None gave very encouraging news. As the injured dragged by, the brass pieces of Griffin's and Ricketts' Union batteries soon were seen wheeling into line on a hill across the open pasture to the west. Supporting the batteries on each side were long lines of blue "as thick as wheat in the field." Shortly after the Union batteries were in place, there was a puff of smoke; then a shell "about the size of a dinner pot" screamed over Jackson's men, falling behind the Confederate line and "plowing up a great trench and throwing a cart load of dirt into the air." With that the Federals announced their next target—Jackson's Brigade.

The two Union batteries blasted the Virginians posted on Henry House Hill for the next one-and-a-half hours. The intense bombardment produced few casualties in the Second Virginia, however, because many of the Yankee missiles failed to explode. "I picked up many which fell to the ground with a dull sound," mused D. B. Conrad, after discovering that the Unionists were failing to cut fuses. Although the shelling caused little damage, for the men of the Second Virginia crouched low in the pine thicket, the experience was "terribly demoralizing."

About mid-afternoon the bombardment ceased. During the next half hour, the Confederates puzzled over the meaning of the silent interlude. Suddenly "the roar of the field pieces sounded louder" than yet heard. Ricketts had moved his battery onto the hill Jackson occupied, and had opened on the Confederate left with grape and canister. "This was more than Colonel Jackson could stand, and the general order was 'Charge and take that battery.'"

Colonel Alfred Cummings' Thirty-third Virginia sprang to its feet, fixed bayonets, and swept toward Ricketts' position. Following a determined Federal resistance, the gallant Thirty-third temporarily seized the offending guns. The advance of the Thirty-third was unprotected, however, and the regiment soon fell back in disorder, leaving the left flank of the Second unprotected. A withering enfilading fire soon poured into Companies C and G on the left of the Second Regiment. Captain William Nelson of Company C dropped during the storm with a ball through the chest. At this juncture, Colonel Allen ordered his three left companies to fall back, reform, and counter the enemy's flank assault. In the smoke, noise, and confusion, the center companies of the Second misunderstood Allen's order as a directive for the whole regiment to fall back. Within moments, "all the line had turned." More confusion ensued when

Colonel Allen was blinded temporarily by a falling pine limb cut off by a shell.

Command devolved on Lieutenant Colonel Francis Lackland, who, seeing that his left had been turned, rallied the Second's right, and with but 100 men, joined the charge of the Fourth Virginia, now advancing to secure the Confederate left and drive Ricketts' battery off the field. Again the Federals abandoned their pieces, and again the Confederates endeavored to bring their captured prizes to the rear. While attempting to draw off a rifled cannon, Lackland's detachment was shredded by a Union counterattack from the right. The drive to and withdrawal from the Federal guns proved costly for the Second Virginia as it suffered its heaviest casualties of the day, nine dead and 34 wounded, during this portion of the fight.

Although exhausted and partially disorganized, the Second Virginia stood firmly with the newly proclaimed "Stonewall" Jackson until victory was won. The regiment had helped Jackson earn his immortal fame, but standing like a stonewall had proved costly:*

Company	A	B	C	D	E	F	G	H	I	K	Total
KIA	—	—	3	4	1	5	—	1	—	1	15
MWIA	2	—	2	—	—	—	3	1	—	—	8
WDED	4	—	10	10	2	8	7	7	4	1	53
POW	—	—	—	—	—	—	—	—	—	—	0
TOTAL	6	0	15	14	3	13	10	9	4	2	76

The Second Virginia's muster rolls disclose that First Manassas produced two records: greatest number killed during a battle (15) and greatest number wounded (53). Records seldom were established in a regiment's first fight, but four more bloody years would never erase the carnage suffered by the Second Infantry on July 21, 1861.

First Manassas. First fire. First blood. First death. Men not yet acclimated to war's horrors never forgot the human wreckage that littered Henry House Hill. When the sun set over the blood-stained fields of Bull

---

*The above table is based on the Compiled Service Records of the Second Virginia Infantry. Abbreviations used for this illustration and throughout this text include: **KIA,** Killed in Action; **MWIA,** Mortally Wounded in Action; **WDED,** Wounded in Action; **POW,** Prisoner of War; and **MIA,** Missing in Action.

The above casualty totals differ substantially from the 90 casualties reported in the **Official Records** (18 killed and 72 wounded). Unless otherwise noted, casualty figures in this text are from the regiment's Compiled Service Records.

Run on the evening of the 21st, some of the survivors in the Second remembered their thoughts on the train to Manassas Junction. Memories only now, for friend Isaac Glaize was dead; neighbor John Fryatt killed; brothers Holmes and Tucker Conrad embraced lifeless on the field; and cousin Peyton Harrison?—they carried cousin Peyton to the morgue so that he could travel home in a coffin. For them, the war had ended. For the others in the Second Virginia, the battle against death had just begun.

—4—

The Second Virginia bivouacked near the battlefield before moving with the brigade on August 2 to Camp Harman, one mile east of Centerville. During the next three months, the men settled into the "tedious and monotonous" routine of camp existence. Only an occasional picket assignment disrupted the daily schedule of morning, afternoon, and evening drill. "There was no better drill officer in the army than our Colonel Allen," bragged an admiring Tom Gold of Company I. In almost the same breath, Gold moaned that for two hours each afternoon Allen practiced his men "until every one was almost worn out."

Worn out or not, Allen deemed the drilling particularly essential to the Second Virginia due to unexpected gaps in his officer corps. Three of Allen's company commanders—Captains Rowan, Nelson, and Clarke—had been wounded at First Manassas, and none had the prospect of an early return to the field. Company I's Captain Strother Bowen resigned his commission, finding that his advanced age made the service "very hard on him."

A severe blow to Colonel Allen and the regiment was the loss of Lieutenant Colonel Francis Lackland. Lackland admitted himself to the brigade hospital at Fairfax Court House in late August, complaining about chest pains and a severe cough. Several days later, on September 4, Lackland died, a victim of heart disease and pneumonia.

With the death of Colonel Lackland, Major Botts advanced to the rank of Lieutenant Colonel and Frank B. Jones, an 1848 graduate of V.M.I. and a classmate of Colonel Allen, was appointed major.

Vacant company commander's positions were not filled as rapidly, however. With the exception of the election of Samuel J. C. Moore as Captain of Company I in November, none of the vacancies were occupied until the regiment's reorganization in April, 1862. For eight months Colonel Allen had to content himself with junior-grade officers in command positions. Fortunately for the Second Virginia, it was a relatively quiet eight months.

The regiment packed up and moved with the brigade in mid-September, transferring its base from Centerville to within one mile of Fairfax Court House. While stationed here, the regiment engaged in three separate picket actions. For eight days near Falls Church, the men eyed the Yankees from a distance. For five days at Braddock Ford on Accotink Creek, the regiment carefully observed Federal positions. The final patrol came along the Little River Turnpike near Germantown. The regiment returned to Centerville on October 16, remaining there for three weeks. On November 8, the men boarded the cars at Manassas Junction with "great joy and delight." The regiment was returning home. All awaited new adventures with Jackson in the Shenandoah Valley.

CHAPTER II

HOME IN THE VALLEY

A cold drenching rain greeted the regiment when the cars crawled into Strasburg on November 9. The mud march that followed north to Winchester dampened few spirits, however, as warm thoughts of family and friends and comfortable quarters preoccupied the minds of all.

As the brigade approached Winchester, pleasant dreams crashed into reality when orders from Jackson notified the men that Winchester was off limits to the returning veterans. Camp would be set up on the outskirts of town, and the militia had strict orders not to allow the regulars to pass into the city.

The indiginity of it! How dare the general banish "the young volunteers to this rural retreat and hard-tack diet, while the old seedy militia had comfortable quarters in the city and feasted on the best in the market." Determined to rebel against this "unjust and arbitrary restriction," Jackson's men connived ingenious schemes to outwit the militia sentries and gain entry into Winchester. When Lieutenant Henry Kyd Douglas tramped into the official campground as the last officer of his regiment, Douglas humorously observed that the Second Virginia had shrunk to one-fifth its normal size. Douglas' friends were "on the road to Winchester."

Thoughout November and December, company officers at Camp Stephenson, five miles north of Winchester, dealt with a steady stream of men who plotted entries into Winchester. When Company G's Captain Moore asked George Flagg and George Baylor why they had been absent without leave for a week when they had been granted permission to attend church in Winchester for only a day, Flagg responded: "Yes, but when we got there we found it was a protracted meeting and lasted all week." The captain, put in good humor, allowed all to escape without punishment.

In mid-December, General Jackson reckoned punishment was necessary for the Chesapeake and Ohio Canal, a major transporter of coal and other supplies to Washington, D.C. One attempt to breach Dam Number 5 on the Potomac had failed earlier in the month due to unexpected Federal resistance. On the night of December 17, with the entire Stonewall Brigade in support, men again commenced work designed to break the dam. The Second Virginia's Raleigh Colston — captain of Company E and a native well acquainted with the dam's structure — volunteered to take charge of the effort. For the next four-and-a-half nights,

18

Colston and his working parties labored through icy waters and annoying Federal artillery and infantry fire. Finally on December 22, after effecting a slight breach in the dam's firmly-constructed masonry, the Second Virginia returned with the brigade to Camp Stephenson where the men enjoyed a subdued and peaceful Christmas.

New Year's Day dawned "fair, bright, mild, and beautiful," a perfect begining to an otherwise miserable and ill-timed expedition to Bath and Romney. Wretched winter weather dominated the movements of this campaign in northwestern Virginia, a campaign that reminded some of Napoleon's retreat from Moscow and convinced others that "General Jackson was crazy" indeed.

For 25 days the men of the Second Virginia and the rest of Jackson's forces battled snow, rain, sleet, and slush in a venture that pitted weather against man. Only an occasional comfort or laugh disrupted the misery of the march. A blazing fire in the banquet hall of the resort hotel at Bath shielded the regiment from the cold one January evening. A timely delivery of overcoats, compliments of the gracious citizens of Clarke County, warmed the soldiers of Companies C and I during a brief pause at Unger's Store. Five inches of snow burying men asleep in a field near Hancock provided some comic relief when Company B's Bill Wintermeyer jumped to his feet, describing the scene with an amazed "Great Jehosophat! The Resurrection!" Nothing brought more cheers, however, than the announcement that the expedition was ending and the columns returning to Winchester. "The shout that went up . . . when we learned this," recalled Company G's George Baylor, "evinced as much heart as lungs, for we were heartily weary of this midwinter tramp without any spoils and with much hardship and discomfort."

The Second Virginia returned to Winchester with the brigade on January 25, 1862, and began preparing winter quarters northeast of town "near the Old Smithfield house." For the remainder of the winter, the men in the regiment "managed to exist most miserably" in quarters composed of tents and chimneys. The penetrating damp chill of Camp Zollicoffer at Winchester in 1862 always reminded the men in later years of the necessity of constructing log and stone huts as winter quarters.

The winter passed quietly as many of the men obtained furloughs to visit their families in the valley. Only the military execution of a cavalryman named Miller from Jefferson County proved eventful. Company I of the Second, detailed to guard the execution, escorted the prisoner and his coffin to a field just south of town. At the command of fire from the lips of provost marshal Lawson Botts, 12 guns flashed and the victim fell dead. "An awful sight," recalled young Tom Gold, "but men became hardened to things of that kind."

"Well-hardened" already described most of the veterans of the Second Virginia. Nearly a year had passed since the "easy and innocent"

19

days of Harpers Ferry in 1861. As the winter melted into spring, most in the regiment quickly agreed that there was nothing romantic about war anymore. Hundreds of miles of marching had blistered their feet. Hundreds of hours of drilling had dulled their enthusiasm. Unhealthy camps and uncontrolled diseases had made them sick. The scarcity of visits to home had made them lonely. Friends had been killed. Others were mangled. Captain George Chambers' home in Harpers Ferry had been looted and burned by Federal raiding parties. Captain John Nadenbousch's extensive mill holdings in Berkeley County had been torched. How much longer would the hardships and misery continue?

No one knew the answer, but all agreed that the war would continue beyond the originial 12 months' enlistment. As the first term of service neared expiration, most in the Second Virginia agreed to re-enlist for three years or the war; but for George Baylor and others, a year for the cause in the infantry was quite enough. About the first of March, Baylor and friends succeeded in obtaining transfers to the cavalry. "On horseback, I felt like a new man," Baylor proclaimed, "and I contemplated the war from a much more favorable standpoint." Others followed Baylor's example, and before the transfers ended, nearly an entire company of cavalry was organized from the ranks of the Second Virginia.

Such a mass exodus punched a hole in the regiment's strength, but before the Second had the opportunity to fill the gaps, the army moved south. Jackson was stirring; a long, arduous spring lie ahead.

—2—

On March 9, 1862, Federal columns under General Nathaniel P. Banks started for Winchester. Two days later Jackson hesitantly moved his forces south, halting finally at Mt. Jackson, 42 miles from Winchester. Major General James Shields shadowed Jackson's march up the Valley, but advanced no further than Strasburg with his own Union division. On the 21st of March, the scouting Turner Ashby reported that the Yankees had evacuated Strasburg. Jackson became concerned. The Federals could not be allowed to leave the Valley. An outnumbered Joe Johnston might be crushed if the bluecoats combined forces east of the Blue Ridge. A chase was necessary. The Federals must not escape without a fight.

Confederate soldiers began racing north at dawn on March 22. With the Stonewall Brigade setting the pace, the men covered 25 miles before encamping for the night at Cedar Creek. Sore legs and tight muscles withstood another pounding on the next day, as Jackson's men tramped another 14 miles before arriving south of Kernstown about 2 p.m. on Sunday the 23rd. Orders were given to bivouac, but heavy gun fire to the north warned Jackson's weary warriors that a fight was close at hand.

Only two-thirds of the Second Virginia stacked arms at Kernstown. Captain John Nadenbousch and Companies D, I and H were campaigning with Turner Ashby in support of his horse artillery. In fact, it was Nadenbousch and friends who were engaged in the ruckus on the Valley Turnpike just north of Jackson's main body. Early on the morning of the 23rd, Nadenbousch and the detached force he commanded had been ordered forward by Ashby to protect Captain R. Preston Chew's three guns from Federal skirmishers posted north of Kernstown. Nadenbousch deployed his detachment and advanced into a woods where the enemy's skirmishers were concealed. After a short volley, the Federals fled in disarray, but heavy columns of blue soon arrived, and Ashby directed the outnumbered Nadenbousch to fall back along the pike and await further developments.

Heavy musketry firing signaled Ashby and Nadenbousch that developments were already under way in the hills to their west and on Jackson's left. Jackson had decided to fight on Sunday the 23rd after learning that the Federal force near Kernstown did not exceed four regiments. Consequently, the Stonewall Brigade had been ordered to turn the enemy's right; to the surprise of all, however, a stiff Federal resistance blocked its path.

Jackson had been misinformed. More than a mere rearguard faced the Valley army. Shields's entire division was on hand, and Jackson's 3,000 suddenly found themselves outnumbered two to one. "One of the most stubborn fights of the war" was in store for the men of the Second Virginia. It would not be a pleasant Sunday afternoon.

Shrieking shells plowed into the regiment as it marched with the brigade across an open field toward a wooded height on the Confederate left. Despite the missiles, the veterans pressed forward, arriving in the woods and then continuing to still another wooded area. At this point the regiment spied a stonewall—a stonewall in possession of the enemy. "My object was to get possession of it," declared a determined Colonel Allen. A hailstorm of lead plastered the Second Virginia as it dodged through the undergrowth. Blinding flashes of flame and smoke pointed the way to the wall as volley after volley of Union musketry peppered the regiment on its advance.

The fury of the battle cut down color-sergeant E. B. Crist as he led the charge forward. Lieutenant John B. Davis of Company K clutched the blood-stained banner, but he too was struck by a ball, and again the colors dropped. Company G's Richard Henry Lee was the next to catch the fallen flag, but he also fell, dangerously wounded in the thigh. Four additional brave standard bearers from the Second fell before Colonel Allen sprang from his horse, grabbed the tattered flag himself, and "gallantly charged at the head of his regiment." Before the day ended, the flag of the Second

21

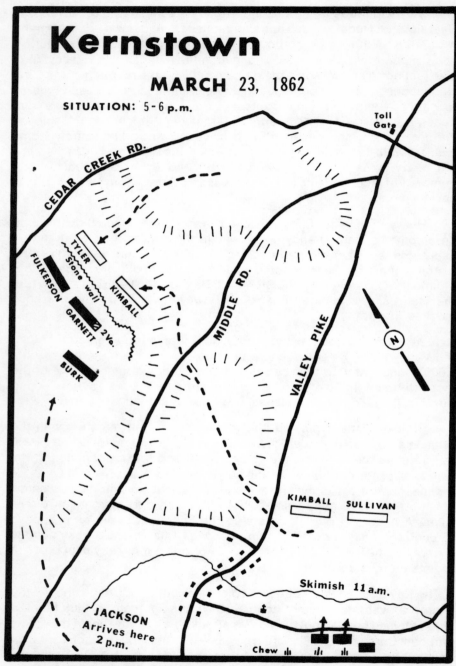

Kernstown

MARCH 23, 1862

SITUATION: 5-6 p.m.

Toll Gate

CEDAR CREEK RD.

TYLER
Stone wall

FULKERSON

KIMBALL

GARNETT   2Va.

BURK

MIDDLE RD.

VALLEY PIKE

N

KIMBALL   SULLIVAN

Skimish 11 a.m.

JACKSON
Arrives here
2 p.m.

Chew

"Nadenbousch detached in A.M. with companies D, H, I. Everything shown in the right corner represents the skirmish on the morning of the 23rd. Nadenbousch was in the 2nd Va.

22

Virginia had proved itself a primary Yankee target. Fourteen bullet holes had shredded the colors and the flagstaff had been shot in two.

Unfortunately for the regiment, so much bloodshed had produced negligible results. Only the right of the regiment had reached the stonewall, and then only temporarily. Shield's right flank remained firm. Mercifully, as dusk neared about 6 p.m., after an hour of futile combat, the regiment received an order to retire.

Losses at Kernstown were severe. No other regiment in the Stonewall Brigade suffered battle tolls as high as the Second Virginia's according to casualty reports filed in the **Official Records.** In one afternoon, the regiment had lost the equivalent of one company of infantry: six men dead, 33 wounded, and a shocking 51 missing. The Kernstown casualties (90 total), as published in the **Official Records,** represented the greatest losses incurred by the Second Virginia Infantry in any single-day action until the regiment's entrapment in the "Bloody Angle" at Spotsylvania on May 12, 1864.

Careful examination of the regiment's Compiled Service Records, however, reveals glaring discrepancies between the numbers reported in the **Official Records** and the figures shown below from the regiment's muster rolls:

Company	A	B	C	D	E	F	G	H	I	K	Total
KIA	1	1	—	—	—	—	—	—	1	—	3
MWIA	—	1	—	—	—	1	—	—	—	—	2
WDED	—	—	1	1	1	—	1	2	2	—	8
POW	8	8	1	3	4	2	1	—	3	4	34
TOTAL	9	10	2	4	5	3	2	2	6	4	47

No explanation exists to account for the differences in casualties reported. Perhaps those tallied in the wounded and prisoner columns in the **Official Records** statement — compiled shortly after the battle — actually included soldiers who later rejoined their regiment unscathed. On the other hand, the lower numbers disclosed by the Compiled Service Records might be the result of incomplete and inadequate reporting on the Second's muster rolls. Whatever the reason for the discrepancies, casualties at Kernstown in the regiment's Compiled Service Records are half the losses noted in the **Official Records.**

Agreement did exist in one area, however. Although the numbers differed, POW's represented the greatest loss in both records. Most of these prisoners had been captured by the Federals during the withdrawal and the ensuing confusion in the early-evening darkness. Most prisoners were shipped to Fort Delaware and there detained until exchanged in August, 1862. Even with the prisoners' release, the tragedy at Kernstown never faded from the memories of the men in the Second Virginia Infantry.

—3—

Silent and sullen survivors retreated south from Kernstown during the night of March 23. Up the Valley the withdrawal continued until Jackson reached Rude's Hill, a strategic point between Mt. Jackson and New Market. Here the army encamped until the third week of April. The lull allowed Jackson the opportunity to replenish his dwindling ranks and to reorganize his forces.

Officers in the Second Virginia welcomed the break. Companies depleted by transfers and the Kernstown disaster needed time to rebuild their strengths. Consequently, while the men were quartered at Rude's Hill, the regiment's company commanders conducted a full-scale recruiting campaign in March and April of 1862; but these enlistment drives in the lower and central valley produced only partial success. Muster roll records revealed that Company G signed 17 volunteers on April 8 and Company E 20 on the following day. Such mediocre results were not nearly enough to fill the gaps in the Second's empty formations. Something more was needed than appeals to man's patriotism.

Help arrived in the form of the Conscription Act passed by the Confederate Congress on April 16, 1862. By the terms of this law, all white males between the ages of 18 and 35 were subject to the draft unless they volunteered instead to join an extant unit of their choice. The law's limited options spurred a renewed interest in voluntarism. Many potential "conscripts" from Augusta and Shenandoah Counties hurridly signed with the Second Virginia Infantry. Company H mustered 21 "interested" prospects when it traveled south to New Market. Company I ventured north to Mt. Jackson and discovered 28 souls "waiting" to fight for their country. The largest enlistment center, however, was near the regiment's base at Rude's Hill. On April 16 alone, the day the Conscript Act took effect, 91 volunteers joined the Second Infantry. Company F grabbed the largest proportion of these Rude's Hill recruits, enrolling 56 of the 91 newcomers on its previously depleted rolls.

Others who did not display a similar patriotic enthusiasm were gathered up and drafted into the weakest companies. Company K was most conspicuous as the conscription company, adding 40 draftees to its ranks in two days. These new recruits shared no affinity for forced soldiering, however; and as a disgusted Tom Gold recalled, several of the draftees fled "on the night after they were mustered in and were never seen again."

Despite some desertion, the regiment greatly bolstered its strength while at Rude's Hill with the addition of 274 fresh bodies (208 through enlistment, 66 by draft). Many new faces had entered the Second, but several of the older, wrinkled veterans discovered that now was their opportunity to leave. One provision in the Conscription Act allowed all those over 35 to be honorably discharged from the service; and although exact numbers are not attainable (due to incomplete records), many of those eligible by the law's definition quit the war during the spring and summer of 1862.

The Conscription Act also instructed the men to elect their officers, but this provision produced no drastic changes in the officer corps of the Second Virginia. The much respected Colonel Allen — whose voice when drilling "could be heard for half a mile" — readily received a vote of confidence from his men. Lieutenant Colonel Botts and Major Frank Jones also received a nod of approval. In addition to confirming staff officers, the elections filled a major void when lieutenants, who had been serving as company commanders since shortly after First Manassas, were officially elected captains on April 20, 1862. The only captain axed by the elections was the aging Vincent Moore Butler of Company B.

With his regiments at full strength and his men rejuvenated, Jackson embarked on the Valley Campaign that would make him and his army "immortal in military history." During the last weeks of April and through the middle of May 1862, the Second Virginia marched and countermarched with Jackson's forces. Up and down, over and across the Shenandoah Valley the men treked, often without knowledge of where they were going or why they were plodding back and forth across the countryside. Despite all this movement, the regiment tasted no combat until Jackson drove toward Winchester on May 24.

Federal defenders at Winchester had been whipped the previous day, and Old Jack intended to complete the rout with a quick strike at Winchester. The Stonewall Brigade led the advance as Confederate forces pushed northward on the night of May 24. Broken and overturned wagons littered the Valley Pike as the Rebels marched north, evidence of a hurried and confused Union flight down the Valley. Federal ambuscades in the darkness north of Newtown slowed Jackson's pursuit and produced "continual skirmishing with an invisible enemy" throughout the night of the 24th and the early-morning of the 25th. Skirmishers from the Second Virginia helped brush aside the resistance, however; and as dawn broke on May 25, Jackson's forces had reached the outskirts of Winchester.

Nathaniel Banks did not intend to abandon Winchester without a fight. The mustachioed Union general had prepared his defense by posting Federal infantry along the crest of a commanding ridge southwest of town. Jackson accepted Banks's challenge and wasted no time in ordering the Stonewall Brigade "to seize that height as speedily as possible."

The Second Virginia, formed in line of battle in the center of the brigade, dashed toward the targeted hill. The Union defenders quickly scattered. Upon reaching the crest, however, the advance abruptly halted. Enemy cannoneers on an opposite ridge only 400 yards distant tugged their lanyards. The murderous close-range artillery fire sent the Stonewall Brigade scurrying for shelter behind the crest of the hill it had recently occupied. The screeching, hissing music of the well-aimed projectiles played a deadly tune for the men of the Second Virginia for nearly two hours. Two men were ripped to pieces when two shells fell and exploded exactly amidst crouching Companies H and I.

Assistance finally arrived when the brigade of General Richard Taylor showed up on the Confederate left. Taylor and the Stonewall Brigade linked forces and charged forward rapidly at the tenacious Federals. As the advance gained speed, the Second Virginia spotted the enemy preparing to defend a stonewall directly in front of Taylor's brigade. In an effort to remove this potential menace, Colonel Allen directed the Second Virginia to fire into the left flank of the Union defenders. Allen's ploy proved successful in driving the Yankees "off at a run" and helped to break the enemy's last line of resistance. With their defenses broken, Union soldiers retreated "in the greatest disorder" through Winchester. The Second Virginia followed closely, pursuing the fleeing bluecoats down Main Street. The regiment left behind three dead and 13 wounded, victims of the battle fought southwest of town.

Hearty cheers greeted the victorious Confederates as they passed through Winchester. Citizens who for more than two months had been suffering under the "hateful surveillance and rigors of military depotism" received Jackson's liberators with "the most enthusiastic demonstrations of joy." Only for a moment, though, did the Second Virginia and the Stonewall Brigade enjoy the merry voices and bright faces of Winchester's grateful populace. Only for a moment did friends and relatives catch a glimpse of their soldier heroes. Only for a moment did Company F return home.

Jackson insisted on a complete rout, and the chase continued five miles north of Winchester before the "fatiguing marches and almost sleepless nights" of the campaign exhausted the victors' endurance.

Banks had been whipped, but the ever-demanding Jackson wanted more. Consequently, on the morning of May 28 Old Jack ordered the Stonewall Brigade to march from Winchester to Charles Town in what Jackson termed "a demonstration toward the Potomac." On the afternoon of the 28th, the Stonewall Brigade reached Charles Town, but the Second Virginia Infantry was not with it. The regiment had remained at Winchester on provost duty. This arrangement proved only temporary, however. On the 29th, the Second rejoined the brigade, and as the main body moved east toward Harpers Ferry to demonstrate against Federal positions on Bolivar Heights, the lower-valley regiment spent the day scaling precipitous and rugged Loudoun Heights. Throughout the 30th of May, the Second Virginia remained perched atop Loudoun Heights, the men enjoying a splendid mountain-top view of Harpers Ferry. On occasion, the Second would interrupt its sight-seeing to pop off an annoying but mostly harmless volley at the Union garrison lying far below.

A messenger bearing troubling news shattered this tranquil and relaxing mountain environment. The courier reported that Federal columns under Shields and Fremont were concentrating a heavy force in Jackson's rear. Obviously the Federals determined to cut the Confederate avenue of retreat up the Valley and figured to entrap Jackson at Winchester. Only the most rapid march south would thwart the enemy's scheme. The race for Strasburg was on.

As the message was delivered to the lonely men on Loudoun Heights, Jackson started up the Valley Pike from Winchester. The general did not wait for the Stonewall Brigade to return from its venture to Harpers Ferry. The veterans of his former command would have to fend for themselves in this adventure. With no time to lose and every hour valuable, the Stonewall Brigade focused all its strength and energy on rendezvousing with Jackson at Strasburg.

As the brigade hurried south from Charles Town, the Second Virginia struggled to catch up. A pounding rain hindered the regiment's progress as it slipped furiously down Loudoun Heights. Crossing the Shenandoah River proved another obstacle. The raging waters at Key's Ferry made a safe crossing impossible. Tom Munford's Second Virginia Cavalry provided the solution to this problem the men of the Second Infantry clung desperately to its horses' tails as they forded the Shenandoah.

Following its difficult start, the regiment rejoined its brigade south of Charles Town and joined in the race for Strasburg. Mile after long mile passed. Fears of a Yankee prison kept the warriors moving at top-speed. Even after thousands upon thousands of dragging steps, weary minds and weak bodies responded to the constant barking of "Press forward! Press forward!"

Finally it ended. About 10 p.m. on the night of May 31, the Stonewall Brigade was ordered to bivouac at Newtown. Ten miles still separated the tired Confederates from Jackson's main force at Strasburg; but the limits of physical endurance had been reached, and a rest was necessary. Exhausted soldiers welcomed the break and fell asleep immediately, despite the relentless rain.

This march rated as a major highlight in the history recorded by the Second Virginia Infantry. Through a drenching rainfall and over slippery, mud-caked roads, the Second had tramped 36 miles in 14 hours! Even more amazingly, after enduring without rations for the two days before the march, the men had traveled this distance on empty stomachs. Chaplain Abner C. Hopkins of the Second summarized this extraordinary episode when he later wrote: "I venture to say there is no military march on record, for distance and unfavorable conditions, equal to that march of Saturday of the Second Regiment of Virginia infantry!"

The regiment deserved Hopkins' praise, but the arduous march had exacted its toll. The May 31 marathon, as revealed in the Second's Compiled Service Records, proved too much for some. The records showed that Federal scouts nabbed at least 18 of the stragglers. The aching muscles of 12 others in the regiment convinced them the war was too painful and they deserted. Despite these findings, the Second's gallop from Loudoun Heights had fairly won for the men the sobriquet of "Jackson's foot cavalry."

The Stonewall Brigade rejoined Jackson about noon on June 1. Forced marches by the Confederates and ineffectual Federal generalship foiled the Union plan to trap Jackson at Winchester. Stonewall had escaped one threat, but another quickly materialized as the separate Federal armies cautiously followed Jackson up the Valley to Harrisonburg. Jackson's new problem was this: if Fremont driving east and Shields moving west were allowed to unite, the combined Federal strength would nearly double Jackson's own numbers. Action had to be taken before the Northerners linked forces.

With this in mind, Jackson marched his legions east from Harrisonburg on June 7. On the following day, Old Jack implemented his strategy of dealing with one Federal opponent at a time. In an engagement at Cross Keys on June 8, General Richard Ewell's division stopped Fremont's columns in their drive from the west. Not a shot was fired by the Second Virginia in the Cross Keys fight, for the regiment was then stationed four miles southeast of that battlefield, comfortably encamped on the grassy knolls north of the village of Port Republic.

June 8 was not a peaceful, late-spring Sunday for the Second, however. About mid-morning, an urgent summons reached Colonel Allen. Federal cavalry had dashed unexpectedly into Port Republic. A crucial bridge had been seized. Jackson's rear was threatened, the ordnance and quartermaster's trains endangered. Could the Second Virginia help to check the enemy's advance?

Allen sounded the alarm. Men sprang from their grassy mattresses, grabbed their weapons, and fell into marching order. Within five minutes of the initial summons, the regiment was en route. When the regiment topped the hill overlooking the disputed bridge (across the North River), the men witnessed a spendid scene. Standing between the enemy horsemen and the Confederate wagon trains was Captain S. J. C. Moore and part of Company I of the Second. Moore's detachment, which had been placed on detached duty guarding the trains, was conducting a stubborn defense that had prevented capture of the prized wagons. The timely arrival of Confederate infantry and artillery provided Moore with the assistance he needed to beat back the invaders. A few well-placed shells and volleys hurled back Shields's advance, and the fight ended with the wagons safe and the bridge secured. Jackson spent the night of the 8th planning the next day's strategy.

The long roll sounded at 3:45 a.m. on June 9. Yawning men in the Stonewall Brigade strapped on their accoutrements and began marching into Port Republic. With the Second Virginia in the lead, the brigade crossed at dawn a temporary bridge spanning the South River, and then proceeded down the river road to "measure strength with Shields's unwhipped army and to settle the account left open since Kernstown."

After an advance of one and one-half miles, contact was made with the enemy's pickets. Companies D and I of the Second were hurled forward as skirmishers, and after a brief encounter the march continued. Moments later, a tornado of shells sliced through the Confederate advance. After a brief consultation, it was determined that the Second and Fourth Virginia regiments should flank the Federal left and silence the Yankee guns that commanded the crucial road upon which the Confederates were advancing.

Colonel Allen embarked on his mission with 177 men in his regiment, guiding them and their cohorts of the Fourth Virginia to within 100 yards of the troublesome battery after clawing his way through a forest tangled with thick undergrowth and laurel thickets. Unfortunately for Allen, standing in support of the six Federal guns were three regiments of blue-clad infantry.

Recognizing its predicament, Allen's force squatted in silence. The enemy battery had to be eliminated, but an attack on the Federals without help would be suicide. Consequently, Allen promptly called for reinforcements and then issued orders to the companies on the left of his regiment (and nearest the guns) to take "deliberate aim and fire at the gunners." Two chance shots from the Fourth Virginia revealed the Confederate flank effort, however, and the surprised Federals countered angrily with volley after volley of canister in such quick succession that Allen's forces were thrown "into confusion."

Outnumbered and outgunned, Allen's detachment crouched nervously in the woods and waited for help to arrive. It was a long wait. Finally in the late afternoon, General Richard Taylor and his Louisiana brigade arrived on the Confederate right, the position Allen had been tenuously holding. After three bloody assaults, Taylor's men silenced the Federal guns and successfully turned the Union left flank. The Second Virginia gratefully fell in behind the Louisianians and helped drive the Yankees from the field. One man was dead in the regiment, and 25 others wounded, but—another victory! Kernstown was avenged!

Jackson's Valley Campaign was over. After resting near Brown's Gap and Weyer's Cave for a week, Stonewall turned his warriors east. The army was on its way to Richmond.

CHAPTER III
HOT DAYS AND HOT FIGHTS

Clouds of dust blanketed Jauman's and Rockfish Gaps as Jackson's Confederates ascended the western slopes of the Blue Ridge on the morning of June 17, 1862. Reports of impending doom at Richmond hastened the pace of the determined veterans racing to rescue the Southern capital from the pinching claws of George B. McClellan and the Army of the Potomac. The urgency of the situation pushed the men forward with cheerful resolve. "We are in fine health and spirits," assured Captain Raleigh Colston of Company E in a letter to his mother, "and trust we shall get down in time to turn the tide of battle."

For eight days, Jackson's forces pressed eastward. By the evening of June 25, Jackson had reached Ashland, just 12 miles north of Richmond. The next day, General Robert E. Lee's Army of Northern Virginia pounced on McClellan's right flank at Mechanicsville. With the opening of the Seven Days Campaign on the 26th, Jackson pushed closer to the action. At Hundley's Corner on the night of the 26th, Jackson's warriors bivouacked in silence. The campfires of that evening would prove memorable to the men of the Second Virginia; it represented the last moments the regiment would share with its colonel—James Allen.

At about 5 a.m. on June 27, Jackson's men began a "slow and tedious" march south and east toward Gaines's Mill and Cold Harbor. General Lee's plan called for the envelopment of the Federal right, but Major General Fitz John Porter and his Union Fifth Corps intended to make Lee's task difficult, if not impossible.

Porter, defender of the Union right at Mechanicsville the previous day, had withdrawn his forces six miles east of the battlefield of the 26th and had positioned the Fifth Corps in a semicircle on a commanding ridge east of Powhite Creek. Marshy swamps, tangled undergrowth, and deep ravines gave additional protection to Porter's front. Despite these natural barriers and Porter's fine defensive position, Lee determined to assault the Federal lines. Consequently, the Battle of Gaines's Mill erupted at 2 p.m. on the afternoon of June 27 with A. P. Hill's division hammering hard at Porter's left and center.

Artillery thundered in the distance as Jackson pushed his forces toward the McGehee House, the anchor of Porter's right. Securing the ground about McGehee's became a crucial Confederate objective; if it could be seized by the Southerners, Porter's right would be broken and the right wing of the Army of the Potomac severely endangered. The Federal position on McGehee's Hill had to be taken.

The Stonewall Brigade rested in reserve in an open field near Old Cold Harbor as Confederates under Jackson, Ewell, and D. H. Hill massed assault after assault against the Union defenders on the Federal right. Porter's forces stubbornly maintained their position, repulsing each successive thrust with a heavy shower of iron and lead from well-placed artillery and infantry. Finally at about 5 p.m., after an hour of unsuccessful Confederate attacks, the Stonewall Brigade was called into action.

First came a directive that detached the Second and Fifth Virginia regiments and ordered them to the support of Purcell's Battery. While in this position, Captain James Burgess of Company F fell with a severe, but not mortal, wound. As 5:30 p.m. approached, the Second and Fifth rejoined the brigade, forming on its left, and moved forward toward the main focus of attention—McGehee's Hill. A swamp and thick undergrowth of laurel disorganized the lines, but the brigade reformed when it reached an open field at the base of McGehee's Hill. Then began the deadly assault up the hill.

The excitement of the attack pushed the Second and Fifth Virginia forward rapidly, so rapidly in fact that the two regiments became detached from the brigade. Enemy batteries and their supports zeroed in on the exposed targets, "thinning their ranks at every step." When the Second Virginia topped the hill near McGehee's House, the regiment's strength numbered a mere 80; and the carnage was not yet complete. While rallying the regiment for a final charge, the thunderous voice of Colonel Allen was silenced most suddenly. A Yankee bullet had pierced Allen's brain, killing the 32-year-old officer instantly. Moments later, a canister round blew away a knee of the regiment's third in command, Major Frank Jones. The ghastly wound would prove fatal. Company E's Raleigh Colston fell when a ball struck him in the thigh. Unlike his fellow officers, however, Colston would survive to command and fight another day. Only the timely arrival of darkness ended the slaughter on McGehee's Hill.

The Confederates had achieved partial success. Porter's right flank had been driven, but not broken. The determined assault of the Stonewall Brigade had pushed the Union defenders 300 yards beyond their original position at McGehee's, but the lines of blue remained intact. During the night, however, Porter withdrew his fighters south. The action near Gaines's Mill had ended.

The Second Virginia remained near McGehee's Hill for the next two days. As Lieutenant Colonel Lawson Botts—the regiment's only surviving field officer—surveyed the human wreckage of the 27th, the men grimly removed their dead and wounded comrades, and assisted also with the more pleasant detail of repairing Grapevine Bridge for the passage of

Jackson's army. Duing the night of June 29, the regiment moved with Jackson's columns across the Chickahominy River and then proceeded past Savage Station and into bivouac near White Oak Swamp at noon on the 30th. The pursuit of McClellan continued on the 1st of July when Jackson advanced first to Frazier's Farm and then pushed onward toward Malvern Hill.

George McClellan had transformed the peaceful slopes of Malvern Hill into an impressive defensive position. Over 250 guns lined the crest of the ridge, their charged tubes staring ominously north at the approaching Confederates. The position was an artilleryman's paradise. Before the Union gunners stretched 300 yards of open field which descended gradually into the swamps and woods of the drainage called Western Run. Supporting the Union cannoneers was that old nemesis Porter and the Third Corps of General Samuel Heintzelman.

Although warned about the strength of McClellan's position, Lee determined to attack. The Confederate leader figured a successful blow here would certainly drive McClellan off the Peninsula and possibly even destroy the Army of the Potomac. With the hope of victory in the air, the initial Rebel drives at Malvern Hill began during the mid-afternoon of July 1. At first Lee tested the Union left, but efforts there were repulsed with heavy losses. Additional assaults occurred when D. H. Hill's division began testing the Federal center about 6:30 p.m.

Hill's advances proved suicidal, and his calls for help triggered into action Jackson's old division and the Stonewall Brigade. Throughout much of the 1st, the Stonewall Brigade had been held in reserve near the Willis Methodist Church, approximately one and one-half miles to the rear of the main battlefield. Even though the heavy fire of Union artillery was "all the while heard in the front," the brigade saw no action until 6:30 p.m., when instructions were received to advance south along the Willis Church Road and to support D. H. Hill's efforts against the Federal center.

Execution of this order to advance produced one of the most futile exercises experienced by the Second Virginia during the entire war. The thick swamp undergrowth, omnipresent on the Peninsula, so entangled the movements of the Second and Fifth regiments that by the time the lead company of the Second had found the Willis Church Road, a frustrated Colonel Botts reported the rest of the Stonewall Brigade "nowhere in sight." Darkness added to the confusion, and the congested Willis Church Road—clogged with retreating infantry and artillery—produced additional disarray.

Determined to find the brigade, Botts and Colonel Baylor of the Fifth Virginia pushed their men forward. The two regiments never succeeded in locating the Stonewall Brigade on July 1, but the lost columns unhappily discovered the Yankee artillery on Malvern Hill. When Botts and Baylor emerged into the open field facing Malvern Hill in the darkness of the 1st,

Federal gunners spied the unsuspecting targets, and within moments an intense bombardment hurled at the Second and Fifth regiments forced the adventurers to seek shelter in a deep ravine 150 yards to the right of the Willis Church Road. With the men relatively safe from the Union missiles, Botts rode out of the ravine and conducted a reconnaissance. No Confederates seen. No Confederates heard. Botts and Baylor, after a brief consultation, determined it prudent to fall back and search for the brigade. Shortly after 6 a.m. on July 2, the orphaned regiments rejoined their brigade, which was then bivouacked some two miles from the front.

Malvern Hill revealed itself to Confederate scouts on the morning of July 2 as a "bare plateau stripped of its terrible batteries." McClellan had withdrawn again, this time to Harrison's Landing, the Army of Potomac's new base of supplies and the Union commander's new stronghold. As McClellan began digging his fortress on the north bank of the James, Lee's army paused and celebrated its successful relief of Richmond. The Second Virginia shared in the rejoicing, but it also mourned. The recent bloodbaths had produced 29 casualties: six men dead, 21 wounded (four mortally), and two veterans missing. Most widely noticed, of course, was the loss of Colonel Allen and Major Jones.

As Lee's Army paused to catch its breath, Daniel Sheetz of the Second Virginia's Company K reflected upon the events of the past week: "I must tell you that we have had a hard time since we were over at Richmond," Sheetz wrote to his family. "I have seen more [hard fighting] than I ever expected to see or ever care about seeing again . . . I am getting tired of soldiering."

Tired soldiers do not end wars, however. A dangerous storm brewed to the north. Another Union army under Major General John Pope began operations in north-central Virginia. Again the Confederacy was threatened. Again Jackson would strike like lightening. Again Daniel Sheetz and his compeers would have to wait for peace.

—2—

John Pope's mission in Virginia sounded simple enough. Strategists in Washington instructed Pope, in part, to demonstrate against Confederate communication and supply lines at Gordonsville and Charlottesville. A Federal move against these key areas, the planners reasoned, would compel Lee to counter these Union threats by removing troops from Richmond. With Lee's army divided, McClellan would have the numerical superiority he demanded to make his operations on the Peninsula successful.

With McClellan squatting comfortably at Harrison's Landing, however, Lee determined to neutralize the Federal scheme. To dispute the advance of Pope's army, Lee ordered Jackson and his two divisions from Richmond to Gordonsville. Stonewall began his northwesterly march on July 14, and five days later he arrived in Gordonsville. Jackson remained at Gordonsville for the next three weeks, carefully observing Pope and awaiting additional reinforcements. Finally on August 7, Jackson's legions splashed across the Rapidan at Barnett's Ford and began moving north toward Culpeper.

Jackson's object was to strike Pope before Pope united his scattered forces. Combined, the three Unions corps that comprised Pope's Army of Virginia swelled to more than 50,000—twice Jackson's strength at Gordonsville; but Pope's command was still separated in early August, and when intelligence sources informed Jackson that Banks's corps of 8,000 was all alone near Culpeper, Jackson determined to crush Banks while the odds were in his favor.

At 3 p.m. on August 9, Jackson and Banks tangled about eight miles south of Culpeper in the vicinity of Slaughter's Mountain. The Stonewall Brigade witnessed little action until late afternoon. At approximately 5 p.m., the brigade received orders to deploy in line of battle at the skirt of a woods. Facing the men as they looked north was a large field, beyond which extended a dense growth of pines and cedars.

As the brigade moved forward, with the Fourth and Second Virginia regiments posted on its left, James M. Hendricks of Company H recalled: "A blue line came out of the timber, rolled over the stake-and-rider fence at the edge of the cornfield, and came on." Guns clicked up and down the line, but no one fired until only 400 yards separated the Confederates from G. H. Gordon's Union brigade. At 400 yards, the Stonewall Brigade pulled its triggers and followed with a spirited charge. After a brief resistance, Gordon's right flank was turned and his men pressed toward the center of the Union line.

The Second Virginia followed the enemy into the pine forest, but when a strong Federal counterattack threatened the right of its brigade, the Second ended its pursuit and came to the support of the Stonewall Brigade's right flank. Additional Confederate reinforcements from A. P. Hill's division stalled the Federal offensive, and with the arrival of darkness, the infantry fighting soon ended.

Jackson remained on the battlefield throughout the 10th. After becoming convinced that Banks had been heavily reinforced, Jackson withdrew south to Orange Court House on August 11, and again diligently eyed Pope's movements in preparation for another strike.

Another blow at Pope was imperative. The Unionists had adopted another strategy, and their new plan threatened to create a formidable monster the Confederates could not easily conquer. The latest Federal policy began with the withdrawal of McClellan from the Peninsula and the return of the Army of the Potomac to Washington. McClellan's forces would then reinforce Pope, swelling Pope's ranks to 130,000.

Lee realized he had to attack Pope before this marriage of Union armies transpired. Accordingly, Marse Robert adopted a bold plan—a plan designed to pass the Confederates around the right flank and to the rear of General Pope's army. Successful execution of Lee's strategy would sever Pope's railroad communication with Washington; but even more importantly, a move on Pope's rear would wedge Lee's command between Pope's army and the Federal capital.

As the Confederate high command plotted its way around Pope, the ranks sensed something was astir. First indications of the upcoming venture occurred on the evening of August 24 when the army received orders to cook three days' rations. The order was accompanied by a message that alerted the men to be "ready to move at anytime." The Second Virginia's James M. Hendricks remembered those final hours before the march: "We baked our slapjacks, and this finished our preparation, for at this time we never cooked our bacon, but ate it raw."

Sixty rounds of ammunition were issued to the troops during the early-morning hours of August 25. Marching orders soon followed: "No straggling; every man must keep his place in ranks; in crossing streams, officers are to see that no delay is occasioned by removing shoes or clothing." As Jackson's veterans left the line of the Rappahannock at dawn on the 25th, each felt that "something extraordinary was contemplated."

"I do not believe that there was a man in the corps that knew our destination except Jackson," mused James Hendricks as the columns marched north. "It looked like madness to march away from our supplies and support," Hendricks continued, "but we had learned to obey and to blindly follow."

Follow they did. Mile after mile, Jackson's warriors pounded, along roads and through fields and woods. Kyd Douglas, now on Jackson's staff, watched admiringly as the column "moved on after its silent leader and asked no questions." Finally, after 26 difficult miles, Jackson reached the hamlet of Salem. Stonewall rested his troops here for the night, and "the men slept on the spot where they halted."

Dawn of August 26 arrived too early for men suffering from blistered feet, aching knees, and hungry stomachs; but despite physical infirmities, the march continued, this time east toward Thoroughfare Gap and Manassas Junction. The rays of the hot August sun mercilessly pelted the column as it marched another grueling 26 miles. Shortly after sunset, Jackson neared Bristoe Station on the Orange and Alexandria Railroad. As the Confederates approached Bristoe, the Second Virginia was placed in advance of the army. After crossing a small stream near the station, the Second encountered a large force of Union cavalry; but after a brief skirmish, the Federals fled. Bristoe Station belonged to Stonewall.

Pleased with his effort, a delighted Jackson informed Lee on the evening of the 26th that his command "was now in the rear of General Pope's Army."

The gamble had succeeded. Pope's flank had been turned, his communications sliced, and his rear endangered—all accomplished by a 54-mile foot race in less than 40 hours. Kyd Douglas marveled at the endurance of Jackson's "mortal men" and proclaimed boldly that "never in the history of warfare had an army shown more devotion to duty and the wishes of one man, than the followers of Jackson exhibited during these days."

Jackson rewarded the gargantuan effort of his soldiers when he seized Pope's supply depot at Manassas Junction and ordered that the captured booty be distributed to the troops. August 27 was a day of feasting for the Second Virginia and most of the rest of Jackson's campaigners. The sights and smells of bacon, cornbeef, salt pork, flour, coffee, and sutlers' stores quickly revived senses numbed by the previous days' march. "We never had rations issued to us so liberally," James Hendricks rejoiced as he helped carry boxes of crackers and bacon to each company of the Second Virginia. Company I's Tom Gold hardly constrained his excitement: "What a time was that," declared Gold, when "half starved and worn out, we suddenly found ourselves turned loose among car loads of everything good to eat and drink and smoke." Kyd Douglas summarized the exhiliration of the day when he wrote that "as a Commissary, Pope was even superior to Banks."

The unbridled celebration soon ended, however. Pope, well aware of the Confederate threat to his hindquarters, started withdrawing his scattered forces northward. Jackson responded quickly, first by torching all remaining Federal supplies at Manassas Junction and then by manuevering his 20,000 men northward also.

After a day of "moving here and there, fronting first one way and then the other," Old Jack finally settled his veterans on commanding ground at the base of Sudley Mountain. Jackson rested in this new position—just north of the Warrenton Turnpike and three-quarters of a mile west of Groveton—and waited patiently for the arrival of Longstreet and the remainder of Lee's army.

Stonewall's halt during the late afternoon of August 28 provided welcome relief to the Second Virginia Infantry. Lawson Botts's men needed rest. The foot campaign of the past three days had depleted the regiment's ranks as effectively as a hard-fought battle. Company I's Tom Gold sadly lamented that "the hard march, the lack of rations and the lack of shoes caused many of the Company and of the army to straggle." Gold counted only 23 present in his company on the afternoon of the 28th. In Company H, only 14 sounded off with "here!"

Company D's Albert Saville loudly announced his presence, however, and with good cause. Saville had been in the army only 16 days, and the endurance he had displayed on the march from Gordonsville to Groveton had earned him the respect of many dubious veterans; but some still challenged Saville's promotion to veteran status. Indeed, the new kid had performed well on the march; but how would he react in battle?

Saville's "place" in the regiment posed an interesting question, but nobody wished for battle on the evening of August 28 to settle the debate. The men desired rest, not a fight. Company E's Francis Pike, in fact, particularly cherished his opportunity to recover. Pike just recently had gained his freedom from the Federal prison at Fort Delaware following five months in captivity after his capture at Kernstown. Pike and 69 other veterans of the Second Infantry, as well as many other Confederates, had been released at Aiken's Landing on August 5 in a mass exchange of prisoners. Although weakened by captivity, Pike and most of his newly freed companions had returned to the regiment in time to participate in Jackson's flank march. The excitement of the campaign had carried Pike to Groveton, but his energy reserves had run dry and Jackson's timely halt near Groveton provided him with a chance to recuperate.

As Private Pike was attempting to regain his strength, "To arms!" resounded urgently through Jackson's resting army. Stonewall had spied a Federal column approaching along the Warrenton Turnpike and promptly had determined to attack it. At about 4 p.m., Old Jack directed his forces to advance through a woods until they reached a commanding position near Brawner's house. The Stonewall Brigade subsequently formed near Jackson's right, facing an open field and peering silently south toward the Turnpike.

Deployed and coiled to strike, Jackson waited — waited for the most opportune moment to pounce on the unsuspecting Federals. A long hour passed. The Second Virginia stood patiently on the left of its brigade, but some of its men found the wait unsettling. William Light of Company D probably nervously rubbed his hand along the scar on his face and neck; Company C's John Weir doubtless glanced at the gash in his left arm. Both men remembered their struggle on Henry House Hill, barely two miles east of their present position. Both had been wounded at First Manassas; and both now wondered, as the upcoming battle approached, if additional war souvenirs would be added to their bodies.

Thoughts of battle turned into reality about 5 p.m. when Jackson advanced his men into the open field. Seconds later the Confederates were firing toward the Warrenton Turnpike and shredding the exposed flank of Rufus King's division. Stonewall's initial sting stunned the surprised Federals, but the men in blue quickly recovered and responded to the Rebel attackers with "a most terrific and deadly fire." For the next four hours, the two opponents squared off in the open field and engaged in a stand-up, knock-'em-down fight that Jackson described as "fierce and sanguinary."

The hot action near the Brawner farm stirred the blood of the Second Virginia's Tom Gold: "On we go, a long line of gray, firing as we advance. From somewhere in front the bullets come thick and fast, the smoke hanging low. We see nothing. At last we reach a fence. We halt — all seem to be falling — the rain of bullets is like hail."

The opposing lines sometimes closed to within 100 yards; but neither side yielded; neither side quit. The Wisconsin and Indiana boys of John Gibbon maintained an "obstinate resistance" in their first fight and Abner Doubleday's Pennsylvanians surrendered no ground to the veteran Virginians of the Stonewall Brigade.

Not until 9 p.m. on the evening of the 28th did the slaughter at Brawner's mercifully end. The Federals finally withdrew; but as Kyd Douglas noted, the Yankees had "punished us severely."

Indeed, the four-hour bloodbath had produced devastating Confederate losses. James Hendricks of the Second Virginia wrote years after the war that the Stonewall Brigade particularly had suffered at Brawner's farm and "ever afterwards was weak in numbers." The Second Virginia's Compiled Service Records support Hendricks' assertion, revealing that in this regiment alone, the August 28 duel had produced at least 39 casaulties (eight killed, 31 wounded — seven mortally).

The wounded included Francis Pike and John Weir. Former POW Pike gasped for air on the blood-stained field, the victim of a bullet through a lung. Another Union missile had downed Weir; and despite two more days of late-August fighting, Weir would become the only man in the regiment to be wounded at both First and Second Manassas. William Light escaped this battle unscathed, but Albert Saville — Albert Saville was dead; the "veteran" of 16 days finally had earned the respect of all his comrades.

The Brawner farm shootout not only had decimated the ranks of the Second Virginia, but it also had wrecked the regiment's officer corps. Colonel Lawson Botts had received a ghastly wound. A speeding minie had knocked him off his horse during the peak of the struggle, the deadly ball having penetrated the colonel's cheek and then exited behind his ear. The feeble Botts survived this initial injury, but died on September 16 from secondary hemorrhage.

The regiment's company commanders had fared better than its commander, but a groin wound had sidelined Company D's Nadenbousch and Moore of Company I needed time to nurse his wounded thigh. The resignation of Company B's Captain Lee Moler (on August 15, 1862) and John Rowan's self-removal (due to the painful recurrence of a foot injury received at First Manassas) had weakened further the regiment's com-

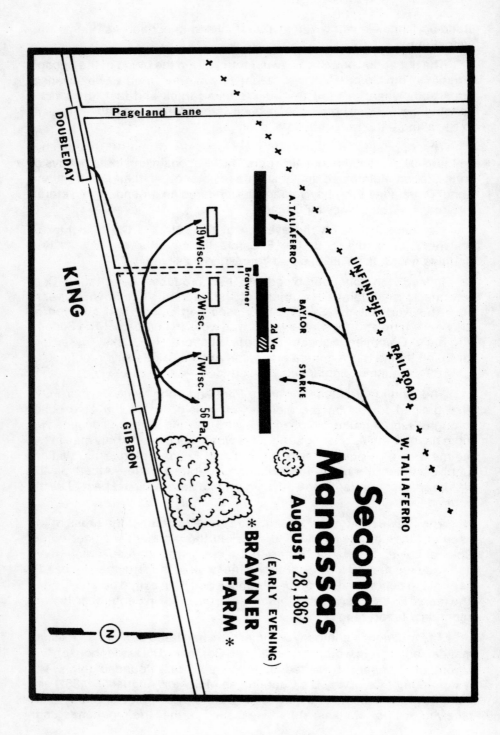

Second Manassas
August 28, 1862
(EARLY EVENING)

BRAWNER FARM

KING

DOUBLEDAY

Pageland Lane

A. TALIAFERRO

19 Wisc.

Brawner

2 Wisc.

BAYLOR

2d Va.

7 Wisc.

STARKE

56 Pa.

GIBBON

UNFINISHED RAILROAD

W. TALIAFERRO

N

mand structure. Thus on the morning of August 29, 1862, the Second Virginia had no field officers and lacked four of its company commanders.

There was no time to fret over losses, however, and no time to fill vacancies. The Second Manassas fight was not over, and as the Second Infantry prepared for action on the 29th, Raleigh Colston controlled the helm of a regiment whose numbers had dwindled to fewer than 100.

Kyd Douglas described August 29 as a "fearfully long day"; but for the Second Virginia—in position on the Confederate right—the second day of Second Manassas proved relatively uneventful. Most of the hard fighting of the 29th focused on the Confederate left. With the exception of intermediate shellings and occasional brushes with Federal skirmishers, the Confederate right witnessed little action.

The Unionists offered no similar reprieve to Jackson's right on the next day. At about 4 p.m. on the 30th, the long blue lines of Fitz-John Porter's Fifth Corps filled the horizon and began approaching Jackson's forces. The Second Virginia, anchoring the right flank of the Stonewall Brigade, watched the Federals advance from a woods parallel with and 200 yards from the cut of an unfinished railroad. As the Union infantry inched forward, Raleigh Colston received orders "to get the regiment into the railroad cut." "The conflict from the woods to the railroad was terrible," Colston reported later, "and it was at this time that casualties in the Second were the greatest."

Wave after wave of Union attackers swept toward the Confederate defenders, but none succeeded in breaching the Rebel position. Porter's thrusts finally ceased after Longstreet crashed into Pope's left flank, forcing the Federal commander to retreat from the field and to withdraw his defeated army to Centerville.

The three-day fight at Second Manassas had crippled severely the Second Virginia Infantry. Casualties had stripped the regiment to a skeleton unit:

Company	A	B	C	D	E	F	G	H	I	K	Total
KIA	4	1	—	1	1	—	—	—	3	3	13
MWIA	1	2	1	5	2	—	3	2	2	1	19
WDED	7	7	5	5	7	1	7	3	4	3	49
POW	—	—	—	—	—	—	—	—	—	—	—
TOTAL	12	10	6	11	10	1	10	5	9	7	81

Casaulties at Second Manassas

Casualties incurred by the regiment at Second Manassas tripled the losses it later received at Gettysburg, the only equivalent three-day battle in which the Second Virginia participated. Only the "Bloody Angle" of Spotsylvania produced more losses in the regiment (100). Most appalling, however, was this statistic: of the estimated 130 men available for duty on August 28, 82 soldiers or 67 percent of the regiment's strength dropped on the field at Manassas in only 48 hours! No other battle produced such a staggering proportion of losses in the regiment.

Despite these damages, the Second Virginia had no time to recuperate. Robert E. Lee had his eyes glued on Maryland. When the Army of Northern Virginia began wading the Potomac on September 5, the 40 or more survivors in the Second Virginia splashed along also, joining their comrades in a resounding chorus of "Maryland, My Maryland." The first major invasion of the North was underway.

CHAPTER IV
MENDING THE HOLES

The Maryland campaign of 1862 is known best for two major events. The first is the Confederate siege and capture of Harpers Ferry; the second the Battle of Antietam. In neither of these actions did the Second Virginia participate. In fact, the regiment's excursion into Maryland lasted but six days.

After crossing the Potomac on September 5, the regiment marched with the brigade to Frederick, encamping on the 7th two miles north of Frederick along the Emmitsburg Road. Several days of inactivity followed; but on the 10th, Stonewall's men broke camp and proceeded west across South Mountain via Turner's Gap and the National Pike. After an evening of rest near Boonsboro, Jackson's forces traveled even further west, recrossing the Potomac on September 11 at Williamsport and then advancing toward Martinsburg on the 12th. The following day, Old Jack's command zeroed in on Harpers Ferry, arriving just opposite Bolivar Heights during the late morning of September 13.

Harpers Ferry was the reason for this circuitous cross-country gallop through Maryland and Virginia. Garrisoned in the lower valley towns of Harpers Ferry and Martinsburg were 14,000 Federals who posed a potential threat to Confederate communication and supply lines into Maryland. In a bold plan outlined in Special Order 191, Lee had plotted to remove the Yankee menace from the Valley, first by herding the Federals into a trap at Harpers Ferry and then by encircling the town with Confederates. Although behind schedule a few days, Lee's scheme worked brilliantly, culminating with the surrender of the Harpers Ferry garrison on September 15, 1862.

The Second Virginia, however, witnessed none of the Harpers Ferry drama. Detached several days before the investment of the Ferry, the regiment remained behind at Martinsburg as Provost guard. This unexpected development especially thrilled Company D, but the Martinsburg homecoming provided benefits and comforts to all in the Second. "We have better times now than we [have] had for a long time," wrote Company K's Daniel Sheetz. "We have good houses to stay in and not much to do."

Thundering artillery at Harpers Ferry and cannon roaring at Sharpsburg interrupted the peace Sheetz and his friends enjoyed in mid-September, 1862; but no bullets were flying at Martinsburg; no men were dying. For the moment, at least, the war was only a sound to the Second Virginia Infantry.

Provost duty at Martinsburg remained the regiment's primary function during the week following September 19—the day Lee's bedraggled Confederates completed their retreat from Maryland. After a brief stay near the Potomac, the army and the Second Virginia moved south to Bunker Hill. Three weeks passed before the regiment changed base again, this time traveling east into Jefferson County and pitching Camp Allen near Rippon on October 20.

The month of October 1862 produced a remarkable revitalization of the Second Virginia Infantry. Soldiers wounded during the summer's campaigns quietly reappeared in the ranks. Sick men absent for months with debilitating diseases returned from the hospitals fully recovered. Stragglers wearied by the summer's strenuous marches ventured into camp on a daily basis. Conscripts and enlisted men absent without leave silently rejoined to perform their duties. Determined draft and recruitment campaigns generated 67 additional bodies for a regiment resolved to rebuild.

When the paymaster finally arrived on October 31, the Second Virginia Infantry mustered 432 men—a phenomenal 1,100 percent increase over the 36 survivors reported in the regiment by Captain John Rowan following the butchery at Second Manassas.

When the regiment headed east toward Fredericksburg on November 22, 1862, its rested and healthy members radiated strength and a new vigor; but despite this resurgence in the Second Infantry, one nagging problem remained: the regiment still lacked a suitable command structure three months after the death of Colonel Lawson Botts. No field officers had been appointed as yet and few promotions had occurred at the company level. The situation was so acute in Company B that command had devolved on Second **Sergeant** Samuel Ray.

Brigadier General E. F. Paxton, the Stonewall Brigade's new commander, recognized that these deficiencies existed in the Second and had designated a Board of Examiners to find suitable replacements for the field-officer vacancies. These positions were still unfilled, however, when fighting erupted at Fredericksburg on December 13.

At daybreak on the morning prior to the battle, the Second Virginia had marched with the brigade from its encampment near Guinea's Depot to Hamilton's Crossing on the Richmond, Fredericksburg and Potomac Railroad. During the afternoon, the men moved westward and were positioned approximately 400 yards behind A. P. Hill's division in a large woods covering the crest of a hill.

When the front line of the Confederate right became hotly engaged on the morning of the 13th, the Stonewall Brigade was ordered to advance. As the brigade pushed forward with the Second Virginia on its right, Captain Nadenbousch observed that "there was no support on our right." Nadenbousch feared that "if the enemy was near at hand they would take advantage of this gap and fall upon our flank at this unguarded point."

Sure enough, as Nadenbousch had predicted, the Federals drove toward "the gap" on the right of the Second with a large force of infantry. The veteran captain responded decisively to this threat, first by filing the regiment to the right and then by presenting the front of the Second to the oncoming Unionists. A sharp fight ensued, but only momentarily, for the Federals soon withdrew. The regiment then rejoined the brigade and continued forward until reaching the R. F. & P. Railroad, where it remained until 7 p.m., when instructions were received ordering a withdrawal from the front for the evening.

In practical terms, the fight at Fredericksburg had ended. Some "lively skirmishing" kept the brigade and the regiment occupied throughtout the 14th but as Kyd Douglas noted, "there was nothing interesting about the Battle."

The Second Virginia had escaped from the Fredericksburg action relatively unscathed. Total casualties for the regiment numbered 20, with two men killed and 18 wounded, two wounds being mortal. The battle at Fredericksburg did establish one record, however. One of the men killed in the Second—John Kiser of Company E—had been in the army only nine days. No other soldier in the regiment served so little time before meeting his death.

With the Federals soundly defeated and winter rapidly approaching, Jackson moved his forces southeast of Fredericksburg and established winter quarters at Moss (or Corbin's) Neck. For the next two months, the "good log huts" of Camp Winder sheltered the Stonewall Brigade and the Second regiment from a winter that was "variable and disagreeable if not severe." Occasionally, a week of picket duty along the Rappahannock interrupted the men in their "comfortably heated" quarters. Tom Gold shivered when he remembered his blustery vigils along the river because "on picket we had no houses or tents and had to do the best we could with shelters made of blankets and oil cloths." Despite these sporadic hardships, moral in the ranks soared because "everybody seemed to be working to get the army into effective condition."

Effective conditioning in the Second Virginia was hampered, however, by a menancing problem. The regiment still had no field officers. Six months had passed since the death of Colonel Botts, and still no colonel, no lieutenant colonel, and no major. Why had the vacancies not been filled?

Raleigh Colston was the first to vent his frustration over this issue. On Christmas Eve, 1862, the usually tranquil Colston fired off a pointed letter to Congressman Alexander R. Boteler: "I commanded the regiment for four months, ranking only as captain," explained Colston to his representative in the Confederate Congress. "Now Nadenbousch is in command, ranking only as captain. . . I wish you would do us the favor to see that the appointments are made and sent on."

Captain Colston had good reason to complain. Six weeks prior to his inquiry to Boteler, a Board of Examiners in the Stonewall Brigade had recommended that Colston be appointed lieutenant colonel of the Second Virginia Infantry. The same Board had chosen Nadenbousch for colonel and Samuel J. C. Moore as major. Brigade commander Paxton had endorsed the Board's selections, as had division commander Jones and corps commander Jackson. Everything seemed in proper order. Why then —asked Colston in a letter to Adjutant General Samuel Cooper on December 27, 1862—had the appointments not been made? What was the problem?

The problem was John W. Rowan, captain of Company A and senior captain in the Second Virginia. Rowan contested the examining board's recommendations, arguing that "as senior captain, I am in the regular order of promotion entitled to the command of the regiment." Incensed by an apparent coup at his expense, the puzzled Rowan presented his grievance in Richmond—just three days after the Board's decision—and campaigned for Congressman Boteler's sympathy and support.

"Upon what grounds or at whose instance is my increased rank withheld?" Rowan queried Boteler in a letter dated November 22, 1863. "I feel most keenly and deeply the injustice which I am compeled to believe has been done me."

Rowan stated his case after declaring adamantly that the War Department never had had the proper facts presented before it. First of all, Rowan informed Boteler that he was senior captain in the regiment because his commission dated to August 1858—14 months before Nadenbousch's appointment in the Virginia militia. Then Rowan emphasized his command of the regiment during four-fifths of the administration of Lawson Botts, due to Botts's feeble health. Rowan continued by asserting confidently that "the voice of the regiment, both officers and men" favored his selection as colonel; to Rowan's knowledge, none of his superior officers opposed his promotion, especially since "they have too much respect for the feelings of a soldier."

Most convincing, however, was Rowan's legal argument. The Captain assuredly reminded Boteler of an act passed during the Fourth Session of the Provisional Congress—an act which stated that after the elections of April 1862, "all vacancies should be filled by regular promotion from the company, battalion, or regiment in which vacancies might occur." Rowan noted further that there were no exceptions to this rule, except in the case of disability or incompetency, neither of which applied to him. Captain Rowan's treastise to Boteler concluded finally with Rowan's firm assertion that he was "legally entitled to the promoted rank."

General E. F. Paxton, though, was not convinced. In letters to Adjutant General Samuel Cooper on January 20, 1863, the Stonewall Brigade commander urged the promotions of Captains Nadenbousch and Colston "to the exclusion of Captain Rowan." The Adjutant General's Office responded on February 9 and informed Paxton that the examining board's recommendations had been submitted to the War Department and that the contestants were "pressing the matter to a final decision."

Suspecting foul play, Rowan informed Boteler of his concern and stated: "From what source the opposition proceeds, as what it's ground and character, I am ignorant but think it do, I should be informed, in order to meet it openly and fairly." Rowan, thoroughly anguished by the "cruel and unjust" ordeal, concluded with emotion: "I would dislike to be thrown out of my regiment a disgraced man."

On March 17, 1863, John Q. A. Nadenbousch and Raleigh T. Colston received their appointments as colonel and lieutenant colonel of the Second Virginia Infantry. The rank of major remained vacant, as Samuel J. C. Moore had received a promotion in the Adjutant General's Department and had transferred out of the regiment. Edwin L. Moore of Company G later occupied the major's position.

Why did the Board of Examiners not recommend John W. Rowan for command of the Second Infantry? The regiment's Compiled Service Records reveal that the Board based its decision primarily on two factors: Rowan's age and the captain's prolonged absences from the field due to a stubborn wound received at First Manassas.

Rowan was 52 in November 1862—the oldest captain in the regiment and one of the older captains in the army. Although he had been in excellent health at the war's beginning, a painful foot wound at First Manassas had sidelined the venerable captain for approximately seven months. Rowan had returned to the regiment three weeks before Kernstown and been re-elected easily as Company A's commander at the April 20, 1862 elections. Rowan had survived the arduous summer of 1862; but on the first day of the Second Manassas fight, he had aggravated his foot wound and removed himself from command. Ten weeks later, as the Board of Examiners conducted its hearings, Rowan still had not returned to the regiment. Despite his early-commission status and his role as a captain in the Mexican War, the Board determined that Rowan's age and his painful disability disqualified him from command of the Second Virginia Infantry.

Rowan's unhappy story had a curious ending. In a petition sent to the Secretary of War and dated March 28, 1863, the officers of the Second Virginia expressed remorse that Rowan's "spirit of honor had been subjected to mortification" and urged the Confederate government to reward Rowan—"and experienced soldier and a practical man"—with command of a post or a camp of instruction. The petition was signed by 36 officers, including Colonel Nadenbousch and Lieutenant Colonel Colston.

This plea apparently brought no response from the government. Rowan's service records disclose that he remained on board as captain of Company A until April 1864, when he then retired to the Invalid Corps and was stationed at Staunton.

With the officer controversy settled, the regiment and the army prepared to face their most formidable enemy yet — the 130,000 bluecoats in Joseph Hooker's reconstituted Army of the Potomac.

CHAPTER V
ADVANCE AND RETREAT

The young clerk in Company C of the Second Infantry scribbled the obvious: "Nothing of mention had occurred since last muster," he wrote cryptically on the front of his company's muster sheet. It was the last day of April 1863; the last day of winter peace for Lee's Army of Northern Virginia.

Messengers had reported a large portion of Hooker's army crossing the Rappahannock west of Fredericksburg and concentrating on the extreme left and to the rear of Lee's outnumbered forces. General Lee promptly responded by withdrawing much of his army from Fredericksburg and redeploying it seven miles to the west, near Chancellorsville.

The Stonewall Brigade arrived near Lee's western front about sunset on May 1. At dawn on the following day, Jackson led his 28,000 Confederates on a flanking maneuver that eventually crushed the unsuspecting Federal right. The Second Virginia and the Stonewall Brigade participated in the 12-mile venture that exposed Hooker's right; and though "the day was very hot and the movement rapid," Colonel Nadenbousch proudly reported "that not a man of the regiment straggled or fell to the rear."

At the completion of this march, the Stonewall Brigade was posted on the extreme right of Jackson's line, along the Plank Road. The brigade and the regiment remained in this position while Jackson's warriors pounced on the Federal Eleventh Corps, "enjoying the novel sensation of watching a running fight without taking part in it." About 6 p.m., however, the Stonewall Brigade moved forward to join the victorious Confederates and spent much of the rest of May 2 changing positions to the right and left of the Plank Road. Nadenbousch remembered that all the movement during that night "deprived the men of the rest so necessary . . . after the wearisome march of the morning."

Vengeful Federals greeted their Rebel flankers at sunrise on May 3 with a "terrific shelling." Despite this bombardment, the brigade and the regiment received orders at about 6 a.m. to advance to a position about 300 yards to the right of the Plank Road. Their mission—to attack and capture some enemy breastworks obstructing the advance on the Confederate right.

An interminable mass of undergrowth, a swamp, and a "destructive musketry fire" made passage toward the breastworks quite difficult; but the determined veterans pressed forward with the watchword "Remember Jackson" (who had been wounded the previous evening), and successfully seized the Federal works. During this advance, the Second Virginia had been detached and had positioned itself upon high ground approximately 100 yards to the right of the brigade. When Union reinforcements massed to retake the contested breastworks, the Second Virginia used its advantage on the higher elevation "to maintain an incessant fire upon the head" of the Yankee counterattack. Following a fierce encounter in which the "tumultuous leaden hail...hissed like darting snakes with fangs," the Federals were driven back. The breastworks belonged to the Stonewall Brigade.

The Second Virginia rejoined its victorious brigade behind the breastworks where the men were supplied with rations and ammunition. At about 3 p.m., the brigade marched north from the Chancellor House toward the United States Ford on the Rappahannock. Confederate strategists hoped to reach the ford and to cut off Hooker's main avenue of escape. The Federals, however, hurled a "terrific fire of grape and shell" at the Rebel advance and maintained a secure stronghold behind their newly-constructed breastworks.

The Stonewall Brigade ventured to within 200 yards of the Union fortifications, but severe artillery fire forced the brigade to retire and to seek shelter during the night of May 3 behind some abandoned Federal works. The following morning, the brigade and regiment transferred to a position three-quarters of a mile east of the road leading to the United States Ford. The men faced the enemy's works and remained here skirmishing until the morning of May 6.

Chancellorsville was a masterful Confederate triumph, but a Pyrrhic victory at best. Raleigh Colston, in a letter to his mother, summed up well the thoughts of many: "I am greatly fatigued from exertion and loss of rest," he wrote. "We have had a glorious victory, but what, except defeat, can be so sad as such a victory,—our great leader [Jackson] severely wounded, our brigadier general [Paxton] killed, and so many of our brave fellows cut down in the prime of life."

Company	A	B	C	D	E	F	G	H	I	K	Total
KIA	1	—	1	2	—	—	1	1	—	2	8
MWIA	—	2	—	1	—	1	—	—	3	1	8
WDED	3	2	2	3	5	2	4	1	9	3	34
POW	—	—	—	—	—	—	—	—	—	—	0
TOTAL	4	4	3	6	5	3	5	2	12	6	50

Casualties at Chancellorsville

Tom Gold of Company I had survived another fight; many of his friends had not. Two years of war had hardened Gold, but not to the point that he no longer mourned the loss of his comrades. Two years of war had taught him, however, that soldiers had little time to grieve. The thought of Chancellorsville made Gold pause, but only for a moment. "The spring was here," observed Gold, "and the time for action had come." Robert Lee agreed, and within weeks, the drive to Pennsylvania had begun.

—2—

"It was thought that if it had not bin for the bush in that part of the country hooker's army bin routed and run into the river. . . ."

Company K's Daniel Sheetz never professed to be a master of the English language. His words, however, typified the assessment of many confident veterans who eagerly discussed their Chancellorsville victory. Morale soared as the Stonewall Brigade and the Second Virginia Infantry rested comfortably near Hamilton's Crossing at Camp Paxton. Most eagerly awaited the army's next campaign.

The drive to Pennsylvania began on June 5. Jackson's corps, now reorganized and commanded by Richard S. Ewell, headed west from Fredericksburg via Culpeper toward the Shenandoah Valley. The journey was "steady and regular" during the next week with marches ranging between ten and 18 miles each day. Division commander Edward Johnson reported that "nothing occurred worthy of particular note during the march," but Tom Gold disagreed—when the column of gray topped the Blue Ridge at Chester Gap, the Shenandoah Valley presented its elegant splendor. It was a moment worth remembering: "What joy in all hearts," reported Gold, "when from the top of a hill we at last saw in the distance the long blue hills. Now all with one accord broke forth into shouts of gladness, homeward bound, for the Valley [was] home."

In honor of this return to the Valley, the Second Virginia and the Stonewall Brigade were ordered to the front to take the advance. "How all stepped out with renewed vigor and pressed forward," Gold proudly boasted, "eager to meet the foe and drive him from our beloved home-land."

The foe, as expected, waited nervously behind its defenses at Winchester. Union general Robert Milroy knew the Confederates were coming, and his 6,000-8,000 men prepared to give the Rebs a hot reception. "Old Baldy" Ewell, on the other hand, planned a different program. Ewell and Jubal Early schemed to rout the Federals from their forts and to gobble them up during their subsequent retreat. Milroy was to be bagged.

At daybreak on Saturday, June 13, 1863, Edward Johnson's division began marching north on the Winchester and Front Royal Turnpike. Johnson placed the Second Virginia Infantry in front of the division about nine miles from Winchester. The advance experienced no opposition until noon when, four miles south of Winchester, the Confederates encountered enemy pickets.

At this juncture, the Second Virginia was detached from the Stonewall Brigade and deployed as skirmishers. General Johnson watched the movement and later complimented the Second: "This regiment advanced handsomely, driving the enemy to a stone fence near the junction of the Millwood and Front Royal roads." The Federal pickets sheltered themselves behind this rock fortification; but when the Second "continued to press them sharply," the bluecoats evacuated their position.

The regiment remained in a skirmish line along the Millwood Pike until 9 p.m. It then rejoined the brigade and later advanced under cover of woods to a position nearer Winchester. During the morning of June 14, Johnson maneuvered his division onto the hills southeast of town. Johnson's diversion focused Milroy's attention on his right and enabled Early to swing around the Federal left in preparation for the main attack against the Union fortifications northwest of Winchester. The Stonewall Brigade suffered no casualties on the 14th since it rested comfortably to the rear of the hills southeast of town under cover of a ravine.

The final stages of the Confederate plan to trap Milroy commenced at nightfall on June 14. General Johnson received instructions to move his division east of town to a point on the Valley Turnpike two and one-half miles north of Winchester and near Stephenson's Depot. Johnson's mission was to interrupt the expected retreat of the enemy; or, if necessary, to attack the Federal fortifications from the north.

To prevent Federal detection of his movement, Johnson marched his division to Stephenson's via the road which led by Jordan Springs. Just before dawn on the 15th, Johnson reached his designated position and rapidly deployed behind a stone fence along the edge of the Winchester and Potomac Railroad and immediately adjacent to the Valley Pike. General Johnson scarcely had completed his dispositions when the unexpected happened—a Federal attack viciously and suddenly swooped down upon his lines. Large flanking parties quickly threatened the Confederate position. "The situation was exceedingly critical," the mortified Johnson reported, "and nothing could have been more timely than the arrival of the Stonewall Brigade."

The Second and Fifth regiments formed in line of battle on the Confederate right and advanced immediately across the railroad and onto the Valley Pike. The dense morning fog and the smoke of burned powder reduced visibility to only a "few steps in front" of the men. Upon reaching the Turnpike, however, the Second and Fifth regiments spied a large body of troops moving north towards Martinsburg. It was the enemy—retreating! The Virginians unloaded a volley; the Federals gave way; and a chase through a woods quickly followed.

52

Frightened Unionists ran for their lives, but only for a moment. With the Confederates hotly pursuing and the situation hopeless, dejected Yanks hoisted the white flag. The battle of Second Winchester had ended.

"We had not much hard fighting to do to get the town of Winchester," exulted the Second Virginia's Daniel Sheetz. "We got all that the enemy had and the greater part of them."

Sheetz was correct. Only Milroy and 200 to 300 of his cavalry had escaped the Confederate pincers. Men in the Second Virginia found themselves the proud possessors of six stands of enemy colors. Colonel Nadenbousch informed headquarters that the following infantry regiments had surrendered to the Second: Eighteenth Connecticut; Fifth Maryland; One hundred and twenty-second Ohio; One hundred and twenty-third Ohio; Eighty-seventh Pennsylvania; and the Twelfth West Virginia. The Second Virginia acquired this remarkable fortune (816) prisoners) at the price of only two men wounded. In no other battle did the regiment gain so much and lose so little.

"You need not to be afraid of the Yankees coming up the Valley laitly," Sheetz wrote to his family while resting with the regiment at Shepherdstown on June 18, 1863. Indeed, the invasion tide had shifted; the wave of war was about to flow into the Union. Worried citizens in Maryland and Pennsylvania's Cumberland Valley watched with anxiety as Lee's drive to the north continued.

—3—

Blackford's Ford evoked some horrible memories. Ten months had passed since the terrible bruising at Sharpsburg, but the hardened veterans of Ewell's Second Corps still remembered the image of Robert E. Lee seated staunchly upon his mount in the middle of the Potomac, watching silently as the tattered remnants of his army retreated sullenly back to Virginia.

Gloom and despair shrouded Blackford's Ford in September 1862; but hope and visions of victory filled the air when Ewell's confident Confederates splashed into Maryland on June 18, 1863. The Second Virginia's Tom Gold shared in this enthusiasm, but the prolific sergeant's attention focused on a more immediate matter. "Fording rivers had become no more a hardship," Gold observed. The comforting water was "cooling and cleansing in its effects on our hot and dusty bodies."

During the night of the 18th, Ewell's forces encamped upon the battlefield at Sharpsburg. The Second Virginia picketed for a brief time at Burnside Bridge where the men ascertained that the areas of hottest action were "where fences and trees showed the rain of bullets upon them."

On the 19th, the command traveled to Hagerstown and then started north for Pennsylvania. "We are a right smart distance in the enemies country," Daniel Sheetz reported from his camp at "Calisle [Carlisle] Pencilvania" on June 28, 1863. "We fare very well here plenty to eat." Young Sheetz noted further that "the people in this state did not know any thing of war times only what they herd and read. . .but they feel the effects of war at this time."

On June 29, Johnson's division countermarched south from Carlisle and raced eastward toward Gettysburg, arriving there too late to participate in the action of July 1. During the late evening hours of the 1st, the Stonewall Brigade and the Second Virginia deployed in a position southeast of town on the extreme left of the Confederate line. The brigade and the regiment remained here—on Culp's farm near the Hanover Road—until 6 p.m. on the evening of the 2nd, at which time the brigade advanced to the north side of the Hanover Road.

During this maneuver, Federal sharpshooters posted in a wheat field and woods opened an annoying fire on the brigade's left flank. The Second Virginia was ordered to drive away these menacing harrassers, and "at a single dash, the men advancing with great spirit," the regiment accomplished its task.

The Second rejoined the brigade—still on the extreme left of the Confederate line—about 8 p.m. on July 2 without Companies I and K, which had been detached "to watch the fellows they had just driven off and to guard the road in the rear of the battle line." At 2 a.m. on the 3rd, the brigade and the regiment crossed to the north bank of Rock Creek and positioned themselves eventually at the base of Culp's Hill, 30 yards in front of some captured enemy breastworks. Two of the three bloody days at Gettysburg had passed and the Second Virginia thus far had burned virtually no powder; within hours, however, the regiment's rifle barrels became red hot.

John Geary's division of the Federal Twelfth Corps charged toward the Confederate left at dawn on July 3. Recapture of the breastworks at the base of Culp's Hill was the Union objective, but the Rebel defenders refused to budge from the works they had taken on the previous night. When it became apparent that one Federal thrust was intended to turn the Confederate flank to the left of the Stonewall Brigade, Colonel Nadenbousch received orders to support the First North Carolina Infantry and to protect the threatened left flank.

Nadenbousch acted quickly. First he detached Company D and sent it south across Rock Creek "for the purpose of attracting the fire of the enemy" and to force the Federals to the right. Company D maneuvered into position, and as expected, when its volley of lead crashed into the Union column, the Federals diverted their advance to the right.

Nadenbousch's strategy had worked perfectly—the new Union route placed the Yankees on a collision course with the Second Infantry.

The regiment waited patiently behind the breastworks the Federals were attempting to recapture. Onward the bluecoats rushed, harder and faster, when suddenly — 25 yards to the left of the contested works — the Federal drive halted abruptly. The Second Virginia had "opened a heated oblique fire" that had stunned and stalled the Union advance.

The Unionists stood stubbornly where they had stopped, compelling Nadenbousch to further divide his regiment. Two companies were detached and sent 60 yards to the rear to annoy the attackers' right flank. The remainder of the regiment joined Company D on the south side of Rock Creek and poured more lead into the Federal front. "With this concentrated fire" combined with the efforts of the First North Carolina, Nadenbousch reported "the enemy was soon forced to retire in confusion."

The Second Virginia did not rejoin the brigade at this juncture, but remained instead on the south side of Rock Creek where it engaged in skirmishing for the rest of the day. The regiment did not participate in the July 3 assults against Culp's Hill; consequently, since it encountered minimal action, the Second Virginia suffered limited casualties during the bloody three days as Gettysburg. Losses included one killed, 14 wounded (three mortally), nine captured and four missing.

Ironically, the only man killed in the Second Virginia at Gettysburg was John Wesley Culp. The 24-year-old Culp — a veteran of Company B since the first day of the war — had returned home to Pennsylvania for the first time in two years. The young Confederate, however, had little time to visit: the fighting of July 3 killed J. W. Culp only a few hundred yards from his family's farm.

About midnight on the 3rd of July, after "all had been done that it was possible to do," a crestfallen Confederate army withdrew to Seminary Ridge. Here the Southerners remained drawn up in line of battle until 11 p.m. of the 4th. The retreat then began slowly and painfully south toward the Valley of Virginia. When Lee's weary veterans finally waded the Potomac near Williamsport on July 13, the Gettysburg Campaign was history.

"I can not say that I am enjoying myself at all at this time," wrote a dejected Daniel Sheetz from his temporary encampment at Darkesville on July 18, 1863. "I am too much waried down from the march that we had in the yankee states . . . it was the hardest times that we had since the war. I was in good hopes that the war would soon be over," Sheetz continued, "but it don't look much like it at this time."

Others in the Second Virginia apparently agreed with Sergeant Sheetz's assessment and decided they had had enough. The regiment's Compiled Service Records discloses 61 deserters from the Second's ranks during the two weeks following the army's reentry into Virginia.

Most of the desertions occurred at Darkesville, a Berkeley County village; consequently, it is not surprising to discover that Company D and Company E—the two Berkeley County units in the regiment—accounted for more than half the desertions noted above (22 skeddadled from Company D; ten from Company E). This massive departure represented nearly one-fifth of the regiment's total number of deserters for the entire war!

Daniel Sheetz desired to return home also, but Sheetz was not a quitter. Sheetz had faith that "the lord will smile upon us and at last give us A glorious victory." In a letter from his new camp at Orange Court House on August 23, 1863, Sheetz reassuringly boasted: "I suppose maby you think that the Yankees have us nearly whipped," he wrote. "You must not get discouraged yet we can fight them long time yet."

Indeed, the fight would continue.

—4—

Little of consequence occurred for the Second Virginia Infantry during the four months following the retreat from Gettysburg. The regiment remained encamped with the brigade at Orange Court House until September 14, and then pitched tents at Morton's Ford on the Rapidan, remaining there until October 8. When fighting erupted at Bristoe Station that month, Johnson's division was in the vicinity, but arrived too late to participate in the action. On the return south to Brandy Station, the regiment helped to destroy the Orange and Alexandria Railroad, eventually returning to Morton's Ford in early November 1863.

One event, however, did startle the regiment—the execution of Layton B. Morris. Private Morris had enlisted in Company D of the Second Infantry on February 9, 1863. His Compiled Service Record ends shockingly and abruptly: "Shot to death by sentence of court-martial for desertion, 26 October, 1863." Why Morris received the maximum penalty for his crime is not entirely clear. His record reveals that he had deserted on May 16, 1863 and was captured in September; but many others had been recovered from desertions of longer periods, and their sentences were much less severe. The court-martial record refers to this "being the second offence" for Morris. Even so, the court only had "two-thirds concurring" in handing down the death sentence.

The Second's Compiled Service Records abound with examples of justice for deserters. Some like John S. Brown of Company G were fined. Brown deserted from Rude's Hill in April 1862, four days after he enlisted. When recovered ten months later, he was fined $25.00 (roughly two month pay) for his absence. Others like Samuel W. Sheetz of Company G—AWOL for five months in 1863—had only their "clothing allowances deducted for time of absence." Henry Jones of Company B suffered a double humiliation for his desertion. Jones received the filthy and dangerous task of working in the government's Nitre and Mining Bureau "without allowances of pay of soldiers." John Taylor experienced a similar fate when he was ordered to sweat it out in an iron foundry following his nine-month absence. Occasionally deserters were sentenced to hard labor with ball and chain—as was Company B's John Estep; but fines and deductions of clothing allowances served as the major penalty for desertion.

Of the 330 men who deserted from the Second Virginia Infantry during the war (or 22.5% of the total number who served in the regiment), only Layton B. Morris received the death sentence. When Morris slumped before the firing squad, the veterans in the Second Virgnia received a grim reminder of army discipline.

—5—

"To arms!" resounded through the camps of General Edward Johnson's division on Thursday morning, November 26, 1863. Scouts had reported Union forces crossing the Rapidan and General Lee desired to have his Confederates ready to meet the expected Federal attack. Accordingly, General Johnson marched his division from its "tolerably comfortable" camp at Morton's Ford and positioned his men behind breastworks near Mine Run on the evening of the 26th.

Early the next morning, with Federal movements indicating an assault against the Confederate right, Johnson's division left the breastworks and hustled southeast to strengthen Lee's right, then anchored near Locust Grove. Just as the head of the column approached its destination, a "sharp but desultory firing" erupted toward the rear of the division. Enemy skirmishers had attacked an ambulance train just to the rear of the Stonewall Brigade. Johnson immediately ordered an about-face and instructed his brigadiers to throw out skirmishers.

Since the Second Virginia was bringing up the rear of the brigade and consequently was nearest the action, Lieutenant Colonel Colston—filling in for the ailing John Nadenbousch—received orders to deploy the Second Virginia in front of the brigade and to "feel out" the enemy's skirmishers. Colston quickly organized his line and rapidly advanced toward the source of agitation. Suddenly, the regiment made a startling discovery: the woods it approached contained more than a handful of Yankee sharpshooters. The entire Twelfth Corps of the Army of the Potomac was preparing for battle!

The Federal Twelfth Corps had unexpectedly collided with Edward Johnson's division, and Raleigh Colston's skirmish line provided the Unionists with an easy target. A tornado of lead smashed into the Second Virginia Infantry. Colonel Colston toppled from his horse, his left leg shattered by a minie. Captain Charles Stewart received command, and Stewart withdrew hastily until the regiment connected its line with the Confederate skirmishers on its right and left. The advance of the enemy opened a heavy skirmish fire against the defending Southerners, but the Twelfth Corps massed no major assaults.

At about 4 p.m. on the 27th, General Johnson ordered an attack "to drive the enemy out of the tangled wilderness in which he had sheltered himself." The Federals moved forward at the same time. The two lines of advancing opponents presented Captain Stewart with a major problem: the Second Virginia—still deployed as skirmishers and in position on the crest of a hill—was "directly in line of fire" from both sides of the field. Stewart rectified this hazard when he ordered the regiment to fall back to the brigade and to reform in its rear.

Johnson's determined Confederates surged forward toward the woods and the open fields of Payne's Farm just beyond. The snarled thicket through which the men scrambled, however, was so dense that it was "found impossible to maintain an unbroken line." Consequently each brigade commander, finding himself unsupported on both flanks, ordered his brigades back to the edge of an open field; here the Confederates remained unmolested for the rest of the evening. At 10 p.m., Johnson withdrew his forces, settling finally on the morning of November 28 on the hills along the western bank of Mine Run.

Men in the Second Virginia remembered the battle of Payne's Farm as "one of the hottest fights of the war." The hard day's struggle—so long and so continuous that a large number in the Second had expended all their ammunition—cost the regiment some of its most seasoned veterans. Tom Gold labeled Payne's Farm "the Battle of the Georges" and explained dolefully that George Patterson, George Riggle, and George Doll were killed in the fight and that badly wounded George Wheeler had died shortly after reaching the hospital. Many others suffered also.

Company	A	B	C	D	E	F	G	H	I	K	Total
KIA	—	—	—	2	—	1	—	—	2	—	5
MWIA	—	1	—	—	—	—	1	—	1	—	3
WDED	2	—	3	—	6	6	9	1	7	3	37
POW	—	—	—	—	—	—	—	—	—	—	0
TOTAL	2	1	3	2	6	7	10	1	10	3	45

Casualties at Payne's Farm

Veterans in the Second Virginia concerned about Raleigh Colston's injury anxiously inquired about their colonel's fate during the days following the Payne's Farm engagement. The regiment rejoiced when it learned that the colonel was looking "remarkably smooth and healthy," but the

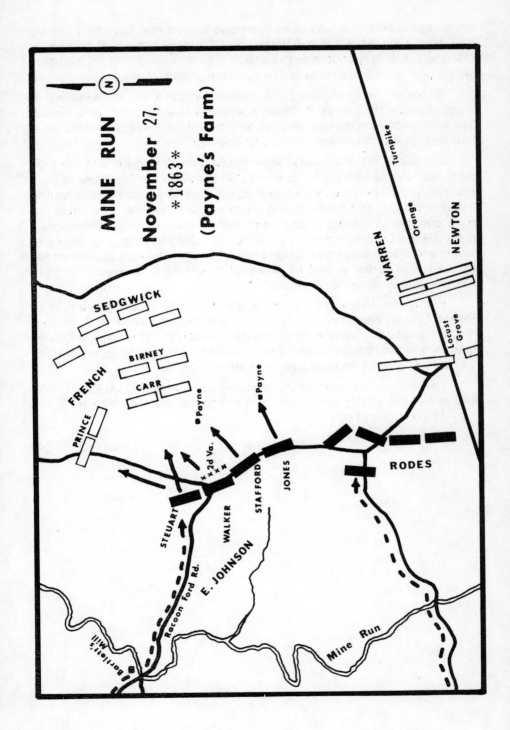

MINE RUN
November 27,
1863
(Payne's Farm)

N

SEDGWICK

FRENCH

BIRNEY

CARR

PRINCE

■Payne

■Payne

Turnpike

Orange

WARREN

NEWTON

Locust Grove

RODES

x x 2d Va.

STEUART

WALKER

STAFFORD

JONES

E. JOHNSON

Racoon Ford Rd.

Bartlett's Mill

Mine Run

cheering became subdued when the news arrived that Colston's left leg had been amputated just below the knee. Saddened, the men prayed for Colston's recovery; but most realized the mutilating wound probably would prevent the colonel's return to the regiment.

Shocking news reached the Second Virginia on the evening of December 23, 1863. Raleigh Colston was dead—a victim of pneumonia. The announcement dampened the Christmas spirit in a regiment that now had lost its fourth colonel in two and one-half years.

About the 1st of January, 1864, the Stonewall Brigade and the regiment settled into new winter quarters at Pisgah Church. Experiences from the two previous winters had taught the men methods of combating Virginia's damp and bone-chilling weather. "Our houses were small log huts, capable of holding three or four men, and were quite comfortable," reported the Second regiment's Tom Gold. "Chimneys built of sticks of wood and plastered on the inside answered well. The roof of clapboards or pieces of tents, a bed of straw of pine shats on pieces of split wood...made us quite luxurious."

Warm and welcomed they were, but the crude and crowded huts of Pisgah Church were poor substitutes for the comforts of home. Tom Gold did not grumble when he fixed his daily ration of corn meal and one-quarter pound of bacon; Daniel Sheetz wrote that he was enjoying himself "as well as [could] be expected for A Rebel Soldier."

The men hoped, however, that the upcoming campaigns finally would end the killing, the misery and the discomfort of civil war.... All they could do was hope.

CHAPTER VI
THE FINAL YEAR

William W. Randolph had just returned from Richmond when he received the good news—he just had been appointed lieutenant colonel of the Second Virginia Infantry.

Randolph had advanced far up the command ladder since first enlisting as a private in Company C on June 6, 1861. The former University of Virginia graduate was a popular selection. Few had forgotten, after all, that in April 1862, Private Randolph unanimously had been elected captain of his company. Again in 1863 Randolph's appeal had reached the voters, this time in an election for a representative to the Virginia Legislature from Clarke County. His experience as a private coupled with his inspiring leadership as a captain made Randolph, in the opinion of most, the perfect successor to the much-liked Raleigh Colston.

Lieutenant Colonel Randolph had little time to acquaint himself, however, with his new position. Ulysses S. Grant and the Army of the Potomac had crossed the Rappahannock on May 4 and the spring campaign had commenced with a race through the Wilderness. General Lee resolved to strike the Federals while they were still entangled in the densly overgrown jungle of the Wilderness. During the late evening hours of May 4, consequently, the Stonewall Brigade packed its bags at Pisgah Church and started east with Johnson's division along the Orange Turnpike. Near noon on the 5th, while near the intersection of the turnpike and the Germanna Plank Road, the advancing Confederates collided with the head of the Federal column and the Battle of the Wilderness began.

No official report detailing the actions of the Second Virginia in the Wilderness fight ever was completed. Tom Gold wrote simply that "after some moving back and forth through the wood, [we] met the enemy and all day long were engaged until the brigade was almost out of ammunition." Gold added, however, that the Second's position was on the extreme left of the brigade and also on the extreme left of Johnson's division. While in this precarious situation, the line of the Second "had to be continually stretched out towards the left" in order to counter repeated Federal flanking attacks.

Colonel Randolph conducted the defense of his position actively and decisively, even ordering the color-bearer at one point to plant the Second's standard beside himself in order to steady the regiment's line. At about 2 p.m., after approximately an hour of hot action, Sergeant Mord Lewis of Company C informed Randolph that Lieutenant Sam Grubbs had been shot in the head and instantly killed while attacking a column of enemy flankers. Randolph quickly assessed his position, and after determining that his men were holding their own, he and Sergeant Lewis darted away to find and to bring off Lieutenant Grubbs's body. Randolph barely had begun his mission when a bullet smashed into his skull, wounding him mortally. Two hours later, the last and the youngest colonel of the Second Virginia Infantry was dead at age 27.

Despite the loss of its colonel, the regiment held its ground on the left of the brigade until relief finally arrived about 5 p.m. When Harry Hays's Louisianians marched onto the field, the Stonewall Brigade dropped to the rear to reorganize and to rearm. Surprisingly, casualties in the Second Virginia—although under fire for nearly five hours—had been relatively light. The regiment's Compiled Service Records showed only one man killed, two wounded mortally, and four more injured in the fight of the Wilderness.

Heavy skirmishing continued along the front until dusk on May 5, but then the firing ceased and shovel handles replaced gunstocks as both sides hastily constructed opposing breastworks. The next two days passed in comparative silence for the regiment and the brigade, which remained securely behind their works. When Grant abandoned his position, however, and started driving toward Lee's right flank, the Confederates moved rapidly to the right also. A "hot and toilsome" 16-hour march eventually brought the Southerners into a position north of Spotsylvania Court House on the evening of May 8.

"A rail fence nearby gave us the foundation" for the new breastworks, recalled Tom Gold as he and the rest of Edward Johnson's division prepared the army's first line of defense at Spotsylvania. "We dug dirt with whatever we could, with our bayonets and one pick; and threw it up the best we could, and in a short time we had it breast high and thick enough to withstand bullets, if not cannon balls."

The five-sided salient which Johnson's men had constructed protruded northward from the center of a Confederate line distinctly resembling a "mule shoe." This unusual fortification received its first test on the evening of May 10, when Emory Upton's brigade of the Federal Sixth Corps pierced the left wall of the salient and went dashing toward the Stonewall Brigade, then posted on the left center of Johnson's line. The Second Virginia—on the far left of the brigade and closest to the Union attackers—initially fell back, but the rest of the brigade and additional reinforcements soon rushed to the rescue and the Federals were repulsed.

Company C's Elliott Weir initially had fallen victim to the Union foray of May 10. When the Federals climbed over the breastworks, Weir was captured and ordered to the rear of the Yankee column. Faced with bayonets and gun muzzles, Weir readily obeyed and leaped over the works. Instead of following instructions, however, the prudent Weir hurled

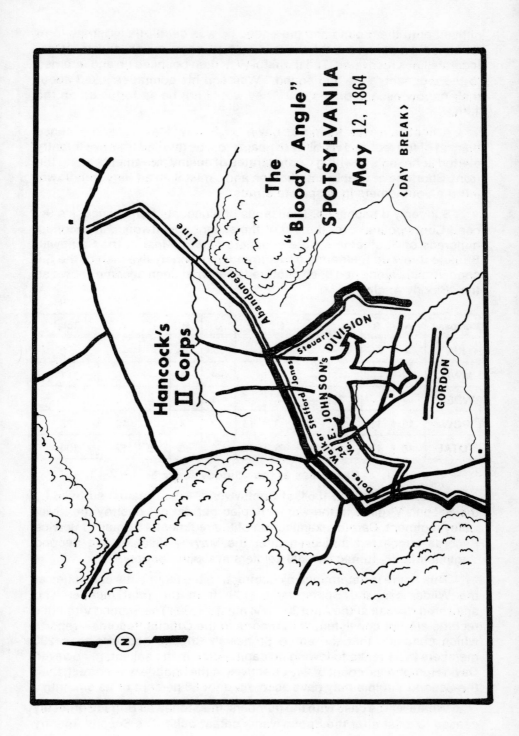

The "Bloody Angle"
SPOTSYLVANIA
May 12, 1864

⟨DAY BREAK⟩

Hancock's
II Corps

Abandoned Line

Stewart

Jones

Stafford

Walker

2d Va.

EDW. JOHNSON's DIVISION

Doles

GORDON

N

63

himself onto the ground and pretended he was dead. His prostrate form remained motionless until the enemy had been driven and the Confederate lines recovered. The thankful Weir then bounced up and returned to the regiment "safe and sound." Weir and his comrades joked about their narrow escape on May 10. They would not be as fortunate on the 12th.

A light rain was falling at dawn on Friday, May 12, and a dense blanket of fog reduced visibility to near zero. The muffled tramp of infantry alerted Johnson's yawning Confederates of enemy movements along the front. Shortage of usable ammunition and a mistaken artillery withdrawal left the Southerners in desperate straits.

Suddenly it happened. Thousands of bluecoats from Hancock's Second Corps poured over the top of the salient breastworks. In seconds, hundreds of Southerners were prisoners of war. Most in the Stonewall Brigade threw up their arms and surrendered. Ninety-five men of the Second Virginia alone had been captured near what soon became known as the "Bloody Angle."

Company	A	B	C	D	E	F	G	H	I	K	Total
KIA	—	—	—	—	—	—	—	—	—	—	0
MWIA	—	—	—	—	—	—	—	1	—	—	1
WDED	—	—	3	—	—	—	1	—	—	—	4
POW	18	11	8	16	3	16	2	4	5	12	95
TOTAL	18	11	11	16	3	16	3	5	5	12	100

Casualties at the "Bloody Angle"

Losses on May 12, 1864, at Spotsylvania—the greatest suffered by the Second Virginia in the war—crippled but did not destroy the lower valley regiment. Careful examination of the regiment's Compiled Service Records suggested that even after the May 12 disaster, the Second Virginia Infantry turned out **200** soldiers available for duty.

This figure is determined by subtracting the regiment's casualties at the Wilderness and Spotsylvania (109) from the total number who answered roll call at the April 30, 1864 muster (309). The Second Virginia's records are not consistent with reports in the **Official Records**—reports which conclude that the entire Stonewall Brigade had **less** than 200 members in its ranks following its capitulation in the salient. If, however, David Humphreys' count of 249 effectives in the brigade was correct, then the Second Virginia may have accounted for 80 percent of its strength.

Whatever the case with the numbers, the Stonewall Brigade **officially** ceased to exist after the Spotsylvania catastrophe. The Second Infantry was consolidated with 13 other regiments and formed into a brigade composed mostly of the remnants of Edward Johnson's division. Indeed, as Tom Gold the prisoner hopelessly recorded: "The 12th of May, 1864, was a day never to be forgotten."

—2—

It is difficult to chronicle the history of the Second Virginia Infantry during the last eleven months of the war. With the exception of several brief mentions in the **Official Records,** little documentation exists detailing the regiment's career from Spotsylvania to Appomattox. It is appropriate, however, to present a concise narrative of the information which is available.

U.S. Grant continued maneuvering against the right flank of Lee's army throughout May and June of 1864. Lee shadowed his stubborn opponent on each move, but the Second Virginia experienced no action when the two armies locked horns at North Anna (May 17) and Cold Harbor (June 3).

When Lee dispatched Jubal Early and the Second Corps to the Shenandoah Valley in mid-June, the regiment marched along (now as a part of John B. Gordon's division) and helped frighten David Hunter's Yankees out of the Valley. In early July, "Old Jube" grasped the initiative and invaded Maryland, climaxing his drive with a demonstration toward Washington. This Confederate offensive stalled, however, when Early's skirmishers collided with veterans from the Army of the Potomac at Fort Stevens. Early then withdrew across the Potomac and moved back to the Valley in late July.

The Second Virginia returned from its excursion into Mayland relatively unscathed by the July 9 fight at Monocacy (nine casualties) and the movement against Fort Stevens (no reported injuries). In mid-August, the regiment settled at Winchester and began a relaxing few weeks of provost duty.

Major General Philip H. Sheridan introduced himself to the Shenandoah Valley in late August 1864. Within one month, the good fortunes Early's Confederates were enjoying rapidly would disappear. On September 19, 1864, Sheridan's 40,000 struck "Old Jube's" greatly outnumbered divisions at Third Winchester, eventually forcing the Southerners to withdraw up the Valley Pike past Strasburg. Sheridan hotly pursued, and three days later at Fisher's Hill, "Little Phil" stampeded Early's left flank and produced a major Confederate defeat.

Early fired back on October 19 when he surprised the Federals at Cedar Creek and initially routed them in confusion. The fiesty Sheridan rallied his troops, however, and unleashed a counterattack that virtually annihilated Early's Second Corps. The lower valley belonged to Sheridan.

The Second Virginia's Compiled Service Records reveal that the regiment suffered only 18 casualties in the three battles against Sheridan. Most of the victims (13) were captured, but two men were killed and three other veterans wounded. The records show, however, that nearly as many were captured between the formal, full-scale engagements—in other words, stragglers, skirmishers, and rear-guard defenders also became victims of Sheridan's Valley Campaign.

Included among the casualties were two of the regiment's company commanders. The Federals nabbed Frank Barnhart of Company A at the Fisher's Hill disaster. Company G's William Shearer fell wounded severely at Cedar Creek.

The most painful loss, however, occurred at Third Winchester. While defending the town during the late afternoon of September 19, the Second Virginia lost its battle flag on the heights north of Winchester. A spirited charge by the Thirty-seventh Massachusetts Infantry (Third brigade, First division, Sixth Corps) cracked the regiment's line and the tattered colors fell. Thirteen battles inscribed across the Stars and Bars proved complete testimony to the regiment's arduous service during three years of war.

When the Second Virginia mustered for the first time in six months on October 31, 1864, 113 members of the regiment stepped forward to receive their meager pay. Evidence of the regiment's deterioration—in addition to its reduction in strength—was disclosed when an inspection report in late November labeled the command "in a most deplorable condition," and warned that clothing and especially overcoats were an "absolute necessity" to prevent much suffering during the coming cold weather. The same inspector also found a "large deficiency" in the regiment's armaments due to the fact that "most of the guns issued to [the Stonewall Brigade] since October 19 [had] been collected from citizens." The report recommended that .58 caliber rifles replace the old .69 smoothbores as soon as possible.

The survivors of Jubal Early's Second Corps left the Shenandoah Valley for the last time as soldiers on December 6, 1864. The columns marched eastward to join Lee at Petersburg. When "Old Jube's" campaigners arrived in mid-December, the Stonewall Brigade was stationed on the Confederate right at Hatcher's Run. Winter quarters hastily were constructed at Camp Ewell near Burgess Mills. For the next four months, the men spent their energy "fighting famine from within and Grant from without."

Cornbread and middling day after day weakened the constitutions of many in the Second Virginia. "Chills and fever and other malarious diseases" sent many from the trenches to the hospital during the winter of 1865. In some ways, however, the regiment's situation improved. An inspection report of the Stonewall Brigade in late February revealed that the arms and accoutrements of the command were "ample" and that all the brigade's units were "well-clad." Only the "great want of soap," the inspector reported, "prevent[ed] that perfect cleanliness which would otherwise be the case."

When the winter began to thaw in late March 1865, the Stonewall Brigade shared in the opportunity to participate in the last offensive thrust of the Army of Northern Virginia. At 4 a.m. on March 25, John Gordon's Second Corps charged toward Fort Steadman in an all-out effort to loosen Grant's stranglehold on Petersburg. Gordon's determined Confederates rushed forward and captured the fort; but confusion followed the initial success, and in a short time Gordon's attackers were raked by a murderous Federal countercharge. Rather than risking the return to their own lines, hundreds of Confederates surrendered, including nine veterans of the Second Virginia Infantry.

Eight days after the Fort Steadman assault, Petersburg fell. The week-long retreat toward Appomattox then began.

It ended on April 9, 1865, when Robert E. Lee surrendered his Army of Northern Virginia. Only 69 men in the Second Virginia Infantry witnessed the end.

A	B	C	D	E	F	G	H	I	K
4	13	7	7	14	0	10	10	2	2

Number Who Surrendered at Appomattox

—3—

A welcome peace descended upon Virginia in the spring of 1865. Whistling minies no longer competed with the pleasant chirping of returning fowl. Acrid powder smoke no longer polluted the freshness of the air. Booming cannon no longer were confused with the distant thunder of an approaching storm. Living replaced killing; happiness transcended sorrow; comfort conquered fear. Peace, indeed, had returned.

Many in the Second Virginia never would return. The wife's husband was dead; the sweetheart's companion was missing; the mother's son rested in the grave. Memories remained, but it sometimes hurt to remember.

Survivors hurried home, however, and many in the Second Virginia struggled to begin life anew in the lower Shenandoah Valley. Some limped when they plowed their fields; some winced when they examined their scars—but they had healed, and it was now time to mend also their lands, their businesses, their families, and their countries.

Soldiers no longer were they; soldiers now only in memory.

CHAPTER VII

COUNTING THE NUMBERS

This chapter presents a brief summary and analysis of statistics derived from the regiment's Compiled Service Records. Analysis will be minimal in most cases, as the numbers speak well for themselves.

According to the official records, 1,631 men served in the Second Virginia Infantry. The regiment reached its greatest strength on June 30, 1861, when 671 soldiers mustered near Winchester. A letter in the file of Captain John W. Rowan reported the regiment's nadir was reached shortly after Second Manassas when only 36 men appeared in the Second Virginia's ranks.

Company I topped the list with the largest company strength when it mustered 92 eager recruits on June 30, 1861. Company D consistently maintained the highest numbers on its roles, however, averaging 59 present for duty during the first three years of the war. The weakest unit in the regiment was Company H, which habitually mustered only 16 men from April 1863 through April 1864. The total number who registered in each company during the war was as follows:

A	B	C	D	E	F	G	H	I	K
130	148	151	202	169	166	184	144	170	145

The vast majority of the men who enrolled in the Second Virginia voluntarily joined the regiment. Conscripts accounted for only 5.2% of the total number who served. Of the 120 who were drafted, 36 men (or a surprisingly low 30%) deserted.

A complete understanding of the personal backgrounds of soldiers in the Second Virginia is impossible, because after the first two months of the war, an individual's age and occupation no longer were recorded. A sample of the regiment's composition was determined, however, from investigation of the records for 790 men who had enlisted by June 30, 1861. This investigation revealed 82 different occupations represented in the regiment and disclosed further that farmers and laborers comprised 36.9% of the Second Virginia's manpower. A more detailed breakdown of the top 15 pre-war occupations follows:

Occupation	Men	Occupation	Men	Occupation	Men
1. Farmer	168	6. Shoemaker	20	11. Teacher	14
2. Laborer	124	7. Tailor	18	12. Painter	14
3. Carpenter	76	8. Printer	18	13. Farmhand	13
4. Student	43	9. Lawyer	17	14. Blacksmith	12
5. Clerk	40	10. Merchant	16	15. Cooper	12

Nearly half of those who fought with the Second Virginia became a casualty at some point during the war. The regiment's service records revealed that 781 men—or 47.9% of the 1,631 who saw action with the Second—either were killed, wounded or wounded mortally, taken prisoner, or declared missing.

Company	A	B	C	D	E	F	G	H	I	K	Total
KIA	6	3	7	10	7	7	3	4	7	6	60
MWIA	3	6	3	10	4	4	8	7	7	3	55
WDED	25	19	39	31	52	26	49	18	37	17	313
POW	55	39	26	53	31	33	21	16	40	30	344
TOTAL	89	67	75	104	94	70	81	45	91	56	772

Second Virginia Casualties

The above table does not include the four men who were reported missing at Gettysburg or the regiment's five field officers who were killed or mortally wounded.

The Second Virginia's battlefield statistics are presented below. The battles with the highest casualties are listed first:

Battle	Date	Total	KIA	MWIA	WDED	POW
1. Spotsylvania	5-12-64	100	—	1	4	95
2. 2nd Manassas	8-28/8-30 1862	83	13	19	49	—
3. 1st Manassas	7-21-61	76	15	8	53	—
4. Chancellorsville	5-3-63	50	8	8	34	—
5. Kernstown	3-23-62	47	3	2	8	34
6. Payne's Farm	11-27-63	46	5	4	37	—
7. 2nd Manassas	8-28-62	39	8	7	24	—
8. Gaines Mill/Malvern Hill	6-27 & 7-1 1862	28	6	4	17	1
9. Port Republic	6-9-62	26	1	—	25	—
10. Gettysburg	7-2 & 7-3 1863	24	1	3	11	9
11. 1st Winchester	5-25-62	22	3	2	11	6
12. Fredericksburg	12-13-62	20	2	2	16	—
13. Salem Church	5-20-64	18	—	—	3	15
14. Gettysburg	7-3-63	16	1	2	5	8
15. 2nd Manassas	8-30-62	14	2	7	5	—
16. Cedar Run	8-9-62	11	—	1	10	—
17. 2nd Winchester	6-15-63	2	—	—	2	—

Several men in the regiment received wounds on three separate occasions. Company E's Charles W. Manor suffered a worse fate. Manor fell victim to a bullet wound for the first time on Henry House Hill at First Manassas. Eleven months later he was wounded again, this time at Gaines's Mill. Manor recovered and returned, but was shot again at Cedar Creek. The Federals captured Manor on the October 19, 1864 battlefield and imprisoned him at Point Lookout after his final wound had healed.

Another killer—disease—proved fatal to only a small proportion of the Second Virginia's manpower. Of the total number who served, 89 or 5.5% succumbed to a variety of illnesses. Typhoid was the leading disease killer, claiming 15 lives; diarrhea killed ten others. The records disclose that 24 of the 89 who fell victim to disease died while in Federal prisoner-of-war camps. Company E's Nathaniel Layman was one of these prisoner deaths—Layman expired at Point Lookout on surrender day, April 9, 1865.

Although the war in Virginia officially ended at Appomattox, it continued for several months for the 99 men of the Second Virginia who had been captured and interred in Federal prisons. Most of these unfortunates returned home in June and July of 1865 after taking the Oath of Allegiance to the United States, a requirement for release.

Charles Kiser of Company B was especially happy to leave prison. Kiser—who had enlisted at age 48 in April of 1861 and had again reenlisted in 1863—was captured during the third day at Gettysburg. Kiser then began an unrequested tour of Federal prisons that included stops at Fort McHenry, Fort Delaware, Point Lookout, Fort Columbus and a return venture to Fort Delaware. Despite his travels, Kiser at least was released in May of 1865.

On the other hand, Joseph Tapscott of Company I remained imprisoned until August 7, 1865. Tapscott was held captive longer than any other prisoner from the ranks of the Second Virginia. He remained a POW for two years and six days.

Nearly one-quarter of the total number who served in the Second Virginia deserted. The records disclosed that 330 of the regiment's members simply quit the war. Company E bore the ignominious distinction of having the greatest number of deserters (53 or 31.4% of its total compliment) while Company H could boast that it had the least (13 or 8% of the total on its rolls).

Nine men who witnessed the action at Harpers Ferry on April 18, 1861, surrendered with the Second at Appomattox. Only two of these—John F. Foley of Company H and Captain Joseph Jenkins of Company H—made it through the war with no apparent injury or illnesses. Jenkins commanded the regiment on April 9, 1865.

Cemetery records reveal that David Aaron Cline of Company D lived to be the oldest veteran of the Second Virginia Infantry. Cline died on March 19, 1920, at the ripe age of 96 years, 1 month, and 19 days.

Officially, the Second Virginia veteran who was the last to die was John Allen Link of Company H. Link expired on June 19, 1935 (at age 93) at his farm near Uvilla in Jefferson County. Unofficially, however, John R. Hooks—who claimed he had served in Company F but was not listed in the Compiled Service Records—was the last survivor of the Second Virginia Infantry. Hooks died on December 6, 1939.

Battle Flag of Second Virginia captured at Third Winchester September 19, 1864

Flag carried by the Second Virginia at First Manassas July 21, 1861

Colonel
John Quincy Adams Nadenbousch

Courtesy Ben Ritter

Captain William N. Nelson
Company C

Courtesy Stuart E. Brown, Jr.

Captain Robert C. Randolph
Company C

Courtesy Stuart E. Brown, Jr.

Captain William W. Randolph
Company C

Courtesy Stuart E. Brown, Jr.

Lieutenant John T. Hull
Company E
*(Note scar on right side of neck from bullet
wound at Chancellorsville)*

Courtesy Larry W. Allen

Captain William L. Clark, Jr.
Company F

Courtesy Ben Ritter

Captain Strother H. Bowen
Company I

Courtesy Stuart E. Brown, Jr.

Captain Samuel J. C. Moore
Company I

Courtesy Stuart E. Brown, Jr.

Captain James H. O'Bannon
Company I

Lieutenant Charles A. Marshall
Company I

Lieutenant Algernon S. Allen
Company I

Private John Wesley Culp
Company B

CHAPTER VIII

"Lost and Not Heard From Since"

The battle is over; the field won or lost. The assessment of war now begins. Commanding officers write their reports. Captains and lieutenants survey their ranks. The examiners report the killed, wounded, and missing. Headquarters' staffers compile the casualties. Reports list the numbers lost and praise the brave. Clerks file the records for safe — keeping.

The above process, as dictated by military protocol, produces brief and concise official battle reports. Statistics and cold, hard facts are the emphasis. Collective actions and collective losses are the focus. Individual's seldom receive mention. Several do receive recognition for heroics; others are noted for extraordinary leadership performance. On the whole, however, the individual fighting man is overlooked.

Consequently, reports of the Second Virginia Infantry in the **Official Records** present only a portion of the regiment's history. The story of the men of the regiment — the individual soldiers of the Second — is revealed primarily by the unit's Compiled Service Records.

These records, which are housed in the National Archives in Washington, D.C., provide a plethora of minute that often includes date and location of enlistment; physical description, age and occupation; rank and promotions; notations of presence or absence; casualty returns and hospitalization; statements of captivity and release; and records of surrender or final parole. Personal information of this type begins the reconstruction of an individual's war record; but this represents only a beginning.

It is impossible to reconstruct completely the annals of soldiers in the Second Virginia because the regiment's Compiled Service Records are incomplete. No muster roll records exist after December 31, 1864; and although the regiment generally mustered for pay on a bi-monthly basis, records in 1862 and 1864 are sketchy and sparse. For example, with the exception of Company B, no other company has muster records for January through June of 1862. Consequently, it is not possible to determine a soldier's record during that period. A similar situation exists for 1864 when the regiment campaigned for six months (from April 30 through October 31) without mustering for pay.

Another void occurs when a record ends abruptly. April 30, 1864 represents the last entry for many soldiers. For these individuals, nothing exists that traces their history for the last year of the war. A more blatant example of a sudden end to all records occurs when 166 men simply "vanish" from the rolls following the December 31, 1861 muster. The cryptic "No further record" or "Last official entry" is used in the accompanying roster to signify the unexplainable and abrupt end to an individual's record.

A soldier's physical description usually is available if he receives a surgeon's discharge or has the misfortune of being captured. Hospital rolls sometimes include descriptive lists and final parole statements also provide good physical descriptions. Descriptions almost always include an individual's heighth, complexion, and eye and hair color. On occasion, a description will mention a man's age, occupation, and place of residence. If a soldier enlisted before June 30, 1861, his age and occupation are noted with minimial exceptions.

Some names appear in this roster that are not included in the Compiled Service Records. Entries of this type will be prefixed with "Unofficial source says" and will be followed with pertinent information that has been discovered in sources other than official records.

Attempts have been made in this roster to carry the individual "from the cradle to the grave." Cemetery records and newspaper obituaries have provided a wealth of data pertaining to births, deaths and burials. Death notices in **Confederate Veteran** and United Daughters of the Confederacy records also have proven helpful in piecing together puzzles of the past.

Sources of this nature have revealed some discrepancies, however, with data that appears in the Compiled Service Records. For example, a soldier's enlistment form may show him 20 years old in 1861. On the other hand, the gravestone of the **same** person reveals his age at only 16 in 1861. Patriotic youth sometimes lied about their ages in order to join the army, and this may explain the four-year discrepancy noted above. Whatever the explanation, a "?" appears in the accompanying roster to denote birth dates found only in the Compiled Service Records.

The researcher is cautioned also that three different Greenhill Cemeteries appear in this roster. One Greenhill is located at Martinsburg, another at Berryville, and a third at Stephens City in Frederick County.

Misspellings in the Compiled Service Records present another major problem. Eight variations of Edward R. Harrell appear in the records and Abraham Voorhees' name is on the register under six different spellings. These two examples represent extremes, but many individuals have several divergent spellings of their names. Meticulous efforts have been made to present names in their most correct form; but on occasion, it has been necessary to hypothesize an individual's proper identification.

When (sic) appears in the roster, the Compiled Service Records present an obvious mistake. For example, the records may show a soldier drafted at Winchester on April 8, **1861.** The actual date is 1862, but the error is identified with (sic) rather than corrected.

Some changes were necessary, however, to prevent confusion. The Compiled Service Records show the regiment recruiting and drafting at Rude's Hill and Rhode's Hill in 1862. Both represent the same location, and since Rude's Hill is the proper spelling, that is the designation that appears throughout the roster.

Company A's muster rolls disclose that on April 18, 1861, 58 men enlisted in the company in front of the Jefferson County Court House. The roster shows the men enlisting at Charles Town.

The November 27, 1863 battle at Payne's Farm is known also as Mine Run or Locust Grove. Payne's Farm is the only designation used in this roster. "Salem Church" is substituted for the Compiled Service Records' "near Spotsylvania" engagement of May 20, 1864. "Fort Steadman" replaces "near Petersburg" for the action on March 25, 1865.

Various grades within rank (such as fifth sergeant or second lieutenant) are listed simply as sergeant or lieutenant. On the other hand, hospital designations (such as Chimborazo #6 or General Hospital #15) are given when known. Chimborazo, incidentally, was a hospital compound located southeast of Richmond.

Specific dates for battle wounds and capture are noted in the roster when the information is available.

The roster assumes a soldier is present for duty unless otherwise indicated. Entries in the Compiled Service Records showing absence without leave (AWOL) and desertion have been scrutinized carefully to insure that an individual's record is not impaired by these ignominious labels. For example, if a person listed as a deserter returns to the regiment by his own volition, his roster entry reports him as AWOL. It is important to note that the records occasionally mistaken prisoners-of-war as AWOL or deserters. A similar error often occurs for those away on special detail or absent sick in the hospital. Where mistakes of this type appear in the records, corrections have been made in the adjoining roster.

Despite the culling of inaccuracies, a substantial number of AWOL's and desertions still remain. These absences are noted accordingly.

Most of the 344 men who were captured from the ranks of the Second Virginia were incarcerated at some point in Northern prisons. The names of these prisons are scattered throughout the roster and their locations are given below:

Camp Chase	Columbus, Ohio	Fort McHenry	Baltimore, Maryland
Camp Douglas	Chicago, Illinois	Johnson's Island	Sandusky, Ohio
Elmira	Elmira, New York	Old Capitol Prison	Washington, D.C.
Fort Columbus	New York Harbor, New York	Point Lookout	Point Lookout, Maryland
Fort Delaware	Fort Delaware, Delaware		

"Lost and not heard from since" is how Thomas B. Clark's service record suddenly ended after he was reported missing following the Battle of Cedar Run. The notation for Clark appropriately introduces the soldiers who served in the Second Virginia Infantry during the Civil War. You are invited to meet the members of the regiment in the pages ahead.

Abbreviations Used in the Roster

AAAG . . . . . Acting Assistant Adjutant General
Adm. . . . . . . Admitted
Apptd. . . . . . Appointed
Asst. . . . . . . Assistant
AWOL . . . . . Away Without Leave
b. . . . . born
bur. . . . . buried
C.S. . . . . Confederate States
Capt. . . . . . . Captain
Cav. . . . . Cavalry
Cem. . . . . . . Cemetery
Co. . . . . Company or County
Col. . . . . Colonel
Corp. . . . . . . Corporal
d. . . . . died
Dept. . . . . . . Department
enl. . . . . enlisted
Ft. . . . . Fort
Gen. . . . . General
Gen. Hosp. . General Hospital
grad. . . . . . . graduated
Inf. . . . . Infantry
KIA . . . . Killed in Action
Lt. . . . . Lieutenant

m. . . . . married
Maj. . . . . Major
Md. . . . . Maryland
MIA . . . . Missing in Action
Mt. . . . . Mount
MWIA . . . . . Mortally Wounded in Action
Nat. . . . . National
N.Y. . . . . New York
Ord. . . . . Ordnance
Pa. . . . . Pennsylvania
POW . . . . . . Prisoner of War
Pt. . . . . Point
Pvt. . . . . Private
QM . . . . Quartermaster
Regt. . . . . . . Regiment
Sgt. . . . . Sergeant
Trans. . . . . . Transferred
U.S. . . . . United States
Va. . . . . Virginia
V.M.I. . . . . . . Virginia Military Institute
Wded. . . . . . Wounded
W.Va. . . . . . West Virginia

Unless otherwise noted, all locations are within Virginia.

ADAMS, GEORGE E.: b. 3/21/43. Confectioner. enl. 4/29/61 in Co. B as Pvt. Absent sick Nov. 1861 and taken POW while on furlough. Exchanged 8/5/62. Surrendered at Appomattox. d. 9/29/05. bur. Elmwood Cem., Shepherdstown, W.Va.

ADDISON, JOHN W.: b. 1846? 5′ 4½ ″, fair complexion, blue eyes, dark hair. Druggist. Residence Baltimore, Md. enl. 3/6/62 in Co. F. as Pvt. To Corp. 1/1/63. POW at Kernstown 3/23/62 (Ft. Delaware). Exchanged 8/5/62. Wded. at Chancellorsville, 5/3/63. Present again July/Aug. 1863. POW at Winchester, 9/19/63 (Ft. McHenry, Point Lookout). Paroled 4/18/65 at Winchester.

ADKINS, ALBERT: b. 1845? 5′9½ ″, sallow complexion, brown eyes, dark hair. Farmer. enl. in Co. H as Pvt. POW Cabell Co., Va.; (Camp Chase, Johnson Island, Point Lookout). Oath of Allegiance to U.S. 1/21/64. Joined U.S. Service 1/24/64.

AISQUITH, ARCHIBALD H.: b. 5/11/45. 5′7 ″, light complexion, brown eyes, dark hair. Clerk. enl. 4/18/61 at Charles Town in Co. G as Pvt. Wded. at Chancellorsville, 5/3/63. Right arm amputated at Gen. Hosp. at Staunton. Listed as unfit for active duty. Attached to Gen. Hosp. Staunton. Last official entry shows him still at same hospital in Sept./Oct. 1864. Paroled 4/22/65 at Winchester. d. 11/3/94. bur. Zion Episcopal Cem., Charles Town, W.Va.

AISQUITH, CHARLES W.: b. 1842? in Jefferson Co. 5′ 8 ″, fair complexion, blue eyes, dark hair. Clerk. enl. 4/18/61 at Charles Town in Co. G as Pvt. To Sgt., date not listed. Wded. in neck at 1st Manassas, 7/21/61. Returned to duty 9/25/61. Absent sick Nov. 1861. Present again 4/30-10/31 1862. Hospitalized 4/5/63, chronic diarrhea. Last official entry shows him commissioned as hospital steward, 6/1/63. d. 4/2/92. bur. Zion Episcopal Cem., Charles Town, W.Va.

ALABAUGH, R. B.: enl. 12/22/62 at Guinea's Depot in Co. D as Pvt. Trans. 2/7/63 to 7th Va. Cav.

ALBIN, JAMES B.: enl. 4/18/61 at Martinsburg in Co. D. as Pvt. Hospitalized at Chimborazo #1, 10/17/61; typhoid fever. Returned to duty 3/12/62. MWIA in head at 2nd Manassas, 8/28/62. d. 9/1/62 or 9/20/62.

ALBIN, MICHAEL (or MILTON) HARVEY: b. 1835. Farmer. enl. 4/20/61 at Martinsburg in Co. D as Pvt. Sick at hospital Sept./Oct.-Nov./Dec. 1861. Unofficial source says trans. to Co. A, 11th Va. Cav., no date given. Postwar, member Turner Ashby Camp #22 at Winchester. d. 4/7/07. bur. Greenhill Cem., Stephens City.

ALEXANDER, GEORGE W.: b. 1844? 5′ 10½ ″, torid complexion, hazel eyes, black hair. Farmer. Residence Winchester. enl. 6/19/61 at Winchester in Co. I as Pvt. To Sgt. 6/1/63. Wded. in head at 1st Winchester, 5/25/62. Gen. Hosp. Mt. Jackson, 6/2/62. To Lynchburg, 6/8/62. To Gen. Hosp. Charlottesville, 6/16/62. Present again by 10/31/62. Chimborazo #9, 6/2/64 (reason not stated.) To Gen. Hosp. Farmville, 6/20/64. Returned to duty, 6/22/64. Gen. Hosp. Charlottesville, 6/25-7/6 1864. POW at Berryville, 8/16/64 (Old Capitol Prison, Elmira). Released 6/14/65.

ALEXANDER, THOMAS B.: b. 1840? Farmer. enl. 4/21/61 at Harpers Ferry in Co. B as Pvt. d. in hospital at Staunton, 6/18 or 6/19, 1862; cerebretis. bur. Thornrose Cem., Staunton.

ALEXANDER, WILLIAM FONTAINE: b. 8/13/41. Druggist. enl. 6/3/61 at Camp Jackson on Bolivar Heights in Co. G as Pvt. Absent sick 9/10/61. Present again Nov./Dec. 1861. Apptd. Hospital Steward, Ladies Relief Hospital, Lynchburg, 5/27/62. Steward at University Hosp., Charlottesville, June 1862. To Ladies Relief Hospital, Lynchburg, 12/62-11/63. "Request that Steward be permanently assigned to duty as druggist" at Chimborazo #5, 2/29/64. Last official entry states he received a furlough from Chimborazo, 9/30/64. d. 4/11/80. bur. Zion Episcopal Cem., Charles Town, W.Va.

ALLEN, ALGERNON S., JR.: b. 1841? Farmer. enl. 4/18/61 at Berryville as Sgt. in Co. I. Elected Lt. 4/20/62. MWIA at Chancellorsville, 5/3/63. d. 5/21/63 at Baptist Female Institute Hospital, Richmond.

ALLEN, CHARLES W.: Drafted 10/1/62 at Bunker Hill in Co. K as Pvt. Deserted 10/12/62.

ALLEN, DAVID W.: enl. 4/14/62 at New Market in Co. H. as Pvt. AWOL 5/30-Nov./Dec. 1862. Present again May/June 1863. Sentenced by court-martial to forfeit 1 month's pay. POW near Petersburg, 3/25/65 (Pt. Lookout). Released 6/19/65.

ALLEN, JAMES M.: b. 12/23/39. Farmer. enl. 6/15/61 at Charles Town in Co. H as Pvt. Wded. Port Republic, 6/9/62. Wded. 2nd Manassas, date not specific. No further record. d. 6/17/09. bur. Episcopal and Masonic Cem., Middleway, W.Va.

ALLEN, JAMES WALKINSON: b. 7/2/29 in Shenandoah Co. 6′3 ″. "One eye lost in childhood when a piece from a spent cap blinded him." Grad. V.M.I. 1849 (#5 of 24). V.M.I. faculty 1852, Asst. Professor of Mathematics. Farmer, Summit Point, Va., 1857. Commissioned Col. 2nd Va. Volunteer Militia, Jefferson Co., 1860. Apptd. Col. 2nd Va. Volunteer Infantry, 4/28/61. KIA when shot through the head at Gaines's Mill, 6/27/62. bur. Hollywood Cem., Richmond. Reentered Liberty, date not known.

ALLEN, JOHN W.: b. 1835? Teacher. enl. 6/15/61 at Harpers Ferry in Co. H as Pvt. To Corp. 11/22/61. Absent sick June/July 1861. Present again Sept./Oct. 1861. Last official entry shows him present, Nov./Dec. 1861.

ALLEN, WILLIAM S.: b. 1840? Boatsman. enl. 5/7/61 at Harpers Ferry in Co. I as Pvt. AWOL 10/18-10/24 1861. Deserted 7/22/63.

ALLENDER, WILLIAM R.: enl. 3/4/62 at Winchester in Co. D as Pvt. POW at Winchester, 6/1 or 6/11 1862 (Ft. Delaware). Oath of Allegiance to U.S., 8/10/62.

ALLEY, W. D.: enl. 10/15/64 at Richmond in Co. C as Pvt. No further record.

ALLSTADT, J. THOMAS: b. 8/24/40. Farmer. Youngest prisoner of John Brown during Brown's raid on Harpers Ferry in Oct., 1859. enl. 4/20/61 at Harpers Ferry in Co. K as Pvt. Deserted 6/2/61. d. 11/2/23, "the last survivor of John Brown." bur. Edge Hill Cem., Charles Town, W.Va.

AMEY, WILLIAM F.: b. 8/15/39. Workman. enl. 6/15/61 at Harpers Ferry in Co. F as Pvt. AWOL 10/29/62. Escaped from Guard House near Winchester, 11/21/62. No further record. d. 3/10/12. bur. Greenhill Cem., Martinsburg, W.Va.

ANDERSON, GEORGE H.: b. 1840? Shoemaker. enl. 4/18/61 at Winchester in Co. F as Pvt. AWOL 7/23/61. Present again Sept./Oct. 1861. AWOL 7/20/63. Trans. to Navy, 9/3/63.

ANDERSON, GEORGE M.: b. 10/27/31. m. Mary Margaret Boustack. "Is on regular muster roll of this company (the Winchester Riflemen), but has disregarded the summons to service." d. 11/29/88. bur. Mt. Hebron Cem., Winchester.

ANDERSON, GEORGE W.: b. 4/19/24. 5'9", light complexion, blue eyes, blonde hair. enl. 3/8/62 at Winchester in Co. C as Pvt. Detailed as Wagoner 12/30/62-May/June 1863. AWOL 9/2/63. Last official entry still shows him AWOL, Nov./Dec. 1864. Paroled 4/21/65 at Winchester. d. 8/22/99. bur. Episcopal and Masonic Cem., Middleway, W.Va.

ANDERSON, JAMES V.: b. 1834? Farmer. enl. 6/12/61 at Harpers Ferry in Co. D as Pvt. Deserted 10/18/62. "Gone to enemy at Bunker Hill."

ANDREWS, WILLIAM J.: b. 1819? "Is on regulation muster roll of this company (the Winchester Riflemen, Co. A, 31st Virginia Militia), but has disregarded the summons to service." One source lists him as a shoemaker on detached service, Nov./Dec. 1861. d. 5/18/78. bur. Mt. Hebron Cem., Winchester.

ANNAN, ROBERDEAU: b. 1844? at Cumberland, Md. 5'11", fair complexion, hazel eyes, black hair. Student. Great grandson of Daniel Roberdeau, a member of the Continental Congress and a signer of the Articles of Confederation. Trans. 8/23/61 into Co. G as Pvt. from Capt. Gaither's Co. of Cav. Detailed as Paymaster's Clerk 6/9-6/30 1862. Discharged 7/23/62 when term of service expired and "his being a Marylander, not subject to the conscript law." Clerk to QM John Ambler, July-Sept. 1862. Clerk in Second Auditor's Office, C.S. Treasury Dept., no date given. No further record.

AREY, GEORGE W.: enl. 4/18/62 at Rude's Hill in Co. B as Pvt. AWOL 4/20-8/24 1862. Deserted 11/25/62. Returned from desertion under guard, 2/21/63. Wded. at Gettysburg, 7/3/63. Last official entry shows him still absent from wound, March/April 1864.

ARGENBRIGHT, JAMES: b. 1843? 5'8", fair complexion, gray eyes, dark hair. Drafted 4/16/62 at Rude's Hill in Co. K as Pvt. Last official entry shows him present, March/April 1864. Paroled 5/15/65 at Staunton.

ARGENBRIGHT, ABRAM B. W.: b. 12/14/36 in Rockingham Co. 5'10", dark complexion, gray eyes, dark hair. Carpenter. enl. 4/16/62 at Rude's Hill in Co. E as Pvt. Wded. 2nd Manassas, 8/30/62. Present again by 10/31/62. Gen. Hosp. #9, Richmond, 2/12/65 (no reason given). Surrendered at Appomattox.

ARMENTROUT, CHARLES A.: 5'5", dark complexion, dark eyes, dark hair. Residence Staunton. enl. 4/16/62 at Rude's Hill in Co. D as Pvt. Wded. in leg at 2nd Manassas, 8/30/62. Present again Sept./Oct. 1863. POW at Spotsylvania, 5/12/64 (Pt. Lookout, Elmira). Released 6/27/65.

ARMONTROUT, JOHN: enl. 4/16/62 at Mt. Jackson in Co. I as Pvt. Last official entry states AWOL since 5/24/62 and dropped as a deserter.

ARMSTRONG, HENRY C.: Gray eyes, dark hair. Only official record is a parole statement that lists him in Co. G as Pvt. Paroled 5/12/65 at Staunton.

ARMSTRONG, JOHN S.: b. 2/29/36 Carpenter. enl. 4/18/61 at Martinsburg in Co. D as Pvt. Wded. slightly in arm at 1st Manassas, 7/21/61. Present again Aug. 1861. Last official entry shows him present, Nov./Dec. 1861. d. 11/6/10. bur. Greenhill Cem., Martinsburg, W.Va.

ARTHUR, WILLIAM: b. 1842? Laborer. enl. 4/18/61 at Halltown in Co. B as Pvt. To Sgt. 12/1/62. POW at Spotsylvania, 5/12/64 (Pt. Lookout, Elmira). Exchanged 3/14/65. Last official entry shows him receiving pay on 3/18/65.

ARVIN or **ARWIN, THOMAS E.:** b. 1840? Armorer. enl. 4/26/61 at Harpers Ferry in Co. K as Pvt. Detailed to work in C.S.A. armory at Richmond, 10/28/61. Deserted 12/8/64 at Bermuda Hundred. Oath of Allegiance to U.S. at Bermuda Hundred, (specific date not given); sent to Washington and then to Frederick, Md.

ASHBAUGH, JOSEPH H.: enl. 3/10/62 at Winchester in Co. A as Pvt. Sick at home in Jefferson Co., 10/31/62. Present again Nov./Dec. 1862. POW at Spotsylvania, 5/12/64 (Pt. Lookout, Elmira). Exchanged 2/9/65. Last official entry shows him present, Feb. 1865.

ASHBY, BENJAMIN A.: 5'10", dark complexion, blue eyes, dark hair. enl. 5/17/61 in Co. I as Pvt. POW at Front Royal, 10/31/64 (Old Capitol Prison, Elmira). Oath of Allegiance to U.S., 5/17/65. "Allowed to join his wife in Merys Co., Ohio; she had made her way through Union lines and was now with her aunt." Residence Newark, Ohio.

ASHBY, CHARLES L.: b. 1835? 5'11", light complexion, gray eyes, light hair. Blacksmith. enl. 4/18/61 at Berryville in Co. I as Pvt. AWOL 8/12-8/26 1861. Fined $11.00 for absence by court-martial. Detailed as regimental blacksmith, Nov. 1862. On furlough July/Aug. 1863. Charged $5.00 for lost bayonet, Nov./Dec. 1863. POW at Spotsylvania, 5/12/64 (Pt. Lookout, Elmira). Exchanged 3/10/65. Paroled 4/22/65 at Winchester.

ASHBY, GEORGE B.: b. 1826. Cooper. enl. 4/18/61 at Duffields in Co. H as Pvt. MWIA in arm and in right breast at 1st Manassas, 7/21/61. d. 8/25/61 in hospital at Orange Court House. "His family very poor."

ASHBY, GEORGE W.: enl. 9/2/61 at Charles Town in Co. K as Pvt. Wded. at Cedar Run, 8/9/62. Admitted Gen. Hosp. Charlottesville, 8/11/62 with flesh wound. Returned to duty 8/30/62. Last official entry shows him present, 10/31/64. Retired to Invalid Corps, 2/20/65; assigned to Staunton, 3/14/65. Paroled 5/1/65 at Harpers Ferry.

ASHBY, JOHN W.: enl. 9/18/61 at Charles Town in Co. K as Pvt. POW at Charles Town, 11/10/62 (Ft. McHenry). No further record.

ASHBY, WILLIAM F.: b. 1843? Blacksmith. enl. 4/20/61 at Harpers Ferry in Co. K as Pvt. Last official entry shows him present, Nov./Dec. 1861.

ASHLEY, R.: Drafted 10/3/62 at Bunker Hill in Co. F as Pvt. Deserted 11/25/62 while on the march from New Market to Fredericksburg.

ASQUITH, CHARLES M.: Listed in Co. G as Sgt. Last official entry shows him "slightly wounded by shell in Battle of Fredericksburg," 12/13/62.

ATHEY, JOHN ROBERT: b. 10/26/42. enl. 3/4/62 at Winchester in Co. I as Pvt. d. 4/28/62 at Gen. Hosp. #2, Lynchburg; pneumonia. "Was never paid anything." Due $44.25. bur. City Cem. (Old Methodist Cem.), Lynchburg.

ATHEY, WILLIAM A.: b. 11/18/36. enl. 3/11/62 at Winchester in Co. I as Pvt. d. 4/23/62 at Gen. Hosp. #1, Lynchburg; typhoid fever. bur. City Cem. (Old Methodist Cem.), Lynchburg.

ATKINSON, WILLIAM S.: Listed in Co. C as Pvt. on undated parole statement. No further record.

ATWELL, JOHN A.: b. 1845? Shoemaker. enl. 4/18/61 at Berryville in Co. I as Pvt. AWOL 7/30-8/9 1861. AWOL 11/26-12/1 1861. AWOL 12/27/61. AWOL 3/1-9/10 1862. POW at Winchester, 8/2/63 (Ft. McHenry, Pt. Lookout). Oath of Allegiance to U.S., 3/14/64; forwarded to Baltimore, Md.

AULICK, CHARLES EUGENE: b. 1/6/39. Moulder. m. Ann Rebecca Kremer. enl. 4/18/61 at Winchester in Co. F as Corp. Detailed in Ord. Dept. at Winchester, July/Aug. 1861. Discharged 10/10/61 due to appenditis. Post war, operated a tinner and stove making business in Washington, D.C. a few years after the close of the war; also conducted a large commercial florist business at his home on South Braddock Street in Winchester. d. 11/26/24. bur. Mt. Hebron Cem., Winchester.

AUSTIN, JOHN T.: b. 1842? Carpenter. enl. 4/18/61 at Martinsburg in Co. D as Pvt. Last official entry shows him present, Nov./Dec. 1861.

AUSTIN, WILLIAM: Drafted 10/1/62 at Bunker Hill in Co. K as Pvt. Deserted 10/4/62.

BACKHOUSE, DAVID H.: b. 1837? Farmer. enl. 4/21/61 at Harpers Ferry in Co. G as Pvt. Fined $11.00 by court-martial, 8/13/61 (reason not stated). Detailed as Regt. teamster, Nov./Dec. 1862. Deserted 5/15/63.

BACKHOUSE, EDWARD C.: b. 1839? Farmer. enl. 4/18/61 in Charles Town in Co. A as Pvt. AWOL 12/1/62 (sic). Deserted 5/31/62.

BACKUS, GEORGE H. C.: b. 11/2/34. 5′10″, light complexion, blue eyes, brown hair. enl. 7/12/61 at Winchester in Co. A as Pvt. AWOL 12/27/61. No record again until March/April 1863 when he "turned up as an assistant in hospital at Lynchburg." Detailed hospital nurse at Lynchburg, 9/1/63. Present in ranks again July/Aug. 1863. POW at Salem Church, 5/20/64 (Pt. Lookout). Exchanged 3/14/65. Paroled 5/25/65 at Charles Town. d. 8/14/86. bur. Edge Hill Cem., Charles Town, W.Va.

BAILEY, JAMES G.: enl. 4/18/62 at Rude's Hill in Co. B as Pvt. Wded. at Gaines's Mill, 6/27/62. Recovering from wounds at home. Returned to duty, 2/18/63. Deserted 7/14/63. Sent north via New Creek, W.Va. by Federals, 9/25/63.

BAILEY, JAMES M.: 5′6″, florid complexion, gray eyes, dark hair. Residence Staunton. enl. 4/16/62 at Rude's Hill in Co. E as Pvt. Absent sick Sept./Oct. 1862. Present again Nov./Dec. 1862. Furloughed 40 days due to illness, 6/5/63. Wded. in leg at Payne's Farm, 11/27/63. Gen. Hosp. Charlottesville, 12/4/63. Gen. Hosp. #9, Richmond, 3/21/64. POW at Spotsylvania, 6/10/64 (Pt. Lookout, Elmira). Oath of Allegiance to the U.S., 6/19/65.

BAKER, HARRISON: b. Augusta Co. enl. 4/14/62 at New Market in Co. H as Pvt. d. 8/30/62 in hospital at Gordonsville; reason not stated.

BAKER, HENRY M.: b. 1825 at Winchester. 6′0″, sallow complexion, blue eyes, light hair. Machinist. enl. 6/22/61 at Winchester in Co. F as Pvt. AWOL July/Aug.-Sept./Oct. 1861. Discharged 12/1/61 for disability; heart disease of the left ventricle. Post war, wheat fan manufacturer. d. 11/7/00. bur. Mt. Hebron Cem., Winchester.

BAKER, JAMES: b. 1842? Laborer. enl. 4/30/61 at Harpers Ferry in Co. K as Pvt. Deserted 6/21/61.

BAKER, WILLIAM H.: b. 1838? Wheelwright. enl. 4/18/61 at Charles Town in Co. A as Pvt. Last official entry shows him present, Nov./Dec. 1861.

BALDWIN, CORNELIUS H.: b. 9/1/40. m. Anna Jones. Unofficial record lists him in Co. F and as a surgeon in the Stonewall Brigade. Postwar, M.D. in Winchester, 1865-1901. d. 1/29/16. bur. Mt. Hebron Cem., Winchester.

BALDWIN, JAMES H.: Unofficial source shows him as John Hopkins Baldwin. b. 1843? Student. enl. 6/1/61 at Winchester in Co. F as Pvt. Last official entry shows him present, Nov./Dec. 1861. Appears on the rolls of 33rd Va. Vol. Inf. as Sgt. Maj., July 1862. Listed as present through last record on 10/31/64. d. 5/27/77 "by his own hand in Baltimore." bur. Mt. Hebron Cem., Winchester.

BALDWIN, JOHN ROBERT: b. 10/17/38 at Shepherdstown. Laborer. enl. 4/18/61 at Halltown in Co. B as Pvt. Detailed as teamster 10/9/61. Detailed as forage master, June/Oct. 1862. Detailed as brigade forage master, Nov./Dec. 1862-May/June 1863. Detailed as QM Sgt., July/Aug. 1863-March/April 1864. Last official entry shows him present, 4/30-10/31 1864. Surrendered at Appomattox. d. 12/19/18 in Warren Co.

BALES, ADAM S.: b. 1833? Mason. enl. 5/24/61 at Camp Jackson on Bolivar Heights in Co. D as Pvt. Deserted 7/5/61. Reenlisted 9/12/62 at Martinsburg in Co. D. Deserted 10/15/62 at Bunker Hill.

BALES, DAVID: enl. 10/1/62 at Bunker Hill in Co. H as Pvt. AWOL since 10/2 or 10/4 1862. No further record.

BALL, EDWARD J.: b. 1841? Laborer. enl. 6/24/61 at Harpers Ferry in Co. K as Pvt. Deserted from Camp Harman, 8/15/61.

BANE, JOHN F.: b. 8/6/23. Merchant. enl. 4/18/61 at Duffields as Pvt. To Sgt., no date given. Elected Lt. 11/23/61. POW at Winchester, 5/3/62 (Ft. Delaware). Exchanged 8/5/62. No further record. d. 4/12/70.

BARD, THOMAS S.: Listed in Co. A as Pvt. POW at Gettysburg, 7/3/63 (Ft. McHenry, Ft. Delaware). No further record.

BARLEY, ADAM: b. 7/18/25. Unofficial source states he served in Co. F. d. 3/30/91. bur. Greenhill Cem., Stephen's City.

BARLEY, NATHANIEL: b. 1826? Carpenter. enl. 4/20/61 at Harpers Ferry in Co. B as Pvt. To Sgt. 12/1/62. Detailed as Commissary Sgt., July/Aug. 1861. AWOL 9/1-10/11 1861. Deserted 3/2/64.

BARNETT, ANDREW J.: enl. 9/6/61 at Camp Harman in Co. D as Pvt. KIA at Payne's Farm, 11/27/63.

BARNETT, GEORGE N.: b. 1835? Farmer. enl. 4/18/61 at Berryville in Co. I as Pvt. Trans. to artillery, 4/20/62.

BARNETT, HARRISON T.: Unofficial source lists him in Co. C. POW Camp Douglas, Chicago. d. 3/8/63. bur. Oak Woods Cem., Chicago, Illinois.

BARNETT, LEONARD A.: b. 1831? Laborer. enl. 6/14/61 at Charles Town in Co. K as Pvt. Last official entry shows him present, Nov./Dec. 1861.

BARNHART, DANIEL E.: b. 1840? Carpenter. enl. 4/18/61 at Halltown in Co. B as Pvt. To Corp. 11/13/61. d. 4/25/62 at Gen. Hosp. #2, Lynchburg; disease. bur. City Cem. (Old Methodist Cem.), Lynchburg.

BARNHART, GEORGE W.: b. 7/28/42; Carpenter. enl. 4/18/61 at Halltown in Co. B as Pvt. Absent sick July/Aug. 1861. Present again Sept./Oct. 1861. KIA at 2nd Manassas, 8/30/62. b. Elmwood Cem., Shepherdstown, W.Va.

BARNHART, HENRY F.: b. 1837? 5′5″, dark complexion, blue eyes, light hair. Carpenter. enl. 4/18/61 at Halltown as Sgt. in Co. B. To Lt. 11/18/62. To Capt. 6/13/63. POW at Fisher's Hill, 9/22/64 (Ft. Delaware). Released 6/16/65. d. 1915. bur. Elmwood Cem., Shepherdstown, W.Va.

BARNHART, HENRY: enl. 2/15/62 at Winchester in Co. H as Pvt. AWOL 5/10/62. No further record.

BARR, DAVID: b. 1843? enl. 4/20/61 at Harpers Ferry in Co. C as Pvt. Escaped from guard house in camp near Fairfax Court House, 10/17/61. No further record.

BARR, DAVID: 5′10¼″, light complexion, gray eyes, auburn hair. Shoemaker. Residence Clarke Co. enl. 4/18/62 at Mt. Jackson in Co. I as Pvt. POW at Winchester, 6/5/62 (Ft. Delaware). Exchanged 8/5/62. AWOL since 8/15/62. POW in Jefferson Co. 2/15/63 (Camp Chase). Exchanged 3/28/63. POW at Gaines Cross Roads, 8/3/63 (Old Capitol Prison). d. 12/10/63 at Old Capitol Prison; cause not stated.

BARR, JOHN: b. 1825? 5′5″, fair complexion, gray eyes, sandy hair. Residence Jefferson Co. enl. 7/1/61 at Camp Myers near Martinsburg in Co. K as Pvt. POW 6/15/62 at Harpers Ferry (Ft. Delaware). Exchanged 8/5/62. AWOL 11/20/62. Court-martialed on 2/2/63 for 23 days AWOL (fine not stated). Deserted 7/26/63. POW (Rebel deserter) near Chambersburg, Pa., 7/27/63. Oath of Allegiance to U.S. at Ft. Mifflin, Pa., 11/17/63.

BARR, JOHN T.: b. 1832. Laborer. enl. 6/18/61 at Winchester in Co. I as Pvt. AWOL 12/27-12/30 1861. Wded. at Fredericksburg, 12/13/62. Right arm amputated at Gen. Hosp. Staunton, Feb. 1863. d. 7/9/63 at Gen. Hosp. Staunton; pulmonitis. bur. Thornrose Cem., Staunton.

BARR, MARTIN L.: b. 2/25/42. Shoemaker. enl. 4/18/61 at Berryville in Co. I as Pvt. AWOL 7/30-8/9 1861. AWOL since 12/27/61. POW at Harpers Ferry, 6/15/62 (Ft. Delaware). Exchanged 8/5/62. Wded. in right thigh at Payne's Farm, 11/27/63. Gen. Hosp. #9, Richmond, 11/29/63. To Chimborazo #1, 11/30/63. To Gen. Hosp. Staunton, 12/29/63. To Gen. Hosp. Charlottesville, 6/25-7/15 1864. POW at Clarkson, Va., 11/27/64 (Old Capitol Prison, Elmira). Paroled 3/14/65. d. 11/28/18. bur. Mt. Hebron Cem., Winchester.

BARR, THOMAS S.: b. 1843? Painter. enl. 4/20/61 at Harpers Ferry in Co. A as Pvt. POW at Strasburg, 6/2/62 (Ft. Delaware). Exchanged 8/5/62. Wded. in hand at Fredericksburg, 12/13/62. Gen. Hosp. #12, Richmond, 12/17/62. To Chimborazo #1. To Danville, 4/21/63. Present again May/June 1863. POW at Gettysburg, 7/3/63 (Ft. Delaware). No further record.

BARRINGER, GEORGE W.: b. 1830? Laborer. enl. 4/18/61 at Duffields in Co. H as Corp. To Pvt. Nov./Dec. 1861. AWOL 7/17-12/13/61. POW 6/10/62. No further record.

BARRINGER, JAMES N.: b. 1835? Laborer. enl. 4/18/61 at Duffields in Co. H as Pvt. AWOL 7/17/61. Returned to ranks 10/15/61. Last entry shows present Nov./Dec. 1861.

BARRY, EDWARD N.: 5′6″, florid complexion, gray eyes, black hair. Residence Pittsburgh. Arrested at Pittsburgh, Pa., 10/28 (year not given), and charged as a ''straggler from Co. F, 2nd Va. Vol.''

BARTON, GEORGE W.: 5′6″, dark complexion, dark eyes, dark hair. Residence Edinburg. enl. 4/16/62 at Rude's Hill in Co. K as Pvt. AWOL 6/10/62. Present again Jan./Feb. 1863. Fined one month's pay for being AWOL 3 months, 15 days. Absent sick July/Aug. 1863. Present again Sept./Oct. 1863. Detailed as ambulance driver for the brigade, March/April 1864-8/31/64. Detailed as Teamster 10/1-11/30/64. Admitted Chimborazo #2, 2/11/65; camp itch. Trans. Chimborazo #1, 3/5/65. POW at Richmond Hospital, 4/3/65 (Jackson Hosp., Libby Prison, Newport News). Oath of Allegiance to U.S. at Newport News, 6/15/65.

BARTON, RANDOLPH J.: enl. 10/1/62 at Bunker Hill in Co. K as Lt. On furlough Jan./Feb. 1863. Wded. at Chancellorsville, 5/3/63. Promoted to Capt. in Adj. Gen. Dept., May/June 1863. Postwar member Turner Ashby Camp #22 at Winchester. Alive in 1893.

BARTON, ROBERT THOMAS: b. 11/24/42. Unofficial source says he enl. May 1861 in Co. F. Same source says discharged June 1861 for disability. Served in Rockbridge Artillery, 1862. C.S.A. Nitre and Mining Bureau, 1863. Postwar, lawyer in Winchester; author of *Barton's Law Practice* and *Barton's Chancery Practice;* Trustee University College of Medicine, Richmond; Va. House of Delegates, 1883; Mayor of Winchester, 1899-1902. Member Turner Ashby Camp #22, Winchester. d. 1/17/17. bur. Mt. Hebron Cem., Winchester.

BARTON, WILLIAM M.: b. 10/2/41. Student. enl. 4/18/61 at Winchester in Co. F as Pvt. To Sgt. 10/3/62. POW at Kernstown, 3/23/62 (Ft. Delaware). Exchanged 8/5/62. Admitted Lovington Hosp., Winchester, 8/18/62. Returned to duty 9/1/62. Detailed on conscript duty, Nov./Dec. 1862. Present again Jan./Feb. 1863. Detailed to Ord. Dept., 8/2/63. Returned to ranks Jan./Feb. 1864. Gen. Hosp. #9, Richmond, 5/15/64 (no reason stated). Retired to Invalid Corps, 9/12/64. Assigned to Staunton. d. 4/14/74. bur. Mt. Hebron Cem., Winchester.

BARTON, WILLIAM STROTHER: b. 11/22/39. Farmer. enl. 5/1/61 at Winchester in Co. F as Pvt. Elected Lt. 4/20/62. Wded. in leg at 1st Manassas, 7/21/61. Absent with leave through Nov./Dec., 1861. Signs roll as commanding co., Nov./Dec. 1862-Jan./Feb. 1863. Wded. in thigh at Payne's Farm, 11/27/63; lower third of right leg amputated. Retired to Invalid Corps, 1/18/65. d. 8/27/68.

BASORE, EMANUEL: b. 1837? Carpenter. enl. 4/19/61 at Hedgesville in Co. E. as Pvt. To Corp., no date given. Detailed on conscript duty, 11/2/62. Present again Jan./Feb. 1863. Chimborazo #1, 5/3-5/18 1863; debility. Deserted 7/18/63.

BAST (BOST) GEORGE M.: b. 1818? Laborer. enl. 4/18/61 at Halltown in Co. B as Sgt. Sick at Shepherdstown since 9/29/61. Present again Nov./Dec. 1861. Surgeon's discharge, 4/27/62. d. 5/2/70. bur. Elmwood Cem., Shepherdstown, W.Va.

BATT, JOSEPH J.: Listed in Co. B as Pvt. POW at South Mountain, 9/17/62 (Ft. Delaware). Exchanged 11/10/62. No further record.

BAUGHER, ISAAC A.: b. 1836? Medical student. enl. 4/20/61 at Harpers Ferry in Co. K as Pvt. To Sgt. 8/12/61. Last official entry shows him present, Nov./Dec. 1861.

BAUN, THOMAS: Listed in Co. E as Pvt. POW at Gettysburg, 7/5/63 (Ft. Delaware). No further record.

BAYLOR, GEORGE: b. 2/14/43 in Jefferson Co. grad. from Dickinson College, 1860. Teacher at Episcopal High School in Fauquier Co. enl. 5/9/61 at Harpers Ferry in Co. G as Pvt. Trans. to Co. B, 12th Va. Cav., March 1862. Postwar, studied law at Washington College at Lexington; practiced 5 years in Kansas City, and then returned to Charles Town; m. Lalla Louise Beatty, 4/30/72; formed law partnership with William L. Wilson in Charles Town until Wilson was elected president of W.Va. University; served as prosecuting attorney for Jefferson Co.; author of *Bull Run to Bull Run* (1900). d. 3/6/02. bur. Zion Episcopal Cem., Charles Town, W.Va.

BAYNE, ISAAC N.: b. 1842? 5′6″, fair complexion, gray eyes, dark hair. Carpenter. enl. 4/19/61 at Hedgesville in Co. E as Corp. To Ensign, 4/17/64. Detailed as Color Sgt. 10/4/62. Wded. at Chancellorsville, no date given. Gen. Hosp., Camp Winder, Richmond, 5/9/63. To Gen. Hosp. Staunton, 6/5/63. To Gen. Hosp. Charlottesville, 8/31/63. To Lynchburg, 9/21/63. Present again Sept./Oct. 1863. Paroled 5/1/65 at Staunton.

BEACH, JAMES H.: enl. 4/16/62 near Mt. Jackson in Co. I as Pvt. AWOL from 7/20-10/31 1862. Absent sick, March/April 1863. AWOL 5/8/63. Present again July/Aug. 1863. Charged $5.00 for lost bayonet and $1.00 for lost scabbard in Nov./Dec. 1863. Absent wded., Jan./Feb. 1864. d. 3/3/64 in Augusta Co.

83

BEADLE, SAMUEL: enl. 4/18/62 at Rude's Hill in Co. B as Pvt. Nov./Dec. 1862 entry says deserted, "time of leaving unknown."

BEALES, ADAM: Pvt. No Co. given. Federal POW records state he deserted "on or about 15 of July while his regiment lay near Washington." Oath of Allegiance to U.S., 8/4/64. Transported to Philadelphia, Pa.

BEALL, ALFRED F.: b. 1/16/31. Machinist. enl. 4/22/61 at Harpers Ferry in Co. D as Pvt. AWOL 5/7/61. Arrested 6/6/61. Sent to Martinsburg on "special business" 7/12/61. "Captured there by Federal troops and required to take oath of allegiance to the Federal Govt.; has since left the state." d. 6/16/84. bur. Greenhill Cem., Martinsburg, W.Va.

BEALL, JOHN YATES: b. 1/1/35 in Jefferson Co. 5' 8", fair complexion, blue eyes, brown hair. Farmer. enl. 4/18/61 at Charles Town in Co. G as Pvt. Detailed to convey a sick soldier to Jefferson Co., Sept./Oct. 1861. Wded. in chest in Battle of Bolivar Heights, 10/16/61. Discharged due to wound, 2/18/63. POW at Accomac Co., 11/16/63. Held as a political prisoner and pirate for his privateering in the Chesapeake Bay (Ft. McHenry, Ft. Monroe, Pt. Lookout). Paroled from Pt. Lookout, 3/3/64. Court-martialed as a guerrilla and spy after captured in his attempt to release Confederate prisoners held on Johnson's Island. Hanged on Governor's Island in New York Harbor, 2/24/65. bur. Zion Episcopal Cem., Charles Town, W.Va.

BEALL, WILLIAM: b. 3/26/44. Student. Brother of John Yates Beall. enl. 6/8/61 at Camp Jackson on Bolivar Heights in Co. G as Pvt. Absent sick 10/3/61. POW near Manassas, 8/27/62. Exchanged and returned 11/20/62. On furlough, Jan./Feb. 1863. Sent to hospital, 4/18/63. Gen. Hosp. Charlottesville, 5/2-7/20 1863; diarrhea. Detailed by Special Order 253 from Secretary of War to report to J. Y. Beall, 10/4/63. POW at Accomac Co., 11/16/63 (Ft. McHenry, Ft. Monroe). Exchanged 3/16/64. Surrendered at Appomattox. d. 6/16/07. bur. Zion Episcopal Cem., Charles Town, W. Va.

BEAN, C. C.: Only record is a parole statement that lists him in Co. F as Sgt. Paroled 4/19/65 at Winchester.

BEARD, ALEXANDER S.: enl. 8/30/61 at Camp Harman in Co. G as Pvt. Detailed to Brig. Surgeon, 12/13/62-9/16/63. Detailed as brig. hosp. steward 12/14/63. Last official entry shows him as hospital steward, 10/31/64. Surrendered at Appomattox.

BEARD, JOHN A.: Listed in Co. G as substitute for John Wright. Deserted near Richmond, 7/9/62.

BEATTY (BEATLEY), WILLIAM: enl. 7/1/61 at Winchester in Co. F as Pvt. Wded. in leg at 1st Manassas, 7/21/61. Last official entry shows him absent with leave recovering from wound, Nov./Dec. 1861.

BEAVERS, BARTON: Listed in Co. C as Pvt. Deserted on march from Winchester, 11/22/62.

BEDINGER, GEORGE R.: b. 1841? Student. enl. 5/15/61 at Harpers Ferry in Co. B as Pvt. Trans. to Rockbridge Artillery, 8/26/61 by Special Order 208 from General Johnston's headquarters.

BEEMER (BEAMER), JOHN W.: b. 1827. enl. 11/1/62 at Opequon in Co. F as Pvt. POW at Spotsylvania, 5/12/64 (Pt. Lookout, Elmira). d. 3/8/65 at Elmira; pneumonia. bur. Woodlawn Nat. Cem., Elmira, N.Y., grave #2457.

BEHRENS, BARRETT: b. 1839? Baker. enl. 5/11/62 (sic) at Harpers Ferry in Co. K as Pvt. Deserted 5/13/61.

BEILLER, MARTIN: enl. 4/18/62 at Rude's Hill in Co. G as Pvt. AWOL 5/22-8/15 1862. Fined $30.43 for absence. Sick in hospital at Winchester and sick at home, Nov./Dec. 1862-6/18/63. Deserted 7/23/63.

BEILLER, SELESTIAL: enl. 4/18/62 at Rude's Hill in Co. G as Pvt. Deserted near New Market, 5/22/62. Brought back from desertion under guard, 5/22/63. Fined $30.43 for absence. Deserted 7/23/63 while on march from Winchester to Front Royal. Recovered from desertion 3/22/64 and confined in guard house. No further record.

BELCHER, GEORGE: b. 1840? 5' 7", fair complexion, blue eyes, light hair. Listed in Co. G as Pvt. Only record is a parole statement showing his parole on 5/9/65 at Charleston (sic), W.Va.

BELL, CHARLES E.: b. 1843. 5' 8", florid complexion, hazel eyes, dark hair. Residence Winchester. m. Jennie Streitt. m. Jennie Randolph. enl. 3/6/62 at Winchester in Co. F as Pvt. POW at Kernstown, 3/23/62 (Ft. Delaware). Exchanged 8/5/62. POW at Spotsylvania, 5/12/64 (Pt. Lookout, Elmira). Oath of Allegiance to U.S., 6/21/65. Postwar, Post Master and merchant, White Hall, Va.; member Turner Ashby Camp #22 at Winchester. d. 4/29/12. bur. Old Stone Church Cem., Greenspring, Frederick Co., Va.

BELL, HENRY: enl. 10/1/62 at Bunker Hill in Co. H as Pvt. Admitted to hospital at Staunton, 3/23/62; scorbutus. Absent sick through 4/30-10/31 1864. Surrendered at Appomattox.

BELL, JAMES M.: 5' 8", florid complexion, hazel eyes, auburn hair. Residence Harrisonburg. enl. 4/18/62 at Rude's Hill in Co. B as Pvt. Absent sick March/April 1862. AWOL 6/30-10/31 1862, "time of leaving unknown." Reenlisted from desertion, 2/26/63. POW at Spotsylvania, 5/12/64 (Pt. Lookout, Elmira). Oath of Allegiance to U.S., 6/27/65.

BELL, J. N.: Federal Register of Refugees and Rebel Deserters is the only record available. Lists him as a Pvt. who was sent from City Point, 4/17/65, and transported to Savannah, Georgia.

BENNETT, MASON: b. 1817? Carpenter. enl. 4/18/61 at Duffields in Co. H as Pvt. AWOL 7/29-10/15 1861. Last official entry shows him AWOL, Nov./Dec. 1861.

BENNICK, JOHN SILVENUS: enl. 4/8/62 at Rude's Hill in Co. G as Pvt. On furlough, Jan./Feb. 1863. Trans. to Co. I, 50th N.C. Inf., 2/10/65; "has three brothers in Co. I of 50th N.C."

BENTZ, WILLIAM T.: b. 1840? Farmer. enl. 4/21/61 at Harpers Ferry in Co. D as Pvt. To Corp. 8/4/61. Last official entry shows him present Nov./Dec. 1861.

BERKELEY, L. C.: Only record is a parole statement that lists him as a Pvt. Paroled 4/26/65 at Ashland.

BERLIN, A. JACKSON: b. 1831? 6' 0", florid complexion, blue eyes, light hair. Carpenter. Residence Winchester. enl. 6/22/61 at Harpers Ferry (sic) in Co. C as Pvt. POW at White Post, 7/25/62 (Ft. Delaware). Exchanged 11/10/62. POW at Spotsylvania, 5/12/64 (Pt. Lookout, Elmira). Oath of Allegiance to U.S., 6/23/65.

BERRY, CHARLES JAMES: b. Sept. 1844 at Charles Town. enl. 7/9/61 at Winchester in Co. G as Pvt. Discharged 10/14/62, no reason given. d. 4/20/89 at Albany, Georgia. bur. Edge Hill Cem., Charles Town, W.Va.

BERRY, GEORGE: drafted 4/16/62 at Rude's Hill in Co. E as Pvt. Admitted Chimborazo #4, 9/17/62. d. 11/3/62 at Chimborazo #5; chronic dysentery.

BERRY, LAWRENCE LEE GRIBBS: b. 7/14/39 at Charles Town. Entered University of Virginia, 1857. grad. in political economy and moral philosophy. enl. 7/9/61 in Co. G as Pvt. KIA 9/21/61 while on picket duty at Natt's Farm on Munson's Hill near Falls Church. bur. Edge Hill Cem., Charles Town, W.Va.

BIDLER, DANIEL W.: drafted 4/9/62 at Rude's Hill in Co. E as Pvt. Detailed as teamster in Ord. Train, 12/4/62. Last official entry shows he remained on this detail through March/April 1864.

BILLEN, AMBROSE: b. 1840? 5′ 1″, fair complexion, blue eyes, light hair. Farmer. enl. May 1862 in Shenandoah Co. in Co. G as Pvt. Only official record is a Federal "Descriptive Roll of Rebel Deserters" that states he gave himself up at Rowlesburg, W.Va. on 7/16/64, and took Oath of Allegiance to the U.S. on the same day.

BILLER, JONAS: drafted 4/13/63 at Camp Winder in Co. G as Pvt. Deserted 5/17/63. "Conscript from Shenandoah Co., Va."

BILLHIMER, JOHN: enl. 4/18/62 at Rude's Hill in Co. B as Pvt. AWOL 11/15/62 and dropped from the roll. No further record.

BILLINGS, HENRY MARTIN: b. 3/28/39 at Winchester. Teacher. enl. 4/18/61 at Duffields in Co. H as Corp. To Sgt. 11/22/62. Elected Lt. 4/20/62. Wded. at 1st Manassas, 7/21/61. Resigned 5/26/63 due to smallness of company. "I consider it my duty to resign, as I feel it an imposition upon the service in having so many commissioned officers in so small a company, and would prefer being a humble private in the cavalry." Unofficial source says he rejoined in the cav. d. 10/26/78. bur. Mt. Hebron Cem., Winchester.

BILLMYER, JAMES F.: b. 5/31/36. 6′ 0″, dark complexion, dark eyes, brown hair. enl. 3/15/62 at Woodstock in Co. I as Pvt. AWOL 5/1-9/10 1862. Deserted 7/16/63. Rebel deserter, Clarksburg, W.Va., 10/15/63. d. 3/22/08. bur. Rockland Cem., Rt. 735, Warren Co.

BLAKE, PETER W.: b. 6/22/37. Laborer. enl. 4/21/61 at Harpers Ferry in Co. D as Pvt. Arrested 5/6/61. AWOL 5/7/61. Present again by 6/30/61. AWOL since 12/25/61. No further record. d. 2/7/19. bur. Old Norborne Cem., Martinsburg, W.Va.

BLAMER (BLEAMER), JAMES W.: b. 2/28/34. 5′ 0″, dark complexion, black eyes, gray hair. Farmer. enl. 4/19/62 at Hedgesville in Co. E as Pvt. York House Hospital, Winchester, 9/11/62. Present again Nov./Dec. 1862. Chimborazo #3, 4/2/65; contusion from shell. Trans. Gen. Hosp. Danville, 4/3/65. Paroled 4/27/65 at Winchester. Alive in 1907 in Peewee Valley, Kentucky.

BLANCHFIELD, OWEN: b. 1841? Stonecutter. enl. 4/20/61 at Harpers Ferry in Co. K as Pvt. Absent sick Nov./Dec. 1861. No further record.

BLOSE, JAMES W.: b. 1826? enl. 4/16/62 at Rude's Hill in Co. F as Pvt. Deserted from near Rude's Hill, 5/1/62. Recovered from desertion 3/8/63. Detailed to work in iron foundry by Secretary of War. Last official entry shows him still on this detail, March/April 1864. No further record. d. 9/23/99. bur. Elk Run Cem., Elkton, Va.

BODINE, JOHN T.: b. 7/24/39. Farmer. enl. at Hedgesville in Co. E as Pvt. No further record. d. 5/25/11. bur. Hedgesville Cem., Hedgesville, W.Va.

BOMAN, D.: enl. 4/16/62 at Rude's Hill in Co. F as Pvt. d. 6/29/62 at Port Republic; disease.

BONHAM, JAMES E.: b. 1843? Farmer. enl. 4/18/61 at Berryville in Co. I as Pvt. Absent sick Sept./Oct. 1861. Present again Nov./Dec. 1861. POW at Kernstown, 3/23/62. Exchanged 8/5/62. Furnished John Whittington as a substitute, 9/1/62, and was discharged.

BONHAM, SEBASTIAN E.: b. 1838. Farmer. enl. 4/18/61 at Berryville in Co. I as Pvt. To Corp. 9/28/62. To Sgt. 1/8/63. AWOL 11/22-11/25 1861. MWIA at Chancellorsville, 5/3/63. d. 5/10/63 at Regt. Hosp. near battlefield.

BONTZ, WILLIAM F.: enl. 4/15/62 at Rude's Hill in Co. A as Pvt. AWOL 7/25/63 and dropped as deserter. Federal "Descriptive Roll of Rebel Deserters" at Clarksburg, W.Va. states he was sent north via New Creek, W.Va., 9/25/63.

BOON, J. W.: Only record is a Federal POW listing that shows him in Co. E as a Pvt. POW under guard at Staunton, 6/8/64, and sent to Wheeling. No further record.

BORDEN, JAMES: b. 1821? enl. 4/16/62 near Mt. Jackson in Co. I as Pvt. Discharged 4/30-10/31 1862, overage. d. 12/27/85.

BOTELER, ALEXANDER R., JR.: b. 1843? in Jefferson Co. 5′ 9½″, dark complexion, hazel eyes, brown hair. Clerk. enl. 6/10/61 at Camp Jackson on Bolivar Heights in Co. B as Pvt. On special duty, 4/18-6/30 1861. Present again July/Aug. 1861. Discharged by Secretary of War, 10/8/61, reason not given. Unofficial source states he served in the Rockbridge Artillery. "Cadet" Boteler assigned to Ord. Office, Hokee's Brigade, Early's Division, 2nd Corps, 4/13/63. Relieved from this duty 8/16/63 and ordered to duty "with some artillery co. in the army."

BOTTS, LAWSON: b. 7/25/25 at Fredericksburg. Attended V.M.I. 1841. Lawyer in Charles Town. m. Sarah Elizabeth Bibb Ranson, 1851. Defense attorney for John Brown during the early stages of Brown's trial. Commissioned Capt. of Botts Greys, pre-war militia Co. from Charles Town, 11/4/59. Capt. Co. G, 2nd Va. Vol. Inf., 5/3/61. To Maj., 6/12/61. To Lt. Col., 9/11/61. To Col. 6/27/62. Provost Marshal at Winchester, Nov./Dec. 1861. MWIA when shot through cheek and mouth at 2nd Manassas, 8/28/62. d. 9/16/62 at Middleburg. bur. Zion Episcopal Cem., Charles Town, W.Va.

BOWEN, STROTHER H.: Residence Berryville. Commissioned Capt. of Clarke Rifles, a pre-war militia Co. in Clarke Co., July 1860. Capt. Co. I, 2nd Va. Vol. Inf., 5/3/61. Absent sick Sept./Oct. 1861. Resigned 11/19/61 due to poor health.

BOWERS, JOHN B.: b. 7/32. Farmer. enl. 6/8/61 at Camp Jackson at Harpers Ferry in Co. A as Pvt. Detailed as teamster, 8/16-8/26 1861. Detailed as ambulance driver, 9/6/61. Last official entry shows him sick in hospital at Winchester and still on detail as ambulance driver, 11/27/61. Paroled 5/2/65 at Winchester. d. 11/9/03. bur. Edge Hill Cem., Charles Town, W.Va.

BOWERS, SAMUEL: b. 1829? in Augusta Co. 5′ 6″, dark complexion, gray eyes, dark hair. enl. 4/14/62 at New Market in Co. H as Pvt. Absent sick Nov./Dec. 1862-Jan./Feb. 1863. Surgeon's discharge for disability, 2/19/63; "disease of spinal column as a result of a fall; subject to convulsions since." d. 10/31/96.

BOWERS, WILLIAM: enl. 4/18/62 at Rude's Hill in Co. B as Pvt. MWIA at 2nd Manassas, 8/28/62. d. 10/1/62 in hospital at Aldie.

BOWLES, HENRY C.: b. 1/4/44. Unofficial source lists him in Co. F. d. 2/17/78. bur. Mt. Hebron Cem., Winchester. Tombstone says "Co. H, 13th Va. Inf."

BOWMAN, D.: Unofficial source says he enlisted 4/16/62 at Rude's Hill in Co. F. d. 6/29/62 at Port Republic, disease.

BOWMAN, GEORGE: Unofficial source lists him in Co. F. No further record.

BOWMAN, ISAIAH: b. 9/28/38. drafted 4/9/62 at Rude's Hill in Co. E as Pvt. Sick in hospital, Sept./Oct. 1862. Present

85

again Nov./Dec. 1862. Absent with leave, July/Aug. 1863. Present again Sept./Oct. 1863. Surrendered at Appomattox. d. 5/30/19. bur. Keller Cem., Shenandoah Co.

BOYD, BENJAMIN REED: b. 2/23/16. Merchant in Martinsburg. Father of Belle Boyd. enl. 5/5/61 at Harpers Ferry in Co. D as Pvt. Detailed as Asst. Commissary, 4/18-6/30 1861. Detailed as clerk for Gen. Garnett, Nov./Dec. 1861. No further record. d. 12/6/63 in Washington, D.C. bur. Greenhill Cem., Martinsburg, W.Va.

BOYENSTEN, J.: Only record is a list of POW's paroled (no date) that shows him in Co. C as a Pvt.

BRABHAM, WILLIAM: b. 1839? Tanner. enl. 5/6/61 at Harpers Ferry in Co. I as Pvt. AWOL 7/27-8/9 1861. AWOL 11/19-11/28 1861. AWOL 5/26-8/15 1862. Fined 1 month's pay for absence by court-martial, Jan./Feb. 1863. Deserted 7/16/63. POW at Harpers Ferry, 7/28/63 (Ft. McHenry, Ft. Delaware). d. 5/15/64 at Ft. Delaware, diarrhea.

BRADY, PETER: enl. 7/16/61 at Winchester in Co. D as Pvt. Detailed on conscript duty, 11/2/62. Present again Dec. 1862. Deserted 7/26/63. bur. Edge Hill Cem., Charles Town, W.Va. (no date of death given).

BRANTER, GEORGE W.: b. 4/4/27. Laborer. enl. 4/18/61 at Duffields in Co. H as Pvt. AWOL July/Aug. 1861. No further record. d. 4/2/84. bur. St. James Lutheran Cem., Uvilla, W.Va.

BREMMERMAN, JOHN L.: b. 1837? 5' 9", florid complexion, hazel eyes, sandy hair. Cooper. enl. 4/20/61 at Harpers Ferry in Co. K as Pvt. Detailed as Co. teamster, 10/15/61. Deserted and gave himself up at Sandy Hook, Md., 9/13/64. Oath of Allegiance to U.S., no date given.

BREWBECK, T. M.: enl. 4/16/62 at Rude's Hill in Co. F as Pvt. Deserted from Rude's Hill, 5/1/62.

BRISCOE, THOMAS W.: b. 9/4/33. Physician. enl. 4/18/61 at Charles Town in Co. G as Pvt. MWIA is chest at 1st Manassas, 7/21/61. d. 7/24/61 at hospital at Culpeper Court House. bur. Zion Episcopal Cem., Charles Town, W.Va.

BROCHES, WILLIAM: b. 1842? Silversmith. enl. 5/18/61 at Harpers Ferry in Co. D as Pvt. Deserted 7/26/63. Oath of Allegiance to U.S., 7/27/63.

BRODERICK, TIMOTHY: enl. 3/8/62 at Millwood in Co. D as Pvt. Deserted Oct. 1862.

BROOKS, R. E.: Pvt., no company listed. Admitted Chimborazo #1, 2/21/65. Deserted 2/27/65. Paroled 5/3/65 at Bowling Green.

BROTHERTON, ROBERT R.: b. 12/23/30. enl. 10/3/62 at Bunker Hill in Co. G as Pvt. Deserted near Bunker Hill, 10/16/62. d. 8/20/12. bur. Edge Hill Cem., Charles Town, W.Va.

BROWN, CHARLES J.: b. 1842? Merchant. enl. 4/25/61 at Harpers Ferry in Co. E as Pvt. Last official entry shows him present Nov./Dec. 1861.

BROWN, JAMES H.: b. 1841. Dept. of the Post Master. enl. 4/18/61 at Charles Town in Co. G as Corp. d. 8/13/61, measles. bur. Zion Episcopal Cem., Charles Town, W.Va.

BROWN, JOHN S.: b. 1828. enl. 4/15/62 at Rude's Hill in Co. G as Pvt. Deserted 4/19/62. Recovered from desertion 2/13/63. Fined $25.00 for absence, March/April 1863. Sent to hospital sick, 3/18/64. Last official entry shows him present 4/30-10/31 1864. d. 3/25/65.

BROWN, JOSEPH F. (H.): b. 3/25/28. Laborer. enl. 4/18/61 at Duffields in Co. H as Pvt. Detailed as teamster for regt., Nov./Dec. 1862. AWOL 4/28/63. Unofficial source says he served in Co. A, 1st Va. Cav. d. 3/19/93. bur. Uvilla Methodist Cem., Uvilla, W.Va.

BROWN, JOSEPH MORRISON: b. 8/20/24. enl. 4/16/62 near Mt. Jackson in Co. I as Pvt. Wded. at Chancellorsville, 5/3/63. Gen. Hosp. #9, Richmond, 5/7/63. Furloughed 7/21/63. Furlough extended 11/7/63. Last official entry for March/April 1864 still shows him absent from wound. d. 10/7/05 in Augusta Co.

BROWN, SAMUEL HOWELL: b. 1/14/31. Surveyor. enl. 4/18/61 at Charles Town in Co. G as Sgt. Detailed as a recruiting officer, 8/2/61. Returned from recruiting 10/11/61. Detailed for special duty under Col. A. W. McDonald by order of Gen. Jackson, Nov./Dec. 1861. Detailed in engineer corps, 4/18/62. Apptd. Lt. in engineer corps, 6/1/63. No further record. d. 1/24/05. bur. Zion Episcopal Cem., Charles Town, W.Va.

BROWN, WILLIAM J.: b. 1831. 5' 7", dark complexion, black eyes, sandy hair, gray, sandy whiskers. Clerk for circuit court of Jefferson Co.; also a lawyer. enl. 4/18/61 at Charles Town in Co. A as Pvt. Sick at hospital, Nov./Dec. 1861. Wded. elbow joint, right arm, 2nd Manassas, 8/28/62. Captured at Charles Town and paroled, Sept./Oct. 1862. Detailed by Secretary of War, 8/4/63, to report to Richmond to serve as clerk for T. C. Green, state collector of C. S. taxes in Va. Given 6 months' disability certificate, 4/19/64, due to permanently disabled right arm. No further record.

BROY, ADDISON: enl. 4/18/62 near Mt. Jackson in Co. I as Pvt. d. 4/30/62; location and cause not stated.

BROY, JAMES F.: b. 1844? Farmer. enl. 4/18/61 at Berryville in Co. I as Pvt. Detailed as wagon driver before 6/30/61. Discharged 7/18/62, under age.

BRYANT, MARBLE: Farmer. enl. 9/17/63 at Orange Court House in Co. D as Pvt. On detached service with Reserve Ord. Train, Sept./Oct. 1863. Gen. Hosp. #3, Lynchburg, Jan./Feb. 1864; "almost total blindness." Surgeon's discharge 5/7/64; "general constitution very anemic and broken down. Unfit for duty in any Department of Government."

BRYARLY, JOHN W.: b. 2/11/26 at Winchester. 5' 5", dark complexion, gray eyes, black hair. Carpenter. m. Maria Broughan of N.Y. enl. 4/18/61 at Winchester in Co. F as Pvt. Absent sick 10/18/61. Last official entry shows him present Nov./Dec. 1861. d. 1/18/03. bur. Mt. Hebron Cem., Winchester.

BUCHANAN, THOMAS E.: b. 1843? enl. 4/18/61 at Martinsburg in Co. D as Pvt. Wded. in shoulder at 1st Manassas, 7/21/61. Last official entry shows him present Nov./Dec. 1861. Reported in Gilmore's Md. Cav., Nov. 1862.

BUCK, THEODORE: enl. 4/18/62 at Rude's Hill in Co. G as Pvt. Left in Valley sick, Nov./Dec. 1862. Gen. Hosp. Staunton, 4/15/63; typhoid. Returned to ranks 8/12/63. Last official entry shows him present, March/April 1864.

BULL, JAMES H.: enl. 4/16/62 at Rude's Hill in Co. K as Pvt. Wded. at Gaines's Mill or Malvern Hill, 6/27 or 7/1 1862. Present again 10/31/62. Last official entry shows him present, March/April 1864.

BURGDON (BRAGDON), HENRY T.: Only record is a POW listing that shows him in Co. A as Pvt. POW at Sharpsburg, Md., 11/10/62 (Old Capitol Prison). Oath of Allegiance to the U.S., 11/22/62.

BURGESS, C. E.: enl. 3/6/62 at Winchester in Co. F as Pvt. Detailed on conscript duty, Nov. 1862. Deserted before the enemy, 12/13/62.

BURGESS, EDWARD OWEN: b. 9/29/42. Farmer. enl. 4/18/61 at Winchester in Co. F as Sgt. KIA at 1st Manassas, 7/21/61. bur. Mt. Hebron Cem., Winchester. Tombstone inscription reads: "He could not bring back his shield, he was brought upon it."

BURGESS, JAMES B.: b. 6/39. Gas fitter. enl. 4/18/61 at Winchester in Co. F as Pvt. To Sgt. 7/22/61. To Lt. 10/25/61. Elected Capt. 4/20/62. Wded. at Gaines's Mill or Malvern Hill, 6/27 or 7/1 1862. On detached service gathering conscripts, 10/27/62. Present again Nov./Dec. 1862. Wded. in right hand and leg at Payne's Farm, 11/27/63. Gen. Hosp. #9, Richmond, 5/30/64. Trans. to Chimborazo #1, 6/1/64; debility. Returned to duty 6/9/64. Gen. Hosp. Winchester, 7/25-7/26 1864. Resigned 11/22/64. Postwar, clerk of county and circuit courts of Frederick Co.; notary public and city magistrate in Winchester; member of Turner Ashby Camp #22 Winchester. d. 4/28/07. bur. Stonewall Cem., Winchester.

BURK, JAMES E.: dark complexion, hazel eyes, black hair. enl. 4/16/62 at Rude's Hill in Co. F as Pvt. Deserted from Rude's Hill, 5/1/62. Recovered from desertion, 3/8/63. Detailed to work in iron foundry by Secretary of War. Last official entry shows him still detailed at iron foundry, March/April 1864. Paroled 5/2/65 at Harrisonburg.

BURK, WILLIAM G.: b. 1827? Comedian. enl. 5/1/61 at Harpers Ferry in Co. F as Pvt. To Corp. 8/2/61. Discharged 9/7/61 and appointed Master's Mate in C. S. Navy at Norfolk Navy Yard.

BURK, W. M.: enl. 4/16/62 at Rude's Hill in Co. F as Pvt. Deserted from Rude's Hill, 5/1/62.

BURKE, JOHN R.: b. 1838? Stonecutter. enl. 4/20/61 at Harpers Ferry in Co. K as Corp. Trans. to 1st Va. Cav., 8/12/61.

BURKE, LEWIS: Listed in Co. G. Discharged 10/14/62. No further record.

BURKE, MATTHEW P.: b. 1841? Stonecutter. enl. 4/20/61 at Harpers Ferry in Co. K as Pvt. Trans. to 1st Va. Cav., 8/12/61.

BURLIN, THOMAS: 5'7", dark complexion, dark eyes, dark hair. Residence Amherst Co. Only record is a POW listing that shows him in Co. A as a Pvt. POW at Richmond Hospital, 4/3/65. Oath of Allegiance to the U.S. at Newport News, 7/1/65.

BURNER, ALBERT A.: 9/3/38. Farmer. enl. 4/16/62 at Rude's Hill in Co. F as Pvt. enl. in Co. C, 6th Va. Cav. at Harrisonburg, 5/28/62. Wded. 5/6/64. Chimborazo, 5/9/64. To Gen. Hosp. Farmville, 4/15/64. Released 5/6/65 from U.S. Hosp., Farmville. d. 10/21/05. bur. Mt. Olivet Cem., McGaheysville, Va.

BURNER, CHARLES E.: b. Rockingham Co. enl. 4/16/62 at Rude's Hill in Co. F as Pvt. Entry for 4/30-10/31 1862 states that he was in Capt. Yancey's Co. of the 12th Va. Cav. without proper authority. The entry for March/April 1863 states that he was recovered from desertion 3/8/63 after being AWOL since 6/5/62. d. 5/21/63 or 5/27/63 at Gen. Hosp. #12, Richmond; typhoid.

BURNER, JOSEPH: enl. 4/9/62 at Rude's Hill in Co. E as Pvt. Left behind sick on retreat from Winchester, 6/6/62. POW at Frederick, Md., 9/14/62 (Ft. Delaware). Exchanged 11/10/62. No further record.

BURNER, LAWTON W.: b. 1842. enl. 4/16/62 at Rude's Hill in Co. F as Pvt. enl. 7/5/62 at Harrisonburg in Co. C, 6th Va. Cav. Wded. in left arm and POW at Cold Harbor, 5/31/64 (Lincoln Gen. Hosp., Washington, D.C., 6/11/64). d. 10/5/64 near McGaheysville.

BURNETT or BENNETT, BAZIL: b. 1837? Laborer. enl. 5/8/61 at Harpers Ferry in Co. C as Pvt. Wded. in right shoulder at 1st Manassas, 7/21/61. Last official entry shows him as returned from sick leave, 11/25/61.

BURNETT, THOMAS D.: b. 9/10/38. Druggist and farmer. enl. 4/18/61 at Charles Town in Co. G as Corp. Detailed as Hospital Steward in 33rd Va. Inf., 9/10/61. d. 3/10/62. bur. Zion Episcopal Cem., Charles Town, Va.

BURNETT, WILLIAM: b. 1837? 5'9", fair complexion, gray eyes, brown hair. Lawyer. enl. 6/19/61 at Winchester in Co. G as Pvt. Absent sick Nov./Dec. 1861. Discharged 2/28/62, reason not stated. d. 5/12/88. bur. Zion Episcopal Cem., Charles Town, W.Va.

BURNS, THORTON: enl. 4/9/62 in Co. E as Pvt. Sent away sick from Gordonsville, 8/1/62. Last official entry says whereabouts unknown in Jan./Feb. 1863.

BURWELL, GEORGE H.: b. 1847? enl. 8/18/61 at Camp Harman in Co. C as Pvt. POW Kernstown, 3/23/62 (Ft. Delaware). Exchanged 8/5/62. Listed as a member of Buckhan's Battery of Horse Artillery, 5/63. In the Mexican Army in 1865.

BURWELL, NATHANIEL: b. 9/8/38. Farmer. enl. 4/18/61 at Millwood in Co. C as Pvt. Absent sick 8/16-11/12 1861. MWIA in right femur at 2nd Manassas, 8/30/62. d. 9/5/62. bur. Old Chapel Cem., Millwood.

BURWELL, ROBERT POWEL PAGE: b. 1/17/44. Student. enl. 4/18/61 at Millwood in Co. C as Pvt. Last official entry shows him present, Nov./Dec. 1861. Tombstone says wounded at Brandy Station, 8/1/63. d. 8/31/63 in Staunton. bur. Old Chapel Cem., Millwood.

BURWELL, ROBERT S.: b. 1843? Student. enl. 4/18/61 at Winchester in Co. F as Pvt. To Corp. 6/24/61. To Sgt. 8/1/61. POW at Kernstown, 3/23/62 (Ft. Delaware). Exchanged 8/5/62. Detailed to Ord. Dept., Nov./Dec. 1862. Present again in ranks, March/April 1864. Detailed again 1/13/65, specific assignment not stated.

BUSER (BOOZER), THEODORE: b. 10/18/33. Miller. enl. 4/18/61 at Martinsburg in Co. D as Pvt. Last official entry shows him present Nov./Dec. 1861. d. 6/13/19. bur. Greenhill Cem., Martinsburg, W.Va.

BUTLER, FRANCIS G.: b. 4/10/21. Farmer. enl. 4/18/61 at Charles Town in Co. G as Pvt. MWIA in chest at 1st Manassas, 7/21/61. d. 7/25/61 at Pringle's House, Manassas. bur. Edge Hill Cem., Charles Town, W.Va.

BUTLER, J. O.: Only record is a Federal register that states he was a Rebel deserter received 3/22/65.

BUTLER, VINCENT MOORE: b. 12/21/20. Physician. Apptd. Capt. of Hamtramck Guards, a pre-war militia company from Shepherdstown, 4/59. Capt. Co. B, 2nd Va. Vol. Inf., 5/3/61. Dropped from the roll, 4/20/62; not re-elected. d. 4/22/64. bur. Elmwood Cem., Shepherdstown, W.Va.

BUTLER, WILLIAM: b. 8/23/41. enl. 4/18/61 at Halltown in Co. B as Pvt. To Corp. 8/17/61. Absent sick Nov./Dec. 1861-March/April 1862. Wded. at 2nd Manassas, date not specific. Present again Jan./Feb. 1863. d. 5/6 or 5/8 1863 at Chimborazo #5, pneumonia. bur. Elmwood Cem., Shepherdstown, W.Va.

BUTT, THOMAS J.: enl. 3/5/62 at Winchester in Co. E as Pvt. Wded. in side at 2nd Manassas, 8/28/62. Present again Nov./Dec. 1862. Deserted 7/18/63.

BUZZARD (BUSSARD), ALBERT: b. 8/14/44. Laborer. enl. 4/20/61 at Harpers Ferry in Co. K as Pvt. Last official entry shows him AWOL, Nov./Dec. 1861. d. 8/29/15. bur. Bolivar Cem., Bolivar, W.Va.

BUZZARD, GEORGE W.: b. 1842? Laborer. enl. at Harpers Ferry in Co. K as Pvt. Last official entry shows him absent sick, Nov./Dec. 1861.

BUZZARD, JOHN W.: enl. 9/18/61 at Charles Town in Co. K as Pvt. To Corp. 7/1/62. Hospitalized at Staunton, 3/23-6/30 1863; diarrhea. Present again July/Aug. 1863. Trans. to C. S. Navy, 4/18/64. No further record.

BYRD, LEWIS S.: 5′ 9″, fair complexion, blue eyes, auburn hair. Residence Winchester. enl. 4/15/62 at Rude's Hill in Co. A as Pvt. POW 6/2/64 at Woodstock (Ft. Delaware). Exchanged 8/5/62. Wded. at Chancellorsville, 5/3/63. Present again May/June 1863. Charged $1.00 for wasting 20 rounds of ammunition, Jan./Feb. 1864. POW at Spotsylvania, 5/12/64 (Pt. Lookout, Elmira). Oath of Allegiance to U.S., 6/14/65.

BYRD, THOMAS T.: b. 1826? Listed in Co. I as 2nd Lt. "Has never reported himself for duty having been injured by fall from horse." Resigned 9/1/61.

CAGE, JAMES D.: b. 7/15/37. 5′ 8″, fair complexion, blue eyes, dark hair. Cabinet maker. enl. 4/18/61 at Martinsburg in Co. D as Pvt. Deserted 7/26/63. Oath of Allegiance to U.S. at Ft. Mifflin, Pa., 11/17/63. d. 3/5/02. bur. Greenhill Cem., Martinsburg, W.Va.

CAGE, RICHARD: enl. 9/6/61 at Camp Harman in Co. D as Pvt. Last official entry shows him AWOL since 12/27/61.

CALLAHAN, J.: Only record is a Parole of Honor that lists him in Co. D as Pvt. POW near Shafen Mills, Md. Paroled 10/30/62 by Office of the Provost Marshal, Army of the Potomac.

CALLAHAN, SAMUEL: b. 7/11/32. enl. 2/28/62 at Martinsburg in Co. D as Pvt. Deserted 10/18/62. d. 8/26/07. bur. Smoketown Cem., north of Martinsburg, W.Va.

CALLEN, OWEN: b. 1838? Laborer. enl. 5/11/61 at Harpers Ferry in Co. K as Pvt. Deserted 5/13/61.

CALVERT, WILLIAM H.: b. in Frederick Co., Va. in early 1830's. Unofficial source lists him in service with this regt. Postwar, cigar manufacturer at Winchester; then entered catering and hotel business. d. 1901.

CAMERON, ALEXANDER B.: b. 1834? Clerk. enl. 6/18/61 at Winchester in Co. B as Pvt. Elected Lt. 4/20/62. Absent sick Nov./Dec. 1861. MWIA at 2nd Manassas, 8/28/62; d. 8/29/62. bur. Elmwood Cem., Shepherdstown, W.Va.

CAMERON, HENRY F.: b. 6/18/24. Tailor. enl. 4/18/61 at Halltown in Co. B as Sgt. Reduced to Pvt. Sept./Oct. 1861. AWOL 7/16-8/24 1861. Discharged 4/30-10/31 1862, overage. d. 11/11/88. bur. Elmwood Cem., Shepherdstown, W.Va.

CAMPBELL, ALFRED: b. 1839? 5′ 8″, dark complexion, hazel eyes, light hair. Only record is his final parole that lists him in Co. E as Pvt. Paroled 5/11/65 at Winchester.

CAMPBELL, EDWIN H.: enl. 8/10/63 at Orange Court House in Co. G as Pvt. Detailed as clerk for brig. Commissary Dept., July/Aug. 1863. Gen. Hosp. Charlottesville, 10/17/63-11/23/63; febris renuttens. Last official entry lists him as clerk for Maj. Sexton in Commissary Dept., Sept./Oct. 1864.

CAMPBELL, JAMES A.: b. 1827? Miller. enl. 4/18/61 at Charles Town in Co. A as Pvt. Last official entry shows him present, Nov./Dec. 1861.

CAMPBELL, JOHN A.: enl. 2/28/62 at Winchester in Co. A as Pvt. POW at Fredericksburg, 5/3/63; sent to Washington, D.C., 5/4/63. Exchanged 5/10/63. Deserted 7/24/63.

CAMPBELL, SAMUEL: b. 1823? Carpenter. enl. 4/23/61 at Harpers Ferry in Co. I as Pvt. AWOL 7/27-8/4 1861. AWOL 12/25-12/30 1861. Drafted at end of 12 months enlistment, 4/62. Deserted 4/18/62.

CARAGAN, JOHN P. b. 1806? Tailor. enl. 5/1/61 at Harpers Ferry in Co. H as Fifer. AWOL 5/10/61. Last official entry shows him AWOL, July/Aug., 1861.

CARLISLE, JAMES A.: b. 1827? Merchant. enl. 4/18/61 at Martinsburg in Co. D as Pvt. Last official entry shows him present, Nov./Dec. 1861.

CARNIGHAN, CHARLES H.: b. 1832? Machinist. enl. 5/1/61 at Winchester in Co. F as Pvt. Trans. to Co. F, 12th Va. Cav., 4/14/62, by an act entitling Marylanders to choose service. POW, location not stated, 8/29/62 (Ft. McHenry). Exchanged 10/2/62. KIA at Brandy Station, 10/11/63. bur. Stonewall Cem., Winchester.

CARPENTER, JOHN W.: b. 1841? 6′ 0″, light complexion, black eyes, brown hair. Carpenter. enl. 4/27/61 at Harpers Ferry in Co. I as Pvt. AWOL 7/25-8/31 1861. Fined $11.00 for absence by court-martial. AWOL 11/26-12/1 1861. Chimborazo #1, 6/12-6/21 1864. Last official entry shows him absent sick, Aug./Dec. 1864. Paroled 4/21/65 at Winchester. d. 1912. bur. Mt. Hebron Cem., Winchester.

CARR, WILLIAM: b. 1832? Laborer. enl. 5/11/61 at Harpers Ferry in Co. K as Pvt. Deserted 5/13/61.

CARRELL, REZIN: b. 1839? Cooper. enl. 6/19/61 at Winchester in Co. I as Pvt. AWOL 8/4-8/11 1861. Fined $11.00 for absence by court-martial. AWOL 12/15-12/21 1861. Wded. in arm at 2nd Manassas, 8/28/62. Last official entry says he deserted, 1/20/64.

CARRELL, WILLIAM: b. 1841? Laborer. enl. 5/6/61 at Harpers Ferry in Co. I as Pvt. AWOL 8/4-8/11 1861. Fined $11.00 for absence by court-martial. AWOL 12/18-12/20 1861. Absent sick, Nov./Dec. 1861. Present again 4/30-10/31 1862. Detailed on conscript duty, 11/15/62. Present Jan./Feb. 1863. Wded. in right thigh at Payne's Farm, 11/27/63. Deserted 1/29/64. Rebel deserter, Bermuda Hundred, 10/24/64. Oath of Allegiance to the U.S., 11/12/64; went to Philadelphia.

CARRIER, SAMUEL N.: b. 1844? enl. 4/8/62 at Rude's Hill in Co. G as Pvt. To Corp. 10/1/62. To Pvt. 6/30/63. Paroled at Appomattox. d. 1920. bur. Riverview Cem., Strasburg.

CARRIGAN, JOHN P.: b. 1818? Tailor. enl. 4/18/61 at Berryville in Co. I as Musician. Deserted 3/11/62.

CASKEY, WILLIAM L.: b. 9/30/21. Laborer. enl. 4/22/61 at Martinsburg in Co. D as Pvt. Left sick in Martinsburg, July/Aug. 1861-Sept./Oct. 1861. Present again Nov./Dec. 1861. Discharged 12/1/62, reason not stated. d. 8/13/65. bur. Greenhill Cem., Martinsburg, W.Va.

CASTLEMAN, CHARLES D.: b. 1832? Lumber dealer. enl. 4/18/61 at Berryville in Co. I as Pvt. AWOL 10/15-10/27, 11/19-11/22, and 12/22-12/30 1861. Wded. at Port Republic, 6/9/62. MWIA in lung at 2nd Manassas, date not specific. d. 11/5 or 11/7 1862.

CAVE, MARION F.: drafted 2/10/63 at Camp Winder in Co. K as Pvt. Deserted from Camp Winder, 4/8/63. Recovered from desertion 10/23/63 and under arrest. Absent under arrest; sent to Richmond to work on fortifications, March/April 1864. Court-martialed 6/30/64. Sentence pardoned 8/31/64. No further record.

CAVE, WILLIAM W.: b. 1837? 5′ 10½″, dark complexion, brown eyes, black hair, dark whiskers. Stonecutter. Residence Culpeper Co. enl. 4/18/61 at Charles Town in Co. A as Pvt. Sick at home July/Aug. 1861. Present again Sept./Oct.

1861. AWOL 12/25-12/28 1861. Gen. Hosp. Charlottesville, 5/13-5/20 1862. POW at Clarke Co., 2/8/63. (Cumberland, Wheeling, Camp Chase). Exchanged 3/28/63. No further record.

CHAMBERS, GEORGE W.: b. 1/6/29. Merchant in Harpers Ferry. Mayor of Harpers Ferry, 1860. Organizer and Capt. of the Floyd Guards, a pre-war militia unit from Harpers Ferry. Capt. of Co. K, 2nd Va. Vol. Inf., 5/3/61. Resigned 4/14/62. d. 2/3/08. bur. Harpers Cem., Harpers Ferry, W.Va.

CHAMBERS, JAMES H.: b. 4/20/17. Farmer. Only record is a POW statement which lists him in Co. E as Pvt., and who was "compelled to do service against his will." POW at Strasburg, 10/19/64 (Pt. Lookout). Oath of Allegiance to U.S., 5/13/65. d. 7/4/00. bur. Old Norborne Cem., Martinsburg, W.Va.

CHAMBERS, JOHN M.: b. 4/30/28. Smith. enl. 4/18/61 at Martinsburg in Co. D as Corp. Absent sick 4/18-6/30 1861. No further record. d. 1/21/98. bur. Greenhill Cem., Martinsburg, W.Va.

CHAMBERS, ROBERT D.: b. 1840? Smith. enl. 4/18/61 at Martinsburg in Co. D as Pvt. Absent sick in Martinsburg, 7/3/61, and arrested by Federal troops and kept as prisoner. No further record.

CHAMBERS, HANBURN: enl. 11/9/62 at Winchester in Co. C as Pvt. Deserted 11/22/62 on march from Winchester.

CHAMBLIN, JAMES B.: b. 1829? Laborer. enl. 6/5/61 at Charles Town in Co. C as Pvt. Wded. at Gaines's Mill or Malvern Hill, 6/27 or 7/1 1862. Present again 10/31/62. AWOL 7/12/63. Deserted 9/5/63.

CHAPMAN, JAMES W.: b. 1833? Blacksmith. enl. 4/19/61 at Duffields in Co. H as Sgt. To Pvt. 11/22/61. Absent sick July/Aug.-Nov./Dec. 1861. AWOL at Bunker Hill, 10/15/62. No further record.

CHAPMAN, JOHN: b. 1839? 6′ 2″, dark complexion, blue eyes, dark hair. Residence Jefferson Co. enl. 4/18/62 near Harrisonburg in Co. G as Pvt. POW at Rippon, W.Va., 9/6/64 (Camp Chase). Oath of Allegiance to U.S., 6/11/65.

CHAPMAN, JOHN W.: enl. 7/17/61 at Winchester in Co. A as Pvt. Sick at home in Jefferson Co., Nov./Dec. 1861. No further record.

CHAPMAN, JOSEPH H.: b. 1840? Laborer. enl. 4/18/61 at Charles Town in Co. G as Pvt. Sent to hospital in Winchester, 12/16/61. Present by 10/31/62. Deserted 7/15/63. d. 8/25/77.

CHAPMAN, THORTON J.: b. 12/28/32. 6′ 0″, dark complexion, blue eyes, black hair. Farmer. drafted 4/15/63 at Camp Winder. Surgeon's discharge for "permanent dislocation of the elbow joint," 9/18/63. d. 3/5/11. bur. Episcopal and Masonic Cem., Middleway, W.Va.

CHEVALLEY, SAMUEL: b. 1838? Gardner. enl. 4/18/61 at Martinsburg in Co. D as Pvt. Chimborazo #1, 10/17/61; debility. Present again Nov./Dec. 1861. No further record.

CHEW, JOHN A.: b. 8/10/38. Farmer. enl. 4/18/61 at Charles Town in Co. G as Sgt. Absent sick 8/21-9/2 1861. Last official entry shows him as absent with leave, Nov./Dec. 1861. No further record. d. 7/4/98. bur. Zion Episcopal Cem., Charles Town, W.Va.

CHILDRESS, _____: enl. 4/16/62 near Mt. Jackson in Co. I as Pvt. Last official entry in Nov./Dec. 1862 shows him AWOL since 6/8/62.

CLAIBORNE, GEORGE: b. 1836? Cooper. enl. 4/19/61 at Hedgesville in Co. E as Pvt. Deserted 7/14/61.

CLANAHAN, SAMUEL: enl. 4/14/62 in Co. H as Pvt. Detailed as teamster, 6/30-10/31 1862 through time of capture. POW at Strasburg, 9/22/64 (Pt. Lookout). Paroled 2/18/65.

CLARK, CHARLES H.: grad. V.M.I., 1859. Teacher. enl. 11/1/62 at Winchester in Co. C as Pvt. POW at Gettysburg, 7/3/63 (Ft. Delaware, Ft. McHenry). No further record. Postwar, editor. d. 1904.

CLARK, SAMUEL G.: b. 1839? Workman. enl. 6/15/61 at Harpers Ferry in Co. F as Pvt. AWOL 7/19/61. Present again Sept./Oct. 1861. Discharged 11/9/61, no reason stated.

CLARK, THOMAS B.: enl. 4/15/62 at Rude's Hill in Co. G as Pvt. MIA Battle of Cedar Run, 8/9/62. "Lost and not heard from since." No further record.

CLARK, WILLIAM H.: Unofficial source lists him as serving in this regt. Alive in 1911 in North McAlster, Oklahoma.

CLARK, WILLIAM LAWRENCE, JR.: b. 1/16/30 at Winchester. grad. Yale University, 1849. Lawyer. m. Mary Johnson Stuart of Staunton. Apptd. Capt. of Winchester Riflemen, a pre-war militia Co. from Frederick Co., 10/7/59. Capt. Co. F, 2nd Va. Vol. Inf., 5/3/61. Wded. in the left thigh about 3 p.m. at 1st Manassas, 7/21/61. Resigned 4/14/62 at New Market because wound made him unfit for active duty. Unofficial source says he worked in the C.S.A. Nitre and Mining Bureau after resignation. Re-instated in Invalid Corps, 3/5/65. Postwar, mayor of Winchester, 1879-1/1/84; Judge of Winchester City Court, 1884-1/1/94; Clerk of Frederick Co. Circuit Court, 1894-6/99. Member Turner Ashby Camp #22, Winchester. d. 12/1/99 at Northport, N.Y. bur. Mt. Hebron Cem., Winchester.

CLARK, GEORGE W.: b. 1837? Carpenter. enl. 5/16/61 at Camp Stephens in Co. A as Pvt. Deserted 6/19/63. Appears on Federal POW list as captured, 7/26/63; "wants to take oath of allegiance." No further record.

CLELAND, THOMAS: enl. 9/16/61 at Camp Harman in Co. E as Pvt. Last official entry shows him present Nov./Dec. 1861.

CLEM, NOAH: enl. 4/18/62 at Rude's Hill in Co. B as Pvt. AWOL from 6/1/62-4/13/63. Fined one month's pay for absence by court-martial. Last official entry shows him in Chimborazo #3, 5/24-6/1 1864. d. about May or June, 1906.

CLEM, WILLIAM: 5′ 7″, florid complexion, blue eyes, auburn hair. Residence New Market. enl. 4/18/62 at Rude's Hill in Co. B as Pvt. AWOL 6/1/62-4/13/63. Fined one month's pay for absence by court-martial. POW at Spotsylvania, 5/12/64 (Pt. Lookout, Elmira). Oath of Allegiance to U.S., 6/27/65.

CLEMENT, FRANCES X.: 6′ 1″, dark complexion, hazel eyes, black hair. Residence Jefferson Co. enl. 3/6/62 at Winchester in Co. A as Pvt. Under arrest, Nov./Dec. 1862, charges not stated. Deserted 7/24/63. POW (Rebel deserter) at Harpers Ferry, 8/10/63 (Old Capitol Prison). Oath of Allegiance to U.S., 9/26/63; sent north to Philadelphia.

CLEVELAND (CLEAVELAND), WILLIAM B.: enl. 4/16/62 near Mt. Jackson in Co. I as Pvt. AWOL 5/24-10/31 1862. Absent wded. May/June 1863. Probably MWIA at Chancellorsville, 5/3/63. d. 6/6/63 at Richmond. bur. Hollywood Cem., Richmond.

CLINE, DAVID AARON: b. 2/28/24. 5′ 10½″, dark complexion, blue eyes, brown hair. Painter or printer. Residence Martinsburg. enl. 4/18/61 at Martinsburg in Co. D as Corp. To Sgt. 8/4/61. Detailed as regt. wagonmaster, Aug. 1862. Present Jan./Feb. 1863. Deserted 1/64. Oath of Allegiance to the U.S., 1/64. d. 3/19/20. bur. Greenhill Cem., Martinsburg.

CLINE, HENRY J.: b. 1842? Laborer. enl. 6/11/61 at Camp Jackson on Bolivar Heights in Co. A as Pvt. Sick at home in Jefferson Co., Nov./Dec. 1861. Present 6/30-10/31 1862. Last official entry shows him at Chimborazo #5, 5/23-6/21 1864, flesh wound in right thigh. No further record.

CLINE, PARRAN R.: b. 1841? Laborer. enl. 6/14/61 at Charles Town in Co. A as Pvt. Last official entry shows him present, Nov./Dec. 1861.

CLINE, THOMAS J.: 5'7", florid complexion, blue eyes, dark hair. Residence Winchester. enl. 4/16/62 at Rude's Hill in Co. E as Pvt. To Corp., date not given. AWOL Nov./Dec. 1862. Present again Jan./Feb. 1862. POW at Spotsylvania, 5/12/64 (Pt. Lookout, Elmira). Oath of Allegiance to U.S., 6/23/65.

CLINE, WILLIAM H.: b. 1834? enl. 4/18/61 at Martinsburg in Co. D as Pvt. Elected Lt. 12/8/61. POW at Winchester, 6/1/62. Exchanged 8/9/62 or 8/25/62. AWOL 11/18/62. Dismissed from rolls, 12/9/62.

CLINEBALL, ADAM: b. 1828? 5'8", fair complexion, blue eyes, light hair. Farmer. Residence Augusta Co. enl. 4/14/62 at New Market in Co. H as Pvt. Deserted 8/24/62. POW (Rebel deserter) at Beverly, 12/6/64. Oath of Allegiance to U.S., 12/12/64.

CLIP (CLIPP), JOHN W.: b. 2/17/34. enl. 10/3/62 at Bunker Hill in Co. F as Pvt. AWOL since 10/12/62. No further record. d. 7/28/23. bur. Edge Hill Cem., Charles Town, W.Va.

CLOUD, AMOS: drafted 10/3/62 at Bunker Hill in Co. C as Pvt. Absent sick 5/3/63. Gen. Hosp. Farmville, 7/15-7/29 1863. Wded. in both hands at Payne's Farm, 11/27/63. Gen. Hosp. Staunton, 12/8/63. Last official entry shows him on detailed service, 11/9/64; duty not stated. Surrendered at Appomattox.

COAKLEY, JOHN: b. 1828? Laborer. enl. 4/20/61 at Harpers Ferry in Co. K as Pvt. Last official entry shows him present, Nov./Dec. 1861.

COCKRILL, DAVID H.: b. 1818? Carpenter. enl. 4/18/61 at Charles Town in Co. A as Lt. Detailed as conscript officer for Jefferson Co., 10/1/62. Detailed by Brig. Gen. Talliferro as chief of Pioneer Corps, 12/19/62; retained on this detail through March/April 1864. Last official entry shows him as commanding Division Provost Guard at Camp Ewell near Burgess Mill, 2/27/65. POW Appomattox, 4/9/65 (Old Capitol Prison). Released 8/8/65. bur. Edge Hill Cem., Charles Town, W.Va.; no dates on stone.

COCKRILL, JOSEPH H.: b. 3/24/44. enl. 2/28/62 at Winchester in Co. A as Pvt. Detailed to work as pioneer entrenching at Buckner's Neck and Hamilton's Crossing, 2/6-6/6 1863. Detailed as pioneer Jan./Feb. 1864. Last official entry shows him present 4/30-10/31 1864. Surrendered at Appomattox.

COFFELT, AARON: drafted 2/22/63 at Camp Winder in Co. C as Pvt. d. 5/12/63 at Chimborazo #1; typhoid fever.

COFFLET, EPHRAIM: b. 1822? 5'8", dark complexion, black eyes, dark hair. Farmer. enl. 4/18/62 at Rude's Hill in Co. B as Pvt. AWOL 6/1-8/15 1862. Discharged 12/8/62, overage.

COFFELT, GIDEON: drafted 4/14/62 at Rude's Hill in Co. K as Pvt. Absent sick 10/15/62 and sent from Bunker Hill to Winchester. Present again Nov./Dec. 1862. Wded. in face at Chancellorsville, 5/3/63. Gen. Hosp. Howard's Grove, Richmond, 5/10/63. To Gen. Hosp. Staunton. Last official entry shows him still absent from wound, March/April 1864.

COFFMAN, REUBEN: drafted 4/14/62 at Rude's Hill in Co. K as Pvt. AWOL 6/3/62-1/25/63. Absent sick Sept./Oct. 1863. Deserted 10/31/63.

COLBERT, GEORGE W.: b. 1838? 5'0", florid complexion, gray eyes, black hair. Farmer. enl. 4/18/61 at Charles Town in Co. G as Pvt. Absent sick since mid-May, 1861. Discharged 11/9/61, no reason stated.

COLBERT, JOHN JAMES: b. 12/18/39. Farmer. enl. 4/18/61 at Charles Town in Co. G as Pvt. Absent sick Nov./Dec. 1861. Killed 9/9/62? bur. Edge Hill Cem., Charles Town, W.Va.

COLBERT, JOSEPH W.: b. 1842? Laborer. enl. 4/18/61 at Duffields in Co. H as Pvt. Wded. at 1st Manassas, 7/21/61. Last official entry shows him on furlough, Nov./Dec. 1861.

COLBERT, RICHARD W.: b. 1844? Laborer. enl. 4/20/61 at Harpers Ferry in Co. K as Pvt. Gen. Hosp. Staunton, 6/18/62; scarlet fever. Present again Nov./Dec. 1862. Detailed as Teamster, Nov./Dec. 1862. Under arrest March/April 1863, no reason stated. Deserted 6/18/63 at Winchester.

COLLINS, DANIEL M.: enl. 3/10/62. Trans. to Co. F as Pvt., 4/8/63, from 4th Va. Inf. POW at Spotsylvania, 5/12/64 (Pt. Lookout). Joined the U.S. Service, 6/8/64.

COLLINS, HENRY: enl. 3/5/62 at Winchester in Co. E as Pvt. Deserted 7/18/63.

COLLINS, JOSEPH P.: b. 1842? Gas fitter. enl. 5/11/62 at Harpers Ferry in Co. K as Pvt. Deserted 5/13/61.

COLLIS, JOSEPH W.: b. 1836? 5'7", light complexion, gray eyes, brown hair. Carpenter. enl. 4/10/61 at Harpers Ferry in Co. K as Pvt. To Sgt. 3/1/63. To Pvt. 11/1/63. Wded. in foot at 2nd Manassas, 8/28/62. Gen. Hosp. Liberty. To Gen. Hosp. Charlottesville, 12/2/62. Detailed to guard Ord. Train, March/April 1863. On detached service with conscript officer in the Valley of Va., July/Aug. 1863. POW at Winchester, 7/29/63 (Camp Chase, Ft. Delaware). Exchanged 9/18/64. Chimborazo #3, 9/22-9/30 1864. Furloughed 40 days from Chimborazo #3, 9/30/64. Trans. to Co. D, 2nd Battalion, Missouri Cav., 1/31/65.

COLSTON, RALIEGH THOMAS: b. 2/18/34 at Richmond. Attd. V.M.I. 1850. Farmer. Capt. of Hedgesville Blues, a pre-war militia Co. from Berkeley Co., Oct., 1859. Capt. Co. E, 2nd Va. Vol. Inf., 5/3/61. To Lt. Col., 3/17/63. Wded. in thigh at Gaines's Mill, 6/27/62. Commanded the regt. following 2nd Manassas through Dec. 1862. Gen. Hosp. Charlottesville, 6/22-7/9 1863, dysentery. MWIA in left leg at Payne's Farm, 11/27/63. Left leg amputated below the knee. d. 12/23/63 at Gen. Hosp. Charlottesville; pneumonia. bur. 12/25/63 in Cem. at University of Virginia, Charlottesville.

COLSTON, WILLIAM BROCKENBROUGH: b. 4/25/36. Farmer. Attd. University of Virgina, 1854-1856. enl. 4/19/61 at Hedgesville in Co. E as Sgt. To Capt. 9/17/62. Absent sick Sept./Oct. 1861. Present again Nov./Dec. 1861; signs roll as commanding Co. Wded. in the hip at Kernstown, 3/23/62. Wded. by shell at Fredericksburg, 12/13/62. Absent recovering from wound until July/Aug. 1863. Retired to Invalid Corps, 4/25/64; "disqualified for marching." Assigned to the Commander of Conscripts for Va. Paroled at Farmville. d. 5/5/19. bur. Old Norborne Cem., Martinsburg, W.Va.

COMPTON, ANDREW J.: b. 1835? 5'8", fair complexion, blue eyes, fair hair. Farmer. Residence Morgan Co. enl. 3/2/62 at Strasburg in Co. D as Pvt. Detailed on conscript duty, 11/2/62. Wded. through both hips at Hatcher's Run, 2/7/65. Chimborazo #4, 2/8/65; POW at Richmond hospital, 4/3/65 (Pt. Lookout). Oath of Allegiance to U.S., 7/25/65.

90

COMPTON, GEORGE W.: enl. 12/22/62 at Camp Nadenbousch in Co. D as Pvt. Last official entry shows him present, March/April 1864.

COMPTON, WILLIAM: enl. 3/2/62 at Strasburg in Co. D as Pvt. Wded. in hand at 2nd Manassas, date not specific. Sick at hosp., July/Aug. 1863. Gen. Hosp. Charlottesville, 11/27/64, rubeola. Trans. to Lynchburg Hosp., 12/3/64. No further record.

CONLEY, WILLIAM H.: b. 1833? Carpenter. enl. 6/15/61 at Camp Whiting in Co. B as Pvt. AWOL 9/3-11/13 1862. Wded. in finger on right hand at Payne's Farm, 11/27/63. POW at Salem Church, 5/20/64 (Pt. Lookout). Exchanged 3/15/65. Chimborazo #2, 3/19/65; scorbutus. POW in Richmond hospital, 4/3/65. Paroled 4/22/65 from Libby Prison.

CONLY, JAMES P.: enl. 2/28/62 at Winchester in Co. B as Pvt. POW at Kernstown, 3/23/62 (Ft. Delaware). Exchanged 8/5/62. No further record.

CONNER, A. J.: enl. 3/4/62 at Winchester in Co. E as Pvt. AWOL Sept./Oct. 1862. No further record.

CONNER, JOHN: enl. 4/14/62 at New Market in Co. H as Pvt. AWOL 6/21/62. Listed as Rebel deserter captured at Hamilton, Va., 10/24/62. Oath of Allegiance to the U.S., 11/12/64. Went to Philadelphia.

CONNER, MORRIS: b. 1831? Laborer. enl. 4/18/61 at Duffields in Co. H as Pvt. Last official entry shows him present, Nov./Dec. 1861.

CONNER, RHODDY: b. 1813? Stonecutter. Residence Augusta Co. enl. 11/1/62 near Berryville in Co. I as Pvt. Wded. at Chancellorsville, 5/3/63. Gen. Hosp. #12, Richmond, 5/8/63. Chimborazo #1, 5/26/63; rheumatism. Trans. to Danville, 6/16/63; returned to duty from Danville, 8/4/63. Wded. in ankle at Payne's Farm, 11/27/63. Present again Dec. 1863. Last official entry shows him absent sick, March/April 1864.

CONRAD, ALEXANDER N.: b. 1842? Boatsman. enl. 6/15/61 at Charles Town in Co. A as Pvt. AWOL 12/25-12/30 1861. POW at Berryville, 7/1/62 (Old Capitol Prison, Ft. Monroe). Exchanged 8/5/62. Reenlisted in Co. A, 9th Va. Cav., Sept./Oct. 1862. No official record of his service in the 9th Va. Cav.

CONRAD, DANIEL BURR: b. 2/24/31. grad. Winchester Academy. grad. Winchester Medical College. Attd. Jefferson Medical College, Philadelphia, Pa. Entered U.S. Navy, 1855, and served on the U.S.S. **Congress** and **Brooklyn.** m. Susie Davis. Assigned as Surgeon to 2nd Va. Vol. Inf., 6/8/61. Requests detachment from regt., 8/13/61. Unofficial source says he was apptd. to Admiral Buchanon's staff, C.S. Navy, date not known. Postwar, superintendent of lunatic asylum at Richmond; superintendent of Western State Hospital, Staunton, April 1886-4/21/89; living in Kansas City, Missouri, 1891; d. 9/20/98. bur. Mt. Hebron Cem., Winchester.

CONRAD, HENRY TUCKER: b. 12/17/39 at Martinsburg. Attd. University of Virginia. Student of Divinity at Episcopal Theological Seminary in Alexandria at outbreak of war. enl. 7/4/61 at Darkesville in Co. D as Pvt. KIA at 1st Manassas, 7/21/61. bur. Old Norborne Cem., Martinsburg, W.Va.

CONRAD, HOLMES ADDISON: b. 9/30/37 at Martinsburg. grad. Winchester Academy. Attd. University of Virginia. Principal of Martinsburg Academy, 1857-1859. enl. 4/23/61 at Martinsburg in Co. D as Sgt. On special duty at telegraph office at Harpers Ferry, 5/7-6/17 1861. KIA at 1st Manassas, 7/21/61. bur. Old Norborne Cem., Martinsburg, W.Va.

CONRAD, JAMES: 5' 11", dark complexion, gray eyes, dark hair. Painter. enl. 10/20/61 at Martinsburg in Co. B as Pvt. AWOL 10/21/62, "supposed to be near Harrisonburg." No further record.

COOKE, BUSHROD W.: b. 1837? 6' 0". Civil Engineer. Nephew of Philip St. George Cooke. enl. 4/18/61 at Charles Town in Co. G as Sgt. Trans. to QM Dept., 6/24/61. Requested transfer to mounted service. No further record.

COOKE, NATHANIEL BURWELL: b. 4/24/45 in Clarke Co. Student. Brother of John Esteen Cooke. enl. 4/18/61 at Millwood in Co. C as Pvt. To Corp., date not given. Trans. to Co. D, 6th Va. Cav., 10/10/62. d. 4/30/18 in Hanover Co.

COOKUS, GEORGE C.: b. 10/11/40. Mason. enl. 4/21/61 at Harpers Ferry in Co. B as Pvt. Absent sick 6/30/61. Present again July/Aug., 1861. Absent sick 9/15/62 at home. POW at Shepherdstown, 4/23/63 (Ft. McHenry, Ft. Monroe). Paroled 4/30/63. Absent sick 5/21/63. Gen. Hosp. #11, Richmond, 6/5/62; diarrhea. Furloughed 60 days, 6/5/63. d. 10/5/63 at home in Shepherdstown, disease. bur. Old Reformed Graveyard, Shepherdstown, W.Va.

COOLEY, SAMUEL: drafted 9/24/62 at Martinsburg in Co. K as Pvt. AWOL 11/24 1862-Jan. 1863. Fined 2 month's pay for absence. KIA at Chancellorsville, 5/3/63.

COONTZ, JAMES R.: b. 9/7/33 at Winchester. 5' 9", dark complexion, blue eyes, dark hair. Wife's name is Mary E. Coontz. enl. 7/1/61 at Winchester in Co. F as Pvt. Wded. in ankle at 1st Manassas, 7/21/61. Present again Sept./Oct. 1861. Reenlisted in Co. G, 11th Va. Cav., 10/31/62. Paroled 4/29/65 at Winchester. d. 9/30/13. bur. Stonewall Cem., Winchester.

COOPER, GEORGE: drafted 11/1/62 at Winchester in Co. C as Pvt. Deserted 12/20/62 from camp near Moss Neck.

COOPER, JAMES W.: enl. 3/2/62 at Cedar Creek in Co. C as Pvt. Wded. in face at 2nd Manassas, 8/30/62. Gen. Hosp. Staunton. Returned from hospital 2/27/63. POW 7/2/63 at Gettysburg. No further record. d. 3/27/00. bur. Wisecarver Cem., Route 625, Clarke Co.

COOPER, JOHN H.: b. 1839? 5' 10", dark complexion, blue eyes, dark hair. Coachsmith. Residence Kernstown. enl. 7/15/61 at Winchester in Co. C as Pvt. POW 5/30/62 at Front Royal. Exchanged 8/5/62. Gen. Hosp. Staunton, 8/15/62-Jan. 1863; nurse. POW Winchester, 1/25/63 (Camp Chase). Exchanged 3/28/63. POW Williamsport, Md., 8/63 (Ft. Delaware, Pt. Lookout). Exchanged 2/18/65. Paroled 4/20/65 at Winchester.

COOTES, BENJAMIN FRANKLIN: b. 1830 at Cootes's Store, Rockingham Co. Lawyer. Unofficial source states he served in this regt. Wded. at Monocacy, 7/9/64. Postwar, employed with Hodges Brothers, wholesale dry goods firm of Baltimore. d. 1880.

COPELAND, PHILIP D.: b. 1838? Carpenter. enl. 4/18/61 at Charles Town in Co. A as Corp. To Pvt. 8/5/61. Sick in Charles Town, Nov./Dec. 1861. POW at Front Royal, 6/6/62. Exchanged 8/5/62. Reenlisted in Blackford's Co. of Cav., Sept./Oct. 1862.

COPENHAVER, JACOB D.: b. 1830? Cooper. enl. 4/18/61 at Martinsburg in Co. D as Pvt. AWOL 28 days, April/June 1861. Last official entry shows him present, Nov./Dec. 1861.

COPENHAVER, RUFUS W.: Trans. into Co. H as Pvt. from 8th Va. Cav. No further record.

COPENHAVER, WILLIAM B.: b. 1843? Miner. enl. 4/18/61 at Millwood in Co. C as Pvt. d. 10/16/61 at home "from sickness contracted in camp"; typhoid fever.

91

CORBIN, WILLIAM H.: b. 1821? Carpenter. enl. 4/18/61 at Winchester in Co. F as Lt. Last official entry shows him present July/Aug. 1861 and commanding the company.

CORRELL, JOHN WILLIAM: b. 8/14/26 at Winchester. Sheriff's deputy in 1860. m. Lucinda Latham. Unofficial source lists him in Co. F. Attd. Winchester Medical College. "Connected with surgical dept. of Jackson's Army, but was obliged to give up this work and then went to North Carolina." Medical degree from University of Maryland. d. 1/20/00 at Baltimore, Md.

COSTBURN, C. D.: Only record shows him in Co. I as Pvt. Wded. at 2nd Manassas, date not specific. No further record.

COUCHMAN, GEORGE W.: b. 12/28/40. enl. 3/5/62 at Winchester in Co. E as Pvt. MWIA in cheek and shoulder at 2nd Manassas, 8/30/62. d. 11/16 or 11/18 1862. bur. Greenhill Cem., Martinsburg, W.Va.

COWLEY, SAMUEL T.: b. 1842? Tailor. enl. 4/18/61 at Charles Town in Co. A as Pvt. AWOL 12/8-12/10 1861. MIA at Gettysburg. POW at Waynestown, Pa., 7/10/63 (Pt. Lookout). Exchanged 12/25/63. Chimborazo #4, 2/10/64; bronchitis. Deserted 2/14/64.

CRAIG, JOHN H.: enl. 12/1/61 at Camp Stephenson in Co. I as Pvt. Deserted 3/1/62. Arrested and brought back to camp under guard, 1/10/63. Fined 12 month's pay for absence by court-martial. d. 4/23/63 at hospital in Gordonsville, reason not stated.

CRAIGHILL, EDWARD D.: b. 11/2/40 at Charles Town. Physician. enl. 4/22/61 at Harpers Ferry in Co. G as Pvt. To Asst. Surgeon, 11/16/61. Detailed as steward in hospital at Winchester, 6/25/61. Detailed as hospital steward at Camp Pickens, Manassas, 9/19/61. Trans. Nov./Dec. 1861, location not stated. Postwar, physician at Lynchburg.

CRAIGHILL, JAMES B.: b. 1839? Student. enl. 6/6/61 at Camp Jackson in Co. G as Pvt. Detailed in Ord. Dept., 7/11/61. Last official entry shows him as an Ord. Sgt. through 2/26/62. No further record.

CRALEY, EDWARD: b. 1842? Laborer. enl. 5/26/61 at Harpers Ferry in Co. H as Pvt. Last official entry shows him present, Nov./Dec. 1861.

CRANE, JOSEPH: b. 6/28/42. Clerk. enl. 5/28/61 at Camp Johnston at Harpers Ferry in Co. G as Pvt. Absent sick 7/15-10/28 1861. Trans. to Co. B, 12th Va. Cav., 11/24/62.

CRAUN, DAVID: enl. 4/15/62 at Rude's Hill in Co. G as Pvt. Discharged 11/62 by furnishing Rhoddy Conner as substitute.

CRIM, JOHN: enl. 12/4/62 at Guinea's Station in Co. D as Pvt. Deserted 12/7/62.

CRIM, JOHN PETER: b. 1827. Carpenter. enl. 10/29/62 at Bunker Hill in Co. F as Sgt. Wded. in left arm near wrist at Payne's Farm, 11/27/63. Chimborazo #4, 11/29-12/9 1863. POW (Rebel deserter) at Milford Road, Va., 11/23/64. No further record. d. 11/9/00. bur. Brucetown Methodist Church Cem.

CRIM, WILLIAM BENJAMIN: 5' 9", light complexion, blue eyes, dark hair. Residence Clarke Co. enl. 3/10/62 at Winchester in Co. I as Pvt. Wded. slightly at Payne's Farm, 11/27/63. Wded. in right side at Ft. Steadman, 3/25/65. Chimborazo #5, 3/26/65. POW at Richmond hospital, 4/3/65 (Jackson Hosp., Libby Prison, Newport News). Oath of Allegiance to the U.S., 7/1/65.

CRIM, WILLIAM H. H.: enl. 4/14/62 at New Market in Co. H as Pvt. AWOL 9/22/62-1/28/63. Fined one month's pay for absence by court-martial. Chimborazo #1, 5/2-6/18 1863; diarrhea. AWOL since 7/1/63. No further record.

CRIZFIELD, JOHN W.: b. 1843? Blacksmith. enl. 4/18/61 at Duffields in Co. H as Pvt. KIA at Chancellorsville, 5/3/63.

CRIST, EPHRAIM B.: b. 1837? Machinist. enl. 5/24/61 at Camp Stephens in Co. A as Pvt. KIA at Kernstown, 3/23/62.

CRISWELL, JOHN: enl. 10/4/62 at Bunker Hill in Co. E as Pvt. Surrendered at Appomattox.

CROCKWELL, JOHN R.: Painter. enl. 4/18/61 at Millwood in Co. C as Pvt. Absent sick 6/30/61. Present again July/Aug. 1861. Discharged by Secretary of War, 11/9/61; no reason stated.

CROFT, ENOCH: b. 1832? in Augusta Co. 5' 11", florid complexion, gray eyes, black hair. Farmer. enl. 4/16/62 near Mt. Jackson in Co. I as Pvt. Detailed as nurse for 2nd Corps hospital at Guinea's Station, 12/19/62. Remained on detached service as nurse with 2nd Corps until trans. to hospital at Liberty Mills, June/July 1863. Then trans. to hospital at Staunton, 7/10/63. Surgeon's Discharge at Staunton, 12/30/63; "paralysis of arms."

CROMER, JOHN H.: b. 1822? in Rockingham Co. 5' 6", fair complexion, blue eyes, light hair. Farmer. enl. 4/18/62 at Rude's Hill in Co. E as Pvt. Discharged 8/3/62, overage.

CROMWELL, RICHARD W.: enl. 10/8/62 at Bunker Hill in Co. A as Pvt. Deserted 12/13/62.

CROW, JACOB B.: b. 11/6/32. 5' 8", fair complexion, blue eyes, dark hair. Residence Jefferson Co. enl. 4/18/61 at Halltown in Co. B as Pvt. To Corp. 8/17/61. To Pvt. Nov./Dec. 1861. AWOL 7/16-8/10 1861. Detailed as teamster, 9/8/61. Detailed as teamster, 6/30-10/31 1862 through Jan./Feb. 1864. Detailed to report to Col. Nadenbousch at Staunton, 2/64. POW near Lexington, 6/11/64 (Camp Chase). Exchanged 3/2/65. No further record. d. 2/24/97. bur. Elmwood Cem., Charles Town, W.Va.

CROWEL, JOSEPH: enl. 12/4/62 at Guinea's Station in Co. D as Pvt. Deserted 5/9/63. Joined U.S. Service, Co. C, 3rd W.Va. Cav., date not known.

CROWN, FREDERICK N.: b. 1842? Miner. enl. 5/5/61 at Harpers Ferry in Co. C as Pvt. Sick in hospital 12/26/64. Discharged 5/23/62, no reason stated.

CULP, JOHN WESLEY: b. 1839? Tailor. enl. 4/20/61 at Harpers Ferry in Co. B as Pvt. Taken POW while absent on furlough, March/April 1862. Exchanged 8/5/62. KIA at Gettysburg on Culp's Hill within sight of the family farm, 7/3/63.

CUNNINGHAM, PHILLIP S.: b. 1822. Farmer. enl. 4/18/61 at Martinsburg in Co. D as Lt. Resigned 11/30/61. d. 1865. bur. St. Joseph's Cem., Martinsburg, W.Va.

CUNNINGHAM, WILLIAM L.: b. 2/14/36. Farmer. enl. 4/19/61 at Hedgesville in Co. E as Pvt. Last official entry shows him present, Nov./Dec. 1861. d. 10/5/11. bur. Falling Waters Cem., Spring Mills, W.Va.

CURL, GEORGE W.: b. 1832? 5' 7", florid complexion, blue eyes, brown hair. Plasterer. Residence Frederick Co. enl. 4/18/61 at Winchester in Co. F as Corp. Detailed as teamster, Nov./Dec. 1861. Detailed as teamster, Jan./Feb. 1863-March/April 1864. Wded. at Ft. Steadman, 3/25/65. POW at Richmond hospital, 4/3/65 (Pt. Lookout). Oath of Allegiance to U.S., 7/7/65. Transportation furnished to Winchester. d. 2/24/06 at Lincoln, Va.

CURRIE, CHARLES W.: b. 1838? Farmer. enl. 4/18/61 at Duffields in Co. H as Pvt. Wded. at Kernstown, 3/23/62. POW near Harpers Ferry, 10/16/62 (Ft. McHenry). Exchanged 10/25/62. Trans. to Co. D, 12th Va. Cav., 12/17/62.

CURRIE, GEORGE E.: b. 3/21/39. Farmer. enl. 4/18/61 at Duffields in Co. H as Pvt. To Sgt. 6/30-10/31 1862. To Lt. Jan./Feb. 1863. Wded. at 1st Manassas, 7/21/61. Present again Sept./Oct. 1861. POW at Spotsylvania, 5/12/64 (Pt. Lookout). Exchanged 3/14/65. d. 2/24/95. bur. Edge Hill Cem., Charles Town, W.Va.

CURRY, ELISHA: b. 1819? 6′ 2″, sallow complexion, gray eyes, black hair. Brick layer. drafted 4/15/62 at Rude's Hill in Co. G as Pvt. Deserted, date not known. Recovered from desertion, 7/11/62, and fined $38.50 for absence by court-martial. Discharged 11/12/62, overage. d. 1/15/96.

CUSTER, EPHRAIM G.: b. 1/16/32. 5′ 6″, fair complexion, gray eyes, brown hair. enl. 4/18/61 at Martinsburg in Co. D as Pvt. To Corp. 8/4/61. To Sgt. 11/1/62. To Pvt. 2/64. On furlough July/Aug. 1863. AWOL since 2/1/64. Reduced to ranks by court-martial and sentenced to forfeit 2 month's pay, Jan./Feb. 1864. POW at Spotsylvania, 5/12/64 (Pt. Lookout, Elmira). Exchanged 3/2/65. Jackson Hosp., Richmond, 3/6/65. Furloughed 30 days, 3/8/65. Paroled 4/25/65 at Winchester. d. 1/1/05. bur. Greenhill Cem., Martinsburg, W.Va.

DAGGY, SAMUEL BROWN: b. 1844? drafted 4/16/62 at Rude's Hill in Co. E as Pvt. Wded. in knee at Gaines's Mill, 6/27/62. Gen. Hospital, Howard's Grove, Richmond, 7/14/62. Furloughed for 30 days, 7/14/62. Last official entry in March/April 1864 shows him still absent due to wound received, 6/27/62. Gen. Hosp. #13, Richmond, 1/17/65; febris intermittens Quartana. To Castle Thunder, 1/19/65. To Chimborazo #2, 2/9/65. To Chimborazo #3, 3/5/65. To Chimborazo #1, 3/5/65. POW at Richmond hospital, 4/3/65. Oath of Allegiance to U.S., 6/29/65. d. March, 1866.

DAILEY, PATRICK: Residence Harpers Ferry. enl. 7/2/61 at Camp Myers in Co. K as Pvt. To Corp. 6/30-10/31 1862. Detailed to arrest deserters, Jan./Feb. 1863. Deserted 4/3/63 "while on detail to arrest deserters in the Valley of Va." POW at Kearneysville, 4/6/63 (Ft. McHenry). Oath of Allegiance to U.S., 4/20/63.

DAILEY, WILLIAM: b. 1834? Laborer. enl. 4/20/61 at Harpers Ferry in Co. K as Pvt. Deserted from Camp Harman, 8/30/61.

DALGARN, STEPHEN S.: b. 8/5/44. 5′ 5″, light complexion, blue eyes, dark hair. enl. 12/4/62 at Guinea's Station in Co. D as Pvt. Last official entry shows him present, 4/30-10/31 1864. Paroled 4/18/65 at Winchester. d. 8/14/04. bur. Edge Hill Cem., Charles Town, W.Va.

DANDRIDGE, EDMOND PENDLETON: b. 1/28/41. Farmer. enl. 4/18/61 at Martinsburg in Co. D as Pvt. Wded. in foot at 1st Manassas, 7/21/61. Present again Sept./Oct. 1861. Last official entry shows him sick in hospital, Nov./Dec. 1861.

DANDRIDGE, PHILIP PENDLETON: b. 11/5/43 in Jefferson Co. Student. enl. 5/1/61 at Winchester in Co. F as Pvt. Discharged 8/6/61, no reason stated. Assigned cadet Co. F, 9th Va. Cav., 10/30/61. Assigned to staff of Gen. W.H.F. Lee, 10/15/63. Promoted to Lt. of Infantry (which organization not stated), 3/3/65. Postwar, civil engineer. d. 1/8/21 at Baltimore, Md. bur. Mt. Hebron Cem., Winchester.

DANIELS, BENJAMIN F.: b. 1831? 5′ 8″, fair complexion, blue eyes, brown hair. Merchant. enl. 6/18/61 at Winchester in Co. B as Pvt. Absent 6/30/61, on leave. Present again July/Aug. 1861. On furlough Jan./Feb. 1862. POW while on furlough (not stated where), March/April 1862. Exchanged 8/5/62. AWOL 8/5/62-1/21/63. POW at Spotsylvania, 5/20/64 (Pt. Lookout). Exchanged 10/30/64. Paroled 4/20/65 at Mt. Jackson.

DARNELL, ANDREW J.: enl. 4/15/62 at Rude's Hill in Co. A as Pvt. AWOL 4/18/62-4/12/63. Sentenced by court-martial to forfeit all pay during time of absence. Wded. 5/3/63 at Chancellorsville. Deserted Jan./Feb. 1864.

DAUGHERTY, CHARLES: enl. 11/25/61 at Camp Stephenson in Co. A as Pvt. d. 7/12/62 at Port Republic; typhoid fever.

DAUGHERTY, JAMES W.: b. 1822? Farmer. enl. 5/13/61 at Harpers Ferry in Co. A as Pvt. In Commissary Dept. 10/19-10/30 1861. Wded. slightly at 2nd Manassas, date not specific. Detailed as teamster, Jan./Feb. 1863-Jan./Feb. 1864. Deserted March/April 1864.

DAUGHERTY, JOHN: enl. 4/16/62 near Mt. Jackson in Co. I as Pvt. KIA 5/25/62 at 1st Winchester.

DAVENPORT, HENRY BEDINGER: b. 9/9/31. Farmer. enl. 4/18/61 at Charles Town in Co. A as Lt. Last official entry in Nov./Dec. 1861 shows him commanding the Co. since 7/21/61 due to the wounding of Capt. Rowan. d. 9/15/01. bur. Edge Hill Cem., Charles Town, W.Va.

DAVIS, GEORGE A. S.: b. 1835. Farmer. enl. 4/18/61 at Charles Town in Co. A as Sgt. To Lt. 10/24/61. Commanding Co. 6/30-10/31 1862 through Nov./Dec. 1862; May/June 1863; Sept./Oct. 1863. Gen. Hosp. Charlottesville, 1/6/63; acute diarrhea. To Gen. Hosp. Lynchburg, 1/9/63. Present again March/April 1863. On furlough July/Aug. 1863. Gen. Hosp. #4, Richmond, 9/16-9/28 1863; chronic diarrhea. Sent to hospital sick, 1/22/64. Present again March/April 1864. Inspector and Mustering Officer for regt., 10/31/64. On detached service, 11/29/64; mission not stated. Resigned 1/18/65 due to smallness of Co. and his inability to march "on account of chronic diarrhea from which I have been suffering for two years." d. 2/12/80. bur. Edge Hill Cem., Charles Town, W.Va.

DAVIS, HENRY C.: b. 5/18/39. Teacher. enl. 4/18/61 at Charles Town in Co. A as Pvt. To. Corp. 11/25/61. In Commissary Dept., 10/19-10/31 1861. Reenlisted in artillery, 6/30-10/31 1862.

DAVIS, JOHN B.: b. 1833? Soldier. enl. 4/20/61 at Harpers Ferry in Co. K as Lt. Discharged 4/18/62, no reason stated.

DAVIS, JOHN D.: enl. 3/25/62 near Mt. Jackson in Co. I as Pvt. KIA at 2nd Manassas, 8/28/62.

DAVIS, JOHN R.: Unofficial source shows him serving in the 2nd Va. Inf. d. 6/5/62. bur. Hollywood Cem.

DAVIS, JOSEPH M.: b. 1833? Laborer. enl. 5/18/61 at Camp Lee in Co. K as Pvt. Last official entry shows him present, Nov./Dec. 1861.

DAVIS, JOSEPH N.: b. 1836? Shoemaker. enl. 4/19/61 at Hedgesville in Co. E as Pvt. Last official entry shows him present, Nov./Dec. 1861.

DAVIS, RICHARD: drafted 10/30/62 at Bunker Hill in Co. G as Pvt. Deserted 11/20/62.

DAVIS, WILLIAM: drafted 4/14/62 at Rude's Hill in Co. K as Pvt. Wded. at 2nd Manassas, 8/28/62. Last official entry in March/April 1864 still shows him absent and in hospital.

DAY, JAMES W.: b. 6/27/33. Plasterer. enl. 4/18/61 at Martinsburg in Co. D as Pvt. Deserted 5/3/61. d. 4/7/78. bur. Greenhill Cem., Martinsburg, W.Va.

DAY, JOHN: enl. 4/14/62 at New Market in Co. H as Pvt. Last official entry shows him AWOL since 8/25/62. No further record.

DEAHL, HORACE PEAKE: b. 3/26/36 at Berryville. Cabinet maker. enl. 4/18/61 at Berryville in Co. I as Lt. Not reelected 4/18/62. Reenlisted as Pvt. in Co. D, 6th Va. Cav. Wded. twice at Brandy Station and once at Trevilion Station (dates not given). POW Jan. 1865 (Ft. McHenry); place of capture not stated. d. 3/25/12. bur. Greenhill Cem., Berryville.

DEAN, JAMES: enl. 4/9/62 at Rude's Hill in Co. E as Pvt. Wded. in upper arm at Gaines's Mill, 6/27/62. Gen. Hosp., Howard's Grove, Richmond, 7/14/62. Furloughed 30 days, 7/14/62. Still absent from wounds, Nov./Dec. 1862. Present again Sept./Oct. 1863. Last official entry shows him present 12/31/64.

DEAN, WILLIAM F.: b. 1/20/28. enl. 4/6/62 at Rude's Hill in Co. F as Pvt. AWOL since 6/1/62. Recovered from desertion, 3/8/63. Detailed to work in iron foundry by Secretary of War., March/April 1863. Last official entry shows him still on detail at iron foundry, March/April 1864. d. 5/4/07. bur. Dean Family Cem., Swift Run, Va.

DEANE (DEAN), WILLIAM M.: b. 6/10/35 at Mechanicsburg, Pa. Plumber. Residence Kernstown. m. Henrietta Long. enl. in Co. F as Pvt. Escaped from Federal captivity, 10/3/62. Wded. in leg at Jordan's Springs near Winchester, 6/13/63. d. 2/4/16. bur. Youngstown, Ohio.

DEARMONT, PETER: b. 1835? Farmer. enl. 4/18/61 at Millwood in Co. C as Pvt. Sick since 11/2/61. Trans. to Co. D, 6th Va. Cav., 6/30-10/31 1862.

DEBTOR, J. L.: b. 1832? 5' 6", ruddy complexion, gray eyes, brown hair. Residence Berkeley Co. enl. 3/4/62 at Winchester in Co. D as Pvt. Gen. Hosp. Mt. Jackson, 6/2/62; bilous fever. Absent sick at hospital, 10/16/62. Detailed as hospital steward at Gen. Hosp. #9, Richmond, 2/11/63-Feb. 1864. Detailed to C. S. Shoe Dept., Richmond, 2/14/64-Aug. 1864. POW at Martinsburg, 9/5/64 (Ft. Delaware). Oath of Allegiance to U.S., 6/14/65.

DECK, EDWARD C.: b. 12/4/39. Blacksmith. enl. 6/15/61 at Harpers Ferry in Co. H as Pvt. Last official entry shows him present, Nov./Dec. 1861. d. 1/18/00. bur. Greenhill Cem., Martinsburg, W.Va.

DECK, JACOB H.: b. 1840? Merchant. enl. 4/19/61 at Hedgesville in Co. E as Corp. Deserted 7/18/61.

DECKER, PALATINE: b. 1837? Armorer. enl. 4/10/61 at Harpers Ferry in Co. K as Sgt. Discharged by Secretary of War, 8/23/61; reason not stated.

DECKER, R. A.: Unofficial source states he served in Co. F for four years.

DELARUE, GUS E.: b. 1844. Unofficial source states he served in Co. K. d. 6/14/08. bur. Hollywood Cem., Richmond.

DELAVIN, PATRICK: b. 1816? Laborer. enl. 4/19/61 at Duffields in Co. H as Pvt. AWOL July/Aug. 1861. Surgeon's Discharge, Sept./Oct. 1861., reason not stated.

DELLINGER, AUGUSTUS: enl. 4/18/62 at Rude's Hill in Co. B as Pvt. Detailed as teamster, 4/28/62. Last official entry in Sept./Oct. 1863 shows him as AWOL since 11/1/62. No further record.

DELLINGER, WILLIAM L.: enl. 4/18/62 at Rude's Hill as Pvt. in Co. B. Absent sick April 1862. AWOL 5/25-9/7 1862. Deserted 11/1/62 and supposed to be in Shenandoah Co. No further record.

DEMARSTER, DANIEL: Residence Augusta Co. enl. 4/16/62 near Mt. Jackson in Co. I as Pvt. AWOL 5/23/62-11/1/63. On detached service, March/April 1864; duty not stated. Chimborazo #1, 6/64. To Gen. Hosp. Farmville, 6/2/64; spinal injury. Furloughed for 60 days, 6/28/64. Gen. Hosp. Charlottesville, 9/25-10/4 1864. Last official entry shows him sick, 12/31/64.

DE PRIESTE, ROBERT H.: b. 4/1/34 in Augusta Co. enl. 4/16/62 near Mt. Jackson in Co. I as Pvt. Lovingston Hospital, Winchester, 8/27/62; dysentery. To Gen. Hosp. Staunton, 9/6/62. Attached as nurse 9/17/62-1/31/63. Present again Feb. 1863. Last official entry shows him present, March/April 1864. d. 1/15/92 in Augusta Co.

DEPUTY, JOHN: drafted 4/18/62 at Rude's Hill in Co. C as Pvt. First official entry shows him returning from desertion, Sept./Oct. 1863. Last official entry shows him present, March/April 1864.

DESPER, JOHN: b. 1826? 5' 8", light complexion, hazel eyes, red hair. enl. 4/16/62 near Mt. Jackson in Co. I as Pvt. AWOL 6/24/62. Does not appear at a muster again, but records show he was detailed 4/18/63 and again on 9/17/63 to Nitre and Mining Bureau. Paroled 5/1/65 at Staunton.

DICKENSON, CHARLES J.: b. 1818? drafted 4/14/62 at Rude's Hill in Co. K at Pvt. Discharged 7/23/62, overage. d. Sept., 1895.

DICKENSON, ROBERT: drafted 4/14/62 at Rude's Hill in Co. K as Pvt. Drummer 6/30-10/31 1862. Detailed as orderly to Capt., Nov./Dec. 1862. Detailed as orderly to Col., Jan./Feb. 1863. Last official entry shows him present, 10/31/64.

DICKSON, JOHN A.: enl. 4/15/62 at Rude's Hill in Co. A as Pvt. Discharged 8/10/62, overage.

DICKSON, SAMUEL M.: enl. 4/15/62 at Rude's Hill in Co. A as Pvt. Discharged 7/30/62, overage.

DIEFFENDEFER, BERNARD: b. 1835? Carpenter. enl. 4/21/61 at Harpers Ferry in Co. D as Pvt. Deserted 5/8/61.

DIFFENDERFER, JOHN W.: b. 6/15/40 in Winchester. 5' 8", fair complexion, blue eyes, dark hair. Carpenter. m. Emma Glenn. enl. 4/18/61 at Winchester in Co. F as Pvt. Absent sick July/Aug.-Sept./Oct. 1861. Surgeon's discharge 12/1/61, heart disease. Living in Winter Park, Florida, in 1916. d. 2/23/19. bur. Palm Cem., Winter Park, Florida.

DINKLE, CHARLES A.: b. 5/27/22. Listed in Co. F, no rank or enlistment date given. Wded. at Port Republic, 6/9/62. No further record. d. 2/26/04. bur. Edge Hill Cem., Charles Town, W.Va.

DINKLE, ENOS: b. 1843. Student. enl. 6/15/61 at Winchester in Co. F as Pvt. Present through Nov./Dec. 1861. Reenlisted in Pifer's Cavalry sometime before 10/31/62. Killed 7/3/63. bur. Stonewall Cem., Winchester.

DINKLE, PETER: b. 3/12/32 in York Co., Pa. 6' 0", dark eyes, dark hair. Farmer. Residence Frederick Co., Va. enl. 6/15/61 at Winchester in Co. F as Pvt. Sick and AWOL since 10/12/61. Present again Nov./Dec. 1861. Reenlisted in Pifer's Cavalry sometime before 10/31/62. POW April 1864 (Camp Chase). Exchanged 3/27/65. Paroled May 1865 at Winchester. Postwar, proprietor Arlington Hotel, Grafton, W.Va. d. 11/17/13 at Winchester. bur. Mt. Hebron Cem., Winchester.

DISHMAN, SCOTT: b. 1834? Laborer. enl. 6/14/61 at Winchester in Co. C as Pvt. MWIA at 1st Manassas, 7/21/61. d. 7/24/61.

DIXON, ROBERT W.: Listed in Co. K as Pvt. Only official record is his parole at Appomattox.

DOBBINS, JOHN J.: b. 1840? enl. 4/18/61 at Berryville in Co. I as Pvt. Farmer. AWOL 7/27-7/31 1861. Present again Sept./Oct. 1861. AWOL 12/25-12/30 1861. KIA at 1st Winchester, 5/25/62.

DOLBY (DOLLY), HARMAN: b. 10/24/16. enl. at Rude's Hill in Co. F as Pvt. Wded. in right hand and arm at Payne's

94

Farm, 11/27/63. Chimborazo #4, Richmond, 11/29/63. To Staunton, 12/7/63. Present again Jan./Feb. 1864. POW at Salem Church, 5/20/64 (Pt. Lookout). Adm. to U.S.A. Gen. Hosp., Pt. Lookout, 1/31/65; remittent fever. Released 5/14/65 from Hammond Gen. Hosp., Pt. Lookout. d. 6/15/82. bur. Mt. Hebron Cem., Winchester.

DOLL, GEORGE H.: b. in Frederick Co. enl. 4/16/62 near Mt. Jackson in Co. I as Pvt. Gen. Hosp. Farmville, 10/1/62; ulcerated leg. Returned to duty 12/12/62. KIA at Payne's Farm, 11/27/63.

DOLL, JOSEPH: drafted 4/14/62 at Rude's Hill in Co. K as Pvt. Discharged 9/6/62, overage.

DOLL, RICHARD McSHERRY: b. 1843? 5' 8", light complexion, gray eyes, dark hair. Clerk. Residence Berkeley Co. enl. 4/18/61 at Martinsburg in Co. D as Pvt. To Sgt. 4/18/62. Absent sick Sept./Oct. 1861. Present again Nov./Dec. 1861. POW ?/25/62 at Martinsburg. Exchanged 8/5/62. Wded. at Chancellorsville, 5/3/63. Present again July/Aug. 1863. POW at Salem Church, 5/20/64 (Old Capitol Prison, Ft. Delaware). Oath of Allegiance to U.S., 6/15/65.

DOLL, SAMUEL: b. 1823? 5' 10", fair complexion, blue eyes, fair hair. enl. 4/8/62 at Rude's Hill in Co. G as Pvt. AWOL 6/14-10/25 1862. Fined $51.70 for absence. Deserted 1/9/63. Recovered from desertion 6/18/63, and in guardhouse. "Released from guard by President's Proclamation," July/Aug. 1863. Fined $58.54 for absence. POW at Monocacy, 7/10/64. (U.S.A. Gen. Hosp. Frederick, 7/10/64; simple dressing. Trans. to Ft. McHenry, 7/27/64). Exchanged 10/30/64. No further record.

DOLL, WILLIAM: drafted 4/14/62 at Rude's Hill in Co. K as Pvt. d. in hospital sometime after 7/1/62; location of death and cause not stated.

DONNELLY, JOHN H.: b. 1843? Student. enl. 4/18/61 at Charles Town in Co. G as Pvt. Wded. at Manassas, 8/30/62. "Missing since that time and supposed dead."

DONOVAN, SAMUEL: Listed in Co. D as Pvt. AWOL 9/15/62 at Bunker Hill. No further record.

DORAN, JOSEPH T.: b. 1838? Butcher. enl. 4/18/61 at Millwood in Co. C as Pvt. AWOL 10/1/61. No further record.

DOREK, JOSEPH E.: Listed in Co. C as Pvt. AWOL 4/17/62, and reported as joined Capt. Myers's Cavalry.

DORSEY, EDWARD W.: b. 1825? Farmer. enl. 4/18/61 at Charles Town in Co. A as Pvt. Chimborazo #1, Richmond, 10/17/61; debility. Returned to duty 10/28/61. Detailed as teamster 11/27/61. No further record.

DOUGLAS, HENRY KYD: b. 9/29/38. grad. Franklin-Marshall College, Pa.; law school at Lexington, 1860. Lawyer. enl. 4/18/61 at Halltown in Co. B as Pvt. Elected Sgt. 6/5/61. Elected Lt. 8/14/61. To Capt. 9/6/62. Detailed to Gen. Jackson's staff, 4/27/62. Detailed as Brig. Inspector, 12/27/62. Detailed as AAAG on Maj. Gen. Johnson's Staff, 5/18/63. Wded. at Gettysburg, 7/3/63. No further record. Postwar, lawyer. Author of *I Rode With Stonewall*. d. 12/18/03. bur. Elmwood Cem., Shepherdstown, W.Va.

DOUGLAS, JOHN B.: b. 1842? 5' 10", dark complexion, gray eyes, black hair. Student. enl. 4/20/61 at Harpers Ferry in Co. B as Pvt. AWOL March/April 1862. No additional record appears until his parole, 4/17/65, at Winchester.

DOUGLAS, JAMES: b. 1844? Clerk. enl. 5/15/61 at Harpers Ferry in Co. G as Pvt. Last official entry shows him present, Nov./Dec. 1861.

DOWDY, P. H.: Unofficial source lists him in Co. F and states he surrendered at Appomattox.

DOYLE, GARRETT: b. 1831? Laborer. enl. 4/20/61 at Harpers Ferry in Co. K as Pvt. POW at Winchester, 6/1/62. Exchanged 8/5/62. POW at Spotsylvania, 5/12/64 (Pt. Lookout, Elmira). Oath of Allegiance to U.S., 5/12 or 5/14 1865.

DREBING, CHARLES L.: b. 1838? 5' 8", dark complexion, gray eyes, dark hair. Rope maker. Residence Berkeley Co. enl. 4/18/61 at Martinsburg in Co. D as Pvt. Shown as Sgt. by 10/31/62. To Lt. 12/9/62. POW at Martinsburg, 7/10/64 (Camp Chase, Pt. Lookout). Paroled at Camp Chase, 2/12/65. Surrendered at Appomattox.

DUGAN, JAMES F.: b. 1/29/41 in Berkeley Co. 5' 7", fair complexion, blue eyes, light hair. Farmer. enl. 4/20/61 in Co. D as Pvt. Shot by accident, 5/28/61. Surgeon's Discharge, 11/5/61; typhoid fever and wound in right breast and lung. d. 6/20/26. bur. Falling Waters Cem., Spring Mills, W.Va.

DUGAN, JAMES W.: b. 1840? Farmer. enl. 4/19/61 at Hedgesville in Co. E as Pvt. POW at Kernstown, 3/23/62 (Ft. Delaware). Exchanged 8/5/62. Wded. in hand and foot at 2nd Manassas, date not specific. Present again Sept./Oct. Wded. at Chancellorsville, 5/3/63. Last official entry shows him still absent from wound, March/April 1864. Discharged from Invalid Corps, 9/22/64; "totally disqualified."

DUGAN, JOHN A.: b. 1834? in Berkeley Co. 5' 8½", fair complexion, blue eyes, brown hair. Clerk. enl. 4/18/61 at Martinsburg in Co. D as Sgt. Wded. in the thigh at 1st Manassas, 7/21/61. Surgeon's Discharge, 12/6/61.

DUKE, PETER T.: Cooper. enl. 6/3/61 at Camp Jackson in Co. I as Pvt. AWOL 12/27/61. Present again 4/30-10/31/62. Deserted 7/23/63. POW (Rebel deserter) 8/8/63 at Sharpsburg, Md. (Ft. McHenry). Oath of Allegiance to U.S., 10/14/64.

DUNN, E.: Unofficial source lists him in Co. E. bur. Stonewall Cem., Winchester.

DUVAL, EVANS: b. 1839 in Anne Arundel Co., Md. Unofficial source states he served in this regt. Postwar, tobacco merchant in Laurel, Md. and Baltimore, Md.

EARSOME, JOSEPH B.: b. 1834? Farmer. enl. 4/21/61 at Harpers Ferry in Co. D as Pvt. Elected Lt., Co. A, 33 Va. Vol. Inf. in Aug. 1862.

EASTERDAY, JOHN S.: b. 11/15/38. Tinner. enl. 4/18/61 at Charles Town in Co. A as Pvt. Present through Nov./Dec. 1861. Reenlisted in Co. B, 12th Va. Cav., sometime before 10/31/62. d. 2/12/19. bur. Edge Hill Cem., Charles Town, W.Va.

EBBERLY, DANIEL: enl. 4/9/62 at Rude's Hill in Co. E as Pvt. AWOL Sept./Oct. 1862-1/15/63. Fined 1 month's pay for absence by court-martial. d. 3/27/63 at Guinea Hosp.; disease.

EDMUNDS, JOSEPH A.: b. 1842? Carpenter. enl. 4/18/61 at Charles Town in Co. A as Pvt. Wded. in the hip at 1st Manassas, 7/21/61. Present again Sept./Oct. 1861. AWOL 12/25-12/30 1861. No further record.

EICHELBERGER, GEORGE F.: b. 12/18/40. 6' 0", dark complexion, brown eyes, dark hair. Student. enl. 4/18/61 at Charles Town in Co. G as Pvt. To Sgt. 4/15/64. Wded. in arm at 2nd Manassas, 8/28/62. Returned to duty 2/20/62. Wded. at Spotsylvania, 5/12/64. Gen. Hosp. Charlottesville, 5/24/64. Furloughed 6/9/64. Paroled 4/24/65 at Charles Town. d. 2/6/10. bur. Edge Hill Cem., Charles Town, W.Va.

EICHELBERGER, LUCIEN: b. 1843? Laborer. enl. 5/15/61 at Harpers Ferry in Co. H as Pvt. Discharged 5/23/62, reason not stated.

95

EICHELBERGER, WEBSTER: b. 3/9/35. Minister. enl. 6/26/61 at Camp Stephens in Co. G as Pvt. Discharged 7/20/62, reason not stated.

ELLIS, BENJAMIN M.: b. 1823? in Henrico Co. 6'0", dark complexion, blue eyes, dark hair. School teacher. enl. 4/15/62 at Rude's Hill in Co. G as Pvt. Discharged 8/18/62. Unofficial source lists him in Co. F, 1st Va. Cav.

ELLIS, JOHN: enl. 4/9/62 at Rude's Hill in Co. E as Pvt. Absent sick 10/4/62-Jan./Feb. 1863. Present again March/April 1863. Wded. in leg near knee at Payne's Farm, 11/27/83. Reported AWOL 3/13/65 in Page Co.

ELEYETT, JAMES: b. 8/28/42. Farmer. enl. 4/18/61 in Co. D as Pvt. Detailed as wagon driver June-Sept./Oct. 1861. Detached service as teamster Nov./Dec. 1862. Last official entry shows him still detached as teamster March/April 1864. d. 3/23/13. bur. Stone's Chapel Presbyterian Church, Clarke Co.

ELMS, ROBERT: b. 1843? Farmer. enl. 4/25/61 at Harpers Ferry in Co. E as Pvt. Deserted out of state sometime before 6/30/61.

EMERSON, RIDGELY: b. 1843? Laborer. enl. 4/20/61 at Harpers Ferry in Co. K as Pvt. Deserted from Camp Harman, 8/15/61.

EMSWELLER, HARRISON: b. 1841? 5'9", fair complexion, blue eyes, brown hair. enl. 4/8/62 at Rude's Hill in Co. G as Pvt. AWOL 5/26-8/12 1862. Fined $27.86 for absence. Wded. with bruised left arm at Locust Hill, 11/27/63. Chimborazo #4, Richmond, 11/29/63. Returned to duty 12/6/63. Last official entry shows him present 10/31/64. Paroled 4/20/64 (sic) at Mt. Jackson.

EMSWELLER, WESLEY: b. 1841? 5'9", fair complexion, gray eyes, black hair. Residence Shenandoah Co. drafted 11/13/62 at Winchester in Co. G as Pvt. Absent sick Jan./Feb. 1863-3/5/63. Listed as an ambulance driver, March/April 1863. Absent sick 7/26-10/1 1863. Wded. at Payne's Farm, 11/27/63. Present again Dec. 1863. Wded. severely at Spotsylvania, 5/5/64, and "not fit for duty." Paroled 4/20/65 at Mt. Jackson.

EMSWILLER, S.: enl. 4/18/62 at Rude's Hill in Co. B as Pvt. d. 5/20/63 at Gen. Hosp. Staunton; pneumonia. Claim filed by his widow Sarah Emswiller. C. S. government paid her $28.88 for his service in the army.

ENGLE, BENJAMIN F.: b. 1843? Farmer. enl. 4/19/61 at Duffields in Co. H as Pvt. Last official entry shows him present, Nov./Dec. 1861.

ENGLE, GEORGE W.: enl. 12/4/62 at Fredericksburg in Co. H as Pvt. Chimborazo #1, Richmond, 1/11/63; diarrhea. To Gen. Hosp. Palmyra, 3/9/63. d. 3/21/63 at Palmyra.

ENGLE, JOHN M.: b. 9/8/22. Farmer. enl. at Duffields in Co. H as Pvt. AWOL sometime before 6/30/61 and never mustered. d. 1/9/97. bur. Edge Hill Cem., Charles Town, W.Va.

ENGLE, WILLIAM F.: b. 1837? Armorer. enl. 4/20/61 at Harpers Ferry in Co. K as Lt. Accidentally wded. at Winchester, 7/14/61. Last official entry shows him still absent Nov./Dec. 1861. Dropped from Register of Commissioned Officers, 4/20/62.

ENGLEBRIGHT, JOHN H.: b. 1838? Laborer. enl. 4/18/61 at Martinsburg in Co. D as Pvt. Deserted 5/19/61.

ENGLEMAN, JAMES: b. 1831? 5'7", light complexion, blue eyes, black hair. Tailor. Residence Staunton. enl. 4/16/62 near Mt. Jackson in Co. I as Pvt. AWOL 5/8/62 and dropped from the roll, Nov./Dec. 1862. On Federal list of Rebel Deserters in Dept. of W.Va., Jan. 1864; "took the oath and sent west via New Creek."

ENGLEMAN, WILLIAM D.: enl. 4/16/62 near Mt. Jackson in Co. I as Pvt. Trans. to Co. C, 5/14/62. No further record.

ENGLISH, ROBERT M.: b. 9/27/24. Farmer. enl. 4/18/61 at Charles Town in Co. G as Lt. Wded. in arm, leg, and breast at 1st Manassas, 7/21/61. Returned to duty 10/25/61. KIA at Port Republic, 6/9/62. bur. Edge Hill Cem., Charles Town, W.Va.

ENSWILLER, FLAV.: enl. 4/18/62 at Rude's Hill in Co. B as Pvt. Deserted sometime before April 1862. Court-martialed for desertion Nov./Dec. 1862, "but sentence not published." Last official entry shows him present Jan./Feb. 1863.

ENTLER, CATO MOORE: b. 1822? Confectioner. enl. 6/18/61 at Winchester in Co. B as Pvt. Sick at Manassas Hosp. 10/21/61. To Chimborazo #5, 11/3/61; diarrhea. To Gen. Hosp. Farmville, 5/7/62; torpor of liver. Returned to duty 7/16/62; however, last official entry shows him absent sick 6/30-10/31 1862.

ENTLER, CHARLES E.: b. 1842? Clerk. enl. 4/20/61 at Harpers Ferry in Co. B as Pvt. Deserted 6/15/61.

ENTLER, DANIEL M.: b. 1835? in Shepherdstown. 5'8", dark complexion, hazel eyes, dark hair. Carpenter. enl. 4/18/61 at Halltown in Co. B as Pvt. Absent sick Nov./Dec. 1861. On furlough Jan./Feb. 1862. POW at Kernstown, 3/23/62 (Ft. Delaware). Exchanged 8/5/62. Detailed as asst. in commissary dept. (temporarily), Nov. 1862. Wded. in arm at Gettysburg, 7/2/63. Sent to Gen. Hosp., 7/15/63; fractured humerus, left arm. To Chimborazo #4, Richmond, 9/28/63. Surgeon's Discharge 12/23/63, "wound is still open at elbow joint."

ENTLER, JOHN PHIL: b. 8/22/26. Carpenter. enl. 4/21/61 at Harpers Ferry in Co. B as Pvt. To Corp. 4/25/62. To Sgt. March 1864. Absent sick July/Aug. 1861. Present again Sept./Oct. 1861. POW at Spotsylvania, 5/20/64 (Pt. Lookout). Exchanged 3/14/65. No further record. d. 12/30/09. bur. Elmwood Cem., Shepherdstown, W.Va.

ENTLER, JOSEPH N.: b. 1841? Boatman. enl. 5/22/61 at Camp Jackson in Co. A as Pvt. Deserted 6/6/61.

ENTLER, WILLIAM M.: enl. in Co. B as Pvt. AWOL 9/20/62. No further record.

ESKRIDGE, JOHN W.: b. 1815? Tailor. enl. 5/15/61 at Harpers Ferry in Co. H as Pvt. Gen. Hosp. Camp Winder, Richmond, 6/28-7/14 1862; remittent fever. Detailed to Staunton Hosp. 2/27/64, "for light duty." To Gen. Hosp. #9, Richmond, 4/26/64; for duty. To Gen. Hosp. Camp Winder, Richmond, 5/1/64; as guard. Deserted 12/22/64.

ESTEP, HARRISON: 5'8½", florid complexion, hazel eyes, dark hair. Residence Winchester. drafted 4/14/62 in Co. K as Pvt. AWOL 11/22/62. Fined 1 month's pay for absence by court-martial. POW at Spotsylvania, 5/12/64 (Pt. Lookout, Elmira). Oath of Allegiance to U.S. 6/14/65.

ESTEP, JACOB: enl. 4/8/62 at Rude's Hill in Co. G as Pvt. Deserted at New Market, 5/22/62. Recovered from desertion 4/1/63 and sentenced by court-martial to forfeit all pay and allowances to 3/30/63. Deserted 6/10/63. Living in Mt. Clifton, Shenandoah Co., July 1901.

ESTEP, JOHN H.: b. 1829? 5'5½", fair complexion, blue eyes, light hair. Farmer. Residence Shenandoah Co. enl. 4/18/62 at Rude's Hill in Co. B as Pvt. AWOL from 5/10-8/1 1862 and from 10/23/62. Recovered from desertion 4/13/63. Fined 1 month's pay and allowances for absence. Deserted 7/26/63. Recovered from desertion 3/8/64. Sentenced by court-martial to 5 months hard labor with ball and chain. POW (Rebel deserter) at Rowlesburg, W.Va. Oath of Allegiance to U.S., 7/17/64.

ESTES, JACKSON J.: enl. 4/14/62 at New Market in Co. H as Pvt. KIA Winchester, 5/25/62. bur. Stonewall Cem., Winchester.

EVANS, JOHN S. (B.): b. 1843? Student. enl. 5/15/61 at Harpers Ferry in Co. C as Pvt. Wded. in foot at Gaines's Mill, 6/27/62. Chimborazo Hosp. #3, 6/30/62. To Madison Court House Hosp., 7/9/62. Returned to duty 3/1/63. POW at Gettysburg, 7/3/63 (Ft. Delaware, Pt. Lookout). Exchanged 2/13/65. No further record. Alive in 1920.

EVERHART, PENDLETON: enl. 6/3/61 at Camp Jackson in Co. I as Pvt. "Minie rifle destroyed by carelessness; barrel busted, stock broken" sometime before 6/30/61. Deserted 7/24/61.

EVERSOLE, ISSAC H.: b. 1840? 5′8½″, fair complexion, blue eyes, light hair. Farmer. Residence Berkeley Co. enl. 4/19/61 at Hedgesville in Co. E as Pvt. Detached to York House Hosp., Winchester, 9/4/62-Jan./Feb. 1863. POW at Winchester, 11/25/62 (Wheeling, Camp Chase). Exchanged 3/28/63. Last official entry shows him present, March/April 1864.

EVERSOLE, JACOB T.: b. 1843? Farmer. enl. 4/19/61 at Hedgesville in Co. E as Pvt. Wded. at Winchester, 5/25/62. Discharged 12/4/62, reason not stated. bur. Georgetown Cem., Little Georgetown, Berkeley Co., W.Va.

EVERSOLE, JOHN WILLIAM: b. 5/6/32. Farmer. enl. 4/19/61 at Hedgesville in Co. E as Pvt. Deserted 7/18/61. d. 11/20/12. bur. Hedgesville Cem.

EWING, MOSES: enl. 12/22/62 at Guinea's Station in Co. D as Pvt. Trans. to Co. A, 1st Va. Cav., 2/7/63.

FAIRBURN, JAMES: drafted 4/16/62 at Rude's Hill in Co. C as Pvt. Requested discharge on grounds he was a Dunker; "disapproved until applicant furnished some proof of the fact." AWOL 8/24/62 at Gordonsville. Next official entry shows him present again, returning from hosp., 4/7/63. POW at Spotsylvania, 5/12/64 (Pt. Lookout, Elmira). d. 2/21/65 at Elmira; diarrhea. bur. Woodlawn Nat. Cem., Elmira, N.Y., grave #2374.

FARRAR, EDWARD T.: b. 1841? Coach maker. enl. April 1861 at Berryville in Co. I as Pvt. AWOL 8/4-8/22 1861. Fined $11.00 for absence by court-martial. Exempted from military duty by Gen. Jackson, 12/2/61; reason not stated. No record appears again until 6/17/64 when he is shown at Gen. Hosp. Charlottesville with bronchitis. Deserted 12/15/64.

FAUGHNDER, JOSEPH H.: b. 1837? Carpenter. enl. 4/18/61 at Charles Town in Co. A as Pvt. Service in Ord. Dept., 10/19-10/30 1861. Gen. Hosp. Charlottesville, 6/20-7/17 1862. Absent sick at home in Jefferson Co. at 10/31/62 muster. Present again Nov./Dec. 1862. Detailed as teamster, 12/20/62. POW at Spotsylvania, 5/12/64 (Pt. Lookout). d. 6/14/64 at Pt. Lookout; cause not stated.

FAY, SAMUEL: Listed in Co. G as Pvt. Wded. slightly at Fredericksburg, 12/13/62. No further record.

FEAMAN, JOHN S.: b. 1825? Carpenter. enl. 4/18/61 at Halltown in Co. B as Pvt. KIA at Kernstown, 3/23/62.

FEAMAN, WELLS A.: b. 1842? Clerk. enl. 6/18/61 at Winchester in Co. B as Pvt. POW while on furlough, Jan./Feb. 1862. Exchanged 8/5/62. Deserted to Md., 11/15/62.

FEELY, WILLIAM A.: b. 9/8/39. enl. 4/9/62 at Rude's Hill in Co. E as Pvt. AWOL Sept./Oct. 1862. Unofficial source says he joined Co. E, 11th Va. Cav. without official transfer. d. 7/4/24. bur. Lebanon Church Cem., Shenandoah Co.

FEELEY, JOHN E.: b. 8/6/36. 5′10″, brown eyes, dark hair. Residence Shenandoah Co. enl. 4/16/62 at Rude's Hill in Co. F as Pvt. Absent sick at Livingston Hosp., Winchester, 7/1/62. To Gen. Hosp. Charlottesville, 1/8/63; debilitis. Returned to duty 1/9/63. Wded. at Chancellorsville, 5/3/63. Chimborazo #1, 5/12/63. Last official entry shows him still absent from wound, Jan./Feb. 1864. Another source says he joined Co. E, 11th Va. Cav. on 10/16/63 at Culpeper Court House as Pvt. Paroled 4/26/65 at Winchester. d. 3/22/25. bur. Lebanon Church, Shenandoah Co.

FEELY, WATSON: b. in Shenandoah Co. enl. 4/16/62 at Rude's Hill in Co. F as Pvt. d. 4/7/63 at Staunton hosp., typhoid.

FEELER, JACOB G.: b. 1818? in Shenandoah Co. 5′5″, fair complexion, blue eyes, light hair. Farmer. enl. 4/18/62 at Rude's Hill in Co. B as Pvt. AWOL 6/1-10/24 1862. Discharged 12/8/62, overage.

FEELER, SAMUEL M.: b. 1831? 5′8″, fair complexion, gray eyes, dark hair. enl. 4/14/62 at New Market in Co. H as Pvt. AWOL since 11/21/62. Not present again until he returned to Co. from Imboden's Command, 4/1/64. POW at Spotsylvania, 5/12/64 (Pt. Lookout). Exchanged 11/1/64. Paroled 4/17/65 at Winchester.

FELTNER, GEORGE W.: b. 11/20/42. Laborer. enl. 6/15/61 at Winchester in Co. I as Pvt. Detailed as wagoner, 9/1/61. Deserted Nov./Dec. 1861. d. 12/15/99. bur. Red Bud Cem., Charity Chapel, Frederick Co., Va.

FERRELL, CHARLES F.: b. 8/23/42. Painter. enl. 4/20/61 at Harpers Ferry in Co. B as Pvt. AWOL 7/17/61 while on march from Winchester to Manassas. Present again Sept./Oct. 1861. POW at Kernstown, 3/23/62 (Ft. Delaware). Exchanged 8/5/62. After exchange, went home without leave, and taken POW at home. On parole as of 10/31/62. Present again Nov./Dec. 1862. Surrendered at Appomattox. d. 5/23/08. bur. Elmwood Cem., Shepherdstown, W.Va.

FIDDLER, JOHN W.: b. 1834? Laborer. enl. 4/21/61 at Harpers Ferry in Co. I as Pvt. AWOL 8/4-8/14 1861. Fined $11.00 for absence by court-martial. Discharged 8/25/61, disability.

FIRTH, JAMES: b. 1833? Laborer. enl. 6/6/61 at Harpers Ferry in Co. K as Pvt. Last official entry shows him present, Nov./Dec. 1861.

FISER, ELI L.: b. 1835? Laborer. enl. 4/21/61 at Harpers Ferry in Co. B as Pvt. Deserted 7/21/61 while on march from Winchester to Manassas.

FISHACH, GEORGE: b. 1838? Laborer. enl. 5/11/61 at Harpers Ferry in Co. K as Pvt. Deserted 5/13/61.

FISHER, BENJAMIN F.: 5′9″, dark complexion, hazel eyes, dark hair. Residence Waynesboro. enl. 4/16/62 at Rude's Hill in Co. D as Pvt. POW at Spotsylvania, 5/12/64 (Pt. Lookout, Elmira). Oath of Allegiance to U.S., 6/30/65.

FISHER, JAMES W.: b. 1842? Laborer. enl. 4/18/61 at Martinsburg in Co. D as Pvt. POW at Spotsylvania, 5/12/64 (Pt. Lookout, Elmira). Exchanged 3/10/65. No further record.

FISHER, JOHN L.: b. 1843? Laborer. enl. 4/18/61 at Martinsburg in Co. D as Pvt. To Corp. 3/26/63. Wded. in groin at Winchester, 5/25/62. Gen. Hosp. Mt. Jackson. To Gen. Hosp. Charlottesville, 6/8/62. To Lynchburg, 6/19/62. Present again 6/30-10/31 1862. MWIA at Chancellorsville, 5/3/63; date of death not reported.

FISHER, SAMUEL P.: b. 1845? 5′8″, light complexion, gray eyes, light hair. enl. 2/25/62 at Martinsburg in Co. D as Pvt. POW at Gettysburg, 7/3/63 (Ft. McHenry, Ft. Delaware, Pt. Lookout). Exchanged 2/13/65. Paroled 4/21/65 at Winchester.

FIZER, JACOB: b. 1837? Farmer. enl. 5/20/61 at Camp Lee in Co. E as Pvt. Deserted 7/31/61.

FLAGG, GEORGE H.: b. 4/9/32. 5'7", light complexion, blue eyes, light hair. Farmer. enl. 4/21/61 at Harpers Ferry in Co. G as Pvt. Elected Lt. 4/20/62. Signs roll as commanding Co., Jan./Feb. 1864. Stuart Hosp., Richmond, 3/26-4/2 1865; rheumatism. Paroled 4/19/65 at Winchester. d. 3/25/00. bur. Zion Episcopal Cem., Charles Town, W.Va.

FLEMING, ABRAHAM: b. 10/5/38 near Timberville, Rockingham Co. 5'6", dark complexion, hazel eyes, dark hair. Residence New Market. enl. 4/16/62 at Rude's Hill in Co. F as Pvt. AWOL 6/2-9/15 1862. POW at Spotsylvania, 5/12/64 (Pt. Lookout, Elmira). Oath of Allegiance to U.S., 5/29/65. Brother of Erasmus and John M. Fleming.

FLEMING, ERASMUS: b. 3/24/44 near Timberville, Rockingham Co. enl. 4/16/62 at Rude's Hill in Co. F as Pvt. AWOL 6/2-9/15 1862. Last official entry shows him present, March/April 1864.

FLEMING, JOHN MICHAEL: b. 5/17/42 near Timberville, Rockingham Co. Laborer. enl. at Rude's Hill in Co. F as Pvt. AWOL 6/2-9/15 1862. KIA by shell at Fredericksburg, 12/13/62.

FLEMMING, JESSE A.: b. 1843? Shoemaker. enl. 4/20/61 at Harpers Ferry in Co. K as Corp. To Pvt. 8/25/61. Elected Lt. 4/20/62. KIA at 2nd Manassas, 8/28/62.

FLETCHER, JOHN J. (I.): b. 1/29/29 at Winchester. 5'6", florid complexion, blue eyes, dark hair. m. Annie Taylor. Unofficial source lists him in Co. F as Lt. Paroled 4/29/65 at Winchester. Postwar, painter and decorator. "A bullet wound had paralyzed his left hand and although it was saved, he never had good use of it." d. 11/5/16 at Winchester. bur. Mt Herbron Cem., Winchester.

FLICKS, JACOB: enl. 4/18/62 at Rude's Hill in Co. B as Pvt. Deserted sometime before 4/30/62.

FOGLE, JACOB: enl. 4/8/62 at Rude's Hill in Co. G as Pvt. Detailed as teamster until Jan./Feb. 1863. Permanently detailed to Pioneer Corps, Jan./Feb. 1863. Last official entry shows him present in Pioneer Corps, March/April 1864.

FOLEY, JOHN: b. 1834? Laborer. enl. 4/20/61 at Harpers Ferry in Co. K as Pvt. Deserted from Camp Harman, 8/8/61.

FOLEY, JOHN F.: b. 10/22/40. Farmer. enl. 4/18/61 at Duffields in Co. H as Pvt. Shown as Sgt. 6/30-10/31 1862. To Lt. 11/18/62 for "exhibition of extraordinary valor and skill in the several battles in which this regt. has been engaged." Signs roll as commanding Co., Nov./Dec. 1863. Surrendered at Appomattox. d. 6/3/26. bur. Harpers Cem., Harpers Ferry, W.Va.

FOLTZ, JACOB: enl. 4/18/62 at Rude's Hill in Co. F as Pvt. Detailed as blacksmith in QM's Dept., 4/30-10/31 1862. Deserted sometime before 10/31/62. According to rolls of 12th Va. Cav., he enl. 1/1/63 in Co. K at Woodstock and was present through 3/31/64.

FONDER, DANIEL B.: b. 1840? Laborer. enl. 6/15/61 at Charles Town in Co. H as Pvt. AWOL before 6/30/61 and never mustered.

FONDER, FENTON L.: b. 1843? Laborer. enl. 6/15/61 at Charles Town in Co. H as Pvt. Last official entry shows him present, Nov./Dec. 1861.

FOREMAN, JOHN: b. 1839? Farmer. enl. 5/11/61 at Harpers Ferry in Co. C as Pvt. Deserted 6/17/61. d. 2/10/77. bur. Piper Cem., near Silver Grove.

FORNEY, GEORGE: b. 1839? 6'0", blue eyes, dark hair. Residence Shenandoah Co. Listed on rolls of Co. F, but he "disregarded the summons to service." Apparently joined Co. A, 11th Va. Cav. on 10/12/62 at Winchester as Pvt. AWOL near Riseyville, 8/23/63. Paroled 4/17/65 at Winchester. d. 2/1/04.

FORSYTH, HENRY H.: b. 1840? in Jefferson Co. 5'11", fair complexion, brown eyes, dark hair. Molder. enl. at Harpers Ferry in Co. K as Corp. Discharged 10/21/61, reason not stated.

FOWLER, SAMUEL H.: b. 6/10/29. Carpenter. enl. 4/18/61 at Martinsburg in Co. D as Sgt. Reduced to ranks 11/9/61 for drunkenness and disobedience of orders. To Corp. 11/1/63. POW at Fisher's Hill, 9/23/64 (Pt. Lookout). Exchanged 3/15/65. d. 3/23/05. bur. Episcopal and Masonic Cem., Middleway, W.Va.

FOWLER, WILLIAM: drafted 10/29/62 at Camp Allen in Co. C as Pvt. Deserted 11/11/62 from Camp Allen near Winchester.

FOX, FERNANDO: enl. 9/25/62 at Martinsburg in Co. C as Pvt. AWOL since 7/15/63. Deserted 9/1/63.

FOX, JOSEPH: b. 1827? Weaver. enl. 5/13/61 at Harpers Ferry in Co. E as Pvt. Deserted 7/14/61.

FOX, WILLIAM B.: Unofficial source stated he served in Co. F for 4 years.

FRANKLIN, JOHN: enl. 4/16/62 at Rude's Hill in Co. D as Pvt. Wded. at Gaines's Mill, 6/27/62, and missing since that fight. No further record.

FRANKS, HENRY: enl. 10/1/62 at Bunker Hill in Co. H as Pvt. AWOL 10/5/62. No further record.

FRAZIER, JAMES H.: b. 1838? Auctioneer. enl. 4/18/61 at Charles Town in Co. G as Pvt. Special duty as harnessmaker, Nov./Dec. 1861. Discharged 7/30/62, reason not stated.

FRAVEL (FREEBLE), GEORGE W.: b. 4/18/40. Carpenter. enl. 4/18/61 at Martinsburg in Co. D as Pvt. Last official entry shows him present, Nov./Dec. 1861. d. 8/26/64. bur. Greenhill Cem., Martinsburg, W.Va.

FREEZE, WILLIAM: b. 1814? Laborer. enl. 4/19/61 at Harpers Ferry in Co. B as Pvt. Absent sick and never mustered; "gone to Md. from Shepherdstown where he was left sick," Nov./Dec. 1861.

FREY (FRY), SAMUEL: b. 4/5/35 in Shenandoah Co. enl. 4/15/62 at Rude's Hill in Co. G as Pvt. Gen. Hosp. #3, Lynchburg, 5/8/63; chronic dysentery. d. 6/6/63 at hosp. in Lynchburg. bur. Salem Lutheran Church, Mt. Sidney.

FRIARY (FIERY), JAMES: b. 1831? Cooper. enl. 4/19/61 at Hedgesville in Co. E as Pvt. To Corp. Nov./Dec. 1862. Gen. Hosp. Charlottesville, 12/23-12/24 1862; debility. Gen. Hosp. Charlottesville, 5/9/64; gunshot wound resulting in a compound fracture of tibia on right leg. (Probably wded. at the Wilderness). d. 5/25 or 5/26 1864 at Charlottesville; pyaemia.

FRIER, FORD: drafted 10/3/62 at Bunker Hill in Co. F as Pvt. MWIA at Fredericksburg, 12/13/62. d. 12/15/62. Unofficial source states he had enl. 6/3/61 in Co. K, 5th Va. Inf. Term of original service had expired.

FRISTO, WILLIAM: enl. 4/9/62 at Rude's Hill in Co. E as Pvt. Wded. at 1st Winchester, 5/25/62. Deserted Sept./Oct. 1862. Bureau of Conscription looking for him in Page Co., 3/13/65.

FRY, ELI: enl. 4/8/62 at Rude's Hill in Co. G as Pvt. Wded. slightly at Port Republic, 6/9/62. Returned to duty 1/19/63. Last official entry shows him present, March/April 1864.

FRY, JOHN: b. 1834? 5' 8", fair complexion, black eyes, light hair. Drafted 4/16/62 at Rude's Hill in Co. C as Pvt. Sick and sent to hosp., 10/10/62. Returned to duty 5/12/63. Wded. at Gettysburg, 7/2/63. All remaining entries show him still absent from wound. POW at Fisher's Hill, 9/22/64 (Pt. Lookout). Exchanged 3/17/65. Paroled 4/20/65 at Mt. Jackson.

FRY, JOHN: Listed in Co. G. MWIA in back at 2nd Manassas; date of wound not specific. d. 9/20/62.

FRY, SOLOMON: 5' 6", ruddy complexion, brown eyes, brown hair. Residence Shenandoah Co. enl. 4/8/62 at Rude's Hill in Co. G as Pvt. AWOL 6/4-10/25 1862. Fined $51.70 for absence. Wded. at Chancellorsville, 5/3/63. Returned to duty 10/1/63. Wded. at Petersburg, 4/2/65. U.S. Lincoln Gen. Hosp., Washington, D.C., 4/10/65; "compound gunshot wound in metatarsal bone of little toe, left foot." Oath of Allegiance to U.S., 6/12/65.

FRYATT, JOHN E.: b. 1842? Carpenter. enl. 6/12/61 at Harpers Ferry in Co. D as Pvt. KIA at Manassas, 7/21/61. bur. Old Norborne Cem., Martinsburg, W.Va.

FULK, WILLIAM: b. 10/19/29. drafted 10/3/62 at Bunker Hill in Co. G as Pvt. Absent sick Oct. 1862-July/Aug. 1863. Listed as deserter, July/Aug. 1863. d. 7/7/03. bur. Elmwood Cem., Shepherdstown, W.Va.

FULLER, JAMES: b. 1841? Laborer. enl. 6/10/61 at Camp Jackson on Bolivar Heights in Co. I as Pvt. AWOL 7/27-7/31 1861. AWOL 9/30-10/8 1861. AWOL 11/20-11/27 1861. No further record.

FUNKHOUSER, JAMES W.: b. 6/12/38. enl. 4/16/62 at Rude's Hill in Co. F as Pvt. AWOL 6/3-10/3 1862. AWOL 11/23/62-3/20/63. AWOL again 7/24/63. No further record. d. 12/22/79. bur. Funkhouser Cem., Rt. 646, Shipe Farm, Shenandoah Co.

FURGESON, HAYS: drafted 10/1/62 at Bunker Hill in Co. K as Pvt. AWOL 10/12/62. Present again July/Aug. 1863. POW at Spotsylvania, 5/23/64 (Pt. Lookout). d. 8/13/64 at Pt. Lookout, cause not stated.

FURR, EPHRAIM: enl. 8/27/61 at Camp Harman in Co. I as Pvt. AWOL 12/27-12/31 1861. Last official entry shows him present, March/April 1864.

FURR, GEORGE: enl. 4/16/62 near Mt. Jackson in Co. I as Pvt. Wded. at 1st Winchester, 5/25/62. Gen. Hosp. Winchester, 5/27/62; shoulder amputated at joint. To Gen. Hosp. Mt. Jackson, 6/1/62. Last official entry shows him still absent wded., March/April 1864.

FURR, JOHN E.: b. 1841? Cooper. enl. 5/12/61 at Harpers Ferry in Co. K as Pvt. Last official entry shows him present, Nov./Dec. 1861.

GAGEBY, DAVID B.: b. 1826? Carpenter. enl. 4/19/61 at Duffields in Co. H as Pvt. To Corp. 8/1/61. To Sgt. 11/22/61. Absent sick 5/30/62-March/April 1863. AWOL 5/1/63. No further record. d. 1901. bur. Elmwood Cem., Shepherdstown, W.Va.

GAGEY, S. P.: Only record lists him in Co. E as Pvt. and states that he was wded. at Gaines's Mill or Malvern Hill, 6/27 or 7/1 1862.

GALL, GEORGE W.: b. 1841? Laborer. enl. 4/18/61 at Duffields in Co. H as Pvt. Wded. in thigh at 1st Manassas, 7/21/61. Present again Sept./Oct. 1861. On furlough Nov./Dec. 1861. Wded. at Port Republic, 6/9/62. Gen. Hosp. Charlottesville, 6/9/62. To Lynchburg, 6/16/62. Nurse at York House Hosp., Winchester, 9/12-Nov./Dec. 1862. POW at Winchester, 12/22/62 (Ft. McHenry, Ft. Monroe). Present again Jan./Feb. 1863. Deserted 7/6/64.

GALLAHER, CHARLES FRANK: b. 11/28/42. 5' 8", dark complexion, black eyes, gray hair. Carpenter. enl. 4/18/61 at Charles Town in Co. A as Pvt. Absent sick at home in Charles Town, 10/15/61. Chimborazo #1, 10/17-10/28 1861; debility. Present again Nov./Dec. 1861. POW at Kernstown, 3/23/62 (Ft. Delaware). Exchanged 8/5/62. POW at Spotsylvania, 5/12/64 (Pt. Lookout, Elmira). Exchanged 3/2/65. Gen. Hosp. Charlottesville, 4/9/65; reason not stated. Paroled 4/22/65 at Winchester. d. 1915. bur. Edge Hill Cem., Charles Town, W.Va.

GALLAHER, CHARLES HORACE: b. 4/17/39. 5' 10½", florid complexion, blue eyes, amber hair. Clerk. enl. 4/18/61 at Charles Town in Co. G as Pvt. To Sgt. 10/13/63. Wded. in head at Payne's Farm, 11/27/63. Chimborazo #3, 11/30/63. To Staunton, 12/8/63. Returned to duty 2/11/64. POW at Spotsylvania, 5/12/64 (Pt. Lookout, Elmira). Exchanged 2/20/65. POW at Staunton. d. 1/29/11. bur. Edge Hill Cem., Charles Town, W.Va.

GALLAHER, JAMES N.: b. 5/2/41. Printer. enl. 4/18/61 at Charles Town in Co. A as Corp. To Pvt. 8/31/61. Wded. at Port Republic, 6/9/62. Trans. to Co. B, 12th Va. Cav., 10/22/62. d. 2/25/85. bur. Edge Hill Cem., Charles Town, W.Va.

GALLAHER, WILLIAM W. B.: b. 3/21/33 at Charles Town. Publisher and Editor of Charles Town's *Virginia Free Press.* enl. 6/22/61 at Camp Stephens in Co. A as Pvt. Discharged 7/28/62, reason not stated. Unofficial source states he served in Commissary Dept. of the 2nd Corps, Army of Northern Virginia, during the rest of the war. d. 8/28/03. bur. Edge Hill Cem., Charles Town, W.Va.

GARBER, ELI: b. 6/15/26. enl. 4/16/62 near Mt. Jackson in Co. I as Pvt. Discharged 6/1/62 after furnishing a substitute. d. 3/22/84.

GARBER, JACOB: enl. 4/15/62 at Rude's Hill in Co. A as Pvt. Detailed as teamster, 6/20/62. AWOL 12/1/62-2/14/63. Fined 1 month's pay for absence by court-martial. Gen. Hosp. Charlottesville, 12/20/64-1/13/65; wound in right thigh. No further record.

GARDNER, GERVIS S.: b. 1843? Printer. enl. 4/18/61 at Martinsburg in Co. D as Pvt. Deserted 7/26/63. POW (Rebel deserter), 7/27/63. Oath of Allegiance to U.S., date not given.

GARRETT, WILLIAM: drafted Nov. 1862 at Camp Bitzer in Co. C as Pvt. Deserted 11/24/62 on march from Winchester to Fredericksburg.

GENTRY, ELI: enl. 4/18/62 at Rude's Hill in Co. A as Pvt. AWOL 4/19/62-3/25/63. Confined in guardhouse, March/April 1863. Fined 11 month's and 6 day's pay for absence by court-martial. Wded. in scalp at Payne's Farm, 11/27/63. Chimborazo #5, 11/29/63. To Staunton, 12/5/63. Absent on furlough Feb. and March, 1864. No further record.

GETTINGER, CHARLES W.: b. 1842? Clerk. enl. 6/12/61 at Harpers Ferry in Co. D as Pvt. Absent sick Sept./Oct. 1861. Present again Nov./Dec. 1861. Absent sick Nov./Dec. 1862. Present again Jan./Feb. 1863. Deserted 7/26/63. POW (Rebel deserter), 7/27/63. Oath of Allegiance to U.S., date not stated.

GETTS, JOSEPH: enl. 12/4/62 at Fredericksburg in Co. H as Pvt. d. 3/30/63 at Guinea's Station, cause not stated.

GIBSON, JAMES GREGG: b. 11/19/42. Farmer. enl. 4/18/61 at Charles Town in Co. G as Pvt. Deserted near Richmond, 7/10/62. Joined C. S. Marine Corps at Savannah, Georgia, 3/1/64. Gen. Hosp. #9, Richmond, 8/22/64. Furloughed 8/23/64. d. 8/30/64 in Madison Co. while on furlough, cause not stated.

99

GIBSON, JOSHUA GREGG: b. 1/3/23. Listed in Co. G, but never mustered "being of bad health" and because he "furnished a substitute uniformed." d. 2/24/94. bur. Edge Hill Cem., Charles Town, W.Va.

GIBSON, MOSES: enl. 7/5/61 at Darkesville in Co. G as Pvt. Last official entry shows him present, Nov./Dec. 1861. Alive in 1906.

GIBSON, SAMUEL J.: enl. 4/14/62 at New Market in Co. H as Pvt. d. 8/5/62 at Gen. Hosp. Charlottesville; dysentery. Claim states he left no wife or children, and that $66.06 was paid for his time in the service to his father William Gibson.

GIBSON, WILLIAM: b. 1827? in Augusta Co. 5' 10", fair complexion, blue eyes, light hair. Farmer. enl. 4/14/62 at New Market in Co. H as Pvt. Absent sick at hosp., 5/7/62-March/April 1863. Surgeon's Discharge, 4/4/63, "because of valvular disease of the heart the result of rheumatism."

GILL, JAMES H.: b. 1841? Coach maker. enl. 4/21/61 at Harpers Ferry in Co. I as Pvt. Chimborazo #1, 10/17-10/27 1861; debility. Present again Nov./Dec. 1861. MWIA in face and hand at 2nd Manassas, date not specific. d. 11/18/62 or 3/20/63.

GILLILAND, J. A.: Carpenter. Residence Halifax Co. enl. 10/15/64 at Richmond in Co. C as Pvt. POW at Ft. Steadman, 3/25/65 (Pt. Lookout). Oath of Allegiance to U.S., 5/12/65.

GILLOCK, DAVID: enl. 4/14/62 at New Market in Co. H as Pvt. Detailed as wagoner in QM's Dept., April 1862, and remained on this detail until March/April 1864. Last official entry shows him as detailed as blacksmith in QM's Dept., 4/30-10/31 1864.

GILMER (GILMORE), RICHARD: enl. 4/16/62 at New Market in Co. H as Pvt. Absent sick 4/30-10/31 1862 through 2/7/63. Absent sick March/April 1863. Detailed to guard Ord. train, April/May 1863. Present again July/Aug. 1863. POW at Spotsylvania, 5/12/64 (Pt. Lookout, Elmira). d. 1/13/65 at Elmira; pneumonia. bur. Woodlawn Nat. Cem., Elmira, N.Y., grave #1454.

GINN, CHARLES L.: b. 1838? Lawyer. Unofficial source says he enl. 4/18/61 at Winchester in Co. F as Pvt. AWOL Sept./Oct. 1861. No further record.

GITTINGS, HENRY M.: b. 1830? Farmer. enl. 4/18/61 at Winchester in Co. F as Pvt. To Sgt. 6/24/61. KIA at 1st Manassas, 7/21/61. bur. Mt. Hebron Cem., Winchester.

GLAIZE, JOHN: b. 10/12/22. m. Selma Baker. Unofficial source lists him in Co. F. Apptd. Capt. and Asst. QM to Gen. Carson commanding the Va. Militia at Winchester, 9/11/61. Assigned to QM's Dept. in the Valley District, 4/28/62. Capt. and Asst. to Forage QM, Army of Northern Va., 9/15/64. Paroled 4/9/65. Postwar, in lumber business in Winchester; sheriff; treasurer; jailor; and magistrate in Winchester; on City Council of Winchester, 1887-1890. d. 1/22/01. bur. Mt. Hebron Cem., Winchester.

GLAIZE, ISAAC N.: b.1830? Farmer. enl. 4/18/61 at Winchester in Co. F as Pvt. KIA at 1st Manassas, 7/21/61. bur. Mt. Hebron Cem., Winchester.

GLASS, GREENBURG: 5' 5½", dark complexion, hazel eyes, dark hair. enl. 10/7/63 at Morton's Ford in Co. D as Pvt. POW at Charles Town, 8/13/64 (Old Capitol Prison, Elmira). Oath of Allegiance to U.S., 5/29/65.

GLENN, WILLIAM Y.: b. 1837? Stonecutter. enl. 5/1/61 at Harpers Ferry in Co. F as Pvt. Wded. at 1st Manassas, 7/21/61. Discharged 9/23/61 after receiving appointment in C. S. Navy.

GLOVER, PORTERFIELD: enl. 4/16/62 at Rude's Hill in Co. D as Pvt. Acquitted by court-martial of desertion, 10/25/62. Absent sick 11/25/62-Jan./Feb. 1863. AWOL March/April 1863. No further record.

GLOVER, THORTON K.: b. 1835? 5' 10", light complexion, dark eyes, gray hair. Carpenter. enl. 4/21/61 at Harpers Ferry in Co. I as Pvt. AWOL 8/4/61. Present again Sept./Oct. 1861. AWOL since 12/22/61. AWOL from 6/15-8/10 1862. Wded. at Chancellorsville, 5/3/63. Gen. Hosp. Charlottesville, 5/11/63. Furloughed for 30 days, 6/23/63. Gen. Hosp. Charlottesville, 8/21/63. Returned to duty, 10/2/63. Absent on detached service, Jan./Feb. 1864; duty not stated. Present again Feb./March 1864. POW at Spotsylvania, 5/12/64 (Pt. Lookout, Elmira). Exchanged 3/2/65. Jackson Hosp., Richmond, 3/7/65; debility. Furloughed for 30 days, 3/9/65. Paroled 4/17/65 at Winchester.

GOHEEN, THOMAS: b. 1832? 5' 3", dark complexion, blue eyes, black hair. Boatsman. Residence Jefferson Co. enl. 5/26/61 at Lemon's Ferry in Co. I as Pvt. Gen. Hosp. Charlottesville, 5/11-5/28 1864; cephalalgia. POW at Strasburg, 10/19/64 (Pt. Lookout). Oath of Allegiance to U.S., 6/13/65.

GOLD, THOMAS DANIEL: b. 2/23/45. 5' 8", light complexion, hazel eyes, dark hair. enl. 4/18/61 at Berryville in Co. I as Pvt. To Corp. 8/13/61. To Sgt. 8/1/62. POW at Kernstown, 3/23/62 (Ft. Delaware). Exchanged 8/5/62. Wded. in arm at 2nd Manassas, 8/28/62. Present again Nov./Dec. 1862. Gen. Hosp. Charlottesville, 10/22/63-1/13/64; typhoid fever. Absent sick Sept./Oct.-Nov./Dec. 1863. On detached duty, Jan./Feb. 1864. Present again March/April 1864. POW at Spotsylvania, 5/12/64 (Pt. Lookout, Elmira). Exchanged 2/20/65. Paroled 4/21/65 at Winchester. Postwar, Va. State Senate, 1899-1903; author of *History of Clarke County and its Connection with the War Between the States* (1914). d. 12/7/15. bur. Greenhill Cem., Berryville.

GOLLADA, SAMUEL: enl. 4/14/62 at New Market in Co. H as Pvt. AWOL from 5/18/62-2/16/63. Sentenced by court-martial to forfeit 1 month's pay and 30 days hard labor. Gen. Hosp. Charlottesville, 4/26/63; epilepsy. Furloughed 6/5/63. Still shown absent sick, Nov./Dec. 1863. Deserted 1/16/64.

GOLLIDAY (GOLLADAY), GEORGE: b. 8/6/30. drafted 4/14/62 at Rude's Hill in Co. K as Pvt. Sent to hosp. 8/11/62. Absent sick through Jan./Feb. 1863. Present again March/April 1863. Wded. slightly in arm at Payne's Farm, 11/27/63. Gen. Hosp. Charlottesville, 11/30/63. To Gen. Hosp. Lynchburg, 12/3/63. Present again March/April 1864. POW at Monocacy, 7/9/64 (Pt. Lookout). Exchanged 10/30/64. No further record. d. 8/28/72.

GOMPF, MARCELLUS: b. 1837? Moulder. enl. 4/20/61 at Harpers Ferry in Co. K as Pvt. To Sgt., date not given. POW at Winchester, 5/24/62. Exchanged 8/2/62, but never reported back to regt. Began work at the C. S. Armory in Richmond, 10/10/62; served in the Armory Battalion (a local defense organization), and remained at the armory until all troops were called out in the field. Master Armorer J. S. Adams wrote that "Mr. Gompf is a valuable mechanic and has rendered the government essential service in devoting his skill to the manufacturing of arms." Detailed to Ord. Dept., 12/6/64. No further record.

GOOD, ALLEN W.: enl. 4/16/62 at Rude's Hill in Co. F as Pvt. AWOL near Swift Run Gap, May 1862. Does not appear on rolls again until Jan./Feb. 1864, when he is listed as present. POW at Spotsylvania, 5/12/64 (Pt. Lookout, Elmira). Exchanged 2/13/65. No further record.

100

GOOD, JOHN: b. in Shenandoah Co. enl. 4/8/62 at Rude's Hill in Co. G as Pvt. Absent sick since 8/15/62. Chimborazo #4, 9/17-10/10 1862. Still shown as absent sick, Nov./Dec. 1862. In guardhouse under sentence of court-martial, Jan./Feb. 1863. Fined 1 month's pay, charges not stated. Wded. slightly in arm at Payne's Farm, 11/27/63. Chimborazo #4, 11/29/63. To Staunton, 12/7/63. d. 1/4/64 at Staunton, cause not stated.

GOOD, MOSES: b. 1835? 5' 5¼", fair complexion, blue eyes, auburn hair. Residence Shenandoah Co. enl. 4/8/62 at Rude's Hill in Co. G as Pvt. Deserted at New Market, 6/4/62. Recovered from desertion, 1/19/63. Sent to hosp. sick, 6/16/63. Last official entry lists him as a deserter, Sept./Oct. 1863. POW (Rebel deserter) at Romney, 9/15/63 (Camp Chase; Rock Island, Illinois). Oath of Allegiance to U.S., 10/17/64.

GOODEN, G. M.: enl. 4/16/62 at Rude's Hill in Co. F as Pvt. Deserted at Swift Run Gap, May 1862.

GOODEN, GEORGE HARVEY: b. 12/29/44 in Rockingham Co. m. Sarah Elizabeth Monger. enl. 4/18/62 at Rude's Hill in Co. F as Pvt. AWOL 5/22/62-2/23/63. Unofficial source says he enl. in Co. I, 10th Va. Inf., 8/10/62 and returned to Co. F, 2/23/63. Wded. at Chancellorsville, 5/3/63. Chimborazo, 5/10/63. Last official entry shows him still absent from wound, March/April 1864. Postwar, farmer who built house in Elkton and who operated a cooper shop. d. 4/24/06. bur. Elk Run Cem., Elkton.

GORRELL, JOSEPH C.: 5' 8", fair complexion, blue eyes, light hair. enl. 2/23/62 at Martinsburg in Co. D as Pvt. AWOL 9/20/62. AWOL 10/25/62-May/June 1863. Present again July/Aug. 1863. AWOL again 2/20/64. Present again March/April 1864. Sentenced by court-martial to forfeit 2 month's pay and to "mark time 1 hour each day for 5 consecutive days." POW at Spotsylvania, 5/12/64 (Pt. Lookout, Elmira). Oath of Allegiance to U.S., 5/15/65.

GRADY, MICHAEL: b. 1828? Laborer. enl. 6/8/61 at Harpers Ferry in Co. D as Pvt. Absent sick 6/30-10/31 1862. AWOL Nov./Dec. 1862 and dropped from roll for continued absence. No further record. d. 1/24/86. bur. St. Joseph's Cem., Martinsburg, W.Va.

GRANGER, JACOB: b. 1844? 5' 8", dark complexion, blue eyes, light hair. enl. 4/16/62 at Rude's Hill in Co. D as Pvt. POW at Strasburg, 6/3/63 (Ft. Delaware). Exchanged 8/5/62. Last official entry shows him present, March/April 1864. Paroled 5/20/65 at Staunton.

GRAVES, CHARLES E.: b. 1830? in Jefferson Co. Silversmith. enl. 4/18/61 at Winchester in Co. F as Lt. Resigned 6/1/61, reason not stated. Unofficial source states he "attended to Confederate postal matters" in the Winchester vicinity during the war. d. 3/27/14. bur. Mt. Hebron Cem., Winchester.

GREEN, JOHN WILLIAM: Unofficial source says he served in this regt.

GREEN, THOMAS CLAIBORNE: b. 11/30/20 at Fredericksburg. Son of John W. Green, a Va. Supreme Court of Appeals judge. Practiced law with Col. Agnus McDonald in Hampshire Co. at Romney. m. Mary Naylor McDonald, Col. McDonald's oldest daughter. Mayor of Charles Town during the John Brown raid in 1859; also served as a defense attorney for Brown. enl. 4/18/61 at Charles Town in Co. G as Pvt. On special duty in telegraph office, June 1861. Elected to Va. Legislature from Jefferson Co., 12/22/61. Apptd. chief collector of Confederate taxes in Va. by President Davis in 1863 and remained in this position until war's end. Postwar, returned to Charles Town; apptd. to W.Va. Supreme Court of Appeals in 1876 and continued in this capacity until his death. d. 12/4/89. bur. Zion Episcopal Cem., Charles Town, W.Va.

GREVER (GREAVER), ROBERT P.: drafted 4/14/62 at Rude's Hill in Co. K as Pvt. KIA at 2nd Manassas, 8/28/62.

GRIFFIN, MICHAEL: Listed as Pvt. in Co. D. MWIA in knee at Gaines's Mill, 6/27/62. Chimborazo #3, 6/30/62. d. 7/24/62.

GRIM, ST. GEORGE TUCKER: b. 10/28/22. 5' 7", dark complexion, gray eyes, gray hair. enl. 3/6/62 at Winchester in Co. F as Pvt. Absent on detached service collecting conscripts, March/April-May/June 1863. Present again July/Aug. 1863. Chimborazo, July 1864; disease. Last official entry shows him present, 10/31/64. Paroled 4/20/65 at Winchester. Postwar, member of Turner Ashby Camp #22 at Winchester. d. 3/1/98. bur. Stonewall Cem., Winchester.

GRIMM, JAMES WILLIAM: b. 4/3/27. Machinist. enl. 4/18/61 at Winchester in Co. F as Pvt. Absent sick July/Aug. 1861. Present again Sept./Oct. 1861. Last official entry shows him present, Nov./Dec. 1861. d. 12/1/01. bur. Mt. Hebron Cem., Winchester.

GRIMSLEY, W.: enl. 4/18/62 at Rude's Hill in Co. B as Pvt. Only official entry shows him absent sick, March/April 1862. No further record.

GROVE, FRANCIS T.: b. 1845? Student. enl. 5/17/61 at Harpers Ferry in Co. B as Pvt. Last official entry shows him AWOL, March/April 1862. d. 1924. bur. Elmwood Cem., Shepherdstown, W.Va.

GROVE, WILLIAM H.: b. 1842? Student. enl. 5/17/61 at Harpers Ferry in Co. B as Pvt. Absent sick July/Aug. 1861. AWOL March/April 1862. Wded. at 2nd Manassas, date not specific. No further record.

GROW, CYRUS: b. 1829? in Augusta Co. 5' 9", fair complexion, gray eyes, light hair. Shoemaker. enl. 4/16/62 near Mt. Jackson in Co. I as Pvt. Wded. in right arm at 2nd Manassas, 8/28/62. Never returned to ranks because arm permanently disabled. Retired to Invalid Corps, 11/29/64. Surgeon's discharge, 1/16/65 "in consequence of a minie ball injuring the median nerve of the right arm which is now paralyzed. He suffers excruciating pain nearly all the time." Paroled 5/10/65 at Staunton.

GRUBB, J. W.: Unofficial source states he served in the regt. d. 3/23/62 (presumably KIA at Kernstown). bur. Stonewall Cem., Winchester.

GRUBBS, CHARLES W.: enl. 9/19/62 at Martinsburg in Co. I as Pvt. Deserted 6/16/63. Recovered from desertion Sept./Oct. 1863 and fined 1 month's pay for absence. POW at Spotsylvania, 5/12/64 (Pt. Lookout, Elmira). Exchanged 2/9/65. Chimborazo #5, 2/22/65; pernio. No further record.

GRUBBS, EPAMINONDAS: b. 1839? Laborer. enl. 4/18/61 at Millwood in Co. C as Pvt. Absent sick sometime before 6/30/61, dates not specific. KIA at 1st Manassas, 7/21/61.

GRUBBS, JAMES M.: b. 1844? Miner. enl. 4/18/61 at Millwood in Co. C as Pvt. Absent sick sometime before 6/30/61, dates not specific. Present again July/Aug. 1861. Last official entry shows him present, Nov./Dec. 1861.

GRUBBS, JAMES T.: b. 1837? 6' 0", fair complexion, blue eyes, light hair. Carpenter. enl. 4/18/61 at Millwood in Co. C as Pvt. Wded. at Cedar Run, 8/9/62. Present again by 10/31/62. Wded. in side at Payne's Farm, 11/27/63. Chimborazo #3, 11/30/63. Furloughed 30 days, 12/30/63. Returned to duty 2/16/64. POW at Ninevah, 11/12/64 (Pt. Lookout). Exchanged 2/13/65. Paroled 5/9/65 at Winchester. Postwar, member of Turner Ashby Camp #22 at Winchester. Alive in 1893.

GRUBBS, JOHN W.: 5'8", fair complexion, gray eyes, light hair. Residence Clarke Co. enl. 9/19/62 at Martinsburg in Co. I as Pvt. Wded. at Chancellorsville, 5/3/63. Episcopal Church Hosp., Williamsburg, 5/19/63. Furloughed for 30 days, 7/6/63. Present again Sept./Oct. 1863. POW at Salem Church, 5/20/64 (Old Capitol Prison, Ft. Delaware). Oath of Allegiance to U.S., 6/20/65.

GRUBBS, MARTIN L.: b. 1839? 5'11", light complexion, blue eyes, light hair. Residence Clarke Co. Wded. at 2nd Manassas, 8/28/62. Absent sick through Oct. 1863. POW at Winchester, 10/4/63 (Wheeling; Camp Chase; Rock Island, Illinois). Enlisted in U.S. Army for frontier service, 10/18/64.

GRUBBS, NATT: Only record lists him in Co. C and states he was wded. at Port Republic, 6/9/62.

GRUBBS, PHILIP L.: b. 1843? 5'8", fair complexion, blue eyes, dark hair. enl. 3/1/62 at Winchester in Co. C as Pvt. Wded. at Cedar Run, 8/9/62. Gen. Hosp. Charlottesville, 8/11-9/11 1862. Wded. in neck 6/2/64. Gen. Hosp. Charlottesville, 6/21/64. Furloughed for 60 days, 6/27/64. POW at Milldale, 10/31/64 (Old Capitol Prison, Elmira). Oath of Allegiance to U.S., 6/21/65. d. 12/8/13 in Warren Co.

GRUBBS, SAMUEL T.: b. 1837? Carpenter. enl. 5/11/61 at Harpers Ferry in Co. C as Pvt. Elected Lt. 9/25/62. Wded. in hand at 2nd Manassas, date not specific. Collecting conscripts in Clarke Co., Nov./Dec. 1862. Last official entry lists him present, March/April 1864.

GRUBBS, WILLIAM: b. 1829? Wheelwright. enl. 4/20/61 at Millwood in Co. C as Pvt. Absent sick 5/12-11/14 1861. Charged $4.29 for losing a cap box and waist belt, March/April 1864. Last official entry shows him present, March/April 1864.

GRUBER, BENJAMIN F.: b. 1845? Laborer. enl. 5/15/61 at Harpers Ferry in Co. H as Pvt. Last official entry shows him present, Nov./Dec. 1861.

GRUBER, R. T.: Only official record lists him in Co. K as Pvt. and states he was KIA at 2nd Manassas, date not specific.

GUARD, THOMAS W.: b. 1835? Tailor. enl. 6/8/61 at Martinsburg in Co. I as Pvt. AWOL since 12/27/61. AWOL 3/12/62. Detailed as nurse at Culpeper Court House and at Lynchburg hospitals, 4/20/62. No further record.

GUIN, JOHN WILLIAM: b. 1836? enl. 4/19/61 at Hedgesville in Co. E as Pvt. Deserted 7/18/61.

GUINN, CHARLES L.: b. 1838? Lawyer. enl. 4/18/61 at Winchester in Co. F as Pvt. Absent July/Aug. 1861. Last official entry shows him AWOL, Sept./Oct. 1861.

GUINN, JAMES M. VAN B.: b. 6/12/42. 5'9", light complexion, gray eyes, black hair. Shoemaker. Residence Berkeley Co. enl. 4/21/61 at Harpers Ferry in Co. E as Pvt. Absent sick Nov./Dec. 1861. Present again Sept./Oct. 1862. Absent sick 11/29/62. Gen. Hosp. Charlottesville, 12/6/62-1/10/63; rheumatism. AWOL July/Aug. 1863. POW (Rebel deserter), 7/2/63 (Ft. Mifflin, Pa.). Oath of Allegiance to U.S., 11/17/63. d. 11/23/06. bur. Hedgesville Cem., Hedgesville, W.Va.

HACKLEY, WILLIAM: b. 1832? Wheelwright. enl. 4/18/61 at Charles Town in Co. A as Pvt. Absent sick at home in Jefferson Co., 9/20/61. Last official entry shows him present, Nov./Dec. 1861.

HADDOX, WILLIAM H.: enl. 6/22/63 at Martinsburg in Co. D as Pvt. Last official entry shows him present, March/April 1864. bur. Old Norborne Cem., Martinsburg, W.Va.

HAGAN, CORNELIUS J.: enl. 8/23/62 at Charles Town in Co. A, 12th Va. Cav. as Pvt. To Regt. Bugler, date not given. POW at Poolesville, Md., 9/2/62 (Ft. McHenry). Exchanged 12/8/62. AWOL 12/31/62. POW at New Franklin, Pa., 7/2/63 (Chambersburg; Harrisburg; Seminary Hosp., Hagerstown; U.S. Gen. Hosp., West Building, Baltimore; Pt. Lookout). Exchanged 3/16/64. Only record in 2nd Va. Inf. states he enl. 9/1/64 in Co. F as Musician.

HAHN, DAVID: enl. 4/9/62 at Rude's Hill in Co. E as Pvt. Wded. in left hand at Gaines's Mill, 6/27/62. Gen. Hosp., Howard's Grove, Richmond. Furloughed for 30 days, 7/14/62. Discharged 11/15/62, reason not stated.

HAINES, GEORGE W.: enl. 4/18/62 at Rude's Hill in Co. F as Pvt. Deserted from Swift Run Gap, 5/1/62. Recovered from desertion, 3/8/63, and detailed to work in iron foundry by the Secretary of War. Last official entry shows him still on detail at iron foundry, March/April 1864.

HAINS (HAINES), JONAS: enl. 4/16/62 at Rude's Hill in Co. F as Pvt. Under arrest since 6/24/62. Absent sick 11/25/62 and sent to hospital. Gen. Hosp. Charlottesville, 1/25/63. Returned to duty 3/2/63. Chimborazo #3, 9/17-9/29 1863; debility. POW at Spotsylvania, 5/12/64 (Pt. Lookout, Elmira). Exchanged 2/20/65. Gen. Hosp. Howard's Grove, Richmond, 3/2/65; diarrhea. No further record.

HALL, EDWARD: b. 1842? 5'8", fair complexion, blue eyes, light hair. enl. 4/16/62 at Mt. Jackson in Co. I as Pvt. POW at Front Royal, 6/7/62. Exchanged 8/5/62. POW at Gaines's Cross Roads, 8/4/63 (Old Capitol Prison, Pt. Lookout). Exchanged 12/25/63. Chimborazo #4, 2/15-2/16, 1864; rheumatism. POW at North Anna, 5/24/64 (Pt. Lookout). Exchanged 2/10/65. Chimborazo #3, 2/25/65; debility. Furloughed 2/22/65. Paroled 5/20/65 at Staunton.

HALSTAR, FLOYD: Unofficial source lists him in Co. C. d. 3/11/63 at Camp Douglas, Illinois. bur. Oak Woods Cem., Chicago, Illinois.

HAMILTON, DAVID H.: b. 1/14/34? 5'4", dark complexion, light eyes, light hair. Baker. m. widow Sidney Striker Conner. enl. 4/18/61 at Winchester in Co. F as Pvt. AWOL since 7/18/61. Present again Sept./Oct. 1861. Detailed to act as cook in hospital at Winchester, 12/11/61. POW at Winchester, 8/3/62 (Ft. Delaware). Exchanged 10/2/62. Detailed to hosp. at Guinea's Station, 2/1-5/31 1863. To hosp. at Liberty Mills, June/July 1863. To hosp. at Orange Court House, Aug./Sept. 1863. At hosp. at Winchester, July/Sept. 1864. POW at Winchester, 9/19/64 (Pt. Lookout). Oath of Allegiance to U.S., 5/13/65. d. 6/12/21 at Winchester. bur. Mt. Hebron Cem., Winchester.

HAMILTON, EDWIN R.: b. 1837? Farmer. enl. 5/11/61 at Harpers Ferry in Co. K as Pvt. Deserted 5/13/61.

HAMILTON, WILLIAM L.: b. 1829? Merchant. enl. 5/2/61 at Harpers Ferry in Co. D as Pvt. To Corp. 8/4/61. Last official entry shows him as detailed 3/12/62, duty not stated. No further record.

HAMMAN (HAMMOND), LEWIS: b. 6/21/28. Wife's name Barbara. enl. 4/16/62 at Rude's Hill in Co. F as Pvt. d. 6/6/62 or 6/17/62 near Middletown; disease. Claim to C. S. government states he left 1 widow and 1 child. Widow received $13.20 for his service. bur. St. Stephen's Lutheran Church Cem., Shenandoah Co.

HAMNER, N. B.: Listed as Pvt. Discharged 10/21/61, underage.

HAMRICK, A. MENEFEE: b. 1/26/32. enl. 4/16/62 at Rude's Hill in Co. D as Pvt. Absent sick at hosp., 11/25/62. Present again Jan./Feb. 1863. Sick at hosp., May/June 1863. POW at School House Hosp., Chambersburg, Pa., 7/5/63

(Harrisburg; Ft. Delaware; Pt. Lookout; U.S. Hammond Gen. Hosp., 10/22/63; scurbutus). Exchanged 3/3/64. Last official entry shows him present, 12/31/64. Surrendered at Appomattox. d. 10/25/30. bur. Salem Lutheran Church Cem., Mt. Sidney.

HAMTRAMCK, SELBY M.: b. 11/24/42. Student. enl. 4/20/61 at Harpers Ferry in Co. B as Pvt. POW at Kernstown, 3/23/62 (Ft. Delaware). d. 6/9/62 at Ft. Delaware, cause not stated. Claim to C. S. government states that he died with no wife or children and that $180.30 was paid to his mother Sallie E. Hamtramck for his service. bur. Finn's Point Nat. Cem., Ft. Delaware or Elmwood Cem., Shepherdstown, W.Va.

HANEY, R. A.: Unofficial source list him in Co. F.

HANNAH, THOMAS W.: enl. 3/10/62 at Winchester in Co. A as Pvt. KIA at 2nd Manassas, 8/28/62. bur. Edge Hill Cem., Charles Town, W.Va.

HANNUM, WILLIAM E.: b. 1838? 6'3", dark complexion, gray eyes, black hair. Laborer. enl. 4/29/61 at Harpers Ferry in Co. I as Pvt. AWOL 11/23-11/28 1861. Absent sick Dec. 1861. AWOL 5/28-9/8 1862. POW at Brandy Station, 8/1/63 (Old Capitol Prison, Pt. Lookout). Exchanged 2/18/65. Paroled 4/25/65 at Winchester.

HANSUCKER, PHILIP: b. 9/8/19. Wagon maker. enl. 4/18/61 at Winchester in Co. F as Pvt. Detailed at Winchester as carpenter, 4/18-6/30 1861. AWOL July/Aug.-Sept./Oct. 1861. Present again Nov./Dec. 1861. Deserted 4/30-10/31 1862. d. 4/20/87 at his home on Shenandoah River in Clarke Co. bur. Mt. Hebron Cem., Winchester.

HARDING, CHARLES B.: enl. 7/15/61 at Winchester in Co. H as Pvt. Last official entry shows him present, Nov./Dec. 1861.

HARDING, SAMUEL D.: enl. 12/4/62 at Fredericksburg in Co. H as Pvt. Absent sick at hosp., May/June 1863. Present again July/Aug. 1863. Deserted 7/6/64. Conscription Bureau reports him in Loudoun Co., 3/15/65.

HARDY, JAMES ARTHUR W.: b. 1829? Residence Berkeley Co. enl. 10/1/62 at Bunker Hill in Co. D as Pvt. Deserted 7/26/63. POW (Rebel deserter) by 7/31/63. Oath of Allegiance to U.S., date not given.

HARLAN, WILLIAM HUNTER: b. 1/24/39. Farmer. enl. 5/22/61 at Camp Jackson on Bolivar Heights in Co. D as Pvt. Reenlisted 4/19/62. Trans. to Co. A, 1st Va. Cav., 9/29/62. d. 11/18/23. bur. Falling Waters Cem., Spring Mills, W.Va.

HARLEY, PATRICK: b. 1838? Laborer. enl. 5/23/61 at Camp Jackson on Bolivar Heights in Co. D as Pvt. MWIA in the thigh and rectum at Gaines's Mill, 6/27/62. d. 8/4/62 at Chimborazo #3.

HARMAN, WILLIAM A.: b. 1829? 5'10", fair complexion, blue eyes, light hair. Plasterer. Residence Martinsburg. enl. 4/22/61 at Harpers Ferry in Co. D as Pvt. Deserted 7/26/63. POW (Rebel deserter) at Ft. Mifflin, Pa., 7/27/63. Oath of Allegiance to U.S., 11/17/63.

HARP, JOHN W.: enl. 4/30/64 at Winchester in Co. H as Pvt. Charged $36.00 for losing his gun, 4/30-10/31 1864. Only official entry shows him present, 4/30-10/31 1864.

HARRELL, EDWARD R.: b. 1829? 5'8", light complexion, blue eyes, dark hair. Residence Charles Town. Drafted 10/1/62 at Bunker Hill in Co. K as Pvt. Apptd. to Sgt. 3/1/63. Wded. in thigh at Chancellorsville, 5/3/63. Moore hosp., Gen. Hosp. #24, Richmond, 5/11-5/26 1863. To Gen. Hosp. #27, Richmond, 5/26/63; gangrene. Furloughed for 60 days, 7/8/63. Gen. Hosp. Staunton, 7/13-Oct. 1863. Next record shows him on detail at Chimborazo #5, 7/5/64-Feb. 1865. POW at Richmond hosp., 4/3/65, (Jackson Hosp., Libby Prison, Newport News). Oath of Allegiance to U.S., 7/1/65.

HARRELL, EDWIN R.: b. 11/20/30. Tinner. enl. 4/18/61 at Charles Town in Co. A as Lt. Deserted 7/14/61 from Winchester. Dismissed from the army in disgrace by court-martial, 10/23/61. bur. Methodist Graveyard, Charles Town, W.Va.

HARRIS, CHARLES SUTTON: b. 1836 in Shenandoah Co. Tinner. enl. 4/18/61 at Winchester in Co. F as Pvt. Elected Lt. 6/1/61. Detailed for recruiting 8/2-8/31 1861. Last official record shows him AWOL, Sept./Oct. 1861. Unofficial source states he served in QM's Dept. d. 1874 at Winchester.

HARRIS, JOHN J.: b. 1836? 5'9½", fair complexion, blue eyes, fair hair. enl. 3/4/62 at Winchester in Co. E as Pvt. Elected Lt. 4/20/62. Wded. at Fredericksburg, 12/13/62. Present again Jan./Feb. 1863. Absent sick July/Aug. 1863. Present again Sept./Oct. 1863. POW at Frederick Co., Va., 11/13/63 (Wheeling, Camp Chase, Ft. Delaware). Oath of Allegiance to U.S., 6/12/65.

HARRIS, ROBERT: b. 1843? 5'8", light complexion, black eyes, black hair. Student. enl. 4/30/61 at Millwood in Co. C as Pvt. Absent sick 12/16/61. Returned from hosp. 11/9/62. POW at Salem Church, 5/20/64 (Pt. Lookout). Exchanged 2/18/65. Paroled 4/20/65 at Millwood.

HARRISON, JAMES ALEXANDER: b. 1837 in Bedford Co., Pa. Unofficial source says he served in this regt. Postwar, farmer. Alive in 1915.

HARRISON, JAMES P.: Unofficial source shows him in Co. D. d. 1/29/64 at Ft. Delaware. bur. Finn's Pt. Nat. Cem., Ft. Delaware.

HARRISON, JOHN S.: b. 1843? Clerk. Residence Martinsburg. enl. 4/27/61 at Harpers Ferry in Co. D as Pvt. Apptd. Lt. 4/20/62. Apptd. Capt., probably on 4/30/64. Detailed as hosp. steward at Camp Pickens at Manassas, 10/9-12/16 1861. Signs roll as commanding Co., 10/31/62. Gen. Hosp. #4, Richmond, 5/21/64; wound in thigh (probably recieved from battle at Salem Church on 5/20/64). Furloughed for 50 days from Gen. Hosp. Staunton, 8/3/64. Stuart Hosp., Richmond, 3/27-4/2 1865; neuralgia. POW at Richmond, 4/3/65. Paroled 4/17/65 at Richmond. Alive in Louisville, Kentucky in 1900.

HARRISON, PEYTON R.: b. June 1832. Lawyer. enl. 4/18/61 at Martinsburg in Co. D as Lt. KIA at 1st Manassas, 7/21/61. Claim to C. S. government for his service provided his widow Sarah with $56.00. bur. Old Norborne Cem., Martinsburg, W.Va.

HARRISON, SAMUEL P.: b. 1816? Manufacturer. enl. 4/18/61 at Martinsburg in Co. D as Pvt. AWOL 6/14/61 and he "claimed discharge." No further record.

HART, NIMROD R. K.: b. 1844? 5'7½", dark complexion, blue eyes, light hair. Farmer. enl. 4/18/61 at Berryville in Co. I as Pvt. AWOL 8/1-8/14 1861. Fined $11.00 for absence by court-martial. Absent sick Nov./Dec. 1861. Wded. at 1st Winchester, 5/25/62. POW at Berryville, 6/18/62 (Ft. Delaware). Exchanged 8/5/62. AWOL 11/26/62. POW in Clarke Co., 2/5/63 (Wheeling, Camp Chase). Exchanged 3/28/63. Returned regt. 4/3/63 and sentenced by court-martial to forfeit 1 month's pay for absence. Deserted 7/23/63. Captured near Winchester, 10/6/63; "engaged in robbing a coach." No further record. d. 5/18/06.

HARWOOD, JOHN M.: b. 1840? Coach painter. enl. 4/18/61 at Berryville in Co. I as Pvt. AWOL 7/18-7/30 and 8/4-8/14

1861. Fined $11.00 for absence by court-martial. Last official entry states he was "exempted from military duty by order of Gen. Jackson," 12/3/61; reason not stated.

HASTINGS, DANIEL B.: b. 1816? Blacksmith. enl. 5/12/61 at Duffields in Co. H as Pvt. Wded. at 1st Manassas, 7/21/61. Absent sick in hosp. at Fairfax Court House, Sept./Oct. 1861; rheumatism. Surgeon's Discharge, 11/7/61.

HAWKS, CORNELIUS: b. 1829? 5′ 2″, dark complexion, gray eyes, gray hair. Ditcher. enl. 4/18/61 at Millwood in Co. C as Corp. Shown as Pvt. 6/30-10/31 1862. Teamster in reserve ambulance train of 2nd Corps, Army of Northern Va., July/Aug. 1864. POW at Strasburg, 10/19/64 (Pt. Lookout). Exchanged 1/17/65. Paroled 4/17/65 at Winchester. d. 10/22/00 at White Post.

HAWKS, WELLS JOSEPH: b. 1814 in Massachusetts. Moved to Winchester circa 1843 and then to Charles Town. Bought an old church in Charles Town and converted it into a carriage manufacturing establishment. Served as commissioner and superintendent of the public schools of Jefferson Co., as mayor of Charles Town, and was elected to the Va. House of Delegates in 1855 and 1857. m. 1) Mary Smith, 2) Sarah Smith, 3) Sarah B. Worthington. Commissary Capt of 2nd Va. Inf. Commissioned Maj. and served as Gen. Jackson's Chief of Commissary, 10/22/61-5/10/63; also on staffs of Generals Ewell, Early, and Lee. Postwar, returned to Charles Town. d. 5/28/73. bur. Edge Hill Cem., Charles Town, W.Va.

HAWN, WILLIAM H. H.: b. 1840? Shoemaker. enl. 6/15/61 at Camp Whiting in Co. B as Pvt. Supposed to have been taken POW while falling back up the Valley, March/April 1862. Absent sick at home since 9/15/62. Present again Nov./Dec. 1862. AWOL 7/14/63. No further record.

HAY, WILLIAM: b. 1/19/33 in Clarke Co. Physician. enl. 4/18/61 at Millwood in Co. C as Lt. Apptd. surgeon of 33rd Va. Vol. Inf., 8/30/61. Detailed to take charge of Gen. Hosp. Staunton, June 1862. Placed on field duty around Petersburg, 1864. d. 6/1/64 at Petersburg; pneumonia. bur. Old Chapel Cem., Millwood.

HAYDEN, JAMES E.: b. 1843? Silversmith. enl. 4/18/61 at Martinsburg in Co. D as Musician. Gen. Hosp. Charlottesville, 4/19/63; cystitis. To Gen. Hosp. Lynchburg, 5/10/63. Deserted 7/26/63. POW (Rebel deserter), 7/27/63. Oath of Allegiance to U.S., date not given.

HAYES, WILLIAM: b. 1828? Laborer. enl. 4/30/61 at Harpers Ferry in Co. K as Pvt. Deserted from Darkesville, 7/2/61.

HAYS, FRANKLIN: enl. 4/16/62 in Co. D as Pvt. AWOL since 9/12/62 at Bunker Hill, "went home sick." Dropped from roll for continued absence Jan./Feb. 1863. No further record.

HEDGES, GEORGE T.: b. 1837? Farmer. enl. 4/19/61 at Hedgesville in Co. E as Pvt. Deserted 7/18/61.

HEDGES, OWEN T.: b. 1816? enl. 11/12/62 at Winchester in Co. D as Pvt. MWIA at Gettysburg, 7/2 or 7/3 1863. d. 7/9 or 7/11 1863. bur. Hedgesville Cem., Hedgesville, W.Va.

HEDGES, THEODORE F.: b. 9/30/44. drafted 10/4/62 at Bunker Hill in Co. E as Pvt. Deserted 11/21/62. Unofficial source states he served in Cav. d. 10/12/63. bur. Hedgesville Cem., Hedgesville, W.Va.

HEFFLEBOWER (HEFFLEBOUR), EDWARD: b. 1844? Miner. enl. 4/18/61 at Millwood in Co. C as Pvt. Absent sick May 1861-12/4/61. Last official entry shows him present, Dec. 1861.

HEISEY, JOSEPH: Listed in Co. E as Pvt. KIA at Gaines's Mill or Malvern Hill, 6/27 or 7/1 1862.

HEISKELL, HENRY L.: b. 1840? Clerk. enl. 4/25/61 at Harpers Ferry in Co. G as Pvt. Left behind sick at Winchester, 7/18/61; "since ascertained to have deserted." No further record.

HELFERSTAY, WILLIAM R.: b. 1840? Laborer. enl. 4/18/61 at Martinsburg in Co. D as Pvt. AWOL 5/7-6/6 1861. Last official entry shows him present, Nov./Dec. 1861.

HELM, JAMES: b. 1844? 5′ 6″, light complexion, blue eyes, dark hair. Only record is a parole statement that indicates he was paroled 5/2/65 at Winchester.

HELPHINSTINE (HELPHESTINE), ANDREW J.: b. 2/25/17. Tailor. Wife's name Ann C. enl. 4/18/61 at Winchester in Co. F as Pvt. AWOL since 7/18/61. No further record. d. 3/11/72. bur. Mt. Hebron Cem., Winchester.

HENDERSON, DAVID E.: b. 6/23/32. Artist. enl. 4/18/61 at Charles Town in Co. G as Pvt. Apptd. Lt. in Topographical Engineers, date not stated. "Employed in making maps since the commencement of the war with the exception of a few weeks preceding the Battle of Manassas." Detailed as draftsman to Gen. Johnston, 8/26/61. Draftsman at Gen. Lee's headquarters, 6/30/62. No further record. d. 11/16/87. bur. Zion Episcopal Cem., Charles Town, W.Va.

HENDERSON, RICHARD: b. 7/26/43. Student. enl. 5/25/61 at Camp Lee in Co. G as Pvt. Absent sick since 10/13/61. Present again Nov./Dec. 1861. Detailed as teamster for QM's train, Nov./Dec. 1862. Last official entry shows him present, 4/30-10/31 1864. Paroled at Appomattox. Postwar, farmer. d. 6/22/05. bur. Zion Episcopal Cem., Charles Town, W.Va.

HENDERSON, ROBARTUS: b. 1820? in Augusta Co. 5′ 9″, fair complexion, gray eyes, dark hair. Farmer. enl. 4/14/62 at New Market in Co. H as Pvt. Absent sick 5/7/62, "not fit for duty." Discharged 2/14/63, overage.

HENDRICKS, DANIEL WEBSTER: b. 7/26/38. Farrier. enl. 4/18/61 at Duffields in Co. H as Pvt. Listed as present through July/Aug. 1861; then no record again until shown absent sick, Sept./Oct. 1863. Also appears on rolls of Co. D, 12th Va. Cav. Present again Jan./Feb. 1864. Last official record shows him present, July/Aug. 1864. Paroled 4/18/65 at Harpers Ferry. d. 2/15/10 near Duffields. bur. Elmwood Cem., Shepherdstown, W.Va.

HENDRICKS, JAMES MADISON: b. 2/6/44. enl. 4/18/61 at Duffields in Co. H as Pvt. Reenlisted in Co. D, 6th Va. Cav., 6/30-10/31 1862. d. 6/12/23. bur. Elmwood Cem., Shepherdstown, W.Va.

HENDRICKS, WILLIAM: b. 12/32/21. Farmer. enl. 4/18/61 at Duffields in Co. H as Pvt. KIA at 1st Manassas, 7/21/61. bur. St. James Lutheran Cem., Uvilla, W.Va.

HENRY, GEORGE WASHINGTON: b. 12/7/43. Listed in Co. D as Pvt. Detailed to drive ord. wagon, 6/12/62. Continued on this detail until he deserted, 7/26/63. POW near Chambersburg, Pa., 8/8/63. No further record. d. 10/30/10. bur. Mt. Hebron Cem., Winchester.

HENRY, JAMES: b. 1827? Laborer. enl. 4/25/61 at Millwood in Co. C as Pvt. Absent sick since 11/20/61. AWOL 6/4-9/4 1862. Deserted 11/22/62 on march from Winchester.

HENRY, NELSON: enl. 4/6/62 at Winchester in Co. F as Pvt. Returned from AWOL, 10/3/62; time of leaving not stated. Deserted 11/24/62. Still living in 1900.

HENSELL, ROBERT S.: enl. 10/1/62 at Bunker Hill in Co. H as Pvt. AWOL since 10/4/62. No further record.

HENSELL, WILLIAM: enl. 7/3/61 at Hainesville in Co. B as Pvt. Absent sick Nov./Dec. 1861. AWOL since 12/15/61. Dropped from the roll 12/22/62. Appears on roll of Co. F, 1st Va. Cav.

HENSON, GEORGE W.: 5'9½", dark complexion, hazel eyes, dark hair. Residence Charles Town. enl. 2/10/62 at Winchester in Co. A as Musician. To Pvt. 8/17/63. POW at Kernstown, 3/23/62 (Ft. Delaware). Exchanged 8/5/62. Charged $1.00 for wasting 20 rounds of ammunition, Jan./Feb. 1864. POW at Spotsylvania, 5/12/64 (Pt. Lookout, Elmira). Oath of Allegiance to U.S., 5/15/65.

HERBERT, ZED M.: b. 7/24/44. enl. 6/30/64 at Winchester in Co. C as Pvt. Surrendered at Appomattox. d. 9/29/19. bur. Riverview Cem., Williamsport, Md.

HESKITT, LANDON C.: b. 1812? Merchant. enl. 4/18/16 at Halltown in Co. B as Lt. AWOL since 7/16/61. Present again Sept./Oct. 1861. Last official entry states he was cashiered from the army by court-martial, Nov./Dec. 1861.

HESS, CHARLES WILLIAM: b. 3/2/44. Farmer. enl. 4/18/61 at Duffields in Co. H as Pvt. Last official entry shows him present, Nov./Dec. 1861. Unofficial source states he trans. to 1st Va. Cav. and died in service from typhoid fever and peritonitis. d. 12/6/63.

HESSEY, CHARLES E.: b. 1836? Tailor. enl. 4/18/61 at Halltown in Co. B as Pvt. Absent sick at Shepherdstown, July/Aug. 1861. d. 1/3 or 1/30 1862 at Shepherdstown; disease. bur. Elmwood Cem., Shepherdstown, W.Va.

HESSEY, EDWARD H.: b. 1826? Brickmaker. enl. 6/9/61 at Camp Jackson on Bolivar Heights in Co. B as Pvt. Absent sick at home in Winchester, March/April 1862-May/June 1863. Nurse at New School Presbyterian Church Hosp., Winchester, 10/20/62. Present again July/Aug. 1863. POW at Spotsylvania, 5/12/64 (Pt. Lookout, Elmira). Exchanged 10/29/64. No further record.

HESSEY, RICHARD AMOS: enl. 7/9/61 at Winchester in Co. B at Pvt. Absent on furlough Nov./Dec. 1861. Present again Jan./Feb. 1862. AWOL since 5/28/62, and dropped from the roll 12/22/62. No further record. bur. Edge Hill Cem., Charles Town, W.Va.

HEWITT (HUYETT) REZIN D.: b. 1842? Farmer. enl. 6/12/61 at Camp Jackson on Bolivar Heights in Co. G as Pvt. Absent sick Nov./Dec. 1861. Discharged by Secretary of War, 5/23/62; reason not stated. Also served in Co. B, 12th Va. Cav. bur. Old Chapel Cem., Millwood.

HIBBARD, JOHN W.: b. 1833? Farmer. enl. 4/18/61 at Millwood in Co. C as Corp. Wded. in thigh at 1st Manassas, 7/21/61. Last official entry shows him still absent from wound, Nov./Dec. 1861. d. 1/21/99.

HICKS, JOSEPH DORSEN: b. 3/13/38. enl. 4/10/62 at New Market in Co. H as Pvt. Wded. slightly at Fredericksburg, 12/13/62. Absent on detached service March/April-May/June 1863; duty not stated. Present again July/Aug. 1863. Last official entry shows him present, March/April 1864. Surrendered at Appomattox.

HIGGINS, ANDREW J.: b. 1840? Laborer. enl. 4/20/61 at Harpers Ferry in Co. K as Pvt. To Corp. 8/25/61. Last official entry shows him present, Nov./Dec. 1861. Appears as Sgt. on rolls of Co. D, 12th Va. Cav.

HIGGINS, EDWARD: b. 1837? Laborer. enl. 4/18/61 at Duffields in Co. H as Pvt. Absent sick Sept./Oct. 1861. Present again Nov./Dec. 1861. AWOL since 5/30/62. No further record.

HILBERT, JOHN E.: b. 9/14/29. Blacksmith. enl. 5/7/61 at Harpers Ferry in Co. G as Corp. Detailed on special duty, 10/10/61; type of duty not specified. Last official entry shows him absent on special duty, 12/28/62. Appears on rolls of Co. B, 12th Va. Cav. d. 10/19/07. bur. Edge Hill Cem., Charles Town, W.Va.

HILL, ABRAHAM R.: 5'5", dark complexion, hazel eyes, dark hair. Residence Martinsburg. enl. 4/24/62 at Swift Run Gap in Co. E as Pvt. Chimborazo #4, 9/17-10/10 1862; diarrhea. Chimborazo #1, 6/14/63; diarrhea. To Danville, 7/17/63. Present July/Aug. 1863. POW at Spotsylvania, 5/12/64 (Pt. Lookout, Elmira). Oath of Allegiance to U.S., 6/30/65.

HILL, JOHN: b. 12/18/20. 5'9", light complexion, blue eyes, black hair. Tailor. Residence Jefferson Co. enl. 4/18/61 at Duffields in Co. H as Pvt. To Corp. 11/22/61. Detailed to Staunton as nurse in hosp., 11/20/62-Nov./Dec. 1863. Deserted 1/16/64. Oath of Allegiance to U.S., date not given. d. 3/13/05. bur. Edge Hill Cem., Charles Town, W.Va.

HILL, JOSEPH G.: b. 12/21/38. Brickmaker. enl. 4/18/61 at Martinsburg in Co. D as Pvt. Surrendered at Appomattox. d. 9/30/15. bur. Rest United Methodist Church Cem.

HILL, MARTIN LUTHER: b. 1841? Residence Berkeley Co. enl. 3/4/62 at Winchester in Co. D as Pvt. Deserted 7/26/63. POW (Rebel deserter), 7/27/63, "who wishes to take the oath." No further record. bur. Greenhill Cem., Martinsburg, W.Va.

HILL, MICHAEL: b. 1837? Plasterer. enl. 4/18/61 at Martinsburg in Co. D as Pvt. Chimborazo #1, 10/17-10/28 1861; debility. Present again Nov./Dec. 1861. Deserted 7/26/63. POW (Rebel deserter), 7/27/63, "who wishes to take the oath." No further record.

HILL, WILLIAM J.: enl. 10/15/64 at Richmond in Co. D as Pvt. Surrendered at Appomattox.

HINES, JAMES E. (W.): b. 1830? Shoemaker. enl. 6/15/61 at Charles Town in Co. F as Pvt. MWIA in leg at 1st Manassas, 7/21/61. d. 8/27/61 at Gen. Hosp. Charlottesville after leg amputated.

HINES, JOHN R.: b. 1837. Shoemaker. enl. 5/1/61 at Harpers Ferry in Co. F as Pvt. Detailed to hosp. to nurse his brother James, July/Aug. 1861. Present again Sept./Oct. 1861. Last official entry shows him present, Nov./Dec. 1861.

HINTON, JOSEPH: enl. 4/15/62 at Rude's Hill in Co. A as Pvt. d. 8/20/62 at hosp. in Albermarle Co.; "camp fever."

HITE, ISAIAH H.: b. Augusta Co. enl. 4/15/62 at Rude's Hill in Co. G as Pvt. Wded. in leg at 2nd Manassas, 8/28/62. Returned to regt. 1/17/63. Chimborazo #5, 12/20/63; catarrah. d. 1/2/64 at Chimborazo #5; continued fever.

HOBSON, JOHN F.: b. 1832? m. Annie R. Deahl. Listed on regular muster roll of Co. F but disregarded the summons to service. enl. 3/11/62 at Winchester in Co. L, 5th Va. Inf. Detailed to hosp. at Lynchburg, 3/5/63, after being declared unfit for field service. Surrendered at Appomattox. d. 12/20/03. bur. Mt. Hebron Cem., Winchester.

HOBSON, WILLIAM C.: b. 1839? Shoemaker. enl. 4/18/61 at Winchester in Co. F as Pvt. Wded. in leg at 1st Manassas, 7/21/61. Still absent from wound, Nov./Dec. 1861. AWOL 5/11/62. Present again Jan./Feb. 1863. Last official entry shows him sick since 6/13/63. No further record.

HODGE, JAMES: b. 1839? 6'2", light complexion, blue eyes, brown hair. Laborer. enl. 6/22/61 at Winchester in Co. C as Pvt. Detailed as wagoner in QM's Dept., 11/25/61. Remained on this same detail through last official entry, 8/31-12/31 1864. Paroled 4/19/65 at Winchester.

HODGES, ISAAC N.: b. 1823? Machinist. enl. 4/23/61 at Harpers Ferry in Co. D. as Pvt. Last official entry shows him present, Nov./Dec. 1861.

HODGES, JOHN: b. 1817? Laborer. enl. 5/7/61 at Harpers Ferry in Co. H as Pvt. Absent sick Sept./Oct. 1861. Last official entry shows him present, Nov./Dec. 1861.

HOERICK, ADAM: 5'5", florid complexion, blue eyes, auburn hair. Residence Winchester. enl. 12/22/62 at Guinea's Station in Co. D as Pvt. Gen. Hosp. Staunton, 3/15-4/21 1863; diarrhea. Absent on detail as Ord. guard, May/June 1863. Present again July/Aug. 1863. POW at Spotsylvania, 5/12/64 (Pt. Lookout, Elmira). Oath of Allegiance to U.S., 6/21/65.

HOFFMAN, EDMOND L.: b. 1839? 5'10", light complexion, brown eyes, brown hair. Farmer. enl. 4/18/61 at Martinsburg in Co. D as Sgt. Elected Lt. 8/14/61. To Capt. 9/17/62. Signs roll as commanding Co., Nov./Dec. 1861. Wded. at Kernstown, 3/23/62. Sick at hosp., 10/25/62. Present again Nov./Dec. 1862. Gen. Hosp. Charlottesville, 5/16/63; diarrhea. To Staunton, 6/12/63. Present again July/Aug. 1863. Absent sick Sept./Oct. 1863-March/April 1864. Retired to Invalid Corps, 4/30/64, and assigned to the Commandant of Conscription in Va., 5/7/64. Paroled 4/24/65 at Winchester. d. 9/27/04. bur. Greenhill Cem., Martinsburg, W.Va.

HOFFMAN, JOHN A.: enl. 6/20/63 at Orange Court House in Co. D as Pvt. AWOL May/June 1863. Present again July/Aug. 1863. Deserted 3/21/64.

HOFFMAN, ROBERT N.: b. 1840? Coach maker. enl. 4/18/61 at Halltown in Co. B as Pvt. AWOL since 7/26/61. AWOL again 9/1-10/16 1861. AWOL again 11/13/61. Present Jan./Feb. 1862. AWOL during July 1862. Detailed as asst. in Commissary Dept., Sept. 1862-Jan./Feb. 1863. Detailed to drive cattle, 6/14/63. AWOL 10/13-10/31 1863. Sentenced by court-martial to forfeit 1 month's pay. Detailed as musician in 2nd Va. regt. band, 12/11/63. POW at Spotsylvania, 5/12/64 (Pt. Lookout, Elmira). Exchanged 3/2/65. Jackson Hosp., Richmond, 3/7/65; debility. Furloughed for 30 days, 3/9/65. Paroled 5/29/65 at Harpers Ferry.

HOFFMAN, SYLVESTER F.: enl. 4/18/62 at Rude's Hill in Co. F as Pvt. Deserted from Swift Run Gap, 5/1/62. Recovered from desertion, 3/8/63. Absent sick March/April 1863. Detailed as guard to Gen. Johnson's headquarters, May/June-July/Aug. 1863. Present again Sept./Oct. 1863. POW at Brandy Station near Kelly's Ford, 11/8/63 (Old Capitol Prison, Pt. Lookout). Exchanged 3/10/64. Chimborazo #4, 3/15/64; diarrhea. Furloughed 30 days, 3/18/64. No further record.

HOFFMAN, THOMAS W.: enl. 4/14/62 at New Market in Co. H as Pvt. AWOL since 6/1/62. No further record.

HOGG, THOMAS R.: b. 1816? Mechanic. enl. 4/21/61 at Duffields in Co. H as Pvt. Deserted 5/15/61.

HOGSHEAD, PRESTON BAILEY: b. 9/9/33. Residence Rockbridge Co. Unofficial source says he served in this regt. d. 7/4/03.

HOLLAND, HARRISON: enl. 4/16/62 at Rude's Hill in Co. D as Pvt. POW at Standardsville, 9/29/64 (Pt. Lookout). Joined U.S. army, 10/15/64.

HOLLAND, JOHN WILLIS: b. 1/1/28. Carpenter. enl. 4/18/61 at Millwood in Co. C as Pvt. Discharged 8/15/62, reason not stated. d. 2/5/92. bur. Old Chapel Cem., Millwood.

HOLLER, GEORGE: drafted 4/14/62 at Rude's Hill in Co. K as Pvt. Sick at hosp., 8/11/62. Still absent sick March/April 1863. AWOL May/June 1863. No further record.

HOLLIDAY, BENJAMIN TAYLOR: b. 2/28/45. Student. enl. 6/15/61 at Winchester in Co. F as Pvt. Absent sick at Fairfax Court House Hosp., Sept./Oct. 1861. Discharged 12/2/61; reason not stated. Unofficial source states he was apptd. to V.M.I., 12/17/61, and later served as a Pvt. in Chew's Battery. Postwar, traveling salesman and orchardist. d. 4/3/18 at Waynesboro.

HOLLIS, JOHN A.: b. 8/6/34. Mason. enl. 4/18/61 at Martinsburg in Co. D as Pvt. Absent sick Sept./Oct. 1861. Last official entry shows him present, Nov./Dec. 1861. d. 7/17/06. bur. Greenhill Cem., Martinsburg, W.Va.

HOLLIS, THOMAS P.: b. 1825? Town sergeant. enl. 4/18/61 at Martinsburg in Co. D as Pvt. Discharged 5/14/61, "being a town sergeant."

HOLLIS, THOMAS W.: b. 1837? Mason. enl. 4/26/61 at Harpers Ferry in Co. D as Pvt. Left sick at Martinsburg 7/3/61, and arrested by Federals. No further record.

HOLMES, JOHN: enl. 1/5/63 at Camp Winder in Co. C as Pvt. Deserted 1/6/63.

HOLTZMAN, JOSEPH W.: enl. 4/14/62 at Rude's Hill in Co. B as Pvt. AWOL 6/10/62-1/31/63. Under guard, Jan./Feb. 1863. MWIA at Chancellorsville, 5/3/63. d. 5/12/63.

HOMRICH (HOMRICK), JAMES M.: b. 10/20/37. Merchant. enl. 4/18/61 at Martinsburg in Co. D as Pvt. Discharged before 6/30/61 since he was a commissioned officer in the state militia since 5/10/61. d. 1/27/15. bur. Greenhill Cem., Martinsburg, W.Va.

HOOE, HOWSON: m. Henrietta Daniell. Unofficial source says he served in this regt.

HOOFF, JAMES LAWRENCE: b. 10/2/25. enl. 7/6/61 at Darkesville in Co. G as Pvt. Last official entry shows him present, Nov./Dec. 1861. One record states he served as a QM Sgt. in the 2nd Va. Inf. and as Asst. QM in the 11th Va. Cav. Postwar, merchant in Charles Town; elected to W.Va. legislature in 1875; later became president of Jefferson Co. Court. d. 8/24/87. bur. Edge Hill Cem., Charles Town, W.Va.

HOOFF, JAMES P.: b. 1841? Carpenter. enl. 6/19/61 at Winchester in Co. I as Pvt. AWOL 7/27-7/31 1861. Absent sick Sept./Oct. 1861. AWOL since 5/28/62. No further record.

HOOFF, WILLIAM A.: b. 1839? 5'8", dark complexion, gray eyes, dark hair. Farmer. enl. 4/18/61 at Charles Town in Co. G as Pvt. Detailed as nurse to Gen. Hosp. #4, Richmond, 1/30/63. Ward master in Gen. Hosp. #4, Richmond, March/April 1863-Jan./Feb. 1864. Returned to regt. 3/14/64. POW at Salem Church, 5/12/64 (Pt. Lookout). Exchanged 3/14/65. Paroled 4/16/65 at Winchester.

HOOK, WILLIAM F.: enl. 4/15/62 at Rude's Hill in Co. A as Pvt. MWIA in leg at 2nd Manassas, 8/28/62. d. 10/11/62.

HOOKS, JOHN R.: b. 2/5/44 in Rockingham Co. Cooper. m. Mary L. Flick. Lived in Elkton most of his life. Unofficial source says he enl. Feb. 1864 in Co. F. Wded. in leg at Spotsylvania, 5/10/64. d. 12/6/39 in Confederate Soldier's Home in Richmond. He was the last surviving member of the regt. bur. Elk Run Cem., Elkton.

HOOPER, EDWARD B.: b. 7/31/19. Butcher. enl. 4/18/61 at Martinsburg in Co. D as Musician. Regt. butcher, April-Aug. 1861. Detailed as brig. butcher by Gen. Jackson, 8/?/61. Absent Nov./Dec. 1861, reason not stated. Present again 6/30-10/31 1862. Last official entry shows him present, 8/31-12/31 1864. Surrendered at Appomattox. d. 10/5/73. bur. Old Norborne Cem., Martinsburg, W.Va.

106

HOPKINS, ABNER CRUMP: b. 10/24/35 in Powhatan Co. grad. Hampden-Sydney College, 1855. Attd. Union Theological Seminary. Minister at Martinsburg Presbyterian Church. m. Anne Pleasants Atkinson, 5/16/61. Commissioned 5/3/62 as chaplain of the 2nd Va. Vol. Inf. To Chaplain of the 2nd Corps, Army of Northern Va. Postwar, pastor of the Presbyterian Church of Charles Town, 1866-1911. d. 2/4/11. bur. Edge Hill Cem., Charles Town, W.Va.

HORN, GEORGE: b. 8/6/19. Farmer. enl. at Duffields in Co. H as Pvt. AWOL and never mustered, 4/18-6/30 1861. No further record. d. 2/2/79. bur. Elmwood Cem., Shepherdstown, W.Va.

HOTTSENPILLAR, MAHLON: enl. 3/4/62 at Winchester in Co. E as Pvt. Wded. in arm at Payne's Farm, 11/27/63. Chimborazo #4, 11/30/63. To Staunton, 12/13/63. Present again March/April 1864. Last official entry shows him present, 8/31-12/31 1864. Surrendered at Appomattox.

HOUCK, JAMES: b. 2/11/21 in Shenandoah Co. 5'3", dark complexion, blue eyes, dark hair. Tailor. enl. 4/16/62 at Rude's Hill in Co. F as Pvt. AWOL 6/5-10/8 1862. Discharged 1/13/63, overage. d. 6/12/96. bur. St. Paul's Lutheran Church Cem., Strasburg.

HOUT, DAVID H.: b. 11/24/20. Carpenter. enl. 4/18/61 at Halltown in Co. B as Corp. To Sgt. 11/13/61. Discharged 4/30-10/31 1862, overage. d. 3/11/05. bur. Elmwood Cem., Shepherdstown, W.Va.

HOUT, GEORGE W.: enl. 6/1/63 near Sharpsburg, Md. in Co. B as Musician. Surrendered at Appomattox. Postwar, went west. d. 2/13/20 at Warrensburg, Mo.

HOWARD, NORMAN DE V.: b. 1842? in Washington, D.C. Teacher. enl. 5/8/61 at Schoolhouse on the Hagerstown Road (just north of Harpers Ferry) in Co. I as Pvt. Absent sick at Fairfax Court House Hosp., Sept./Oct.-Nov./Dec. 1861. POW at Woodstock, 6/3/62 (Pt. Lookout). Exchanged 8/5/62. On detached service as clerk in hosp. at Staunton, Sept. 1862. Absent sick Jan./Feb. 1863. Present again March/April 1863. Apptd. hosp. steward and assigned to 33rd Va. Inf., 5/1/63. To Asst. Surgeon at Mt. Jackson and Richmond hospitals, dates not given. Postwar, physician in St. Louis; moved to Florida in 1883. Alive 1898 in Florida.

HOWELL, DAVID, JR.: b. 8/25/38. Farmer. enl. 6/15/61 at Charles Town in Co. G as Pvt. Elected Lt. 10/1/62. Signs roll as commanding Co., March/April 1864. Wded. Aug. 1864, exact battle and date not given. Sent to Richmond to forward recruits to army, 11/23/64. Retired to Invalid Corps, 3/6/65, and stationed at Newtown. Paroled 4/21/65 at Charles Town. d. 1/31/03. bur. Zion Episcopal Cem., Charles Town, W.Va.

HUDSON, SAMUEL: b. 1834? Sailor. enl. 4/20/61 at Harpers Ferry in Co. K as Pvt. Last official entry shows him present, Nov./Dec. 1861.

HUDSON, SAMUEL S.: b. 1837? Carpenter. enl. 4/19/61 at Harpers Ferry in Co. B as Pvt. POW at Kernstown, 3/23/62 (Ft. Delaware). Exchanged 8/5/62. Present again by 10/31/62. AWOL 7/27/63, and dropped from the roll as a deserter. No further record.

HUFF, BENJAMIN F.: enl. 4/16/62 at Rude's Hill in Co. D as Pvt. To Corp., date not given. Sick at hosp., March/April-May/June 1863. Last official entry shows him present, March/April 1864.

HUGHES, A. J.: enl. 12/11/62 at Guinea's Station in Co. D as Pvt. Detailed as teamster in Ord. train, 12/11/62. Remained on this detail until he was left sick behind enemy lines, July 1863. No further record.

HUGHES, JOHN T.: b. 1844? Laborer. enl. 4/25/61 at Millwood in Co. C as Pvt. Surgeon's Discharge, 5/20/61; reason not stated.

HULL, DALLAS S.: b. 3/5/44. 5'7½", light complexion, hazel eyes, light hair. enl. 2/14/62 at Winchester in Co. E as Pvt. Wded. in ankle at Payne's Farm, 11/27/63. Chimborazo #4, 11/30/63. To Staunton, 12/15/63. Last official entry shows him still absent from wounds, March/April 1864. Paroled 5/8/65 at Winchester. d. 7/31/11 at Soldier's Home in Richmond. bur. Hedgesville Cem., Hedgesville, W.Va.

HULL, GEORGE M.: b. 1838? 5'5", light complexion, hazel eyes, brown hair. Carpenter. Residence Berkeley Co. enl. 4/19/61 at Hedgesville in Co. E as Pvt. Detailed to hosp., 11/1/62-Jan./Feb. 1863. Present again March/April 1863. Wded. in foot at Payne's Farm, 11/27/63. Chimborazo #4, 11/30/63. To Staunton, 12/15/63. Present again 4/30-10/31 1864. POW at Ft. Steadman near Petersburg, 3/25/65 (Pt. Lookout). Oath of Allegiance to U.S., 6/13/65.

HULL, JOHN T.: b. 3/25/39. Carpenter. enl. 4/19/61 in Co. E as Sgt. To Lt. 9/17/62. Absent sick Sept./Oct.-Nov./Dec. 1861. Wded. at Port Republic, 6/9/62. Present Sept./Oct. 1862. Wded. in neck at Chancellorsville, 5/3/63. Still absent in hosp., 10/30/64. Retired to Invalid Corps, 1/11/65. Assigned to Camp of Instruction at Camp Lee near Richmond, 3/16/65. No further record. d. 10/16/25. bur. Hedgesville Cem., Hedgesville, W.Va.

HULTZ, JACOB: b. 1828? enl. 4/16/62 at Rude's Hill in Co. D as Pvt. Wded. 6/9/62 at Port Republic. Surgeon's Discharge from hosp., 8/24/62. d. 2/3/90.

HUMPHREYS, DAVID: b. 5/2/32 at Charles Town. Farmer. enl. 5/14/61 at Harpers Ferry in Co. G as Pvt. Unofficial source states he was injured during drill in camp at Centreville (1861); disabled and discharged. Absent on special duty since 11/19/61. Reenlisted in Co. B, 7th Va. Cav. Postwar, merchant; moved to Norfolk in 1869 and entered insurance business; helped with the development of Norfolk and was a member of the town council; author of *Heroes and Spies*. d. 7/5/05. bur. Edge Hill Cem., Charles Town, W.Va.

HUMRICKHOUSE, GEORGE W.: enl. 6/21/63 near Sharpsburg in Co. B as Musician. Surrendered at Appomattox.

HUMRICKHOUSE, SAMUEL P.: b. 1830? in Shepherdstown. 5'3", fair complexion, gray eyes, dark hair. Tailor. enl. 6/18/61 at Winchester in Co. B as Pvt. POW at Kernstown, 3/23/62 (Ft. Delaware). Exchanged 8/5/62. Absent sick 8/5-Nov./Dec. 1862. Present again Jan./Feb. 1863. On furlough March/April 1863. Discharged 5/26/63 by reason of insanity; he was "taken very sick with Typhoid Fever."

HUNSICKER, JAMES W.: enl. 10/8/62 at Bunker Hill in Co. A as Pvt. Chimborazo #1, 3/21/63; fever. d. 4/2 or 4/3 1863 at Chimborazo #1.

HUNTER, ABELL: b. 1846? 5'8", light complexion, blue eyes, light hair. enl. 7/16/63 at Darkesville in Co. E as Pvt. Detailed in Signal Corps, Nov./Dec. 1863. Last official entry shows him still on detail in Signal Corps, March/April 1864. Paroled 5/1/65 at Staunton.

HUNTER, ANDREW: b. 1835? Physician. enl. 6/5/61 at Camp Jackson on Bolivar Heights in Co. C as Pvt. Trans. to Culpeper Court House as a Surgeon, 9/25/61. No further record.

HUNTER, DAVID: b. May 1840. Teacher. enl. 5/9/61 at Harpers Ferry in Co. D as Pvt. To Sgt., no date given. Wded. slightly in left arm at 1st Manassas, 7/21/61. Wded. in right breast at 2nd Manassas, 8/28/62. Present again

Nov./Dec. 1862. Detailed to Lexington to arrest deserters, Jan./Feb. 1863. KIA at Cedar Creek, 10/19/64. bur. Old Norborne Cem., Martinsburg, W.Va.

HUNTER, HENRY CLAY: b. 1831? attd. V.M.I., 1849. Lawyer. enl. 4/18/61 at Charles Town in Co. A as Pvt. Commissioned Lt. in Provisional Army of Va., 7/14/61. No further record. Postwar, teacher. d. 12/3/86. bur. Zion Episcopal Cem., Charles Town, W.Va.

HUNTER, JAMES H. L.: b. 4/9/30. Merchant. Capt. of Letcher Riflemen, a pre-war militia Co. in Jefferson Co., 11/25/59. To Capt., Co. H, 2nd Va. Vol. Inf., 5/3/61. Last official entry shows him present, Nov./Dec. 1861. Dropped from Register of Commissioned Officers, 5/18/62; reason not stated. Paroled 4/26/65 at Ashland. d. 8/17/91. bur. Edge Hill Cem., Charles Town, W.Va.

HUNTER, JOHN C.: b. 1831? Printer. enl. 4/18/61 at Martinsburg in Co. D as Corp. To Sgt. 8/4/61. To Lt. 12/8/61. Last official entry shows him present, Nov./Dec. 1861. Dropped from Register of Commissioned Officers, 5/18/62; reason not stated.

HUNTER, ROBERT: b. 1836? Tobacconist. enl. 5/11/61 at Schoolhouse on the Hagerstown Road (north of Harpers Ferry) in Co. I as Pvt. Absent sick in hosp., Sept./Oct. 1861. AWOL 10/13-10/27 1861. Trans. to Medical Dept., 4/18/62.

HUNTER, ROBERT WATERMAN: b. 1837? Teacher. enl. 4/18/61 at Martinsburg in Co. D as Lt. Apptd. adjutant of 2nd Va. Inf., 6/17/61. Last official entry shows him present, Nov./Dec. 1861. Unofficial source says he later served as chief of staff to Gen. John B. Gordon. Postwar, member of Turner Ashby Camp #22 at Winchester. d. 4/4/16. bur. Mt. Hebron Cem., Winchester.

HUNTER, THOMAS C.: 5' 11", light complexion, hazel eyes, dark hair. Residence Jefferson Co. enl. 7/3/61 at Martinsburg in Co. D as Pvt. Listed as hosp. steward, 4/30-10/31 1862 through March/April 1863. Absent sick at hosp., May/June 1863. Commissioned hosp. steward, 8/28/63; place of service not stated. Present again Sept./Oct. 1863. Last official entry states he was trans. to the surgeon at Gen. Long's headquarters, 4/30-10/31 1864. Paroled 4/10/65 at Barkelsville Junction.

HURST, JAMES A.: b. 12/19/29. Farmer. enl. 4/18/61 at Duffields in Co. H as Lt. AWOL 9/20-11/1 1861. No further record. d. 7/24/91. bur. Edge Hill Cem., Charles Town, W.Va.

HURST, JOHN HARRY: b. 6/5/38. Farmer. enl. 4/18/61 at Harpers Ferry in Co. A as Corp. Trans. to Cav., 6/14/61. d. 11/21/64. bur. Edge Hill Cem., Charles Town, W.Va.

HURST, THOMAS N. C.: b. 7/23/26. Farmer. enl. 4/18/61 at Charles Town in Co. A as Pvt. MWIA in abdomen, at 1st Manassas 7/21/61. d. 8/1 or 8/8 1861 at Orange Court House Hosp. bur. Edge Hill Cem., Charles Town, W.Va.

HUSKEY, W. H.: Unofficial source says he served in this regt. Wded. at Port Republic, 8/9/62. Wded. at Gettysburg, date not specific. Alive in 1898 in Tennessee.

HUTCHINSON, SAMUEL: b. 3/21/25. enl. 6/20/63 at Sharpsburg, Md. in Co. D as Musician. Surrendered at Appomattox. d. 9/27/73. bur. Old Norborne Cem., Martinsburg, W.Va.

HUTSON, JACOB: b. 1843? Carpenter. enl. 4/19/61 at Harpers Ferry in Co. B as Pvt. Taken POW while on furlough, March/April 1862; or AWOL since 3/15/62 and dropped from the roll as a deserter, 12/22/62. No further record.

HUTSON, ROBERT: b. 1842? Blacksmith. enl. 4/18/61 at Halltown in Co. B as Pvt. d. 7/19/61 at hosp. in Winchester.

HUTTLE, G.: enl. 4/18/62 at Rude's Hill in Co. F. Deserted from Swift Run Gap, 5/1/62.

ISLER, CHARLES H.: b. 1830? Farmer. enl. 4/18/61 at Charles Town in Co. G as Pvt. Wded. at 1st Manassas, 7/21/61. Last official entry shows him still absent from wound, Nov./Dec. 1861. Appears on rolls of Co. B, 12th Va. Cav. bur. Edge Hill Cem., Charles Town, W.Va.

JACKSON, ABNER: Listed in Co. K as Pvt. Gen. Hosp. Petersburg, 6/2/62; rubeola and diarrhea. d. 6/24/62 at hosp. at Petersburg.

JACKSON, JOHN A.: b. 1825? enl. 6/15/61 at Winchester in Co. F as Pvt. AWOL since 8/28/61. Absent sick without leave, 10/12/61. Last official entry lists him AWOL, Nov./Dec. 1861.

JACKSON, SOLOMON R.: enl. in Co. I as Pvt. "Marched with the company from Berryville, 18 April, 1861, and served with the company until 18 May, 1861, when he was rejected by the surgeon for physical disability." No further record.

JACOCK, J. J.: Conscript from Camp Lee, Richmond, assigned 10/15/64 to Co. H as Pvt. Surrendered at Appomattox.

JAMESON, HENRY: enl. 4/16/62 at Rude's Hill in Co. F as Pvt. Detailed to work in woolen factory, 10/19/62. Last official entry shows him absent, still on detail in woolen factory, Jan./Feb. 1864.

JANNEY, JAMES CAMPBELL: b. 5/2/45. enl. 2/7/62 at Camp Zollicofer in Co. I as Pvt. Detailed as nurse to Gen. Hosp. Staunton, 3/4/62-6/30/63. Gen. Hosp. Staunton, 2/16/63; hernia. Rejoined regt. July/Aug. 1863. Henningson Hosp., 10/25/63; continued fever and debility. Furloughed 30 days, 10/30/63. Gen. Hosp. Charlottesville, 11/28/63-1/6/64; typhoid fever. Present again Jan./Feb. 1864. Last official entry shows him present, March/April 1864. d. 12/20/15. bur. Edge Hill Cem., Charles Town, W.Va.

JENKINS, ALEXANDER: b. 1841? Laborer. enl. 5/1/61 at Harpers Ferry in Co. H as Pvt. Deserted 6/3/61.

JENKINS, ASA: 5' 6½", dark complexion, blue eyes, light hair. Residence Berkeley Co. enl. 10/15/61 at Centerville in Co. E as Pvt. Wded. in finger at 2nd Winchester, date not specific. POW at Salem Church, 5/20/64 (Old Capitol Prison, Ft. Delaware). Oath of Allegiance to U.S., 6/14/65.

JENKINS, GEORGE EDWARD: b. 11/10/37. 5' 8½", dark complexion, black eyes, black hair. Machinist. Residence Frederick Co., Va. m. Sarah Cornelia Baker. enl. 4/18/61 at Winchester in Co. F as Pvt. Sent to hosp. sick from Bunker Hill, 10/11/62. Present again Nov./Dec. 1862. AWOL since 7/20/63. POW (Rebel deserter) near Chambersburg, Pa., 7/27/63 (Ft. Mifflin, Pa.). Oath of Allegiance to U.S., 11/17/63. Postwar, tobacco merchant and cigar manufacturer in Winchester; member of Winchester City Council; friend of President William McKinely. d. 5/28/06. bur. Mt. Hebron Cem., Winchester.

JENKINS, JOHN R.: b. 1840? 5' 5", sallow complexion, blue eyes, auburn hair. Coach trimmer. Residence Winchester. enl. 4/18/61 at Winchester in Co. F as Corp. To Pvt. 8/3/61. AWOL July/Aug.-Sept./Oct. 1861. Present again Nov./Dec. 1861. Deserted from Rude's Hill, 4/18/62. Recovered from desertion, 2/1/63, and under arrest. Gen. Hosp.

Staunton, 4/15/63; debility. Present again July/Aug. 1863. POW at Spotsylvania, 5/12/64 (Pt. Lookout, Elmira). Oath of Allegiance to U.S., 6/27/65. d. 4/3/85. bur. Greenhill Cem., Martinsburg, W.Va.

JENKINS, JOSEPH J.: b. 1832? Shoemaker. enl. 4/18/61 at Duffields in Co. H as Sgt. Elected Capt. 4/20/62. Surrendered at Appomattox.

JENKINS, WILLIAM R.: b. 1833? Laborer. enl. 4/18/61 at Duffields in Co. H as Pvt. AWOL since 6/1/61. No further record.

JOHNSON (JOHNSTON), BENJAMIN: b. 2/14/42? enl. 4/16/62 at Rude's Hill in Co. E as Pvt. Deserted 4/19/62.

JOHNSON (JOHNSTON), HENRY: b. 1838? enl. 4/16/62 at Rude's Hill in Co. F as Pvt. MIA at Gettysburg. Last official entry shows him AWOL since 7/15/63. Next appears as a POW at New Market, 10/1/64 (Pt. Lookout). Exchanged 3/17/65. No further record. d. 1/7/95. bur. Chestnut Grove Cem., Oak Hill, W.Va.

JOHNSON, JOHN W.: b. 1843? 6'0", dark complexion, dark eyes, gray hair. Cooper. Residence Jefferson Co. Drafted 10/3/62 at Bunker Hill in Co. G as Pvt. Absent sick Nov./Dec. 1862. Arrested and POW at Leetown. 12/29/62; "said to be at home when taken making barrels for the Confederate army." (Wheeling, Camp Chase). Exchanged 3/28/63. Present again 4/8/63. Chimboraz #2, 6/11/64; diarrhea. To Lynchburg, 7/9/64. Paroled 4/20/65 at Winchester. d. 11/29/26. bur. Stonewall Cem., Winchester.

JOHNSTON, ABRAHAM: b. 1825? 5'11", dark complexion, dark eyes, gray hair. Only record is his parole statement that lists him in Co. E as Pvt. Paroled 5/20/65 at Staunton.

JOHNSTON, FRANCIS: b. 1837? Boatsman. enl. 5/26/61 at Lemon's Ferry in Co. I as Pvt. AWOL since 12/27/61 and dropped from roll as a deserter.

JOHNSTON, GEORGE THOMAS: b. 1832? drafted 10/3/62 at Bunker Hill in Co. F as Pvt. Deserted 11/22/62 from camp near Winchester. d. 1/3/02. bur. Mt. Hebron Cem., Winchester.

JOHNSTON, SAMUEL DAY: b. 11/10/36. drafted 10/3/62 at Bunker Hill in Co. F as Pvt. Deserted 11/22/62. d. 5/11/76. bur. Red Bud Cem., Charity Chapel, Frederick Co., Va.

JOHNSTON, WILLIAM: b. 1821? Farmer. enl. 6/6/61 at Camp Jackson on Bolivar Heights in Co. E as Pvt. Wded. in chin at 2nd Manassas, date not specific. POW at Aldie or Middleburg hosp. and paroled. Absent on detached service, 12/4/62. Present again Jan./Feb. 1863. AWOL July/Aug. 1863. Last official entry says he trans. to Cav., March/April 1864.

JOLLIFFE, JOHN MARSHALL: b. 5/13/43. Student. enl. 4/18/61 at Millwood in Co. C as Sgt. Wded. at Chancellorsville, 5/3/63. Gen. Hosp. #18, Richmond, 5/10/63. To Stanton, 5/18/63. Absent on detail 12/9/63, duty not stated. Last official entry shows him still absent on detail, 8/31-12/31 1864. Absent on detail 12/9/63, duty not stated. Last official entry shows him still absent on detail, 8/31-12/31 1864. d. 5/18/99. bur. Old Chapel Cem., Millwood.

JONES, CHARLES MARSHALL: b. 6/30/40 at New Orleans, Louisianna. Student. enl. 6/15/61 at Winchester in Co. F as Pvt. Discharged by medical board, 9/6/61, reason not stated. Applied for cadetship from his native state of Louisianna, 12/27/61, having "recovered from disability according to application." Reenlisted 2/24/62 in Co. F. Detailed as nurse at York House Hosp., Winchester, 9/24/62. Discharged 10/11/62 on account of physical disability. d. 4/14/83 at Berryville. bur. Greenhill Cem., Berryville.

JONES, FRANCIS BUCKNER: b. 6/14/28 in Frederick Co., Va. grad. V.M.I., 1848. Farmer. Apptd. Maj. of 2nd Va. Inf., 8/26/61. MWIA at Gaines's Mill, 6/27/61. d. 7/9/62. bur. Stonewall Cem., Winchester.

JONES, HENRY: enl. 4/18/62 at Rude's Hill in Co. B as Pvt. AWOL 6/9/62-3/25/63. Detailed by Secretary of War to work in Nitre and Mining Bureau "without allowance of pay of soldiers," 4/6/63. Last official entry shows him absent and still on detail in Nitre and Mining Bureau, March/April 1864.

JONES, HENRY: enl. 12/11/62 at Guinea's Station in Co. D as Pvt. Detailed as driver in Ord. train, 12/11/62-Nov./Dec. 1863. Last official entry lists him as a deserter, Jan./Feb. 1864.

JONES, JAMES K. P.: b. 1843? Mason. enl. 6/14/61 at Charles Town in Co. A as Pvt. Surgeon's Discharge, 8/14/62; disability.

JONES, JOHN W.: b. 1842? Blacksmith. enl. 4/18/61 at Charles Town in Co. A as Pvt. Wded. at Chancellorsville, 5/3/63. Present again July/Aug. 1863. POW at Spotsylvania, 5/12/64 (Pt. Lookout, Elmira). Exchanged 3/2/65. Chimborazo #2, 3/10/65; pneumonia. Furloughed 60 days, 3/19/65. No further record.

JONES, JOHN W.: b. 1835? Farmer. enl. 4/18/61 in Co. B as Pvt. Detailed as teamster, 6/30-10/31 1862. MWIA at Payne's Farm, 11/27/63. d. 12/3/63.

JONES, OSBURN ALLEN: b. 8/24/41. Farmer. enl. 6/21/61 at Camp Myers in Co. I as Pvt. Surrendered at Appomattox. Postwar, prosperous farmer in Clarke Co. d. 1/5/79. bur. Brucetown Methodist Church Cem.

JONES, WILLIAM: drafted 4/14/62 at Rude's Hill in Co. K as Pvt. Lovingston Hosp., Winchester, 8/8/62; rheumatism. Present again by 10/31/62. Absent sick March/April 1863. Present again May/June 1863. POW at Spotsylvania, 5/12/64 (Pt. Lookout). d. 5/24/64 at Pt. Lookout, cause not stated.

JORDAN, HUDSON: enl. 4/16/62 near Mt. Jackson in Co. I as Pvt. Lovington Hosp., Winchester, 8/27/62; typhoid fever. To Gen. Hosp. Staunton, date not given; bronchitis. d. 10/19/62 at Lynchburg. bur. City Cem. (Old Methodist Cem.), Lynchburg.

JORDAN, WILLIAM: b. 1828? Farmer. enl. 4/19/61 in Co. E as Pvt. Deserted 7/14/61.

JOY, ANDREW J.: b. 1844? Wheelwright. enl. 4/21/61 at Harpers Ferry in Co. I as Pvt. Discharged 7/18/62, underage.

JOY, GEORGE: enl. 3/5/62 at Winchester in Co. E as Pvt. AWOL since 6/1/62. No further record.

JOY, GEORGE W.: b. 1841? Merchant's clerk. enl. 4/18/61 at Berryville in Co. I as Pvt. AWOL 6/1-8/5 1862. Wded. at Chancellorsville, 5/3/63. Present again June 1863. Absent sick at hosp. at Lynchburg, July/Aug. 1863-Sept./Oct. 1863. Detailed to Gen. Hosp. Lynchburg, 11/18/63; suffering from dysentery and "unfit" for duty. Last official record shows him still on duty at Gen. Hosp. #2, Lynchburg, 2/19/65.

JOY, JOHN F.: b. 1815? Laborer. enl. 4/18/61 at Martinsburg in Co. D as Pvt. Never mustered, "being over age and of ill health."

JOY, JOHN W.: b. 1837? Farmer. enl. 4/19/61 at Hedgesville in Co. E as Pvt. Deserted out of state sometime before 6/30/61.

KANODE, BLACKFORD W.: b. 12/31/36. 5' 7", fair complexion, black eyes, dark hair. Residence Charles Town. enl. 10/8/62 at Bunker Hill in Co. A as Pvt. Detailed to Commissary Dept., 12/5/62. Present again Jan./Feb. 1863. Absent sick since 4/10/63. Present again May/June 1863. POW at Spotsylvania, 5/12/64 (Pt. Lookout, Elmira). Oath of Allegiance to U.S., 5/17/65. d. 11/5/18. bur. Edge Hill Cem., Charles Town, W.Va.

KEARFOTT (KEARFOOT), JAMES L.: b. 4/1/42. Farmer. enl. 4/18/61 at Martinsburg in Co. D as Pvt. Absent sick Nov./Dec. 1861. AWOL 9/13/62 at Bunker Hill and reported in Gilmore's Co. of Cav. No further record. d. 3/18/64. bur. Greenhill Cem., Martinsburg, W.Va.

KEARFOTT (KEARFOOT), WILLIAM P.: b. 1825? Shoemaker. enl. 4/18/61 at Martinsburg in Co. D as Pvt. To Sgt. 6/30-10/31 1862. Detailed to QM's Dept. at Richmond, 12/17/62 and reduced to ranks. Last official entry shows him still on detail in QM's Dept., March/April 1864.

KAUFMAN, JACOB: enl. 4/8/62 at Rude's Hill in Co. B as Pvt. AWOL 5/23/62-1/24/63 and still under guard, Feb. 1863. Discharged 3/25/63, reason not stated.

KAUFMAN, WILLIAM: enl. 4/18/62 at Rude's Hill in Co. B as Pvt. AWOL since 6/1/62 and dropped from roll. No further record.

KEBLER, D.: drafted 4/16/62 at Rude's Hill in Co. C as Pvt. Deserted 6/1/62.

KEEFE, JOHN WILLIAM: b. 7/6/28. 5' 8½ ", muddy complexion, blue eyes, dark hair. Residence Berkeley Co. enl. 11/1/62 at Winchester in Co. D as Pvt. Wded. at Chancellorsville, 5/3/63. Present again July/Aug. 1863. Charged $12.86 for ord. lost, Nov./Dec. 1863. POW at Spotsylvania, 5/12/64 (Pt. Lookout, Elmira). Oath of Allegiance to U.S., 2/20/65. d. 7/21/03. bur. Greenhill Cem., Martinsburg, W.Va.

KEELER, DAVID: b. 1839? Carpenter. enl. 4/18/61 at Millwood in Co. C as Sgt. To Lt. 9/9/61. Absent sick since 12/16/61. KIA at Gaines's Mill, 6/27/62.

KEERL, JOHN D.: b. 1840? Clerk. enl. 4/18/61 at Charles Town in Co. G as Pvt. To Sgt. 9/1/63. Wded. at Chancellorsville, 5/3/63. Returned from sick furlough, 7/23/63. Last official entry shows him present, March/April 1864.

KEERL (KEEL), ROBERT DOUGLAS: b. 11/30/45. Trans. from Co. K, 24th Ga. Inf., 11/15/62 (sic) at Culpeper Court House and joined Co. G as Pvt. Only official entry states he was present 4/30-10/31 1864. Surrendered at Appomattox. d. 6/19/26. bur. Edge Hill Cem., Charles Town, W.Va.

KEERL, WILLIAM L.: b. 1843? Clerk. enl. 6/6/61 at Camp Jackson on Bolivar Heights in Co. G as Pvt. Charged $2.00 for pair of shoes received, 8/29/61. Hosp. near Fairfax Court House, Sept./Oct. 1861; fever. Present again by 10/31/61. Wded. in forehead at 2nd Manassas, date not specific. Present by 10/31/62. Wded. when slightly bruised by shell at Fredericksburg, 12/13/62. Present again Jan./Feb. 1863. Last official entry shows him present, 4/30-10/31 1864. Surrendered at Appomattox.

KEESECKER, ISAAC N.: b. 1841? Shoemaker. enl. 4/19/61 at Hedgesville in Co. E as Pvt. To Sgt., date not given. Wded. at Cedar Run, 8/9/62. Gen. Hosp. Charlottesville, 8/11/62. To Lynchburg, 9/1/62. Present again by 10/31/62. Gen. Hosp. Charlottesville, 4/26-5/16 1863; typhoid fever. Last official entry shows him present, March/April 1864. d. 12/16/64 at Mt. Jackson, cause not stated.

KELLER, JACOB: enl. 4/24/62 at Swift Run Gap in Co. E as Pvt. KIA at 2nd Manassas, 8/30/62.

KELLER, NOAH: Trans. 10/27/63 from Imboden's command and placed in Co. E as Pvt. Sent back to Gen. Imboden by order of Gen. Lee, March/April 1864.

KEELER, WILLIAM NEWTON: b. July 1837. m. 1) Mary Carper, 2) Belle Ritter. Drafted 10/3/62 at Bunker Hill in Co. F as Pvt. Deserted 11/22/62. Postwar, for 25 years a contractor on the Berryville Turnpike; moved to Martinsburg, W.Va., in 1907. d. 1/17/10 at Martinsburg. bur. Red Bud Cem., Charity Chapel, Frederick Co. Va.

KELLEY (KELLY), JOHN: b. 1840? Harness maker. enl. 4/18/61 at Berryville in Co. I as Pvt. To Musician, 8/2/61. AWOL from 3/21/62-2/12/63. Sentenced by court-martial to forfeit 1 month's pay and allowances. Chimborazo #1, 5/6/63; vulnus contusum (probably wded. at Chancellorsville, 5/3/63). To Lynchburg, 5/9/63. Last official entry states he deserted from hosp. at Richmond sometime in Nov. 1863. POW (Rebel deserter) at Camp Hamilton, Va., 10/26/64. Released 11/12/64, "went to Philadelphia."

KELLY (KELLEY), GEORGE WILLIAM: b. 1841? Farmhand. enl. 4/29/61 at Harpers Ferry in Co. I as Pvt. Wded. in leg at 1st Manassas, 7/21/61. Present again by 8/31/61. Wded. at Port Republic, 6/9/62. Gen. Hosp. Charlottesville, 6/17/62; debility. To Gen. Hosp. Lynchburg, 8/11/62. Absent due to wound through May/June 1863. Last official entry says he deserted, 6/16/63.

KELLY, JOHN: b. 1821? Saddler. enl. 4/18/61 at Millwood in Co. C as Sgt. Resigned 6/27/61. bur. Old Chapel Cem., Millwood.

KELLY, JOHN: Only record lists him in Co. G and states he deserted 6/24/62 from Louisa Court House.

KENIFORD, FRANK: drafted 10/29/62 at Camp Allen in Co. C as Pvt. Deserted 11/8/62 from Camp Bitzer near Winchester.

KENNAH, H.: drafted 10/29/62 at Camp Allen in Co. C as Pvt. Deserted 11/10/62 from Camp Allen.

KENNAN, WILLIAM: drafted 10/29/62 at Camp Allen in Co. C as Pvt. Deserted 11/22/62 on march from Winchester.

KENNDEY, WILLIAM: b. 1841? Laborer. enl. 4/20/61 at Harpers Ferry in Co. K as Pvt. POW at Winchester, 6/6/62 (Ft. Delaware). Oath of Allegiance to U.S., 8/10/62.

KENNEY, CHRISTOPHER: enl. 5/20/62 at Franklin in Co. C as Pvt. POW near Woodstock, 6/4/62 (Ft. Delaware). Exchanged 8/5/62. Detailed in shoe factory at Staunton as shoemaker, Jan./Feb. 1863. Remained on this detail through Sept. 1864. Deserted 10/14/64.

KENNEY, JAMES: Listed in Co. C as Pvt. Only official record states he was surrendered at Appomattox.

KENNEY, W.: drafted 4/16/62 at Rude's Hill in Co. C as Pvt. Deserted 6/1/62. Recovered from desertion 11/1/62. Absent sick 4/30-10/31 1864. Returned from hosp., 11/15/64. Last official entry shows him present, 12/31/64.

KEPHART, JACOB: b. 1834? Farmer. enl. 6/15/61 at Charles Town in Co. H as Pvt. Absent on special duty, July/Aug. 1861. Present again Sept./Oct. 1861. AWOL Nov./Dec. 1861. No further record.

KERFOOT, AZARIAH: Residence Berkeley Co. enl. 4/19/61 at Martinsburg in Co. D as Pvt. POW at Kernstown, 3/23/62 (Ft. Delaware). Exchanged 8/5/62. Wded. at Chancellorsville, 5/3/63, and absent wded. May/June 1863. AWOL since 7/21/63. POW (Rebel deserter), 7/27/63. Oath of Allegiance to U.S., date not given.

KERFOOT, DANIEL: b. 1843? Miner. enl. 6/22/61 at Winchester in Co. C as Pvt. Absent sick since 11/12/61. AWOL and "killed by enemy," 8/20/62.

KERFOOT, HENRY W. D.: b. 1/10/46 in Clarke Co. Farmer. enl. 4/18/61 at Berryville in Co. I as Pvt. Absent sick July/Aug.-Sept./Oct. 1861. Present again Nov./Dec. 1861. Trans. to Co. D, 6th Va. Cav., 4/30/62. Postwar, studied medicine at Belluvue College in N.Y.; practiced medicine 12 years in Fauquier Co., then in Clarke Co. d. 4/9/03. bur. Greenhill Cem., Berryville.

KERFOOT, ANDREW JACKSON: b. 1834? 5'8", fair complexion, blue eyes, light hair. Carpenter. enl. 4/25/61 at Harpers Ferry in Co. C as Pvt. To Corp., date not given. POW 5/12/64 at Spotsylvania (Pt. Lookout, Elmira). Oath of Allegiance to U.S., 6/16/65. d. 10/7/04.

KERFOOT, JAMES FRANKLIN: b. 9/2/32. Farmer. enl. 4/18/61 at Millwood in Co. C as Pvt. Apptd. QM Sgt., 12/10/61. Last official entry shows him present, Nov./Dec. 1861. Unofficial source states he trans. to 6th Va. Cav. d. 1/20/15. bur. Berryville Baptist Church Cem.

KERFOOT, JUDSON C.: b. 6/12/34. Farmer. enl. 4/18/61 at Millwood in Co. C as Pvt. Last official entry shows him absent sick without leave, 12/3/61. d. 12/22/07. bur. Old Bethel Church Cem., Rt. 625, Clarke Co.

KERN, JOHN: Listed in Co. E as Pvt. KIA at Gaines's Mill or Malvern Hill, 6/27 or 7/1 1862.

KERNS, JOSEPH: b. 1824? Laborer. enl. 4/21/61 at Harpers Ferry in Co. D as Pvt. Deserted 5/20/61.

KESSUCKER, J. W.: b. Mt. Jackson in Shenandoah Co. Unofficial source says he served in this regt.

KEYES, WILLIAM H.: b. 7/15/41. Carpenter. enl. 4/18/61 at Halltown in Co. B as Pvt. Trans. to 1st Va. Cav., 7/14/61. KIA at Jenning's Landing on the James River, 3/24/64. bur. Old Reformed Graveyard, Shepherdstown, W.Va.

KEYSER, CHARLES A.: b. 1813? Tailor. enl. 6/15/61 at Camp Whiting in Co. B as Pvt. Discharged 6/30-10/31 1862, overage.

KEYSER, C. M.: Unofficial source lists him in Co. F and states he served 6 months.

KIBLER, DANIEL: drafted 4/14/62 at Rude's Hill in Co. K as Pvt. d. 4/10/63 in hosp. at Guinea's Station, cause not stated; "his effects delivered to his father."

KIBLER, HENRY: drafted 4/14/62 at Rude's Hill in Co. K as Pvt. Deserted 6/3/62.

KIDD, THOMAS: b. 1843? Guilder. enl. 5/1/61 at Harpers Ferry in Co. F as Pvt. Wded. in back at 1st Manassas, 7/21/61. Present again Sept./Oct. 1861. Last official entry shows him present, Nov./Dec. 1861.

KILMER, GEORGE W.: b. 3/15/31. Farmer. enl. 4/18/61 at Martinsburg in Co. D as Pvt. Detailed brig. butcher, 6/30-10/31 1862 through Jan./Feb. 1863. Deserted 2/9/64. d. 4/27/07. bur. Old Norborne Cem., Martinsburg, W.Va.

KIMES, HENRY: b. 1816? Painter. enl. 4/18/61 at Halltown in Co. B as Pvt. Absent sick at home in Shepherdstown, Sept./Oct. 1861. Present again Nov./Dec. 1861. Last official entry states he was taken POW while on furlough, March/April 1864. b. Elmwood Cem., Shepherdstown, W.Va.

KIMES, WILLIAM: b. 1821? 5'5½", dark complexion, hazel eyes, black hair. Painter. Residence Jefferson Co. enl. 6/14/61 at Charles Town in Co. A as Pvt. Absent sick at home, July/Aug. 1861. Surgeon's discharge, 11/9/61; disability. Reenlisted 2/18/62 at Winchester in Co. B. POW at Kernstown, 3/23/62 (Ft. Delaware). Exchanged 8/5/62. POW at Spotsylvania, 5/12/64 (Pt. Lookout, Elmira). Released 2/20/65. POW at Ft. Steadman near Petersburg, 3/25/65 (Pt. Lookout). Oath of Allegiance to U.S., 6/14/65.

KINDIG, H. H.: enl. 4/16/62 near Mt. Jackson in Co. I as Pvt. Discharged 11/1/62; furnished Rhoddy Conner as substitute.

KINDIG, JOHN E.: Residence Augusta Co. enl. 4/16/62 near Mt. Jackson in Co. I as Pvt. AWOL 5/15/62. Gen. Hosp. Staunton, 8/15/62; fever. Also listed as guard at Gen. Hosp. Staunton. Present again Jan./Feb. 1863. Chimborazo #1, 6/5-6/21 1863; diarrhea. Present again July/Aug. 1863. Last official entry shows him present, March/April 1864. Arrested 4/13/65 (Wheeling). Oath of Allegiance to U.S. at Clarksburg, W.Va., 4/14/65.

KENSEY, SAMUEL: b. 1831? Coach trimmer. enl. 4/18/61 at Winchester in Co. F as Sgt. To Lt. 4/20/62. Absent sick July/Aug. 1861. Wded. at Gaines's Mill or Malvern Hill, 6/27 or 7/1 1862 and absent sick through Jan./Feb. 1863. Present again March/April 1863. AWOL March 1964. No further record.

KIRACOFE, JOHN H.: b. 1821? in Rockingham Co. 6'0", dark complexion, dark eyes, dark hair. Farmer. drafted 4/14/62 at Rude's Hill in Co. C as Pvt. Discharged 2/24/63, overage.

KISER, CHARLES: 5'7", muddy complexion, blue eyes, gray hair. enl. 6/25/63 near Chambersburg, Pa. POW at Gettysburg, 7/3/63 (Ft. McHenry; Ft. Delaware; Pt. Lookout; Ft. Columbus, N.Y. Harbor). Oath of Allegiance to U.S. at Ft. Delaware, May 1865.

KISER, JOHN: enl. 12/4/62 near Guinea's Station. KIA at Fredericksburg, 12/13/62.

KITE, HARVEY: enl. 4/9/62 at Rude's Hill in Co. E as Pvt. Wded. at Fredericksburg, 12/13/62. Present again by 12/31/62. Gen. Hosp. Staunton, 3/22/63; fever. Present again May/June 1863. POW at Gettysburg, 7/3/63 (Ft. McHenry, Ft. Delaware). Exchanged 7/31/63. Absent as paroled POW, July/Aug.-Sept./Oct. 1863. Present again Nov./Dec. 1863. Last official entry shows him present, March/April 1864.

KITE, JAMES F.: b. 1844 in Shenandoah Co. 5'6", fair complexion, blue eyes, light hair. Residence Page Co. enl. 4/9/62 at Rude's Hill in Co. E as Pvt. Absent sick March/April-May/June 1863. POW at White Post, 9/1/64 (Camp Chase). Oath of Allegiance to U.S., 6/12/65. d. 1/27/24 at Elkwood.

KITE, WILLIAM: 5'11", florid complexion, blue eyes, dark hair. Residence Winchester. enl. 4/16/62 at Rude's Hill in Co. F as Pvt. Deserted from Rude's Hill, 4/18/62. Rejoined from desertion, 4/1/64. POW at Spotsylvania, 5/12/64 (Pt. Lookout, Elmira). Oath of Allegiance to U.S., 6/12/65.

KLEIN, CHARLES: Listed in Co. F as Pvt. Only official record is a Federal POW register that states he deserted from the C. S. Ordnance Dept., 10/21/64, and was captured at Bermuda Hundred, 10/22/64. Sent to N.Y.

KLEIN, JOSEPH: drafted 10/20/62 at Camp Allen in Co. C as Pvt. Deserted 11/9/62.

KNIGHT, JOHN: Unofficial source lists him in Co. H. d. 1862. bur. Hollywood Cem., Richmond.

KOINER, LIVINGSTON R.: enl. 4/16/62 at Eck River in Co. D as Pvt. Wded. in head at 2nd Manassas, date not specific. Present by 10/31/62. Wded. at Chancellorsville, 5/3/63 and absent due to wounds through July/Aug. 1863. Present again Sept./Oct. 1863. POW at Spotsylvania, 5/12/64 (Pt. Lookout, Elmira). Exchanged 3/2/65. Chimborazo #2, 3/10/65; diarrhea. POW at Richmond Hosp., 4/3/65. d. 4/10/65 at Jackson Hosp., Richmond; typhoid fever.

KREGLOW, GEORGE T.: b. 1/20/39. Farmer. enl. 4/19/61 at Hedgesville in Co. E as Corp. Deserted 7/18/61. d. 9/9/15 bur. Hedgesville Cem., Hedgesville, W.Va.

KREGLOW, JACOB: enl. 11/4/61 at Centerville in Co. E as Pvt. Only official entry shows him present, Nov./Dec. 1861.

LACKLAND, FRANCIS: b. 5/20/30 near Charles Town. grad. V.M.I., 1849. Employed in Engineer Corps of the Alabama Railroad. Entered C. S. service May 1861 at Harpers Ferry as Capt. in Engineer Corps. To Lt. Col., 2nd Va. Inf., June 1861. Hosp. 1st Brigade, Fairfax Court House, Sept./Oct. 1861; pneumonia. d. 9/5/61 at Fairfax Court House; "pneumonia supervening upon organic disease of the heart." bur. Zion Episcopal Cem., Charles Town, W.Va.

LAMBERT, ALBERT R.: enl. 4/16/62 at Rude's Hill in Co. E as Pvt. Gen. Hosp. Staunton, 4/7/63; typhoid fever. Last official entry shows him dead of disease, Sept./Oct. 1863.

LAMBERT, J.: drafted 4/6/62 at Rude's Hill in Co. C as Pvt. Deserted 6/1/62.

LAMBRIGHT, GEORGE W.: b. 7/6/47 at Hancock, Md. enl. 7/20/64 at Winchester in Co. H as Pvt. Last official entry shows him present, 10/31/64. Surrendered at Appomattox. Postwar, spent 6 years in W.Va. and then moved to Knoxville, Tennessee, where he was a merchant.

LAMDEN, GEORGE W.: b. 1832? Carpenter. enl. 4/18/61 at Winchester in Co. F as Pvt. AWOL since 7/18/61 and listed as deserter, Nov./Dec. 1861. Next record shows him as a POW at St. Joseph, Missouri, 2/11/64 (Military Prison at St. Louis). Oath of Allegiance to U.S., 5/5/64. Postwar, member of Turner Ashby Camp #22 and Henry Heth Camp #119; residence 704-5th St., Washington, D.C.; alive in 1895.

LAMDEN, JAMES W.: b. 1838? Machinist. enl. 4/18/61 at Winchester in Co. F as Pvt. AWOL since 7/18/61 and listed as a deserter, Nov./Dec. 1861. Drafted 4/18/62 at Rude's Hill in Co. F as Pvt. Deserted 11/22/62.

LANDRUM, GEORGE N.: Unofficial source lists him in Co. F.

LANGFORD, WILLIAM: enl. 4/16/62 near Mt. Jackson in Co. I as Pvt. AWOL 5/8/62-1/10/63. Sentenced by court-martial to forfeit 1 month's pay, Jan./Feb. 1863. Absent sick at hosp., March/April-Sept./Oct. 1863. Last official entry in Nov./Dec. 1863 says "sent to hospital March 1863 and never heard from since—supposed dead."

LANHAM, JEREMIAH: b. 1843? 5' 6", fair complexion, hazel eyes, black hair. Farmer. Residence Martinsburg. enl. 5/11/61 at Harpers Ferry in Co. E as Pvt. Absent July/Aug. 1861 and under arrest in Winchester; tried by court-martial and acquitted (charges not stated). Present again Sept./Oct. 1861. Absent sick Nov./Dec. 1861. AWOL Sept./Oct.-Nov./Dec. 1862. Present again Jan./Feb. 1863. Deserted 7/18/63. POW (Rebel deserter), 7/25/63 (Ft. Mifflin, Pa.). Oath of Allegiance to U.S. 1/1/64.

LANHAM, THOMAS B.: b. 1842? Farmhand. enl. 5/6/61 at Harpers Ferry in Co. I as Pvt. Absent sick at home, July/Aug.-Sept./Oct. 1861. AWOL since 12/27/61. AWOL from 6/1-8/1 1862. Deserted 1/29/64.

LARKINS, THOMAS: b. 1846 in Allegeny Co., Md. Laborer. enl. 4/21/61 at Harpers Ferry in Co. D as Pvt. POW at Martinsburg, 6/14/62. Exchanged 8/5/62. Gen. Hosp. Charlottesville, 1/6-3/4 1863; disease. Present again March/April 1863. POW at Gettysburg, 7/28/63 (Ft. McHenry; Ft. Delaware; Pt. Lookout; Ft. Columbus, N.Y. Harbor). Exchanged 2/13/65. No further record. d. 1926 at Martinsburg. bur. St. Joseph's Cem., Martinsburg, W.Va.

LARUE, WILLIAM G.: enl. 9/8/61 at Camp Harman in Co. G as Pvt. Discharged 5/28/62, reason not stated.

LASHORN, JACOB V.: b. 1842? Carpenter. enl. 4/18/61 at Martinsburg in Co. D as Pvt. Wded. slightly in head at 1st Manassas, 7/21/61. Furloughed for 20 days, 7/30/61. Last official entry shows him on sick furlough at Martinsburg, Sept./Oct. 1861.

LASHORN, WILLIAM R.: 5' 8½", fair complexion, blue eyes, dark hair. Residence Martinsburg. enl. 2/23/62 at Martinsburg in Co. D as Pvt. POW at Spotsylvania, 5/12/64 (Pt. Lookout, Elmira). Oath of Allegiance to U.S., 5/15/65.

LASVIE, W.: Unofficial source lists him in Co. A. d. 7/5/62. bur. Hollywood Cem., Richmond.

LAWRENCE, JOHN W.: b. 1837? 5' 6", light complexion, hazel eyes, dark hair. Farmer. Residence Fauquier Co. enl. 4/18/61 at Charles Town in Co. A. Detailed as teamster, 4/30-10/31 1862. Last official entry shows him still detailed as teamster, 4/30-10/31 1862. POW at Ft. Steadman near Petersburg, 3/25/65 (Pt. Lookout). Oath of Allegiance to U.S., 6/14/65. bur. Edge Hill Cem., Charles Town, W.Va.

LAWYER, ADAM: b. Jan. 1834. enl. 12/22/62 at Guinea's Station in Co. D as Pvt. Trans. 2/15/63 to Co. H, 7th Va. Cav. KIA 6/11/64 at Staunton.

LAYMAN, NATHANIEL: enl. 4/1/64 at Pisgah Church in Co. E as Pvt. POW at Fisher's Hill, 9/22/64 (Pt. Lookout). d. 4/9/65 at Pt. Lookout, cause not stated.

LEATHERS, JOHN HESS: b. 4/27/43 at Middleburg. enl. 8/21/61 at Camp Harman in Co. D as Pvt. To Sgt. 4/19/62. To Sgt. Maj. Nov./Dec. 1862. POW at Woodstock, 6/25/61 (sic). Exchanged 8/5/62. Absent March/April 1863, reason not stated. Present again May/June 1863. Wded. at Gettysburg, date not specific. Gen. Hosp. Charlottesville, 8/3-8/21 1863; wounded. Absent through Jan./Feb. 1864. Present again March/April 1864. POW at Spotsylvania, 5/12/64 (Pt. Lookout). Exchanged 2/13/65. No further record. Postwar, banker in Louisville, Kentucky; became president of Banking Association of Kentucky. d. 6/29/23 at Louisville. bur. 2nd Presbyterian Church Cem., Louisville Kentucky.

LEAVELL, JOHN W.: enl. 4/15/62 at Rude's Hill in Co. A as Pvt. Surgeon's discharge, 8/20/62; disability.

LEAVITT, CHARLES P.: b. 1842? Machinist. enl. 4/20/61 at Harpers Ferry in Co. K as Pvt. Discharged 12/2/62, "his labor being required for other important government work."

LEE, RICHARD HENRY: b. 8/24/21, grandson of Richard Henry Lee, mover of the Declaration of Independence in the Continental Congress. Lawyer. Residence Charles Town. enl. 4/18/61 at Charles Town in Co. G as Lt. Absent sick 8/26-9/13 1861. Wded. severely at Kernstown, 3/23/62. Recommended for service on a military court, Oct. 1862. Later became Judge Advocate and Col. in the 2nd Corps, Army of Northern Va. d. 6/18/02. bur. Old Chapel Cem., Millwood.

LEFTWICH, JOHN S.: Unofficial source lists him in Co. F as Lt.

LEGG, JOHN W.: b. 1839? Armorer. enl. 4/20/61 at Harpers Ferry in Co. K as Sgt. POW at Kernstown, 3/23/62 (Ft. Delaware). Exchanged 8/5/62. No further record.

LEMON, ALEX: Unofficial source lists him in Co. B. bur. Elmwood Cem., Shepherdstown, W.Va.

LEMASTER, JOHN H.: b. 1842? Saddler. enl. 4/18/61 at Charles Town in Co. A as Pvt. Deserted 7/21/63. d. 1924. bur. Greenhill Cem., Martinsburg, W.Va.

LEVERY, H.: Unofficial source lists him in Co. H. d. 6/29/62. bur. Hollywood Cem., Richmond.

LEVI, GEORGE W.: b. 11/23/42 in Jefferson Co. Farmhand. enl. 5/22/61 at Harpers Ferry in Co. I as Pvt. Absent sick Nov./Dec. 1861. Disabled by disease and dropped from the roll, 4/18/62. Postwar, farmer; Clarke Co. sheriff for 10 years; U.S. Marshal for Western District of Va. until 1890. d. 3/1/20 at Berryville.

LEWIS, JACOB: b. 1836? 5' 10¼", fair complexion, hazel eyes, light hair. Farmer. Residence Berkeley Co. enl. 3/5/62 at Winchester in Co. E as Pvt. AWOL 7/18/63. Arrested in Berkeley Co. by Federals, 11/4/63 (Wheeling; Camp Chase; Rock Island, Illinois). Exchanged 3/20/65. No further record. d. 5/20/98. bur. Edge Hill Cem., Charles Town, W.Va.

LEWIS, JOHN H. B.: b. 10/19/19. enl. 4/18/61 at Charles Town in Co. G as Pvt. To Ord. Sgt. 4/30-10/31 1862. Absent sick since 11/12/62. No record again until Sept./Oct. 1863 when he is listed as present. Gen. Hosp. Charlottesville, 6/17-6/28 1864; febris remittens. Gen. Hosp. Charlottesville, 9/26/64; debility. Retired to Invalid Corps, 3/3/65, and stationed at Lexington. No further record. d. Dec. 1870. bur. Lewis-Muse Graveyard, Jefferson Co., W.Va.

LEWIS, LEWIS: enl. 3/4/62 at Winchester in Co. D as Pvt. MWIA at 2nd Manassas, 8/28/62. d. 9/3/62. bur. White Church Graveyard, Middleway, W.Va.

LEWIS, MORDECAI: b. 1843? Student. enl. 4/18/61 at Millwood in Co. C as Pvt. To Corp. 11/9/61. To Sgt. 6/30-10/31 1862. Gen. Hosp. Staunton, 7/27/63; debility. Present again Aug. 1863. Chimborazo #1, 3/3-3/13 1865. Surrendered at Appomattox. bur. IOOF Cem., Clarksburg, W.Va.

LEWIS, WALTER: enl. 3/4/62 at Winchester in Co. D as Pvt. MWIA at 2nd Manassas, 8/28/62. d. 10/15/62. bur. White Church Graveyard, Middleway, W.Va.

LEWIS, WILLIAM: drafted 10/1/62 at Bunker Hill in Co. K as Pvt. Deserted 10/12/62.

LEWIS, WILLIAM H. T.: b. 4/30/32. Farmer. enl. 5/5/61 at Harpers Ferry in Co. G as Pvt. Elected Lt. 6/16/61. Last official entry shows him present, Nov./Dec. 1861. Dropped from Register of Commissioned Officers, 5/18/62, reason not stated. d. 5/31/05. bur. Edge Hill Cem., Charles Town, W.Va.

LICKLINDER, GEORGE T.: b. 12/9/38. Farmer. enl. 6/20/61 at Charles Town in Co. H as Pvt. Absent, under arrest at Manassas Junction, July/Aug. 1861; reason not stated. Present again Sept./Oct. 1861. Last official entry shows him present, Nov./Dec. 1861. d. 2/6/05. bur. Elmwood Cem., Shepherdstown, W.Va.

LIGHT, WILLIAM E.: enl. 3/10/62 at Winchester in Co. E as Pvt. Gen. Hosp. Danville, 4/3/65; fever. No further record. d. 9/6/07. bur. St. Joseph's Cem., Martinsburg, W.Va.

LIGHT, WILLIAM H.: b. 1830? Engineer. enl. 4/21/61 at Harpers Ferry in Co. D as Pvt. To Sgt. 6/30-10/31 1862. To Lt. 3/25/63. Wded. in face and neck at 1st Manassas, 7/21/61. Present again Sept./Oct. 1861. Absent sick at hosp., May/June 1863. Present again July/Aug. 1863. Signs roll as commanding Co., July/Aug. 1863. Surrendered at Appomattox.

LINDAMOOD, JOHN F.: enl. 4/8/62 at Rude's Hill in Co. G. Detailed as shoemaker for 1st Va. Brig., Nov./Dec. 1862. Absent on detail in Shenandoah Valley, Jan./Feb. 1863; duty not specified. Absent on conscript duty in Shenandoah Valley, March/April 1863. Present again 6/30/63. Surrendered at Appomattox. Living in Jerome, Shenandoah Co., June, 1901.

LINDEMOOD, G. B.: enl. 4/9/62 at Rude's Hill in Co. E as Pvt. Detailed in Mathew's Factory, 10/20/62-July/Aug. 1863. Present again Sept./Oct. 1863. Surrendered at Appomattox.

LINDEMOOD, ROBERT: enl. 4/9/62 at Rude's Hill in Co. E as Pvt. Detailed in Mathew's Factory, 10/20/62-July/Aug. 1863. Present again Sept./Oct. 1863. Surrendered at Appomattox.

LINDWAY, GEORGE J.: b. 1842? Farmer. enl. 6/19/61 at Camp Jackson on Bolivar Heights in Co. G as Pvt. Absent sick 8/16/61. Discharged 8/24/61, reason not stated. Reappears again as POW at Charlottesville, 4/17/62 (Ft. Delaware). Released 5/31/62. No further record.

LINDSEY, JOSEPH B.: b. 1837? Farmer. enl. 5/11/61 at Harpers Ferry in Co. C as Pvt. Absent sick since May 1861. Last official entry shows him AWOL, Nov./Dec. 1861.

LINEWEAVER, JACOB: drafted 4/14/62 at Rude's Hill in Co. K as Pvt. Gen. Hosp. Charlottesville, 5/30-6/13 1863; debility. Gen. Hosp. Charlottesville, 5/11/64; wounded left thigh. d. 5/24/64 at Gen. Hosp. Charlottesville; "gangrene existed when received in hospital."

LINGAMFELTER, WALTER HEDGES: b. 2/9/30 in Bedford Co., Pa. 5' 6¼", light complexion, brown eyes, dark hair. Farmer. Residence Jefferson Co. enl. 4/19/61 at Hedgesville in Co. E as Pvt. To Sgt. by Sept./Oct. 1862. Absent on special service, July/Aug. 1861. Present again Sept./Oct. 1861. Wded. in head at Monocacy, 7/9/64. POW at Frederick, Md., 7/9/64 (U.S. Hosp. at Sandy Hook, Md., 7/12/64; Old Capitol Prison; Elmira). Exchanged 10/29/64. Present again 10/31/64. POW at Ft. Steadman near Petersburg, 3/25/65 (Pt. Lookout). Oath of Allegiance to U.S., 6/14/65. d. 4/13/01. bur. Hedgesville Cem., Hedgesville, W.Va.

LINK, ADAM, JR.: b. 10/16/17. Farmer. enl. 4/18/61 at Duffields in Co. H as Pvt. Surgeon's discharge, 5/15/61, "for inability." d. 3/27/62. bur. St. James Lutheran Cem., Uvilla, W.Va.

LINK, ADAM CRUZEN: b. 11/30/32. Farmer. enl. at Duffields in Co. H as Pvt. AWOL July/Aug. 1861. No further record. d. 3/28/62 at New Market; measles. bur. 1st at St. Matthew's Lutheran Church Cem., New Market; body later moved to St. James Lutheran Cem., Uvilla, W.Va.

LINK, JOHN ALLEN: b. 4/21/42. Farmer. enl. at Duffields in Co. H as Pvt. AWOL July/Aug. 1861. No record again until he appears as wded. in stomach at Fredericksburg, 12/13/62. Absent wded. Jan./Feb. 1863. Wded. in hand at Chancellorsville, 5/3/63. Last official entry shows him still absent wded. and at home, 4/30-10/31 1864. Postwar, farmer. d. 6/19/35 at Uvilla, W.Va. "Last surviving Confederate veteran in Jefferson Co." bur. Elmwood Cem., Shepherdstown, W.Va.

LINK, THOMAS: b. 4/2/27. Farmer. Residence Duffields. enl. 4/18/61 at Duffields in Co. H. Elected Lt. 11/22/61. Absent sick in hosp. near Centerville, July/Aug.-Sept./Oct. 1861. Last official entry shows him present, Nov./Dec. 1861. Dropped from Register of Commissioned Officers, 4/18/62. d. 4/21/74 at Duffields.

LINTHICUM, JOHN M.: b. 1830? drafted 4/16/62 at Rude's Hill in Co. C as Pvt. Returned from desertion, 4/13/63 (initial desertion date not stated). Absent sick since 6/9/63. Last official entry shows him still absent sick, 8/31-12/31 1864. d. 5/25/92. bur. Old Norborne Cem., Martinsburg, W.Va.

LIPPITT (LIPPETT), CHARLES EDWARD: b. 1/3/28. Physician. enl. 4/18/61 at Charles Town in Co. G as Pvt. On special duty in telegraph office, June 1861. On special duty at surgeon's apothecary, July/Aug. 1861. Promoted to asst. surgeon, Sept. 1861. Trans. 9/2/61, destination not stated. Unofficial source states he served as surgeon in 57th Va. Inf. and as surgeon to Armistead's Brig. d. 12/20/07. bur. Greenhill Cem., Berryville.

LITTLE, CLINTON L.: b. 1842? Coach trimmer. enl. 4/23/61 at Harpers Ferry in Co. I as Pvt. AWOL 8/4-8/14 1861. Fined $11.00 for absence by court-martial. Absent sick Sept./Oct. 1861. Present again Nov./Dec. 1861. AWOL since 2/10/62 and dropped as a deserter.

LITTLE, COLUMBUS M.: b. 1838? Coach painter. enl. 6/8/61 at Camp Jackson on Bolivar Heights in Co. I as Pvt. AWOL from 7/3-8/14 1861. Deserted 9/3/61.

LITTLE, GILBERT: b. 1845? Farmhand. enl. 5/22/61 at Harpers Ferry in Co. I as Pvt. Deserted 6/29/61.

LITTLE, OSCAR P.: b. 1844? in Washington, D.C. 5' 9", fair complexion, blue eyes, auburn hair. Coach maker. enl. 4/28/61 at Harpers Ferry in Co. I as Pvt. AWOL 7/30-8/14 1861. AWOL 9/16-11/1 1861. Surgeon's discharge, 12/3/61; disability; "an injury to the right knee, said to have been received in infancy, occasioning a dislocation of the knee cap."

LLOYD, ISAAC: enl. 4/8/62 at Rude's Hill in Co. G as Pvt. Deserted 5/22/62 at New Market. Recovered from desertion, 4/1/63. Sentenced by court-martial to forfeit all pay and allowances to 3/30/63. Chimborazo #1, 6/14-6/24 1863; fever. Absent sick at hosp., July/Aug.-Nov./Dec. 1863. Last official entry lists him as a deserter, Jan./Feb. 1864.

LLOYD, JOHN D.: b. 1840? Farmer. enl. 5/11/61 at Harpers Ferry in Co. C as Pvt. Absent sick since 12/16/61. Present again 6/30-10/31 1862. POW at Berry's Ferry, 7/21/63 (Pt. Lookout). Exchanged 3/3/64. Returned from imprisonment, 3/9/64. Last official entry shows him present, March/April 1864.

LLOYD, J. W.: enl. 10/1/62 at Berry's Ferry in Co. C as Pvt. Deserted 9/1/63.

LOCKE, WILLIAM M.: b. 9/17/37. Farmer. enl. 6/2/61 at Camp Jackson on Bolivar Heights in Co. G as Pvt. Last official entry shows him absent on special duty in Commissary Dept. since 11/6/61. Apptd. 9/9/62 Capt. of Commissary, 62nd Va. Partisan Rangers. POW at Hardy Co., 11/9/62 (Camp Chase). Exchanged at Vicksburg, Mississippi, 12/8/62. Promoted to Major and Commissary, 1/28/63, in Imboden's Brig. Paroled 5/8/65 at Winchester. d. 5/16/92. bur. Edge Hill Cem., Charles Town, W.Va.

LONG, CONRAD: enl. 4/18/62 at Rude's Hill in Co. B as Pvt. AWOL since 5/1/62 and dropped from the roll 12/10/62. No further record.

LONG, WILLIAM A.: b. 1826 in Rockingham Co. 5' 9', fair complexion, blue eyes, light hair. Farmer. enl. 4/16/62 at Rude's Hill in Co. F as Pvt. Deserted 5/24/62. Recovered from desertion 3/8/63. Surgeon's discharge, 8/31/63; disability.

LONGERBEAM, JOHN: enl. 10/1/62 at Bunker Hill in Co. H as Pvt. AWOL since 10/7/62. No further record.

LOOKER, THOMAS BARRYMAN: enl. 4/16/62 at Rude's Hill in Co. F as Pvt. Wded. at Port Republic, 6/9/62. Still absent wded. May/June 1863. AWOL July/Aug. 1863. No further record.

LOOKER, WILLIAM PENN: b. 11/4/27. 5' 6", dark complexion, dark eyes, dark hair. Residence Lacy Springs. enl. 4/16/62 at Rude's Hill in Co. F as Pvt. Deserted 11/23/62. Recovered from desertion, 3/8/63. POW at Spotsylvania, 5/12/64 (Pt. Lookout). Oath of Allegiance to U.S., 6/27/65. d. 11/19/02. bur. East Point Cem., Harrisonburg.

LOUTHAN, CARTER MCKEIN: b. 5/11/38 at Millwood. Attd. University of Virginia. Teacher. enl. 5/25/61 at Harpers Ferry in Co. I as Pvt. Absent sick July/Aug.-Sept./Oct. 1861. Present again Nov./Dec. 1861. Discharged March 1862 for disability. Unofficial source says he later joined Poague's Battalion of Artillery. Postwar, superintendent of Clarke Co. schools; moved to Charlottesville in 1901. d. 10/13/13 at Charlottesville. bur. Maplewood Cem., Charlottesville.

LOUTZ, NICHOLAS: b. 1839? Confectioner. enl. 5/11/61 at Harpers Ferry in Co. K as Pvt. Deserted 5/13/61.

LOYNS, HENRY M.: b. 1839. enl. 10/16/64 at Richmond in Co. H as Pvt. Surrendered at Appomattox. d. 1910. bur. Elmwood Cem., Shepherdstown, W.Va.

LUCAS, ANDREW: Listed in Co. G. Only official entry says he was discharged 8/7/62. d. 9/3/87.

LUCAS, BENJAMIN F.: b. 1838? Boatman. enl. 4/18/61 at Halltown in Co. B as Pvt. AWOL since 4/20/62 and dropped from roll, 12/22/62. No further record.

LUCAS, EDWARD D.: b. 1842? Lawyer. enl. 6/15/61 at Camp Whiting in Co. B as Pvt. Gen. Hosp. Charlottesville, 5/11-7/4 1864; wounded. Surrendered at Appomattox.

LUCAS, JOHN M.: b. 1822? in Augusta Co. 6' 1½", fair complexion, blue eyes, light hair. enl. 4/8/62 at Rude's Hill in Co. G as Pvt. Deserted near Port Republic, 6/6/62. Recovered from desertion, 1/14/63. Sentenced by court-martial to forfeit 1 month's pay and allowances. Discharged 2/28/63, overage.

LUCIUS, PHILIP B.: b. 1842? 5' 11", ruddy complexion, hazel eyes, dark hair. Farmhand. Residence Loudoun Co. enl. 5/14/61 at schoolhouse on Hagerstown Road (north of Harpers Ferry) in Co. I as Pvt. AWOL 7/27-8/2 and 8/4-8/23 1861. Fined $11.00 for absence by court-martial. Absent sick Nov./Dec. 1861. Gen. Hosp. Charlottesville, 6/10-7/21 1862; rheumatism. AWOL since 9/1/62. No further record until listed as POW at Harpers Ferry, 7/25/63 (Ft. McHenry, Ft. Delaware, Pt. Lookout). Oath of Allegiance to U.S. at Ft. Delaware, 5/10/65.

LUCUS, DAVID J.: b. 1827? in Augusta Co. 6' 0", dark complexion, dark eyes, black hair. enl. 4/14/62 at New Market in Co. H as Pvt. MWIA at 1st Winchester, 5/25/62; d. 6/1/62 or 8/17/62 in hosp. at Winchester. Claim to C. S. government shows $70.46 due for his service.

LUDWIG, HENRY P.: b. 3/21/32. 5' 7", fair complexion, gray eyes, dark hair. Residence Winchester. enl. 4/16/62 at Rude's Hill in Co. E as Pvt. To Corp., date not given. Wded. at Port Republic, 6/9/62. Listed as present, Sept./Oct. 1862. POW at Spotsylvania, 5/12/64 (Pt. Lookout, Elmira). Oath of Allegiance to U.S., 6/27/65. d. 9/30/98. bur. Riverview Cem., Strasburg.

LUMPKINS, THOMAS: Only record is a parole statement that lists him in Co. A as Pvt. Paroled 4/23/65 at Richmond.

LUTZ, BALTZER: enl. 4/16/62 at Winchester in Co. E as Pvt. AWOL since 4/19/62. No further record.

114

MADDOX, JAMES E.: b. 1821? Carpenter. Residence Jefferson Co. enl. 4/18/61 at Duffields in Co. H as Sgt. Elected Lt. 11/22/61. POW at Leetown, 5/3/62 (Ft. Delaware). Exchanged 8/5/62. No further record.

MADDOX, JAMES D.: b. 1821? Cooper. enl. 4/18/61 at Duffields in Co. H as Drummer. Last official entry shows him present, Nov./Dec. 1861.

MAGAHA, JACOB: enl. 2/18/62 at Winchester in Co. B as Pvt. Wded. at 2nd Manassas, date not specific. Present again by 10/31/62. d. 5/26/63 in hosp. at Richmond "from wound."

MAGAHA, JOHN W.: b. 1844? 5'8", fair complexion, blue eyes, light hair. Laborer. enl. 6/27/61 at Camp Allen in Co. B as Pvt. Wded. at Port Republic, 6/9/62, and absent from wound until 1/1/63 when he returned to the regt. Detailed to drive cattle, Sept./Oct. 1863. Nurse at Gen. Hosp. Staunton, 1/22/64; "being unfit for field service." Last official entry shows him still on detail at Gen. Hosp. Staunton, March/April 1864. Paroled 4/18/65 at Winchester.

MAGAHA, WILSON H.: b. 1830. 6'0", light complexion, gray eyes, brown hair. Carpenter. Residence Charles Town. enl. 4/18/61 at Charles Town in Co. A as Pvt. Detailed as teamster, 10/15-10/31 1861. Gen. Hosp. Staunton, 3/10/63; typhoid fever. Present again May/June 1863. Wded. at Gettysburg, 7/2/63. POW at Gettysburg, July 1863 (DeCamp Gen. Hosp., David's Island, N.Y. Harbor; Ft. Wood, Bedloe's Island, N.Y. Harbor where "lower one-third of right thigh amputated."). Paroled from Hammond Gen. Hosp., Pt. Lookout, date not specific. Chimborazo #1, 3/7/64. Furloughed 3/8/64 for 60 days. Gen. Hosp. Charlottesville, 3/22/64. To Staunton, 5/30/64. No further record. d. 1900. bur. Edge Hill Cem., Charles Town, W.Va.

MAKIN, PATRICK: b. 1843? Laborer. enl. 4/20/61 at Harpers Ferry in Co. K as Pvt. Absent sick Sept./Oct. 1861. Present again Nov./Dec. 1861. POW at Kernstown, 3/23/62 (Ft. Delaware). Exchanged 8/5/62. No further record.

MANNING, CHARLES JAMES: b. 6/21/31. Student. enl. 6/10/61 at Camp Jackson on Bolivar Heights in Co. G as Pvt. Absent sick since 10/4/61. Hosp. of 1st brig., Fairfax Court House; disease. Last official entry shows him present again Nov./Dec. 1861. Appears on rolls of Co. B, 12th Va. Cav. Postwar, member of Turner Ashby Camp #22 at Winchester. d. 2/14/03. bur. Zion Episcopal Cem., Charles Town, W.Va.

MANNING, GEORGE UPSHAW: b. 12/15/44 at Vinton. Student. enl. 4/18/61 at Charles Town in Co. G as Pvt. Absent sent to hosp. by surgeon, 10/15/61. Last official entry shows him present again, Nov./Dec. 1861. Appears on rolls of Co. B, 12th Va. Cav. KIA at Brandy Station, 6/9/63. bur. Zion Episcopal Cem., Charles Town, W.Va.

MANNING, WILLIAM PRICE: b. 12/8/44 in Jefferson Co. Student. enl. 4/22/61 at Harpers Ferry in Co. G as Pvt. Wded. in breast and face at 1st Manassas, 7/21/61. Absent due to wound through Sept./Oct. 1861. Last official entry shows him absent on special duty. Appears on rolls of Co. B, 12th Va. Cav. Postwar, received medical degree from University of Md. in 1869; physician at Shepherdstown until 1882; then moved to Washington, D.C.

MANOR, CHARLES W.: b. 10/24/37. 5'8", dark complexion, gray eyes, dark hair. Millwright. enl. 4/19/61 at Hedgesville in Co. E as Pvt. To Sgt., date not given. Wded. in the face at 1st Manassas, 7/21/61. Present again by 8/31/61. Absent sick Nov./Dec. 1861. Wded. at Gaines's Mill or Malvern Hill, 6/27 or 7/1 1862. Present Sept./Oct. 1862. Absent sick at Lynchburg Hosp., March/April 1863. Present again May/June 1863. Wded. in right thigh and left leg at Cedar Creek, 10/19/64. POW at Cedar Creek, 10/19/64 (Pt. Lookout, U.S. Hammond Gen. Hosp.). Exchanged 2/10/65. Furloughed 2/10/65 for 60 days. Paroled 5/8/65 at Winchester. d. 10/5/08. bur. Hedgesville Cem., Hedgesville, W.Va.

MANOR, DAVID H.: b. 2/18/39. Millwright. enl. 4/19/61 at Hedgesville in Co. E as Lt. KIA at 1st Manassas, 7/21/61. bur. Hedgesville Cem., Hedgesville, W.Va.

MAPHIS, HENRY: drafted 4/14/62 at Rude's Hill in Co. K as Pvt. Discharged 7/23/62, due to provisions of conscript act.

MARMADUKE, JAMES J.: b. 1835? Farmer. enl. 6/15/61 at Camp Whiting in Co. B as Pvt. AWOL since 10/14/61. Present again Nov./Dec. 1861. POW at Manassas, 8/27/62, and paroled. Absent sick at home since 9/21/62. AWOL since 11/10/62. Arrested (Rebel deserter) at Baltimore, 6/29/63 (Ft. McHenry). Oath of Allegiance to U.S., 8/26/63.

MARMADUKE, LUTHER: b. 1838? Tanner. enl. 6/18/61 at Winchester in Co. B as Pvt. Detailed as Musician to 2nd Regt. Band, May/June 1863. POW at Spotsylvania, 5/12/64 (Pt. Lookout, Elmira). d. 10/1/64 at Elmira; typhoid fever. bur. Woodlawn Nat. Cem., Elmira, N.Y., Section 9, grave 532.

MARQUIS, JAMES: b. 1829? Laborer. enl. 4/18/61 at Duffields in Co. H as Pvt. Absent on detached service, March/April 1863. Present again July/Aug. 1863. POW at Spotsylvania, 5/12/64 (Pt. Lookout, Elmira). Exchanged 10/29/64 and present again in the regt. 10/31/64. Chimborazo #4, 2/9/65; wounded right knee. d. 3/6/65 at Chimborazo #4.

MARSH, C. W.: Unofficial source lists him in Co. F. Alive in 1920.

MARSHALL, ALFRED C.: b. 1840? Farmer. enl. 4/23/61 at Harpers Ferry in Co. I as Corp. To Pvt. 8/16/61 when he resigned as Corp. Absent sick July/Aug. 1861-Nov./Dec. 1861. Still absent sick 4/18/62 and dropped from roll due to disability.

MARSHALL, CHARLES A.: b. 1842? Merchant. enl. 4/18/61 at Berryville in Co. I as Corp. To Sgt. 8/13/61. To Lt. 9/27/62. Assigned to command of Co. A, Jan./Feb. 1863. Present again in Co. I, March/April 1863. Signs roll as commanding Co., Sept./Oct. 1863. Wded. in right hand at Payne's Farm, 11/27/63. Absent on detached duty, Jan./Feb. 1864. Present again March/April 1864 and signs roll as commanding Co. Gen. Hosp. Staunton, 6/23/64, and furloughed for 60 days to "gunshot wound above elbow joint injuring muscles and paralyzing hand." Still absent 1/28/65 and reported as POW that had been exchanged. No further record.

MARSHALL, ISSAC: drafted 4/14/62 at Rude's Hill in Co. K as Pvt. AWOL since 9/20/62; "got sick leave and never came back." Discharged 2/1/63 "having furnished an approved substitute in the person of Abraham Sharpe."

MARSHALL, WILLIAM H.: b. 1818. Only record lists him in Co. G and states he was discharged 10/14/62, reason not stated. d. 4/15/93 in Augusta Co.

MARTIN, JOHN: Only record lists him in Co. B and shows him absent on detached service in Nov. 1862 with orders to report to Lt. Cockrill, Conscript Officer, Jefferson Co.

MASON, JAMES MURRAY: b. 8/25/39. Unofficial source lists him in Co. F. d. 1/10/23. bur. Zion Episcopal Cem., Charles Town, W.Va.

MASON, JOHN A.: b. 1840? Farmer. enl. 4/18/61 at Winchester in Co. F as Pvt. Absent sick at Winchester sometime before 6/30/61. AWOL July/Aug. 1861. Discharged 10/25/61, reason not stated. Unofficial source says he was Capt. and Inspector Gen. of Long's Artillery.

MATHENY, BUSHROD: b. in Jefferson Co. drafted 10/3/62 at Bunker Hill in Co. G as Pvt. Detailed as shoemaker in 1st Brig., Nov./Dec. 1862. Absent sick and sent to hosp. 1/2/63. Last official entry states he died in hosp. at Lexington, no date given.

MATHEWS, HENRY C.: b. 12/19/30. Printer. enl. 4/18/61 at Martinsburg in Co. D as Pvt. AWOL for 16 days, 4/18-6/30 1861. AWOL since 12/22/61. No further record. d. 3/26/94 bur. Old Norborne Cem., Martinsburg, W.Va.

MAUCK, DANIEL: enl. 4/16/62 at Winchester in Co. E as Pvt. AWOL, "assigned but never reported to company."

MAUPIN, ALGERMAN T.: b. 1836? Printer. enl. 4/18/61 at Martinsburg in Co. D as Pvt. AWOL since 7/1/61; "finger shot off by accident and he has not returned to duty." Still AWOL Sept./Oct. 1861, "has been since arrested and upon parole of honor to report to his captain was released; parole was forfeited." No further record.

MAURY, MAGRUDER: b. 1836? Student. enl. 6/15/61 at Charles Town in Co. G as Pvt. Trans. to Rockbridge Artillery, 8/15/61.

MAURY, THOMPSON B.: b. 1838? Student. enl. 6/12/61 at Camp Jackson on Bolivar Heights in Co. G as Pvt. Trans. to Rockbridge Artillery, 8/15/61.

MAY, BENJAMIN A.: b. 1833? Boatman. enl. 6/3/61 at Camp Jackson in Co. I as Pvt. Wded. in the cheek at 1st Manassas, 7/21/61. Present by 8/31/61. AWOL 12/27-12/30 1861. AWOL since 3/17/62 and dropped from the roll, Nov./Dec. 1862. No further record.

McARDLE, OWEN: b. 1827? Stonecutter. enl. 4/20/61 at Harpers Ferry in Co. K as Corp. KIA at 1st Manassas, 7/21/61.

McCABE, JAMES: b. 1841? Laborer. enl. 4/20/61 at Harpers Ferry in Co. K as Pvt. To Sgt. 10/1/62. Wded. at 1st Manassas, 7/21/61. Present again Sept./Oct. 1861. Absent on detached service, March/April 1863; duty not stated. Present again May/June 1863. Last official entry lists him present, 4/30-10/31 1864.

McCARTY, JOSEPH M.: b. 1843? Millwright. enl. 6/15/61 at Winchester in Co. F as Pvt. To Sgt. 7/1/62. Wded. at Port Republic, 6/9/62. Present again before 10/31/62. Wded. at Gettysburg, date not specific. Missing since 7/5/63. No further record.

McCARTY, TIMOTHY: b. 1840? in Frederick Co. 5' 9", fair complexion, blue eyes, dark hair. Cooper. enl. 4/24/61 at Winchester in Co. F as Pvt. Chimborazo #3, 5/29/62; fever. Present again by 10/31/62. Absent on leave since 2/25/63. Present again March/April 1863. Wded. at Wilderness, 5/5/64. Surgeon's Discharge from Gen. Hosp. Lynchburg, 3/31/65 due to disability "due to gunshot wound necessitating amputation of right arm." Paroled 4/28/65 at Winchester.

McCLEARY, CHARLES F. M.: b. 1841? Clerk. enl. 6/6/61 at Harpers Ferry in Co. D as Pvt. Wded. in thigh at 1st Manassas, 7/21/61. Gen. Hosp. Charlottesville, 7/22/61. Furloughed 9/1/61 for 30 days. Present again by 10/31/61. AWOL since 11/8/62 at Winchester and reported in Gilmore's Cav. No further record.

McCORD, JAMES ARTHUR: b. 1830. Wagonmaker. enl. 4/18/61 at Winchester in Co. F as Pvt. Absent sick 10/18/61. Present again Nov./Dec. 1861. KIA at Kernstown, 3/23/62. bur. Mt. Hebron Cem., Winchester.

McCORMICK, JOHN W.: b. 1834 in Clarke Co. 5' 4", fair complexion, gray eyes, dark hair. Farmer. enl. 4/18/61 at Millwood in Co. C as Corp. To Sgt. 11/9/62. To Pvt., date not given. Absent sick since 12/22/61. Wded. at Gaines's Mill or Malvern Hill, 6/27 or 7/1 1862. Absent sick since 10/15/62. Returned from hosp., 1/15/63. Absent on detail, May/June-July/Aug. 1863; duty not stated. Present again Sept./Oct. 1863. Chimborazo #1, 10/17-11/26 1864; diarrhea. Last official entry shows him present, 12/31/64. Surrendered at Appomattox. d. 12/4 or 12/18 1896. bur. Old Chapel Cem., Millwood.

McCORMICK, PHILIP J.: b. 1837? Brickmaker. enl. 4/20/61 at Harpers Ferry in Co. K as Pvt. To Corp. 8/12/61. To Pvt. 10/18/61. Last official entry shows him present, Nov./Dec. 1861.

McCORMICK (McCORMACK), WILLIAM STEELE: b. 1/18/25 in Augusta Co. Physician. enl. 4/14/62 at Winchester in Co. H as Pvt. MWIA at 1st Winchester, 5/25/62. d. 5/28/62. bur. Stonewall Cem., Winchester.

McDANIEL, JOHN: drafted 12/9/62 at Guinea's Station in Co. C as Pvt. AWOL since 7/15/63. Deserted 9/1/63.

McDANIEL (McDONALD), ENOS: b. 1828? 6' 1½", fair complexion, gray eyes, light hair. Laborer. Residence Berkeley Co. enl. 6/6/61 at Harpers Ferry in Co. D as Pvt. POW at Martinsburg, 6/12/62. Exchanged 8/5/62. Deserted 7/26/63. POW (Rebel deserter) at Chambersburg, 7/28/63 (Ft. Mifflin, Pa.). Oath of Allegiance to U.S., 11/17/63. d. 9/10/91. bur. St. Joseph's Cem., Martinsburg, W.Va.

McDANIEL, JOHN P.: enl. 7/16/61 at Winchester in Co. D as Pvt. To Corp. 1/1/64. Chimborazo #4, 10/28-11/13 1861; diarrhea. POW at Spotsylvania, 5/12/64 (Pt. Lookout, Elmira). Exchanged 3/2/65. Jackson Hosp., Richmond, 3/7/65; debility. Furloughed 3/8/65 for 30 days. No further record.

McDANIEL, MARSHALL: b. 1841? 6' 0", fair complexion, blue eyes, dark hair. Laborer. enl. 5/12/61 at Harpers Ferry in Co. C as Pvt. AWOL 12/26/61-1/10/62. Absent gathering conscripts, Nov./Dec. 1862. Returned from illness at hosp., 1/7/63. Wded. at Spotsylvania, 5/18/64. Last official entry shows him still absent from wound, 8/31-12/31 1864. Paroled 4/29/65 at Winchester.

McDONALD JOHNSTON P.: b. 1830? 5' 10", fair complexion, gray eyes, gray hair. Only record is a parole statement that lists him in Co. B. Paroled 4/23/65 at Winchester.

McDONALD, WILLIAM NAYLOR: b. 2/4/34 in Hampshire Co. Received Master's Degree from University of Virginia and became a professor of rhetoric and principal of a high school in Louisville, Kentucky; then became a lawyer in Charles Town. enl. 4/18/61 at Charles Town in Co. G as Pvt. Absent on special duty in Cav. of Angus W. McDonald, Nov./Dec. 1861. Last official record shows him on detail to engineer service, 3/26/62. Resigned from this and trans. to Co. D, 11th Va. Cav. Later promoted to capt. of artillery and assigned to Ord. Dept. Wded. in side at Wilderness, 5/6/64. Another source says he also served on the staffs of Rosser and Mahone. Postwar, teacher; founder and principal of Shenandoah University School at Berryville; founder of Cool Spring School; author of *The Laurel Brigade*. d. 1/4/98. bur. Greenhill Cem., Berryville.

McDONOUGH, CHARLES T.: b. 1844? in Loudoun Co. Light complexion, blue eyes, brown hair. Tailor. enl. 4/18/61 at Charles Town in Co. A as Pvt. Absent sick at home since 9/5/61. Surgeon's discharge, 12/8/61; disability.

McENDREE, DANIEL M.: b. 1838? in Jefferson Co. 5' 9", fair complexion, gray eyes, brown hair. Clerk. enl. 4/27/61 at Harpers Ferry in Co. B as Pvt. Absent sick Nov./Dec. 1861. Present again Jan./Feb. 1862. AWOL since 5/1/62. Discharged 7/27/62, being a "citizen of Kentucky and having served 90 days after expiration of this term."

McENDREE, WILLIAM H.: b. 1841? Clerk. enl. 5/29/61 at Lemon's Ferry in Co. B as Pvt. To Sgt. 4/18/62. Absent sick Jan./Feb. 1862. AWOL during July 1862 and since 9/20/62. AWOL 10/10-12/1/62. Detailed clerk for QM of 2nd Va. Inf., Dec. 1861. Remained on this detail through last official entry which shows him present, 4/30-10/31 1864. Surrendered at Appomattox.

McGAREY, WILLIAM H.: Residence Berkeley Co. enl. 4/18/61 at Martinsburg in Co. D as Pvt. To Sgt. 3/26/63. Wded. in neck at 1st Manassas, 7/21/61. Gen. Hosp. Charlottesville, 7/22/61. Furloughed 9/1/61 for 30 days. Absent sick at hosp., May/June 1863. Deserted 7/26/63. POW (Rebel deserter), 7/27/63. No further record.

McGUIRE, DAVID HOLMES, JR.: b. 1843. Clerk. enl. 4/18/61 at Berryville in Co. I as Pvt. Wded. in arm at 1st Manassas, 7/21/61. Last official entry shows him still absent sick from wound, Nov./Dec. 1861. Dropped from roll due to disability, 4/18/62. Postwar, lawyer and editor. d. March 1874. bur. Old Chapel Cem., Millwood.

McGUIRE, EDWARD: b. 1837? Student. enl. 4/18/61 at Harpers Ferry in Co. F as Pvt. Absent on detail at hosp., July/Aug. 1861. Present again Sept./Oct. 1861. AWOL from Rude's Hill, 4/18/62. Unofficial source says he was detailed to C. S. Navy and was captured while engaged in operations in the Chesapeake Bay. Same source also says he was involved in C. S. Secret Service operations in Canada. Postwar, returned to Winchester in 1865. d. 9/6/82 at Eastern State Hosp., Williamsburg.

McGUIRE, JAMES: enl. 4/16/62 at Rude's Hill in Co. E as Pvt. AWOL Sept./Oct. 1862-2/15/63. Sentenced by court-martial to forfeit 1 month's pay. Chimborazo #1, 4/4/63; typhoid fever. d. 4/17/63 at Chimborazo #1, typhoid.

McGUIRE, HUNTER HOLMES: b. 10/11/35. m. Mary Stuart. Unofficial source lists him in Co. F as Pvt. To surgeon and medical director of the Army of the Shenandoah, July 1861. To Medical Director of 2nd Corps, Army of Northern Va. and Gen. Jackson's personal surgeon. d. 9/19/00 at Richmond. bur. Hollywood Cem., Richmond.

McINTIRE, JOHN F.: b. 1836? Mason. enl. 4/18/61 at Martinsburg in Co. D as Pvt. To Corp. 1/1/64. POW at Spotsylvania, 5/12/64 (Pt. Lookout, Elmira). Exchanged 10/29/64. Present again by 10/31/64. Surrendered at Appomattox.

McINTYRE (McINTIRE), RICHARD W.: b. 1843? 5' 8", fair complexion, blue eyes, brown hair. enl. 10/8/62 at Bunker Hill in Co. A as Pvt. Sent to hosp. sick, 10/28/63. Present again Jan./Feb. 1864. Last official entry shows him present, 4/30-10/31 1864. Paroled 4/18/65 at Winchester. Alive in 1920.

McINTYRE, THOMAS B.: b. 1837? Mason. enl. 4/18/61 at Charles Town in Co. A as Sgt. KIA at 2nd Manassas, 8/28/62.

McKENNEY (McKINNEY), FRANCIS E.: b. 1841? Florid complexion, hazel eyes, black hair. Farmer. Residence Jefferson Co. enl. 4/18/61 at Charles Town in Co. A as Pvt. POW at Kernstown, 3/23/62 (Ft. Delaware). Exchanged 8/5/62. Absent sick at home in Jefferson Co. 9/5/62-May/June 1863. Shown as AWOL since 6/13/63. POW at Leetown, 10/12/63 (Pt. Lookout). Oath of Allegiance to U.S., 4/23/64. POW at Harpers Ferry, 4/26/64 (Camp Chase). Oath of Allegiance to U.S., 6/1/65. bur. Greenhill Cem., Martinsburg, W.Va.

McMULLEN, LAMBERT: b. 1840? Clerk. enl. 6/12/61 at Harpers Ferry in Co. D at Pvt. Wded. in arm at 1st Manassas, 7/21/61. Gen. Hosp. Charlottesville, 7/23/61. Furloughed 7/30/61 for 20 days. Present again Sept./Oct. 1861. Last official entry shows him absent sick, Nov./Dec. 1861.

McVEIGH, T. J.: Commissioned chaplain of the 2nd Va. Inf., Sept. 1861. Vouchers indicate he was paid in this capacity through 6/30/62. No further record.

McWHARTER, JAMES W.: enl. 7/16/61 at Winchester in Co. D as Pvt. AWOL since 8/6/61. Last official entry states he is commissioner of revenue for Berkeley Co., Sept./Oct. 1861.

McWILLIAMS, JOSEPH G.: b. 1828? Clerk. enl. 5/15/61 at Harpers Ferry in Co. H as Pvt. To Sgt., Jan./Feb. 1863. Surrendered at Appomattox.

McWILLIAMS, WILLIAM: 5' 11½", dark complexion, hazel eyes, black hair. Residence Winchester. Listed in Co. B as Pvt. AWOL 5/1/62-2/16/64. POW at Spotsylvania, 5/12/64 (Pt. Lookout, Elmira). Oath of Allegiance to U.S., 6/14/65.

MEACHEM, RICHARD: enl. 12/22/62 at Guinea's Station in Co. D as Pvt. KIA at Chancellorsville, 5/3/63.

MEADE, DAVID: b. 1/21/33. Farmer. enl. 4/18/61 at Millwood in Co. C as Lt. Absent sick sometime before 6/30/61. Present again July/Aug. 1861. Absent sick since 12/25/61. Apptd. Asst. QM, 11th Va. Cav., 7/17/62. d. 6/6/06. bur. Meade Memorial Episcopal Church Cem., White Post, Clarke Co.

MEADE, RICHARD KIDDER: b. 10/4/41 in Clarke Co. 5' 2", fair complexion, blue eyes, light hair. Attd. Washington College, Lexington. Student. enl. 4/18/61 at Winchester in Co. F as Pvt. Wded. in right arm at 1st Manassas, 7/21/61. Surgeon's discharge, 12/4/61; disability due to amputation of right arm. Unofficial source says he later served on staffs of Jackson and Talliferro. Postwar, teacher. d. 1/20/09. bur. Old Chapel Cem., Millwood.

MEDLAR, NAPOLEON B.: b. 1840? Gunsmith. enl. 4/18/61 at Charles Town in Co. G in Pvt. Detailed as musician for 2nd regt., July/Aug. 1861. Gen. Hosp. Howard's Grove, Richmond, 7/21/63; severe contusion of left thigh by a fall. To Gen. Hosp. Charlottesville, 8/3/63. Present again Sept./Oct. 1863. Next official record shows him as an armorer in a repairing establishment at Charlottesville, 3/19-Aug. 1862. Final record shows him as an armorer at the C. S. Carbine Factory, Richmond, 3/19/64. No further record.

MELVIN, JACOB S.: b. 1/6/30. Farmer. enl. 4/18/61 at Duffields in Co. H as Lt. Last official entry shows him present, Nov. Dec. 1861. Vouchers for the fall of 1862 list him as a Capt. and Asst. Commissary. d. 1/25/12. bur. Elmwood Cem., Shepherdstown, W.Va.

MELVIN, WILLIAM: b. 8/27/41. enl. 3/18/63 at Camp Winder in Co. H as Pvt. Wded. by shell in left side of back below shoulder blade at Monocacy, 7/9/64. POW at Monocacy, 7/9/64 (U.S. Gen. Hosp. West Buildings, Baltimore; Ft. McHenry). Exchanged 2/16/65. Surrendered at Appomattox. d. 2/17/12. bur. Elmwood Cem., Shepherdstown, W.Va.

MERAKLE, GEORGE W.: enl. 4/19/61 at Martinsburg in Co. D as Pvt. POW at Kernstown, 3/23/62 (Ft. Delaware). Exchanged 8/5/62. Wded. at Gettysburg, date not specific, and left behind enemy's lines. Last official entry shows him as a POW, March/April 1864.

MERAKLE, JOHN B.: en. 7/16/61 at Winchester in Co. D as Pvt. Absent sick hosp., Nov./Dec. 1861. MWIA at 2nd Manassas, 8/30/62. d. 9/8/62.

MERAKLE, SMITH: enl. 3/8/62 at Winchester in Co. D as Pvt. KIA at Payne's Farm, 11/27/63.

MERAKLE, THOMAS P.: b. 1835? 6' 1½", fair complexion, hazel eyes, black hair. enl. 7/16/61 at Winchester in Co. D as Pvt. To Sgt. 11/1/63. Last official entry shows him present, March/April 1863. Paroled 4/25/65 at Winchester.

MERCER, DAVID: enl. 3/19/62 at Woodstock in Co. I as Pvt. Gen. Hosp. Charlottesville, 4/12/63; pneumonia. d. 4/25/63 at Gen. Hosp. Charlottesville.

MERCER, JESSE: b. 1840? Farmhand. enl. 6/19/61 at Winchester in Co. I as Pvt. Left at Winchester sick, 7/18/61. Present again Sept.-Oct. 1861. AWOL since 3/12/62. No further record.

MERCHANT, ISAAC N.: b. 1838. 5′8″, fair complexion, hazel eyes, brown hair. Residence Berkeley Co. enl. 10/4/62 at Bunker Hill in Co. E as Pvt. Wded. at Chancellorsville, 5/3/63, and continued absent through March/April 1863. Last official entry shows him present, 4/30-10/31 1864. POW at Ft. Steadman near Petersburg, 3/25/65 (Pt. Lookout). Oath of Allegiance to U.S., 6/15/65. d. Oct. 1933. bur. Arlington Nat. Cem., Arlington.

MERCHANT, SEWELL: b. 1844? 5′9″, dark complexion, gray eyes, dark hair. enl. 10/4/62 at Bunker Hill in Co. E as Pvt. Absent on detail as pioneer, March/April 1863. Present again May/June 1863. Absent on detail as pioneer, July/Aug. 1863. Present again Sept./Oct. 1863. Last official entry shows him absent on detail as pioneer, March/April 1864. Paroled 5/10/65 at Winchester.

MERICA, D.: enl. 4/16/62 at Rude's Hill in Co. F as Pvt. Deserted from Rude's Hill, 4/18/62.

MERICA, HIRAM: enl. 4/16/62 at Rude's Hill in Co. F as Pvt. Deserted from Rude's Hill, 4/18/62. Recovered from desertion 3/8/63. Detailed to work in iron foundry by Secretary of War, March/April 1863. Last official entry shows him still on detail in iron foundry, March/April 1864.

MERICA, P. N.: enl. 4/16/62 at Rude's Hill in Co. F as Pvt. Deserted from Rude's Hill, 4/18/62.

MERICA, ROBERT: enl. 4/16/62 at Rude's Hill in Co. F as Pvt. Deserted from Rude's Hill, 4/18/62. Recovered from desertion 3/8/63. Detailed to work in iron foundry by Secretary of War, March/April 1863. Last official entry shows him still on detail in iron foundry, March/April 1864.

MERK, THOMAS: Listed in Co. D as Pvt. Only record shows him AWOL since 10/15/62 at Bunker Hill.

MICHAEL, ANDERSON: enl. 4/16/62 at Rude's Hill in Co. F as Pvt. Wded. in arm at 2nd Manassas, 8/28/62. Absent sick from wound until 3/8/63 when he returned to regt. Wded. in right side and rib broken at Payne's Farm, 11/27/63. Present again Jan./Feb. 1864. POW at Spotsylvania, 5/12/64 (Pt. Lookout). No further record.

MICHAEL, G. W.: Unofficial source says he enl. 4/16/62 at Rude's Hill in Co. F. Deserted 4/30/62.

MICHAEL, PETER A.: b. 8/26/40. enl. 4/16/62 at Rude's Hill in Co. F as Pvt. AWOL from 6/1/62-2/20/63. Sentenced by court-martial to forfeit 1 month's pay. Last official entry shows him present, March/April 1864. d. 6/26/06. bur. Mt. Olivet Cem., McGaheysville.

MICHAEL, ROBERT: enl. 4/16/62 at Rude's Hill in Co. F as Pvt. To Corp. 1/1/63. Absent sick May/June-July/Aug. 1863. Present again Sept./Oct. 1863. Last official entry lists him present, March/April 1864. Unofficial source states he died 7/10/64 as POW at Elmira, N.Y.

MICHAEL, R. H.: 5′8″, dark complexion, blue eyes, dark hair. Residence Harrisonburg. enl. 4/16/62 at Rude's Hill in Co. F as Pvt. Wded. at Cedar Run, 8/9/62. Gen. Hosp. Charlottesville, 8/11/62. To Gen. Hosp. Lynchburg, 9/1/62. Wded. at Payne's Farm, 11/27/63. POW at Spotsylvania, 5/12/64 (Pt. Lookout, Elmira). Oath of Allegiance to U.S., 6/27/65.

MICHAEL, SAMUEL: enl. 4/16/62 at Rude's Hill in Co. F as Pvt. Deserted 6/1/62. Recovered from desertion 3/8/63. Detailed to work in iron foundry by Secretary of War, March/April 1863. Last official entry shows him still on detail in iron foundry, March/April 1864.

MIDDLEKAUFF, HENRY D.: b. 1833? Harness maker. enl. 4/18/61 at Charles Town in Co. G as Sgt. Charged $2.00 for pair of shoes received, July/Aug. 1861. Detailed for harness making, 10/10/61. Last official entry shows him absent on detail as harness maker, Nov./Dec. 1861.

MIDDLETON, WILLIAM: enl. 4/9/62 at Winchester in Co. E as Pvt. AWOL 5/20/62-2/12/63. Sentenced by court-martial to forfeit 1 month's pay. Deserted 4/14/63 at Camp Winder.

MICKLE, G. W.: enl. 4/16/62 at Rude's Hill in Co. F as Pvt. Deserted from Rude's Hill, 4/18/62.

MILLBURN, HENRY: b. 1841? Carpenter. enl. 4/18/61 at Charles Town in Co. A as Pvt. AWOL 12/27-12/30 1861. Last official entry shows him present, 12/31/61.

MILLER, AMOS: b. in Shenandoah Co. drafted 4/14/62 at Rude's Hill in Co. K as Pvt. Absent sick in hosp., Nov./Dec. 1862. Present again Jan./Feb. 1863. MWIA at Chancellorsville, 5/3/63. d. 5/6/63.

MILLER, BENJAMIN: enl. 4/18/62 at Rude's Hill in Co. B as Pvt. AWOL 4/20-8/1 1862. No further record except parole statement that says he was paroled 4/20/65 at Mt. Jackson.

MILLER, DAVID: drafted 4/16/62 at Rude's Hill in Co. C as Pvt. Absent sick at hosp., no dates given. Returned to regt. from hosp., 10/22/62. Absent on detail to hosp. on Surgeon's Certificate, Nov./Dec. 1862. Returned to regt. from detail, 2/25/63. Absent on detail as nurse at Chimborazo #3, 3/23/63-June 1864. Last official entry shows him still absent on detail to Richmond hosp., 8/31-12/31 1864.

MILLER, GEORGE E.: enl. 4/18/62 at Rude's Hill in Co. B as Pvt. AWOL since 5/1/62 and dropped from the roll 12/10/62. No further record.

MILLER, EMMANUEL: b. 1817? Shoemaker. enl. 4/18/61 at Duffields in Co. H as Pvt. AWOL and never mustered, 4/30-6/30 1861. No further record.

MILLER, GEORGE W.: b. 2/20/41. enl. 4/19/61 at Hedgesville in Co. E as Pvt. Wded. at 1st Manassas, 7/21/61, and absent sick through Nov./Dec. 1861. Next official entry lists him in Co. F and states he was AWOL 6/1/62-2/20/63. Sentenced by court-martial to forfeit 1 month's pay. Absent sick, March/April 1863. AWOL 6/13-July/Aug. 1863. Absent under sentence of hard labor for war, Sept./Oct. 1863. Gen. Hosp. #13, Richmond, 11/23/63; catarrhus. To Castle Thunder 12/14/63. No record again until admitted to hosp. at Salisbury, N.C., 1/6/65; cut toe. Paroled POW 3/7/65. d. 1/4/17. bur. Mill Creek Church of the Brethren, Port Republic.

MILLER, HARVEY ALLEN: b. 9/12/35. Farmer. enl. 4/19/61 at Hedgesville in Co. E as Pvt. Last official entry for Sept./Oct. 1862 states he trans. to Cav. d. 11/08/02. bur. Falling Waters Cem., Spring Mills, W.Va.

MILLER, JOHN H.: drafted 4/14/62 at Rude's Hill in Co. K as Pvt. To Corp. 8/1/63. To Pvt. 4/1/64. POW at Spotsylvania, 5/12/64 (Pt. Lookout, Elmira). d. 1/8/65 at Elmira; typhoid fever. bur. Woodlawn Nat. Cem., Elmira, N.Y., grave #1284.

MILLER, JONATHAN: b. 4/18/30. 5′10½″, fair complexion, gray eyes, sandy hair. Cabinet maker. Residence Martinsburg. enl. 4/18/61 at Martinsburg in Co. D as Pvt. Under arrest for desertion, Nov./Dec. 1862. Court-martialed 12/27/62, sentence not stated. Gen. Hosp. Staunton, 3/10/63; rheumatism. Present again May/June 1863. POW at Spotsylvania, 5/12/64 (Pt. Lookout, Elmira). Oath of Allegiance to U.S., 5/17/65. d. 11/6/04. bur. Greenhill Cem., Martinsburg, W.Va.

118

MILLER, J. WESLEY: enl. 12/22/62 at Guinea's Station in Co. D as Pvt. Gen. Hosp. Staunton, 3/26/63; diarrhea. Present again July/Aug. 1863. AWOL since 4/21/64. No further record.

MILLER, MILTON B.: b. 1832? Shoemaker. enl. 4/18/61 at Duffields in Co. H as Pvt. Last official entry shows him present, Nov./Dec. 1861.

MILLER, NOAH: b. 3/2/44 at Jerome. 5′3″, fair complexion, blue eyes, auburn hair. Residence Winchester. enl. 4/16/62 at Rude's Hill in Co. K as Pvt. Wded. at Gaines's Mill, 6/27/62. Present again Jan./Feb. 1863. Wded. in left upper arm resulting in fracture of the humurus at Spotsylvania, 5/12/64. POW at Spotsylvania, 5/12/64 (Old Capitol Prison, Elmira). Oath of Allegiance to U.S., 6/30/65. d. 1/26/16 at Jerome.

MILLER, SAMUEL: enl. 4/18/62 at Rude's Hill in Co. B as Pvt. AWOL 4/20-8/1 1862. Last official entry shows him present, 10/31/62.

MILLER, SAMUEL: drafted 4/14/62 at Rude's Hill in Co. K as Pvt. POW at Spotsylvania, 5/12/64 (Pt. Lookout, Elmira). d. 2/28/65 at Elmira; chronic diarrhea. bur. Woodlawn Nat. Cem., Elmira, N.Y.

MILLER, WILLIAM: 5′7″, dark complexion, hazel eyes, dark hair. Residence Winchester. enl. 4/16/62 at Rude's Hill in Co. E as Pvt. Absent sick at hosp., 11/9/62. Not present again until 3/1/64, when he "rejoined from desertion." POW at Spotsylvania, 5/12/64 (Pt. Lookout, Elmira). Oath of Allegiance to U.S., 6/30/65.

MILLER, WILLIAM M.: b. 1830? Farmer. enl. 5/17/61 at Harpers Ferry in Co. B as Pvt. Last official entry shows him AWOL, March/April 1862.

MILLHON (MILLHORN), JOSEPH: b. 1838? Millwright. enl. 4/18/61 at Winchester in Co. F as Pvt. To Sgt. 10/25/61. Absent sick Nov./Dec. 1861. POW at Winchester, 3/12/62. Exchanged 8/5/62. No further record.

MILTON, WILLIAM TAYLOR: b. 1838. Farmer. enl. 4/18/61 at Berryville in Co. I as Sgt. Elected Lt. 11/19/61. Not reelected 4/18/62; joined the Cav. d. 1923. bur. Greenhill Cem., Berryville.

MITCHELL, CHARLES M.: b. 1839? Machinist. enl. 4/18/61 at Winchester in Co. F as Pvt. KIA at 1st Manassas, 7/21/61. bur. Stonewall Cem., Winchester.

MIZER, ADAM: 5′8″, florid complexion, blue eyes, auburn hair. Residence Staunton. drafted 4/14/62 at Rude's Hill in Co. K as Pvt. POW at Spotsylvania, 5/12/64 (Pt. Lookout, Elmira). Oath of Allegiance to U.S., 6/27/65.

MOBLEY, GEORGE W.: enl. 9/13/61 at Charles Town in Co. K as Pvt. AWOL Nov./Dec. 1861. Last official entry says he deserted 11/20/62. d. 1899. bur. Harpers Cem., Harpers Ferry, W.Va.

MOCK, H.: drafted 4/16/62 at Rude's Hill in Co. C as Pvt. Wded. at 1st Winchester, 5/25/62. Deserted 6/1/62.

MOLER, DANIEL: b. 1840? 5′8″, dark complexion, gray eyes, dark hair. Farmer. enl. 4/25/61 at Harpers Ferry in Co. G as Pvt. To Corp. 7/61. Absent sick at hosp., July/Aug.-10/25/62. Wded. at Gaines's Mill or Malvern Hill, 6/27 or 7/1 1862. Present again by 10/31/62. Wded. slightly by shell at Fredericksburg, 12/13/62. Present by 12/31/62. Absent sick at hosp., 4/13/63. Gen. Hosp. Charlottesville, 5/2-6/9 1863; debility. Wded. in neck at Payne' Farm, 11/27/63. Chimborazo #3, 11/30/63. To Staunton, 1/6/64. Returned to regt. 3/8/64. POW at Salem Church, 5/20/64 (Pt. Lookout, Elmira). Exchanged 3/14/65. Paroled 4/25/65 at Winchester.

MOLER, HENRY CLAY: enl. 12/8/62 at Camp Moss Neck in Co. B as Pvt. Wded. at Chancellorsville, 5/3/63. Present again Sept./Oct. 1863. Detailed in Pioneer Corps, Johnson's Division, Jan./Feb. 1864. Last official entry shows him present, 4/30-10/31 1864.

MOLER, LEE H.: b. 3/12/37. Farmer. enl. 4/18/61 at Halltown in Co. B as Lt. Elected Capt. 4/20/62. Resigned 8/15/62 due to "an old and large hernia at the left side." d. 10/28/08. bur. Elmwood Cem., Shepherdstown, W.Va.

MOLER, RALEIGH V.: b. 9/4/40. Farmer. enl. 6/14/61 at Charles Town in Co. A as Pvt. AWOL 1/27-12/2 1861. Last official entry shows him present, 12/31/61. d. 10/16/17.

MONROE, ALBERT MARSHALL: b. 11/25/40 in Clarke Co. Farmer. enl. 4/18/61 at Winchester in Co. F as Pvt. To Lt. 4/20/62. Absent sick and AWOL since 10/10/61. Present again 6/30-10/31 1863. Dropped from the roll by order of Secretary of War, 12/1/63; reason not stated. Postwar, m. a Miss Taylor of Augusta Co; moved to Rockbridge Co. in 1881; farmer. d. 5/10/13 at Lexington. bur. Stone's Chapel Cem., Clarke Co.

MONROE, GEORGE B.: b. 8/8/18. Painter. enl. 4/18/61 at Charles Town in Co. G as Pvt. Absent on special duty, 4/18-6/30 1861. Absent sick since 7/1/61. Discharged 11/9/61 for disability. d. 2/18/67. bur. Zion Episcopal Cem., Charles Town, W.Va.

MONROE, JAMES T.: b. 1837? Farmer. enl. 4/18/61 at Winchester in Co. F as Pvt. Last official entry shows him as a deserter, Nov./Dec. 1861.

MONTAGUE, LAWRENCE: b. 1836? 5′5″, light complexion, gray eyes, brown hair. enl. 2/23/62 at Martinsburg in Co. D as Pvt. POW at Gettysburg, 7/3/63 (Ft. Delaware, Pt. Lookout). Exchanged 2/13/65. Paroled 4/21/65 at Winchester. bur. St. Joseph's Cem., Martinsburg, W.Va.

MOODY, JOHN P.: b. 1831? 5′7″, light complexion, gray eyes, brown hair, sandy whiskers. Wool manufacturer. Residence Berkeley Co. enl. 4/18/61 at Martinsburg in Co. D as Pvt. Absent on detail in factory at Martinsburg, Nov./Dec. 1861. Present again 6/30-10/31 1862. POW at Martinsburg, 2/17/63 (Wheeling, Camp Chase). Exchanged 3/28/63. Present again April 1863. Deserted 7/26/63. POW (Rebel deserter), 7/27/63; "desires to take the oath." No further record.

MOORE, ALBERT L.: b. 12/29/45. Student. enl. 4/18/61 at Charles Town in Co. A as Pvt. Absent sick at home, Nov./Dec. 1861. No further record. d. 4/14/34. bur. Edge Hill Cem., Charles Town, W.Va.

MOORE, BERKELEY W.: b. 7/30/44 at Charles Town. Clerk. enl. 5/4/61 at Harpers Ferry in Co. K as Pvt. To Sgt. Maj., 2nd Va. Inf., 5/4/61. To Lt. 4/20/62. To Capt., date not given. Signs roll as commanding Co., 6/30-10/31 1862. Wded. slightly by shell at Fredericksburg, 12/13/62. Signs roll as commanding Co. Nov./Dec. 1863-March/April 1864. Last official entry shows him present, March/April 1864. Surrendered at Appomattox. d. 3/27/22 at Richmond. bur. Edge Hill Cem., Charles Town, W.Va.

MOORE, CLEON: b. 11/24/40. Teacher. enl. 4/18/61 at Charles Town in Co. G as Pvt. To Corp. 8/23/61. To Lt. Nov./Dec. 1862. Absent sick at hosp., 10/15/61. Present again Nov./Dec. 1861. Last official records state he was on duty with Provost Guard, 10/12-Nov. 1864. Surrendered at Appomattox. Postwar, lawyer. d. 12/26/14. bur. Edge Hill Cem., Charles Town, W.Va.

MOORE, EDWIN L.: b. 2/14/31. Banker. enl. 4/18/61 at Charles Town in Co. G. Elected Capt. to succeed Capt. Botts,

6/13/61. To Maj. 9/16/62. Signs roll as commanding 2nd Va. Inf., 10/31/62. Absent on detail as acting inspector, 1st Division, 2nd Corps, Army of Northern Va., Nov./Dec. 1862-May/June 1863. Next official record lists him as AAG to Trimble's Division, 1/6/64. No further record. d. 12/11/81. bur. Zion Episcopal Cem., Charles Town, W.Va.

MOORE, FONROSE M.: b. 1844? Student. enl. 6/14/61 at Charles Town in Co. A as Pvt. Last official entry shows him present, Nov./Dec. 1861.

MOORE, SAMUEL JOHNSTON CRAMER: b. 6/29/26 in Charles Town. Lawyer. m. Ellen Kownslar. enl. 4/18/61 at Berryville in Co. I as Lt. Elected Capt. 11/19/61. Last official entry shows him absent due to wound in thigh at 2nd Manassas, 8/28/62. Detailed as Judge Advocate, Army of Northern Va., 8/25/62? Gen. Hosp. Charlottesville, 5/13-7/25 1863; hemorrhoid. Gen. Hosp. Charlottesville, 5/9/64. To Front Royal, 6/27/64. Served as Asst. Inspector Gen., 2nd Corps, dates not given. Assigned as Adj. Gen. to Gen. Early and the Valley Army, 7/29/64 to Appomattox. Postwar, Clarke Co. lawyer and judge. d. 12/19/08. bur. Greenhill Cem., Berryville.

MOORE, VINCENT G.: b. 4/15/43. Student. enl. 4/18/61 at Charles Town in Co. G as Pvt. Last official entry shows him absent sick, 12/16/61. No further record. d. 12/11/25. bur. Elmwood Cem., Shepherdstown, W.Va.

MOORE, WILLIAM H.: b. 10/29/41 in Jefferson Co. 5′ 8″, dark complexion, blue eyes, brown hair. Laborer. Wded. in leg at Port Republic, 6/9/62. Gen. Hosp. Charlottesville, 6/20-8/13 1862. Trans. to C. S. Navy, 4/6/64. d. 2/25/10. bur. Edge Hill Cem., Charles Town, W.Va.

MORALES, JULIAN: b. 1834? 5′ 2½″, dark complexion, dark eyes, dark hair. Carpenter. Residence Winchester. enl. 6/19/61 at Winchester in Co. I as Pvt. AWOL 12/27-12/30 1861. POW at Berryville, 7/1/62 (Old Capitol Prison, Ft. Monroe). Present again by 10/31/62. Wded. at Chancellorsville, 5/3/63. Present again by June 1863. Absent on detached service, Jan./Feb. 1864, duty not stated. Present again March/April 1864. POW at Spotsylvania, 5/12/64 (Pt. Lookout, Elmira). Oath of Allegiance to U.S., 6/23/65. d. 1921. bur. Greenhill Cem., Berryville.

MORAN, BERNARD: b. 1836? Laborer. enl. 4/25/61 in Co. K as Pvt. Deserted 4/26/61.

MORELAND, LEWIS F.: b. 1842? Farmhand. enl. 4/29/61 at Harpers Ferry in Co. I as Pvt. AWOL 7/27-8/4 1861. AWOL 12/25-12/30 1861. Deserted 7/18/63.

MORNINGSTAR, SAMUEL: b. 1827? 5′ 11″, dark complexion, black eyes, dark hair. drafted 10/1/62 at Bunker Hill in Co. K as Pvt. AWOL since 10/12/62. Present again Nov./Dec. 1862. Absent on detail as teamster, 1/6/63. Last official entry shows him still absent on detail as teamster, March/April 1864. Paroled 4/27/65 at Winchester.

MORRIS, LAYTON B.: enl. 2/9/63 at Camp Nadenbousch in Co. D as Pvt. Deserted 5/16/63. Shot to death by sentence of court-martial for desertion, 10/26/63.

MORRIS, WILLIAM H.: enl. 3/6/62 at Greenbrier in Co. H as Pvt. Only official record states he trans. from 8th Va. Cav. to 2nd Va. Inf. sometime between 4/30-10/31 1864.

MORRISON, BENJAMIN: enl. 10/1/62 at Bunker Hill in Co. H as Pvt. AWOL since 11/22/62. No further record.

MOWERY, D.: enl. 4/16/62 at Rude's Hill in Co. F as Pvt. Deserted from Rude's Hill, 4/18/62.

MOWERY, JAMES: enl. 3/3/64 at Pisgah Church in Co. E as Pvt. Only official entry shows him present, March/April 1864.

MOWRY, EPHRAIM: enl. 4/15/62 at Rude's Hill in Co. G as Pvt. Wded. at Port Republic, 6/9/62. AWOL 1/1-5/26 1863 and brought back to regt. under guard. Fined $53.54 for absence. POW 10/19/64 at Fisher's Hill (Old Capitol Prison, Elmira). d. 4/14/65 at Elmira, diarrhea. bur. Woodlawn Nat. Cem., Elmira N.Y., grave #2601.

MUHLENBURG, CHARLES A.: b. 1839? 5′ 11″, fair complexion, gray eyes, dark hair. Printer. Residence Morgan Co. enl. 5/18/61 at Harpers Ferry in Co. D as Pvt. Absent sick July/Aug. 1861. Present again Sept./Oct. 1861. Absent sick at hosp., March/April 1863-July/Aug. 1863. Gen. Hosp. Charlottesville, 7/10/63; pleurisy. To Lynchburg, 9/21/63. Present again by 10/31/63. POW at Salem Church, 5/20/64 (Old Capitol Prison, Ft. Delaware). Oath of Allegiance to U.S., 5/10/65.

MUMAN, GEORGE W.: enl. 8/10/62 at Orange Court House in Co. H as Pvt. AWOL 11/21/62 at Mt. Jackson. No further record.

MUMAN, JESSE: enl. 4/18/62 at Rude's Hill in Co. B as Pvt. AWOL since 5/12/62. Dropped from roll as a deserter, 12/10/62. No further record.

MUMAN, WILLIAM: Listed in Co. E as Pvt. AWOL Nov. 1862, "never reported." No further record.

MUNSALL, ADDISON: b. 1826? "Yankee School Master." enl. 4/18/61 at Millwood in Co. C as Pvt. Deserted 6/17/61.

MUNSON, ROBERT A. D.: b. 1839? Physician. enl. 4/18/61 at Winchester in Co. F as Pvt. To Asst. Surgeon, 2nd Va. Inf., 1/6/62. Absent on detail in hosp. at Winchester, 4/18-6/30 1861. Present again July/Aug. 1861. Absent on detail as Surgeon's Steward, 9/21/61. Last official entry shows him absent on furlough and on detail as regt. steward, Nov./Dec. 1861.

MUNT, H. F.: Unofficial source says he enl. Jan. 1863 in Co. F.

MURAY, RICHARD: b. 1820? Laborer. enl. 4/20/61 at Harpers Ferry in Co. I as Pvt. Deserted 5/20/61.

MURPHY, JOHN: enl. 12/?/62 at Guinea's Station in Co. C as Pvt. Chimborazo #1, 1/12/63; typhoid fever. d. 1/26/63 at Chimborazo #1.

MURPHY, MOSES B.: b. 1838? Farmhand. enl. 5/3/61 at Harpers Ferry in Co. I as Pvt. AWOL since 8/23/61 and fined $5.00 for absence by court-martial. Present again Sept./Oct. 1861. Absent sick Nov./Dec. 1861. Present again 4/30-10/31 1862. Absent on detail as teamster, Nov./Dec. 1862-March/April 1863. Deserted 3/1/63. Arrested (Rebel deserter) at Bermuda Hundred, 10/9/64. Sent to Washington, D.C. and then to Baltimore, Md. Oath of Allegiance to U.S., 10/12/64.

MURPHY, PATRICK: b. 1846. enl. 4/18/62 at Rude's Hill in Co. B as Pvt. Deserted, date not known, and dropped from roll 12/10/62. d. 1933. bur. Sacred Heart Cem., Winchester.

MURPHY, SMITH: b. 1842? 5′ 7″, light complexion, black eyes, brown hair. Carpenter. enl. 6/14/61 at Charles Town in Co. A as Pvt. To Sgt. 7/1/62. Wded. in thigh at 2nd Manassas, date not specific. Last official entry shows him present, March/April 1864. Paroled 4/26/65 at Charles Town.

MURRY, JOHN: enl. 10/20/62 at Martinsburg in Co. B as Pvt. AWOL since 10/21/62, and dropped from the roll as a deserter, 12/10/62.

MUSGROVE, JOHN: b. 1825? 5′8″, fair complexion, blue eyes, fair hair. enl. 9/25/61 near Fairfax Court House in Co. B as Pvt. Absent sick since 12/15/63. Gen. Hosp. Charlottesville, 1/7/64. Furloughed 1/8/64. Charged $1.50 for lost accoutrements, Nov./Dec. 1863. Absent on detail as guard at Gen. Hosp. Lynchburg, 10/25/64. Present again March/April 1864. Last official entry shows him present, 4/30-10/31 1864. Gen. Hosp. Farmville, 2/25/65; dysentery. Paroled 4/23/65 at Mt. Jackson.

MYERS, AARON H.: b. 1839? Farmer. enl. 4/19/61 at Hedgesville in Co. E as Lt. Deserted 7/18/61.

MYERS, ALFRED: Unofficial source lists him in Co. B. d. between 9/9-10/24 1863 at Ft. Delaware.

MYERS, CROMWELL: b. 1827? Farmer. enl. 4/19/61 at Hedgesville in Co. E as Lt. Deserted 7/18/61.

MYERS, CROMWELL L.: b. 2/7/35. Tinner. enl. 4/19/61 at Hedgesville in Co. E as Pvt. POW at Kernstown, 3/23/62 (Ft. Delaware). Exchanged 8/5/62. d. 10/24/62; disease. bur. Hedgesville Cem., Hedgesville, W.Va.

MYERS, EVAN T.: enl. 4/16/62 near Mt. Jackson in Co. I as Pvt. Nurse at Gen. Hosp. Staunton, 7/16/62-1/13/63. Wded. in left thigh at Chancellorsville, 5/3/63. Gen. Hosp. Howard's Grove, Richmond, 5/10/63. To Staunton, 5/24/63. Present again Jan./Feb. 1864. POW at South Anna, 5/24/64 (Pt. Lookout, Elmira). Exchanged 10/29/64. d. 11/3/64 at Ft. Monroe, Va.; cause not stated.

MYERS, GEORGE N.: b. 2/16/43. Student. enl. 6/14/61 at Charles Town in Co. A as Pvt. MWIA at 1st Manassas, 7/21/61. d. 8/12/61 at Gen. Hosp. Culpeper Court House. bur. Edge Hill Cem., Charles Town, W.Va.

MYERS, JAMES: enl. 3/10/62 at Winchester in Co. E as Pvt. Only official entry shows him as a deserter, Sept./Oct. 1862.

MYERS, JAMES W.: b. 1842? Printer. enl. 4/18/61 at Charles Town in Co. A as Pvt. To Sgt. Nov./Dec. 1862. Wded. at Cedar Run, 8/9/62. Gen. Hosp. Charlottesville, 8/11/62. To Gen. Hosp. Lynchburg, 9/1/62. Present again by 10/31/62. POW at Spotsylvania, 5/12/64 (Pt. Lookout, Elmira). Exchanged 3/2/65. Jackson Hosp., Richmond, 3/7/65; debility. Furloughed 3/9/65 for 30 days. No further record.

MYERS, SAMUEL B.: b. 6/27/41. 5′6″, sandy complexion, gray eyes, sandy hair. Carpenter. enl. 4/18/61 at Charles Town in Co. A as Pvt. Absent sick at home 8/2/61-Sept./Oct. 1861. Present again Nov./Dec. 1861 and detailed as orderly to Col. Allen. Absent on detail as Post Master of 1st Division, 10/25/62-March/April 1863. Gen. Hosp. Charlottesville, 6/9-7/6 1864; debility. Last official entry shows him present, 4/30-10/31 1864. Paroled 4/24/65 at Winchester. d. 5/11/74. bur. Edge Hill Cem., Charles Town, W.Va.

NADENBOUSCH, JOHN QUINCY ADAMS: b. 10/31/24 in Berkeley Co. Miller. Capt. of Berkeley Border Guards, a pre-war militia Co. from Berkeley Co. To Capt., Co. D, 2nd Va. Inf., 5/3/61. Apptd. Col. 3/17/63, but to rank as such since 9/17/62. Absent on detail as provost marshal at Martinsburg, Nov./Dec. 1861-Jan./Feb. 1862. Wded. in groin at 2nd Manassas, 8/28/62. Assigned to command post at Staunton, 8/12/63. Resigned 4/12/64, "being permanently physically disabled for duty in the field with my regiment." d. 9/13/92. bur. Old Norborne Cem., Martinsburg, W.Va.

NASH, JAMES L.: Only record lists him in Co. G and states he was discharged 8/2/62.

NAUMAN, WILLIAM: enl. 4/16/62 at Winchester (sic) in Co. E as Pvt. Listed as deserter Sept./Oct. 1862. No further record.

NELSON, HENRY: b. Jan. 1836. Unofficial source shows him in Co. F. Alive in 1900.

NELSON, O. S.: Only record lists him in Co. C and says he was wded. at Port Republic, 6/9/62.

NELSON, PHILIP W.: b. 2/1/35. Attd. University of Virginia. Farmer. enl. 4/18/61 at Millwood in Co. C as Pvt. Elected Lt. 9/25/62. Absent sick sometime before 6/30/61. Present again July/Aug. 1861. Wded. at 2nd Manassas, 8/28/62. Returned to regt. 1/25/63. Signs roll as commanding Co., Jan./Feb. 1863; July/Aug.-Nov./Dec. 1863. Absent on detached service, 2/19-3/4 1864; duty not stated. Wded. in right shoulder at Spotsylvania, date not specific. Gen. Hosp. Charlottesville, 5/14-10/17 1864. Last official entry shows him present through 12/31/64 with him signing the roll as inspector and mustering officer for the regt. Surrendered at Appomattox. Postwar, farmer in Albermarle Co. d. 9/27/08 in Albermarle Co. bur. Grace Episcopal Church Cem., Crismont, Albermarle Co.

NELSON, WILLIAM N.: b. 1825. Farmer. Capt. of Nelson Rifles, a pre-war militia Co. from Clarke Co. To Capt., Co. C, 2nd Va. Inf., 5/3/61. Wded. in the left breast at 1st Manassas, 7/21/61. Wounded so severely he was unable to return to command his Co. Officially dropped from the Register of Commissioned Officers, 5/18/62. d. 1/12/94. bur. Old Chapel Cem., Millwood.

NEWLAND, JOSEPH F.: Unofficial source says he served in Co. E. Still living in Edinburg, July 1901.

NICELY, CHARLES A.: b. 7/1/43. Clerk. enl. 4/18/61 at Duffields in Co. H as Corp. Last official entry shows him present, Nov./Dec. 1861. d. 3/12/67. bur. Elmwood Cem., Shepherdstown, W.Va.

NICESWARNER (NISWANNER), WILLIAM A.: b. 1822? Butcher. enl. 4/18/61 at Berryville in Co. I as Pvt. Absent for 6/30/61 muster. Bayonet wound in arm and breast at 1st Manassas, 7/21/61. Present again by 8/31/61. AWOL 10/13-10/26 1861. Absent on detached service as butcher since May 1862. Deserted 12/1/62.

NICEWARNER, J. B.: enl. 4/18/62 at Rude's Hill in Co. B as Pvt. AWOL since 5/1/62 and dropped from the roll 12/10/62. No further record.

NICEWARNER, THOMAS: drafted 10/29/62 at Camp Allen in Co. C as Pvt. Deserted 11/22/62.

NICHOLS, FRANCIS M.: enl. 12/1/62 at Guinea's Station in Co. A as Pvt. Stuart Hosp., Richmond, 7/6/64; diarrhea. Jackson Hosp., Richmond, 7/29/64. Furloughed 7/29/64 for 30 days. Last official entry shows him present for 10/31/64 muster and states he was detailed to division Ord. train. No further record.

NICHOLSON, THOMAS A.: enl. 7/18/61 at Winchester in Co. D as Pvt. Absent on detail with surgeon to help attend sick at hosp., July/Aug. 1861. Present again Sept./Oct. 1861. Last official entry shows him present, Nov./Dec. 1861.

NICKOL, R.: Only official record lists him in Co. F and states he was wded. at Cedar Run, 8/9/62.

NIPE, JAMES P.: enl. 3/4/62 at Winchester in Co. E as Pvt. AWOL 6/3/62 at Woodstock. No further record.

NOEL, ISAAC: enl. 4/16/62 at Rude's Hill in Co. F as Pvt. Deserted 11/1 or 11/15 1862.

NOLAN, P. E.: Only record is a POW register that lists him in Co. G and states he was captured 1/24/62 at Blomery Gap and sent to Vicksburg for exchange, 11/22/62.

NOLAND, GEORGE WILLIAM: b. 1838. 5′7″, dark complexion, gray eyes, brown hair. Painter. Residence Jefferson Co. enl. 4/18/61 at Charles Town in Co. A as Pvt. To Corp. 8/5/61. To Sgt. 9/1/62. To Pvt. 10/31/63. POW at Spotsylvania, 5/12/64 (Pt. Lookout, Elmira). Exchanged 3/14/65. Paroled 4/22/65 at Winchester. d. before 1900 at Baltimore, Md.

NOLAND, GILMORE: b. 1824? Painter. Wded. in thigh at 1st Manassas, 7/21/61. Returned to regt. 10/20/61. Last official entry shows him present, Nov./Dec. 1861.

NOLAND, JAMES HENRY: b. 12/7/34. Machinist. enl. 4/18/61 at Charles Town in Co. G as Pvt. On duty at Col. Allen's headquarters, Sept./Oct. 1861. Last official entry shows him absent sick in hosp., Nov./Dec. 1861. Unofficial source states he served in medical dept. Postwar, member of Turner Ashby Camp #22 at Winchester. d. 12/7/98. bur. Edge Hill Cem., Charles Town, W.Va.

NOLAND, SAMUEL C.: b. 1/10/41. Farmer. enl. 4/18/61 at Charles Town in Co. A as Pvt. Gen. Hosp. #7, Richmond, 11/26/62; bronchitis. To private quarters at Camp Winder, 12/8/62. Present at 12/31/62 muster. Absent on detail as courier for Gen. Ewell, 6/16/63. Last official entry shows him still absent on this same detail with detail as courier, July/Aug. 1864. d. 9/28/06. bur. Edge Hill Cem., Charles Town, W.Va.

NORMAN, JOHN P.: 5'8", light complexion, hazel eyes, light hair. Residence Page Co. enl. 3/26/62 at New Market in Co. K as Pvt. First official entry shows him returning from AWOL, 2/21/63. POW Luray, July 1863 (Ft. Delaware): release date not given. POW at Martinsburg, 12/7/63 (Ft. Delaware). Oath of Allegiance to U.S., 5/11/65.

NULTON, JOSEPH ABRAHAM: b. 11/27/37. 5'8", light complexion, gray eyes, dark hair. m. Virginia Clark. Clerk. enl. 4/18/61 at Winchester in Co. F as Pvt. AWOL since 8/17/61. Present again Sept./Oct. 1861. Absent sick May/June 1863. Present again July/Aug. 1863. Last official entry shows him present, March/April 1864. Paroled 4/22/65 at Winchester. Postwar, Capt. of Winchester Light Infantry in 1880's; twice elected Clerk of Circuit Court in Frederick Co.; member of Turner Ashby Camp #22, Winchester. Son was Admiral Louis McCoy Nulton, U.S. Navy. d. 3/3/93. bur. Mt. Hebron Cem., Winchester.

NUNN, JOHN R.: enl. 3/10/62 at Winchester in Co. I as Pvt. To Lt. 1/7/63. Wded. at Malvern Hill, 7/1/62. Present again by 10/31/62. Wded. at Chancellorsville, 5/3/63. Gen. Hosp. #4, Richmond, 5/10/63. To Staunton, 6/13/63. Present again Sept./Oct. 1863. Detailed on 60 days light duty at Staunton, 11/1/63. Last official entry shows him still absent on detached duty, March/April 1864.

O'BANNON, GEORGE M. D.: b. 1844? Student. enl. 4/18/62 at Charles Town in Co. A as Pvt. To Corp., Nov./Dec. 1863. Reenlisted 4/18/62 in Co. I. AWOL Jan./Feb. 1864. Last official entry shows him present again, March/April 1864.

O'BANNON, HENRY C.: b. 1841? Miller. Residence Charles Town. enl. 6/14/61 at Charles Town in Co. A. Wded. in forearm at 2nd Manassas, 8/28/62. POW at Charles Town, 11/10/62 (Ft. McHenry). Paroled 11/12/62. Present again Nov./Dec. 1862. Gen. Hosp. Charlottesville, 1/6-1/8 1863; debility. Absent on detail to Gen. Ewell's headquarters, 6/16/63. Present again July/Aug. 1863. Absent on detail as guard at hosp. in Staunton, 10/3/63. Last official entry shows him still on detail as guard at hosp. in Staunton, March/April 1864. POW at Staunton, 9/26/64 (Pt. Lookout). Oath of Allegiance to U.S., 5/12/65.

O'BANNON, JAMES H.: b. 1840? 5'8", ruddy complexion, black eyes, dark hair. Printer. Residence Jefferson Co. enl. 4/18/61 at Berryville in Co. I as Corp. To Lt. 9/2/61. To Capt. 9/2/62. Absent sick Sept./Oct. 1861. Present again Nov./Dec. 1861. Absent on furlough Jan./Feb. 1863. Present again March/April 1863. Absent sick Jan./Feb. 1864. Present again March/April 1864. POW at Snicker's Gap, 7/25/64 (Old Capitol Prison, Ft. Delaware). Oath of Allegiance to U.S., 6/14/65.

O'BANNON, WILLIAM A.: b. 1843? Butcher. enl. 6/14/61 at Charles Town in Co. A as Pvt. AWOL 6 days in Dec. Last official entry shows him present, Nov./Dec. 1861. enl. 6/1/62 at Charles Town in Co. A, 12th Va. Cav. POW in Jefferson Co., 12/4/63 (Ft. Delaware). Oath of Allegiance to U.S., 6/19/65.

OBOUGH, GEORGE: Only official entry lists him in Co. G and says he was discharged 6/30-10/31 1862. d. 4/27/91 in Augusta Co.

O'CONNELL (O'CONNER), MICHAEL: enl. 12/24/61 at Camp Stevenson in Co. E as Pvt. Wded. in left shoulder at 1st Winchester, 5/25/62. Gen. Hosp. Charlottesville, 6/8/62. To Gen. Hosp. Lynchburg, 6/16/62. Wded. at Cedar Run, 8/9/62. Gen. Hosp. Charlottesville, 8/11/62. To Gen. Hosp. Lynchburg, 9/1/62. Present again by 10/31/62. Gen. Hosp. Farmville, 6/20/64; wound through achilles. To Lynchburg, 7/5/64. Last official entry shows him present again, 8/31-12/31 1864. Surrendered at Appomattox. bur. St. Joseph's Cem., Martinsburg, W.Va.

ODEN, ARCHIBALD: b. 1843? in Martinsburg. 5'7", dark complexion, dark eyes, dark hair. Clerk. enl. 4/20/61 at Harpers Ferry in Co. D as Pvt. Surgeon's discharge, 9/28/62; disability. bur. Old Norborne Cem., Martinsburg, W.Va.

OGDEN, RANDOLPH K.: b. 1843. Carpenter. enl. 6/14/61 at Charles Town in Co. A as Pvt. To Corp. 9/1/62. To Sgt. 10/31/63. Wded. in the hip at 1st Manassas, 7/21/61. Present again Sept./Oct. 1861. POW at Front Royal, 6/12/62. Paroled at Winchester, June 1862. Present again by 10/31/62 muster. POW at Winchester, 11/27/64 (Pt. Lookout). Released 6/16/65. d. 1904. bur. Greenhill Cem., Berryville.

OSBORN, R.: drafted 10/19/62 at Bunker Hill in Co. C as Pvt. Deserted 11/1/62 from Camp Allen.

OSBOURN, ALEXANDER LINK: b. 11/1/44. Farmer. enl. 4/18/61 at Duffields in Co. H as Pvt. Trans. to Co. D, 12th Va. Cav. d. 11/9/11 at Shenandoah Jct. bur. Elmwood Cem., Shepherdstown, W.Va.

OSBOURN, JAMES S. ALLEN: Unofficial source shows him in Co. H. d. 9/29/01. bur. Elmwood Cem., Shepherdstown, W.Va.

OSBOURN, NATHAN: b. 1820? Farmer. enl. 6/18/61 at Winchester in Co. B as Pvt. Absent sick July/Aug. 1861. Present again Sept./Oct. 1861. Last official entry shows him absent sick, March/April 1862.

OVERTON, JAMES W.: b. 1843? 5'9½", florid complexion, gray eyes, dark hair. Printer. Residence Shepherds-town. enl. 4/18/61 at Charles Town in Co. A as Pvt. POW at Kernstown, 3/23/62 (Ft. Delaware). Exchanged 8/5/62. POW at Spotsylvania, 5/12/64 (Pt. Lookout, Elmira). Oath of Allegiance to U.S., 5/17/65.

PADGETT, JAMES E.: enl. 10/1/62 at Bunker Hill in Co. H as Pvt: KIA at Wilderness, 5/5/64.

PADGETT, REUBEN: enl. 4/16/62 at Rude's Hill in Co. D as Pvt. AWOL since 9/19/62. Does not appear again until Nov./Dec. 1863 when he is shown as absent on detail as teamster at Brook's Furnace since 11/2/63. Last official entry shows him still absent on detail as teamster at Brook's Furnace, March/April 1864.

PAGE, RICHARD L.: b. 1840? Clerk. enl. 4/30/61 at Harpers Ferry in Co. G as Pvt. MWIA in arm and abdomen at 1st Manassas, 7/21/61. d. 7/26/61 at Gen. Hosp. at Pringle's House, Manassas.

PAGE, ROBERT POWELL: b. 3/12/38 in Clarke Co. grad. William & Mary. grad. Medical College of University of Va., 1860. Attd. University of Pa. and received M.D. from there in June 1861. Unofficial source says he was attached to Stonewall Brigade as Asst. Surgeon. Postwar, returned to Berryville and continued his practice as physician.

PAINTER, JAMES H.: b. 1841? Laborer. enl. 5/11/61 at Harpers Ferry in Co. G as Pvt. Wded. in the thigh at 1st Manassas, 7/21/61. Returned to regt. 10/1/61. Last official entry shows him present, Nov./Dec. 1861. d. 1910. bur. Greenhill Cem., Stephens City.

PAINTER, LEWIS: drafted 10/1/62 at Bunker Hill in Co. K as Pvt. Deserted 10/28/62.

PAINTER, RICHARD McS.: b. 1837? Carpenter. enl. 4/22/61 at Harpers Ferry in Co. D as Pvt. Deserted 7/26/63. POW (Rebel deserter) near Chambersburg, Pa., 7/28/63 (Ft. Mifflin). Released 10/13/63.

PANNILL, GEORGE D.: b. 1838? 5′6″, fair complexion, gray eyes, brown hair. enl. 2/12/64 at Orange Co. in Co. D as Pvt. Absent under arrest, Feb. 1864. Present again March/April 1864 and sentenced to 3 months hard labor in Corps Guardhouse for desertion. Sentence remitted 6/11/64. Last official entry shows him present, 8/31-12/31 1864. Paroled 5/15/65 at Strasburg.

PARE, JAMES. b. 1816? 5′9″, dark complexion, blue eyes, auburn hair. Residence Berkeley Co. enl. 10/4/62 at Bunker Hill in Co. E as Pvt. Gen. Hosp. #8, Richmond, 1/6/63; diarrhea. To Chimborazo #1, 2/18-3/23 1863; diarrhea. Present again March/April 1864. Deserted 7/18/63. POW (Rebel deserter) near Chambersburg, Pa., 7/28/63 (Ft. Mifflin). Oath of Allegiance to U.S., 12/21/63.

PARKENS, ALEXANDER: b. 1829? Actor. enl. 5/10/61 at Harpers Ferry in Co. C as Pvt. MWIA in left arm at 1st Manassas, 7/21/61. d. 8/7/61.

PARKER, D. M.: Unofficial source says he served in Co. F for four years.

PARKER, JOHN: Unofficial source says he served in Co. F for four years.

PARKER, THOMAS S.: b. 1840? Lawyer. enl. 4/18/61 at Harpers Ferry in Co. D as Pvt. AWOL 10/17/62, "gone to U.S." No further record.

PARKER, WILLIAM: b. 1836? Laborer. enl. 6/10/61 at Camp Jackson on Bolivar Heights in Co. C as Pvt. Absent sick since 11/9/61. Deserted 10/30/62 at Bunker Hill.

PARROTT, PHILIP H.: enl. 4/16/62 at Rude's Hill in Co. E as Pvt. Absent sick since 8/15/62. Next official entry shows him rejoining from desertion, Sept./Oct. 1863. AWOL March/April 1864. No further record.

PATTERSON, GEORGE W.: enl. 3/14/62 near Woodstock in Co. I as Pvt. Lovingston Hosp., Winchester, 8/14-9/6 1862; reason not stated. KIA at Payne's Farm, 11/27/63.

PATTERSON, JOHN T.: 5′7½″, florid complexion, blue eyes, auburn hair. Residence Decauter, Michigan. drafted. 10/3/62 at Bunker Hill in Co. F as Pvt. Absent sick since 6/13/63. Present again July/Aug. 1863. POW at Spotsylvania, 5/10/64 (Old Capitol Prison, Elmira). Oath of Allegiance to U.S., 6/14/65.

PAYNE, JOHN: enl. 3/15/62 at Winchester in Co. E as Pvt. AWOL Sept./Oct. 1862. No further record.

PAYNE, THOMAS: enl. 3/5/62 at Winchester in Co. E as Pvt. Gen. Hosp. Charlottesville, 5/3-6/11 1862; "old contusion." Absent sick, sent to hosp. 8/15/62. Shown as AWOL Jan./Feb.-Sept./Oct. 1863. Listed as deserter, 10/1/63. bur. Falling Waters Cem., Spring Mills, W.Va.

PENCE, HARRISON: enl. 4/16/62 at Rude's Hill in Co. F as Pvt. POW at Spotsylvania, 5/12/64 (Pt. Lookout, Elmira). d. 8/12/64 at Elmira; diarrhea. bur. Woodlawn Nat. Cem., Elmira, N.Y., grave #44.

PENDLETON, BENJAMIN S.: b. 3/28/42. Clerk. enl. 6/18/61 at Winchester in Co. B as Pvt. Absent on leave 10/31/62. Absent on detail as brig. orderly, 11/26/62-May/June 1863. Last official entry shows him present, 4/30-10/31 1864. Surrendered at Appomattox. d. 1/19/31. bur. Elmwood Cem., Shepherdstown, W.Va.

PENDLETON, JAMES ALBERT: b. 5/8/44. Printer. enl. 6/9/61 at Camp Jackson on Bolivar Heights in Co. A as Pvt. POW at Kernstown, 3/23/62 (Ft. Delaware). Exchanged 8/5/62. KIA at 2nd Manassas, 8/30/62. bur. Elmwood Cem., Shepherdstown, W.Va.

PENN, JAMES J.: Unofficial source says he served in Co. F for one year.

PENN, THOMAS F.: Only record says he was a POW that was captured at Shepherdstown, Sept. 1862, and paroled 9/27/62.

PEREGOY (PERRIGORE), WILLIAM R.: b. 1844. enl. 10/4/62 at Bunker Hill in Co. E as Pvt. Surrendered at Appomattox. d. 1926. bur. Harpers Cem., Harpers Ferry, W.Va.

PERKINS, W. H.: Residence Wheeling. Only record is a parole statement that lists him as a Pvt. Paroled 4/20/65 at Richmond.

PERROW, HARLOW: enl. 6/23/63 at New River in Co. H as Pvt. Only record says he trans. from 8th Va. Cav. and shows him present, 4/30-10/31 1864.

PERRY, VAN LEAR: b. 4/29/37 at Cumberland, Md. grad. Franklin-Marshall College and Jefferson Medical School. Physician. enl. 5/29/61 at Camp Jackson on Bolivar Heights in Co. G as Pvt. Charged $2.00 for pair of shoes received, 8/29/61. Promoted to Asst. Surg., 10/15/61 and trans. Served as surg. of 57th Va. Inf. Postwar, surgeon in West Indies. d. 10/26/69 in Nassau, West Indies. bur. Edge Hill Cem., Charles Town, W.Va.

PERVEIL (PERVEILL), LEIGHTON: b. 1839? Tobacconist. enl. 5/1/61 at Harpers Ferry in Co. F as Pvt. AWOL since 8/23/61. Present again Sept./Oct. 1861. Last official entry shows him present, Nov./Dec. 1861. Next record lists him as a deserter who was arrested in Dept. of Henrico, 8/13/62. Unofficial source says he was arrested at Charlotte, N.C. and returned to Co. at Winchester. No official record of his service beyond Nov./Dec. 1861.

PETERFISH, ANDREW JACKSON: b. 3/12/43. Light complexion, blue eyes, dark hair. Laborer. Residence Rockingham Co. enl. 4/16/62 at Rude's Hill in Co. F as Pvt. Deserted 4/18/62. POW (Rebel deserter) Dept. of W.Va., 1/25/64. Oath of Allegiance to U.S., 1/25/64. d. 4/16/13. bur. St. Peter's Union Church Cem., Elkton.

PETTIT, ALLEN: b. 1840? Carpenter. enl. 5/1/61 at Harpers Ferry in Co. F as Pvt. Last official entry shows him absent sick in hosp. at Winchester, Nov./Dec. 1861.

PHILLIPS, SIMON: b. Shenandoah Co. drafted 4/14/62 at Rude's Hill in Co. K as Pvt. Wded. in arm at 2nd Manassas, date not specific. Present again by 10/31/62. KIA at Chancellorsville, 5/3/63.

123

PHILLIPS, WILLIAM: b. 1830. Tailor. enl. 4/18/61 at Martinsburg in Co. D as Pvt. Surgeon's discharge, 5/12/61; crippled in leg. d. 12/17/97. bur. Greenhill Cem., Martinsburg, W.Va.

PHILLIPS, WILLIAM: drafted 4/14/62 at Rude's Hill in Co. K as Pvt. Last official entry shows him present, March/April 1864.

PIET, AMBROSE: b. 1841 in Perry Co., Missouri. Dark complexion, dark eyes, dark hair. Farmer. enl. 11/1/61 at Centerville in Co. D as Pvt. Surgeon's discharge, 7/25/62; "ulcers on right leg from hip to ankle."

PIFER, WILLIAM: enl. 4/15/62 at Rude's Hill in Co. A as Pvt. KIA at 2nd Manassas, 8/28/62. Claim to C. S. government says $65.01 due for his services.

PIFER, WILLIAM F.: enl. 4/18/62 at Rude's Hill in Co. K as Sgt. Absent sick May 1862-2/25/63. Discharged 2/2/63 (sic). Unofficial source says he possibly joined Co. C, 11th Va. Cav. d. 2/7/97 in Missouri.

PIKE, FRANCIS H.: enl. 3/4/62 at Winchester in Co. E as Pvt. POW at Kernstown, 3/23/62 (Ft. Delaware). Exchanged 8/5/62. Wded. in lung at 2nd Manassas, 8/28/62. Present again May/June 1863. Last official entry shows him present, 8/31-12/31 1864. Surrendered at Appomattox.

PINE, DANIEL: enl. 3/3/63 at Camp Winder in Co. C as Pvt. Absent sick 4/25/63. Chimborazo #1, 5/4/63; typhoid fever. d. 5/15/63 at Chimborazo #1; typhoid.

PINE, J.: Only record lists him in Co. I and says he was KIA at 2nd Manassas, date not specific.

PINE, NATHAN H.: b. 1839? Bricklayer. enl. 4/20/61 at Harpers Ferry in Co. I as Pvt. Absent sick July/Aug. 1861. Present again Sept./Oct. 1861. Wded. at 2nd Manassas, 8/28/62. Last official entry says he deserted 6/15/63.

PIPER, GEORGE W.: enl. 9/14/61 at Charles Town in Co. K as Pvt. Last official entry shows him AWOL, Nov./Dec. 1861. Next record shows him as POW near Harpers Ferry, date not given. Paroled at Warrenton, 11/12/62. No further record.

PIPER, JOHN R.: b. 6/8/32. Laborer. enl. 4/21/61 at Harpers Ferry in Co. D as Pvt. Last official entry shows him present, Nov./Dec. 1861. d. 1/22/70. bur. Old Norborne Cem., Martinsburg, W.Va.

POISAL, JACOB: enl. 11/30/61 at Camp Stevenson in Co. E as Pvt. Only official entry shows him present, Dec. 1861.

POLK, SIMON: enl. 4/16/62 at Rude's Hill in Co. F as Pvt. Absent sick and sent to hosp. from Bunker Hill, 10/11/62. d. 9/18/62 (sic) at hosp. in Martinsburg; disease.

POLLARD, E. W.: enl. 4/16/62 at Winchester in Co. E as Pvt. "Assigned and never reported." No further record.

POPE, CHARLES W.: b. 1834? Druggist. enl. 4/20/61 at Harpers Ferry in Co. K as Sgt. Chimborazo #3, 11/5/61; debility. Last official entry shows him present, Nov./Dec. 1861.

POPE, JOHN M.: b. 1831. 5'9", dark complexion, hazel eyes, black hair. enl. 3/11/62 at Winchester in Co. I as Pvt. AWOL 5/30-9/12 1862. Wded. in right shoulder at Payne's Farm, 11/27/63. Chimborazo #5, 11/30/63. To Staunton, 1/18/64. To Gen. Hosp. Charlottesville, 6/25-7/15 1864. Paroled 4/13/65 at Winchester. d. 12/31/92. bur. Greenhill Cem., Berryville.

POPE, WASHINGTON: b. 1843? 5'6", dark complexion, blue eyes, dark hair. Laborer. Residence Clarke Co. enl. 4/18/61 at Charles Town in Co. A as Pvt. Gun stock intentionally broken sometime before 6/30/61. AWOL 7 days Nov./Dec. 1861. AWOL 5/15-9/15 1862. Gen. Hosp. Charlottesville, 4/26-5/8 1863; pleuritis. AWOL since 6/16/63. Present again July/Aug. 1863. POW at Clarke Co., 7/17/64 (Wheeling, Camp Chase). d. 12/23/64 at Camp Chase. bur. at Camp Chase, grave #655.

POPE, WILLIAM H.: b. 1841? 5'10", fair complexion, brown eyes, light hair. Laborer. Residence Clarke Co. enl. 6/2/61 at Camp Jackson on Bolivar Heights in Co. A as Pvt. Wded. at 1st Winchester, 5/25/62. Present 6/30-10/31 1862. POW at Clarke Co., 2/9/63 (Wheeling, Camp Chase). Exchanged 3/28/63. Absent sick at Staunton Hosp., 6/1/63. Present again July/Aug. 1863. POW at Spotsylvania, 5/12/64 (Pt. Lookout, Elmira). Released 6/21/65.

PORTERFIELD, CHARLES A.: enl. 10/4/62 at Bunker Hill in Co. E as Pvt. Wded. by shell at Fredericksburg, 12/13/62. Present again by 12/31/62. Charged $36.00 for losing gun, Nov./Dec. 1863. Last official entry shows him present, March/April 1864.

PORTERFIELD, JACOB M.: enl. 10/4/62 at Bunker Hill in Co. E as Pvt. Last official entry shows him present, March/April 1864.

POTTS, A. A.: Unofficial source says he served in Co. F.

POTTS, JOHN L. (or M.): enl. 12/4/62 at Fredericksburg in Co. H as Pvt. Gen. Hosp. Lynchburg, 4/19/63. d. at Lynchburg hosp., date and cause not stated. bur. City Cem. (Old Methodist Cem.), Lynchburg.

POWELL, LLOYD F.: b. 1835. Clerk. enl. 6/15/61 at Winchester in Co. F as Pvt. KIA at 1st Manassas, 7/21/61. bur. Christ Church, Alexandria.

PRATER, DENTON: enl. 10/1/62 at Bunker Hill in Co. H as Pvt. AWOL since 10/4/62. No further record.

PRATT, THOMAS W.: b. 1841? Farmhand. enl. 4/18/61 at Berryville in Co. I as Pvt. AWOL 7/27-8/2 1861. AWOL since 6/1/62. No further record.

PRICE, SAMUEL J.: enl. 5/10/63 at Camp Winder in Co. K as Pvt. POW in Md., location and date not stated. Paroled 6/24/63. Present again July/Aug. 1863. POW on Rapidan River, 10/1/63 (Old Capitol Prison). Oath of Allegiance to U.S., date not given; remained in Washington, D.C.

PRINCE, GIDEON: enl. 4/9/62 at Winchester in Co. E as Pvt. Wded. at Port Republic, 6/9/62. Wded. at Gaines's Mill, 6/27/62. Listed as AWOL May/June-Sept./Oct. 1863. Final entry shows him as a deserter, Nov./Dec. 1863.

PRINCE, WILLIAM: enl. 4/9/62 at Winchester in Co. E as Pvt. Deserted Sept./Oct. 1862.

PRITCHARD, WILLIS: enl. 3/17/62 at Cedar Creek in Co. I as Pvt. AWOL since 5/24/62 and dropped from the roll, Nov./Dec. 1862.

PROPHIT, J. K.: b. 1828? 6'0", dark complexion, gray eyes, black hair. Laborer. Residence Shenandoah Co. POW in Shenandoah Co., 6/13/62 (Wheeling, Camp Chase). d. 9/3/62 at Camp Chase, cause not stated.

PROPST, JOEL: enl. 4/15/62 at Rude's Hill in Co. G as Pvt. Deserted 6/20/62 at Waynesboro. Recovered from desertion 3/27/63. Sentenced by court-martial to forfeit all pay and allowances through 3/30/63. POW at Salem Church, 5/20/64 (Pt. Lookout, Camp Chase). d. 6/26/64 at Camp Chase; gastro enterites.

124

PRYOR, JOHN: b. 1842? Stone mason. enl. 6/20/61 at Martinsburg in Co. E as Pvt. POW at Kernstown, 3/23/62 (Ft. Delaware). Exchanged 8/5/62. Wded. at 2nd Manassas, 8/30/62. Gen. Hosp. Charlottesville, 12/7/62-1/25/63; wounded thigh. Present again Jan./Feb. 1863. Gen. Hosp. Camp Winder, 5/9/63; bronchitis. To Staunton, 6/5/63. POW 7/27/63, location not stated; "wishes to take oath." No further record. bur. St. Joseph's Cem., Martinsburg, W.Va.

PUGH, J. H.: Unofficial source says he served in this regt. d. 6/26/64. bur. Hollywood Cem., Richmond.

PULLEN, WILLIAM G.: b. 1843. Unofficial source shows him serving in this regt. d. 1907. bur. Hollywood Cem., Richmond.

PULLER, BUSHROD: b. 1832? Laborer. enl. 4/18/61 at Millwood in Co. C as Pvt. Absent sick 4/18-6/30 1861. Present again July/Aug. 1861. AWOL 9/1/61. Discharged 11/9/61; reason not stated.

PURCELL, MORDECAI F.: enl. 3/8/62 at Winchester in Co. I as Pvt. Sent to hosp. 4/10/62 and "not heard from since." No further record.

PURCELL, WILLIAM: Unofficial source lists him in Co. B. d. 5/3/62. bur. Thornrose Cem., Staunton.

PYLE, THOMAS N.: b. 1838? Cooper. enl. 4/29/61 at Co. I as Pvt. AWOL 7/18-8/24 1861. Fined $11.00 for absence by court-martial. AWOL 10/15-10/24 1861. AWOL 12/25-12/30 1861. AWOL 5/26-9/10 1862. Deserted 7/16/63.

PYLE, WILLIAM FRANKLIN: b. 1842. enl. 9/10/62 at Martinsburg in Co. I as Pvt. Sentenced by court-martial to have 3 month's pay taken from him, Feb. 1863; reason for sentence not stated. Gen. Hosp. Lynchburg, 4/19/63. Discharged from hosp., June 1863. Listed as deserter, Nov./Dec. 1863. d. 11/19/22. bur. Old Chapel Cem., Millwood.

RACEY, MORGAN: b. 1843? 5' 10", fair complexion, gray eyes, light hair. Laborer. enl. 4/29/61 at Harpers Ferry in Co. I as Pvt. AWOL 7/27-8/2 1861. AWOL 11/23-11/28 1861. POW at Brandy Station, 8/1/63 (Old Capitol Prison, Pt. Lookout). Exchanged 12/24/63. Returned to regt. 1/8/64. Absent on detached duty, Jan./Feb. 1864; duty not stated. Last official entry shows him present, March/April 1864. Paroled 5/9/65 at New Creek.

RAMSBURG, GEORGE: b. 12/3/35. enl. 10/1/62 at Bunker Hill in Co. H as Pvt. AWOL since 10/15/62 at Bunker Hill. No further record. d. 1/1/97. bur. Greenhill Cem., Martinsburg, W.Va.

RANDOLPH, ROBERT CARTER, JR.: b. 7/14/40. Farmer. enl. 4/18/61 at Millwood in Co. C as Lt. Absent sick since 9/6/61. Present again Nov./Dec. 1861, and signs roll as commanding Co. at 12/31/61 muster. Signs roll as commanding Co. at 12/31/61 muster. Signs roll as commanding Co. at 10/31/62 muster. Absent sick since 2/16/63. Present again March/April 1863. Wded. at Chancellorsville, 5/3/63. Gen. Hosp. Charlottesville, 6/5/63. To Staunton, 6/16/63. Gen. Hosp. Charlottesville, 8/6/63. To Danville, 8/15/63. Returned to regt. from hosp., 1/20/64. KIA at Cedar Creek, 10/19/64. bur. Old Chapel Cem., Millwood.

RANDOLPH, THOMAS HUGH BURWELL: b. 4/5/43. 6' 2", light complexion, blue eyes, light hair. Student. Residence Millwood. enl. 4/18/61 at Millwood in Co. C as Corp. To Lt., date not stated. Wded. in left breast at 1st Manassas, 7/21/61. Returned to regt. from sick leave, 12/3/61. Absent on detail on Gen. Pendleton's staff, 5/1-Nov./Dec. 1862. POW along Rappahannock River, 12/5/62 (Old Capitol Prison). Exchanged 3/29/63. Next official record shows him as a POW in Clarke Co., 10/26/63 (Wheeling, Camp Chase, Johnson's Island). Paroled 6/12/65 from Johnson's Island. d. 4/25/00. bur. Old Chapel Cem., Millwood.

RANDOLPH, WILLIAM WELFORD: b. 2/20/37 in Clarke Co. Attd. University of Virginia. Laborer. enl. 6/1/61 at Camp Jackson on Bolivar Heights in Co. C as Pvt. Elected Capt. 4/20/62. To Lt. Col. 4/26/64. Absent with leave at 6/30/61 muster. Absent on recruiting detail, 8/2-11/19 1861. Absent on special duty, 10/26-11/9 1862; duty not stated. Absent with leave to serve in Va. Legislature, 9/1/63-3/12/64. KIA at Wilderness, 5/5/64. bur. Old Chapel Cem., Millwood.

RANSON, THOMAS DAVIS: b. 5/19/43 at Charles Town. Attd. Washington College. Student. enl. 4/18/61 at Charles Town in Co. G as Pvt. Trans. 8/16/61 to Co. I, 52nd Va. Inf. Wded. severely at Cross Keys, 6/8/62. After recovering from wounds, served as scout for 12th Va. Cav. In 1863-1864, Capt. in charge of scouts in the secret service dept. Reported directly to Generals Stuart and Lee. Also served as aide to Generals Edward Johnson and William L. Jackson. Postwar, grad. University of Pa.; lawyer at Staunton; m. 1) Mary Fontaine Alexander in 1871; 2) Janetta Ravenscroft Harrison; 3) Margaret Fisher Warren in 1900. Alive in 1912.

RAWLINS, DOLPHIN T.: b. 1841 in Jefferson Co. Printer. enl. 4/18/61 in Co. A as Pvt. To Corp. 11/25/61. To Sgt. 7/1/62. KIA at Chancellorsville, 5/3/63.

RAWLINS, FAYETTE W.: b. 1839? Painter. enl. 5/9/61 at Harpers Ferry in Co. G as Pvt. Wded. severely by shell at Fredericksburg, 12/13/62. Gen. Hosp. #11, Richmond, 12/19/63. Gen. Hosp. #21, Richmond, 2/20/63. Gen. Hosp. #1, Richmond, 4/9/63. Still absent and declared unfit for duty, July/Aug. 1863. Detailed to QM, 11/2/63. Last official entry still shows him absent on detail to QM, Sept./Oct. 1864.

RAWLINS, JOSEPH E.: b. 1844? Printer. enl. 6/9/61 at Camp Jackson on Bolivar Heights in Co. A as Pvt. Wded. at 2nd Manassas, 8/28/62. Absent sick in Richmond hosp., 12/23/62. Returned to regt. 2/13/63. Charged $.70 for wasting 14 rounds of ammunition, Jan./Feb. 1864. Last official entry shows him present, March/April 1864. Chimborazo #5, 5/23/64; wound in right leg. (Probably Wded. at Salem Church, 5/20/64.) Furloughed 5/28/64 for 60 days. Assigned to light duty at headquarters, Valley District, 12/3/64, due to disability. No further record.

RAY, JOHN: b. 1845 in Jefferson Co. Shoemaker. m. Mary Ellen Funk. enl. 6/15/61 at Camp Whiting in Co. B as Pvt. To Corp. 12/1/62. Absent sick Jan./Feb. 1862. Present again 6/30-10/31 1862. Gen. Hosp. Richmond, 5/18/64; wound in left thigh. Furloughed 7/9/64 for 30 days. POW at New Market, 9/24/64 (Pt. Lookout). Exchanged 3/17/65. No further record. Postwar, member of Turner Ashby Camp #22, Winchester. d. 10/23/05. bur. Mt. Hebron Cem., Winchester.

RAY, SAMUEL H.: b. 1838? Carpenter. enl. 4/18/61 at Halltown in Co. B as Pvt. To Lt. 11/18/62. Signs roll as commanding Co. as 2nd Sgt. at 10/31/62 muster. Absent with leave Sept./Oct. 1863. Present again Nov./Dec. 1863. Surrendered at Appomattox.

REARDON, JOHN: b. 1842? Laborer. enl. 4/25/61 at Harpers Ferry in Co. C as Pvt. Absent sick at 10/31/62 muster. Returned to regt. from hosp., 11/10/62. POW at Spotsylvania, 5/12/64 (Pt. Lookout, Elmira). d. 9/13/64 at Elmira; diarrhea. bur. Woodlawn Nat. Cem., Elmira, N.Y.; grave #252.

REASER, W. H.: Only record lists him in Co. G and says he was MWIA in back and buttocks at 2nd Manassas, 8/30/62. d. 8/31/62.

RECTOR, EDWARD W.: b. 1838? Clerk. enl. 4/18/61 at Charles Town in Co. G as Pvt. Absent on special duty in commissary dept., 4/18-6/30 1861. Last official entry shows him still absent on special duty in commissary dept., Nov./Dec. 1861.

REDMAN, WILLIAM R.: Only record is a POW statement that lists him in Co. A as Lt. POW 1/7/65 at Baltimore; "Rebel officer and spy." (Old Capitol Prison, Alexandria). "Alias Jackson Wallace. Alias Jerry Bissell." No further record.

REED, GEORGE W.: b. 1843? 5'3", light complexion, blue eyes, light hair. Silversmith. enl. 6/9/61 at Harpers Ferry in Co. D as Pvt. Surgeon's discharge, 9/9/61; reason not stated.

REED, JAMES M.: b. 1844? 5'8", dark complexion, blue eyes, red hair. Printer. Residence Martinsburg. enl. 6/5/61 at Harpers Ferry in Co. D as Pvt. POW at Strasburg, 6/2/62. Exchanged 8/5/62. POW Kelly's Ford, 11/8/63 (Old Capitol Prison). Released on oath of amnesty, 3/15/64.

REED, JOHN J.: b. 1834? Lawyer. enl. 4/18/61 at Halltown in Co. B as Pvt. Discharged 10/12/61, reason not stated.

REED, WILLIAM B.: b. 1842? Farmer. enl. 6/5/61 at Charles Town in Co. H as Pvt. Wded. at 2nd Manassas, date not specific. Wded. at Fredericksburg, 12/13/62. Gen. Hosp. #23, Richmond, 12/19/62. To Gen. Hosp. #20, Richmond, 1/1/63. Gen. Hosp. Camp Winder, Richmond, 4/3/63; bronchitis. To Staunton, 4/22/63. Absent on detached service, May/June 1863-Sept./Oct. 1863; duty not stated. AWOL since 11/4/63. No further record.

RIANHART, J.: enl. 4/16/62 at Rude's Hill in Co. F as Pvt. Deserted 4/18/62 from Rude's Hill.

RICAND, BENJAMIN R.: b. 1816? Tailor. enl. 4/29/61 at Harpers Ferry in Co. I as Pvt. Absent tending to a sick man, Nov./Dec. 1861. Present again 4/30-10/31 1862. Last official entry shows him present, 8/31-12/31 1864. No further record.

RICE, GEORGE R.: b. 1842 in Montgomery Co., Md. Unofficial source shows him in this regt. Postwar, farmer at Travillah, Md.

RICHARDS, CHARLES H.: b. 1827? Saddler. enl. 4/18/61 at Millwood in Co. C as Pvt. KIA at Chancellorsville, 5/3/63.

RICHARD, JAMES R.: b. 2/21/28. Residence Shepherdstown. enl. 6/20/63 near Sharpsburg, Md. in Co. B as Musician. Last official entry shows him absent in hosp. at Lynchburg, 4/30-10/31 1864. Paroled 4/14/65 at Lynchburg. d. 8/26/09. bur. Elmwood Cem., Shepherdstown, W.Va.

RIDDLE, JOHN N.: b. 1845. enl. 7/10/63 at Darkesville in Co. E as Pvt. KIA near New Market, 9/24/64. bur. Old Norborne Cem., Martinsburg, W.Va.

RIDER, JOHN WILLIAM: b. 4/1/40. Teacher. enl. 4/18/61 at Charles Town Co. G as Pvt. Appears as Sgt. at 10/31/62 muster. Wded. in arm and chest at Harpers Ferry, 10/16/61. Wded. at 1st Winchester, 5/25/62. Gen. Hosp. Mt. Jackson, 6/1/62. Present again by 10/31/62. Detailed as Sgt. in charge of ambulances, May/June 1863-March/April 1864. Last official entry shows him present, 4/30-10/31 1864. Surrendered at Appomattox. d. 12/31/23 at Halltown. bur. Edge Hill Cem., Charles Town, W.Va.

RIDGEWAY, SAMUEL: drafted 10/3/62 at Bunker Hill in Co. G as Pvt. Deserted 11/20/62.

RIELEY (RILEY), CHARLES B.: b. 1822? Laborer. enl. 6/16/61 near Charles Town in Co. I as Pvt. AWOL 7/27-8/4 1861. AWOL since 12/25/61. POW at Kernstown, 3/23/62 (Ft. Delaware). Exchanged 8/5/62. KIA at 2nd Manassas, 8/28/62.

RIELEY, JOHN J.: b. 1833? Painter. enl. 6/15/61 near Charles Town in Co. I as Pvt. AWOL since 12/25/61. AWOL since 3/23/62. No further record.

RIGGLE, GEORGE: b. 1836? Coach trimmer. enl. 4/18/61 at Berryville in Co. I as Pvt. KIA at Gaines's Mill, 6/27/62.

RIGGLE, JOHN W.: b. 1839? Miller. enl. 4/18/61 at Berryville in Co. I as Pvt. AWOL 8/4-8/14 1861. Fined $11.00 for absence by court-martial. Absent sick Nov./Dec. 1861. POW at Bruceville, 6/17/62. Exchanged 8/5/62. Present again by 10/31/62 muster. Deserted 7/18/63.

RIGHTSTINE, ADAM: enl. 10/10/62 at Bunker Hill in Co. B as Pvt. Absent sick 5/31/63. Last official entry shows him still absent sick, March/April 1864.

RILEY, JAMES: enl. 4/14/62 at New Market in Co. H as Pvt. AWOL since 6/7/62. No further record.

RILEY, LESTER WILLIAM: b. 8/27/16 in Clarke Co. enl. 3/5/62 at Winchester in Co. C as Pvt. Deserted 9/1/63. d. 8/1/06 at White Post.

RINEAL, EVERHART: b. 1824? Carpenter. enl. 4/18/61 at Martinsburg in Co. D as Corp. Discharged from service for ill health before 6/30/61 muster.

RINKER, J. F.: b. 1837. enl. 4/16/62 at Rude's Hill in Co. F as Pvt. Deserted from Rude's Hill, 4/18/62. d. 11/8/06 at Middletown. bur. Mt. Carmel Cem., Middletown.

RINKER, J. W.: enl. 4/16/62 at Rude's Hill in Co. F as Pvt. Deserted from Rude's Hill, 4/18/62.

RIPPON, JOHN J.: enl. 7/1/61 at Darkesville in Co. I as Pvt. AWOL 11/23-12/1 1861. AWOL since 5/30/62 and dropped from the roll, Nov./Dec. 1862. No further record.

RISSCHER, J. A.: Only record lists him in Co. E and states he was wded. at Cedar Run, 8/9/62.

RISSLER, GEORGE L.: b. 10/11/27 in Frederick Co. 5'10½", florid complexion, blue eyes, brown hair. Farmer. enl. 4/18/61 at Charles Town in Co. G as Pvt. AWOL since 12/19/61. No further record. d. 7/20/16. bur. Edge Hill Cem., Charles Town, W.Va.

RISSLER, SAMUEL J. (or L.): b. 9/30/30. 5'9", dark complexion, brown eyes, dark hair. drafted 12/4/62 at Guinea's Station in Co. G as Pvt. Detailed as ambulance driver for 2nd Regt., 12/14/62-July 1864. POW near Harpers Ferry, 7/2/64 (Old Capitol Prison, Elmira). Exchanged 3/10/65. Paroled 4/19/65 at Charles Town. d. 9/3/05. bur. Edge Hill Cem., Charles Town, W.Va.

RITENHOUR, NOAH D.: enl. 4/9/62 at Rude's Hill in Co. E as Pvt. Wded. in hand at Fredericksburg, 12/13/62. Gen. Hosp. Charlottesville, 12/15/62-3/4/63. Absent on detail in Richmond, 4/1/63; duty not stated. Absent on detail until discharged March/April 1864 "on account of wound."

RITTER, JACOB: b. 1828? Miller. enl. 4/18/61 at Millwood in Co. C as Fifer. AWOL since 6/27/61. Trans. to Newtown Cav., Col. Stewart commanding, Sept./Oct. 1861.

RITTER, SAMUEL: b. 1817? Farmer. enl. 4/18/61 at Millwood in Co. C as Pvt. Wded. in breast, neck, and arm at 1st Manassas, 7/21/61. Still absent from wounds, Nov./Dec. 1861. Next official record shows him wded. 7/2/62 (sic) near Malvern Hill. Last official entry shows him still absent from wound, 8/31-12/31 1864. d. 9/9/99.

ROBERTS, WILLIAM: b. 1821 in Berkeley Co. 5'9", dark complexion, blue eyes, dark hair. Farmer. enl. 4/16/62 at Rude's Hill in Co. D as Pvt. Discharged 12/8/62, overage.

ROBERTSON, MYRTILLO STEPTOE BRENT: b. 5/29/26. Tailor. enl. 4/18/61 at Charles Town in Co. A as Sgt. Absent on detail guarding baggage wagons, 10/7/61. Present again Nov./Dec. 1861. Detailed as commissary Sgt., 10/10/62. Last official entry shows him present and still on detail as commissary Sgt., 4/30-10/31 1864. Paroled at Farmville, date not specific. d. 2/16/86 at Charles Town, W.Va.

ROBEY, JOHN N.: enl. 4/15/62 at Rude's Hill in Co. A as Pvt. Gen. Hosp. Staunton, 4/15/63; typhoid fever. Deserted 7/18/63. Oath of Allegiance to U.S., 8/14/63; "then began working in Franklin County, Pa."

ROBINSON, FREDERICK M.: b. 1831? Tailor and postal worker in Charles Town. enl. 5/9/61 at Harpers Ferry in Co. G as Pvt. AWOL since 12/27/61. Gen. Hosp. #13, Richmond, 10/31-11/15 1862; rheumatism. Gen. Hosp. Camp Winder, Richmond, 11/17-11/27 1862; acute diarrhea. Absent on detail with extra baggage, Jan./Feb.-May/June 1863. Absent on detail with Ord. train, May/June-8/6/63. AWOL 2/1-3/20 1864. Chimborazo #5, 3/12/64; gonorrhea. To Chimborazo #2, 4/10/64. To Farmville, 5/5/64. To Chimborazo #4, 5/19-9/20 1864. Last official entry shows him present again by 10/31/64. POW (Rebel deserter) at Brandy Station, 4/6/65. Took oath and sent to New York City.

ROBINSON, ISRAEL: b. 1819. Unofficial source says he served in Co. D as Sgt. d. 10/25/63 at Richmond.

ROBINSON, JAMES B.: b. 3/27/37. Farmer. enl. 5/15/61 at Harpers Ferry in Co. H as Pvt. Last official entry shows him present, Nov./Dec. 1861. d. 6/22/85. bur. Elmwood Cem., Shepherdstown, W.Va.

ROBINSON, JOHN: b. 1817? 5' 11", fair complexion, blue eyes, brown hair. enl. 4/14/62 near New Market in Co. H as Pvt. Discharged 11/18/62, overage.

ROCKWELL, GEORGE F.: enl. 3/8/62 at Winchester in Co. E as Pvt. Elected Lt. 4/8/63. Signs roll as commanding Co., Jan./Feb. 1864. Last official entry shows him present, March/April 1864. Paroled 4/26/65 at Winchester.

RODEFFER, SAMUEL: enl. 4/18/62 at Rude's Hill in Co. B as Pvt. AWOL 6/30-10/31 1862. Listed as a deserter and dropped from the rolls, 12/10/62.

RODEHEFFER, JOHN: enl. 4/15/62 at Rude's Hill in Co. A as Pvt. Absent on detached duty in the Valley District, 1/1/63. Present again May/June 1863. AWOL since 7/25/63. POW (Rebel deserter), place of capture not stated; "sent north via New Creek."

RODES, J. A.: Only record is a parole statement that lists him in Co. I as Pvt. Paroled 5/20/65 at Staunton.

RODGERS, L. T.: Only record is a parole statement that lists him in Co. B. Paroled June 1862 at Winchester.

RODGERS, PATRICK: b. 1818? Laborer. enl. 4/18/61 at Millwood in Co. C as Pvt. Discharged 4/25/62.

ROGERS, J. P. G.: Residence Berkeley Co. 5' 11½ ", dark complexion, blue eyes, dark hair. enl. 5/12/62 at Gordonsville in Co. D as Pvt. Wded. at Gettysburg, date not specific. Chimborazo #1, 7/29-8/24 1863; wounded. POW at Kelly's Ford, 11/8/63 (Old Capitol Prison, Ft. Delaware). Oath of Allegiance to U.S., 6/14/65.

RONEMOUSE, LEWIS: b. 1826? Farmer. enl. 4/18/61 at Duffields in Co. H as Pvt. Last official entry shows him present, Nov./Dec. 1861.

RONEMOUSE, WILLIAM: b. 1817? Farmer. enl. at Duffields in Co. H, date not given. Listed AWOL at both 6/30 and 8/31 musters. No further record.

ROOTS, MARTIN V.: enl. 4/16/62 at Rude's Hill in Co. D as Pvt. MWIA at 2nd Manassas, 8/29/62. d. 9/2/62 at Aldie.

ROW, JOHN: enl. 4/18/62 at Rude's Hill in Co. B as Pvt. Absent sick at 4/30/62 muster. Deserted 6/20/62.

ROWAN, JOHN W.: b. 8/3/10. 5' 10", dark complexion, blue eyes, black hair. Mason. Capt. of Co. K, 2nd Battalion, Va. Regt. U.S. Army, Mexican War. Capt. of Jefferson Guards, a prewar militia Co. from Jefferson Co., since May, 1858. To Capt. of Co. A, 2nd Va. Inf., 5/3/61. Wded. in the ankle at 1st Manassas, 7/21/61. Still absent at home in Charles Town, Nov./Dec. 1861. Absent sick at Charles Town since 9/15/62, "complaining of wound received at Manassas." Present again Jan./Feb. 1863. Retired to Invalid Corps, 4/26/64 because of wound. Assigned to Staunton where he assisted Provost Marshal. Paroled 4/30/65 at Staunton. d. 12/24/72. bur. Edge Hill Cem., Charles Town, W.Va.

ROWE, AMOS: b. in Augusta Co. 5'8", fair complexion, gray eyes, dark hair. Shoemaker. enl. 4/15/62 at Rude's Hill in Co. G as Pvt. Permanently disabled by accidental wound, 5/1/62. Discharged by Medical Board, 3/31/63; valvular disease of the heart.

ROWE, EDWARD: enl. 8/26/61 at Camp Harman in Co. H as Pvt. Last official entry shows him present, Nov./Dec. 1861.

ROWE, OLIVER J.: b. 1833. Listed in Co. F. On regular muster roll of the Winchester Riflemen but he disregarded the summons to service.

ROY, RICHARD R.: b. 1840? in Marion Co. 5' 6", light complexion, blue eyes, light hair. Farmhand. enl. 4/29/61 at Harpers Ferry in Co. I as Pvt. AWOL 10/15-10/24 1861. AWOL 12/27-12/30 1861. Wded. at Kernstown, 3/23/62. Discharged 12/21/63 due to wounds received at Kernstown.

ROYSTON, MATHEW: b. 1836? Carpenter. enl. 4/18/61 at Millwood in Co. C as Pvt. AWOL since 10/1/61. AWOL since 12/28/61. No further record. Postwar, carpenter.

ROYSTON, WILLIAM P.: Listed in Co. C as Pvt. Only record shows him AWOL 4/17/62 and says he joined Capt. Myers's Cav.

RUCKER, HENRY: Unofficial source lists him in Co. E. d. 8/2/06.

RUNKLE, CHARLES E.: enl. 4/16/62 at Rude's Hill in Co. F as Pvt. To Corp., date not given. Wded. at Port Republic, 6/9/62. Present again Jan./Feb. 1863. Absent sick March/April-July/Aug. 1863. Present again Sept./Oct. 1863. POW at Spotsylvania, 5/12/64 (Pt. Lookout, Elmira). d. 9/16/64 at Elmira of continued fever. bur. Woodlawn Nat. Cem., Elmira, N.Y.

RUNKLE, JACOB W.: b. 1835. enl. 4/16/62 at Rude's Hill in Co. F as Pvt. Deserted from Rude's Hill, 4/18/62. d. May 1895.

RUPERT, SAMUEL: Only record shows him in Co. G and says he deserted at New Market, 6/4/62.

RUSHBUSH, SAMUEL: enl. 4/15/62 at Rude's Hill in Co. G. d. 5/17 or 5/22 1862 of disease. Claim states he was from Augusta Co.

RUSMISELL, G. B.: b. 1829? 5' 11", dark complexion, gray eyes, dark hair. enl. 10/15/64 at Richmond in Co. C as Pvt. Last official entry shows him present at 12/31/64 muster. Paroled 5/15/65 at Staunton.

127

RUSSELL, JOHN: enl. 10/31/61 at Centerville in Co. G as Pvt. Sent home sick in Feb. Recovered from illness, but never returned to regt. Listed as a deserter at 10/31/62 muster.

RUST, HENRY D.: b. 1833? Carpenter. enl. 4/18/61 at Charles Town in Co. A a Sgt. To Pvt. 7/1/62. Wded. in arm and foot at 2nd Manassas, 8/28/62. At hosp. in Lynchburg since 11/20/62. Gen. Hosp. Liberty, 12/13/62. Present again Sept./Oct. 1863. Wded. in hand and thumb at Payne's Farm, 11/27/63. Last official entry shows him still absent from wound, March/April 1864. bur. Zion Episcopal Cem., Charles Town, W.Va.

RUST, THOMAS G.: b. 1839. 5' 4", dark complexion, blue eyes, dark hair. Carpenter. Residence Harpers Ferry. enl. 4/18/61 at Charles Town in Co. A as Pvt. POW at Spotsylvania, 5/12/64 (Pt. Lookout, Elmira). Oath of Allegiance to U.S., 5/20/65. d. 1908. bur. Edge Hill Cem., Charles Town, W.Va.

RUST, WILLIAM: b. 1840? Carpenter. enl. 4/21/61 at Harpers Ferry in Co. D as Pvt. Last official entry shows him present, Nov./Dec. 1861.

RUTHERFORD (RETHERFORD), GEORGE W.: b. 3/18/42. Printer. enl. 6/6/61 at Harpers Ferry in Co. D as Pvt. Last official entry shows him present, Nov./Dec. 1861. d. 4/4/14. bur. Old Norborne Cem., Martinsburg, W.Va.

RUTHERFORD, GERARD DAVID: b. 1841? 5'8", dark complexion, hazel eyes, brown hair. Farmer. Residence Jefferson Co. enl. 4/18/61 at Charles Town in Co. A as Pvt. Absent sick at home in Jefferson Co., Nov./Dec. 1861. Last official entry says he deserted, 5/31/62. When captured at Petersburg, however, he is listed in Co. D, 12th Va. Cav. POW at Petersburg, 10/29/62 (Wheeling, Camp Chase). Exchanged 12/2/62. No further record.

RUTHERFORD, JOHN A.: b. 1843? Carpenter. enl. 4/18/61 at Duffields in Co. H as Pvt. Last official entry shows him present, Nov./Dec. 1861.

RUTHERFORD, THOMAS W.: b. 1838? Laborer. enl. 4/20/61 at Duffields in Co. H as Pvt. Wded. in arm at 2nd Manassas, 8/28/62. Absent sick at home Nov./Dec. 1862-Nov./Dec. 1863. AWOL 2/1/64. No further record.

RUTTER, EDWIN M.: b. 1838? 5' 7¼ ", light complexion, dark brown eyes, dark brown hair. Coach painter. Residence Clarke Co. enl. 4/26/61 at Harpers Ferry in Co. I as Pvt. Absent sick Sept./Oct. 1861. Present again Nov./Dec. 1861. Gen. Hosp. Charlottesville, 12/2/62-1/26/63; pneumonia. Wded. in left leg at Payne's Farm, 11/27/63. Chimborazo #4, 11/29/63. Present again 4/30-10/31 1864. POW at Burkesville, 4/6/65 (Pt. Lookout). Oath of Allegiance to U.S., 6/17/65.

RUTTER, GEORGE W.: b. 1808? Tailor. enl. 4/18/61 at Millwood in Co. C as Drummer. Last official entry shows him absent on detail to cut mens' clothing, Nov./Dec. 1861.

RYAN, ISAAC: 5' 7½ ", sallow complexion, blue eyes, dark hair. Residence Winchester. enl. 4/16/62 at Rude's Hill in Co. F as Pvt. To Corp., date not given. POW at Middletown, 6/5/62. Exchanged 8/5/62. POW at Spotsylvania, 5/12/64 (Pt. Lookout, Elmira). Oath of Allegiance to U.S., 6/19/65.

RYAN, PATRICK: Only record lists him in Co. G as a substitute for David Reeves. KIA at Port Republic, 6/9/62.

RYAN, PATRICK: b. 1828? Laborer. enl. 6/4/61 at Camp Jackson on Bolivar Heights in Co. K as Pvt. To Corp., date not given. POW at Kernstown, 3/23/62. Exchanged 8/5/62 or Oath of Allegiance to U.S. at Ft. Delaware, 8/10/62. No further record.

RYMAN, JOHN: drafted 4/18/62 at Rude's Hill in Co. C as Pvt. Wded. in foot at 2nd Manassas, 8/28/62. Absent from wound and he returned to regt., 4/6/64. POW at Spotsylvania, 5/12/64 (Pt. Lookout). Exchanged 3/15/64. No further record. d. Dec. 1893 in Shenandoah Co.

RYMAN, MOSES: drafted 4/13/62 at Camp Winder in Co. G as Pvt.; "conscript from Shenandoah Co." Absent sick at hosp., 6/1-Nov./Dec. 1863. Deserted 5/10/64.

SADLER, JOHN N.: b. 11/26/29. enl. 6/1/62 at Winchester in Co. G as Pvt. Absent sick, captured at Charles Town, and paroled by 10/31/62. Absent sick at Staunton hosp., Jan./Feb.-5/24/63. Gen. Hosp. Staunton, 1/24/63; typhoid fever. Gen. Hosp. Staunton, 4/13/63; phthisis. Gen. Hosp. Charlottesville, 8/5/63; pneumonia. To Lynchburg, 9/21/63. Returned from sick leave, 10/3/63. Wded. in neck at Payne's Farm, 11/27/63. Chimborazo #3, 11/30/63. To Staunton, 12/8/63. Listed as unfit for active service, Sept./Oct. 1864. On "duty" at Gen. Hosp. #9, Richmond, 1/23/65. No further record. d. 1/18/95. bur. Zion Episcopal Cem., Charles Town, W.Va.

SADLER, LEONARD L.: b. 4/16/32. Merchant. enl. 6/14/61 at Charles Town in Co. A as Pvt. Last official entry shows him absent sick, Nov./Dec. 1862. No further record. d. 9/22/98. bur. Zion Episcopal Cem., Charles Town, W.Va.

SAGER, MORRIS: enl. 4/14/62 at New Market in Co. H as Pvt. AWOL since 6/1/62. No further record.

SALES, RICHARD: b. 1841? Laborer. enl. 6/6/61 at Harpers Ferry in Co. D as Pvt. d. 8/31/61 in hosp. near Camp Harman; typhoid fever.

SALMES, F.: Only record lists him as a substitute in Co. I and says he deserted in a few days.

SAMPSON, HENRY: Unofficial source says he enlisted in Co. F, Oct. 1861.

SAMPSON, WILLIAM J.: 5' 6", dark complexion, dark eyes, dark hair. Residence Harrisonburg. enl. 4/16/62 at Rude's Hill in Co. A as Pvt. POW at Spotsylvania, 5/12/64 (Pt. Lookout, Elmira). Oath of Allegiance to U.S., 6/27/65.

SANBORN, JOHN J.: b. 1841? Teacher. enl. 4/18/61 at Charles Town in Co. G as Pvt. Lost one bayonet sometime before 6/30/61. Fined $11.00 by court-martial, 8/15/61; reason not stated. Last official entry shows him present, Nov./Dec. 1861.

SANDY, JOHN H.: enl. 4/18/62 at Rude's Hill in Co. B as Pvt. Wded. at 2nd Manassas, 8/28/62. Absent from wounds through Jan./Feb. 1863. Present again March/April 1863. Charged $1.50 for lost accoutrements, Nov./Dec. 1863. Last official entry shows him present, 4/30-10/31 1864.

SANDY, TILMON: enl. 4/18/62 at Rude's Hill in Co. B as Pvt. Gen. Hosp. Charlottesville, 1/19-3/14 1863; acute diarrhea. Last official entry shows him present, March/April 1864. Next record shows him retiring in Invalid Corps, 1/17/65, and being assigned to a Gen. Hosp. at Harrisonburg. No further record.

SAPPINGTON, GEORGE W.: b. 1827? Laborer. enl. 4/18/61 at Duffields in Co. H as Pvt. To Corp. Aug. 1861. To Sgt. 11/22/61. To Lt. 4/20/62. Wded. at Kernstown, 3/23/62 and still absent from wounds at 10/31/62 muster. Dismissed from C.S.A. service, 12/16/62; reason not stated.

SAUM, ELIAS: b. 7/20/20. drafted 4/14/62 at Rude's Hill in Co. K as Pvt. POW at Woodstock, 6/2/62. Exchanged 8/5/62. Discharged before 10/31/62, overage. d. 3/28/98. bur. Saumsville Christian Church Cem., Saumsville, Shenandoah Co.

128

SAUM, WILLIAM: drafted 4/14/62 at Rude's Hill in Co. K as Pvt. d. 5/30/62 in hosp. at Charlottesville; typhoid fever.

SAVILLE, ALBERT: enl. 8/12/62 at Gordonsville in Co. D as Pvt. KIA at 2nd Manassas, 8/28/62.

SAVIN, EDWARD: b. 1834? Laborer. enl. 4/20/61 at Harpers Ferry in Co. K as Pvt. Deserted 5/13/61.

SCARLET, JOHN W.: enl. 9/4/61 at Charles Town in Co. K as Pvt. AWOL Nov./Dec. 1861. No further record.

SCHMIDT, CONRAD: b. 1823? Laborer. enl. 4/20/61 at Harpers Ferry in Co. B as Pvt. Discharged before 10/31/62 (date not specific); overage.

SCOTT, MICHAEL: b. 1838? enl. 4/20/61 at Harpers Ferry in Co. K as Pvt. Deserted 9/20/61.

SECRIST, CHARLES N.: enl. 4/18/62 at Rude's Hill in Co. B as Pvt. Absent sick since 4/13/63. Present again May/June 1863. POW at Spotsylvania, 5/12/64 (Pt. Lookout, Elmira). d. 10/6/64 at Elmira; chronic diarrhea. bur. Woodlawn Nat. Cem., Elmira, N.Y.; grave #571.

SEIBERT, JOSEPH M.: 5' 9", dark complexion, dark eyes, dark hair. Residence Edinburg. enl. 4/14/62 at Rude's Hill in Co. B as Pvt. Wded. at 2nd Manassas, 8/28/62. Absent from wounds through Jan./Feb. 1863. Present again March/April 1863. POW at Spotsylvania, 5/12/64 (Pt. Lookout, Elmira). Oath of Allegiance to U.S., 6/27/65.

SEIGLER, SOLOMAN: enl. 4/9/62 at Winchester in Co. E as Pvt. Assigned to Co. but never reported.

SELDON (SELDEN), JOHN: b. 2/24/22 in Loudoun Co. 6' 0", florid complexion, blue eyes, light brown hair. enl. 4/18/61 at Charles Town in Co. G as Pvt. Absent sick since 8/1/61. Discharged 12/5/61, "unfit for duty." d. 1/8/96. bur. Zion Episcopal Cem., Charles Town, W.Va.

SHAFFER, HENRY: b. 1826? 5' 8", dark complexion, blue eyes, gray hair. enl. 4/16/62 at Winchester in Co. E as Pvt. AWOL 5/20/62-1/6/63. AWOL 7/15/63. No further entries. Paroled 4/19/65 at Winchester.

SHAFFER, H. I.: Unofficial source lists him as serving two years in Co. F as Pvt.

SHANER, ALEXANDER J.: b. 1/27/28. Carpenter. enl. 4/18/61 at Halltown in Co. B as Pvt. Absent with leave at 6/30/61 muster. Present again July/Aug. 1861. AWOL since 5/15/62. No further record. d. 9/26/20. bur. Elmwood Cem., Shepherdstown, W.Va.

SHANER, SEBASTION: Only record is his final parole that lists him in Co. B. Paroled 5/31/65 at Campbell.

SHANK, J. W.: enl. 4/9/62 at Winchester in Co. E as Pvt. Wded. at Port Republic, 6/9/62. AWOL since 8/1/62 at Gordonsville. No further record.

SHANK, PHILIP: enl. 4/9/62 at Winchester in Co. E as Pvt. AWOL since 6/15/62 at Brown's Gap. No further record.

SHANK, W. J.: enl. 4/9/62 at Winchester in Co. E as Pvt. AWOL 6/9/62 at Brown's Gap. No further record.

SHARFF, JACOB K.: b. 3/2/24. Laborer. enl. 4/18/61 at Duffields in Co. H as Pvt. Detailed as cook with surgeon, Nov./Dec. 1862. Surrendered at Appomattox. d. 3/1/11. bur. Episcopal and Masonic Cem., Middleway, W.Va.

SHARFF, PETER: b. 1/30/38. enl. 10/4/62 at Bunker Hill in Co. E as Pvt. Only entry shows him present at 10/31/62 muster. No further record. d. 5/4/16. bur. Greenhill Cem., Martinsburg, W.Va.

SHARRER, GEORGE: b. 1828? Carpenter. enl. 4/18/61 at Martinsburg in Co. D as Pvt. Deserted 5/18/61. Arrested 6/30/61 and in custody. No further record.

SHAY, WILLIAM: Residence Woodstock. enl. 2/1/63 at Camp Winder in Co. K as Pvt. Substitute for Isaac Marshall. Wded. in middle third of front right thigh at Payne's Farm, 11/27/63. Robertson Hosp., Richmond, 11/29/63. Furloughed 5/3/64 for 60 days from Robertson Hosp. Chimborazo #3, 9/8-9/12 1864; debility. Retired to Invalid Corps, 9/9/64 and stationed at Harrisonburg. No further record.

SHEA, J. M.: Listed in Co. C as Pvt. Only entry shows him AWOL 4/17/62 at Winchester. No further record.

SHEADRICK, THEODORE: Listed in Co. G as Pvt. Only entry says he was detailed as cook for officer's mess, Nov./Dec. 1862. No further record.

SHEARER, JAMES MADISON: b. 7/30/35. Wheelwright. enl. 4/18/61 at Millwood in Co. C as Pvt. AWOL since 10/1/61. Present again Nov./Dec. 1861. No record again until he is shown as wded. at Gettysburg, date not specific. No further record. d. 7/27/94. bur. Old Chapel Cem., Millwood.

SHEARER, PHILIP: b. 7/27/43. "Boy." enl. 4/18/61 at Millwood in Co. C as Pvt. AWOL since 10/20/61. Present again Nov./Dec. 1861. Wded. at Gettysburg, 7/2/63. Absent from wounds through March/April 1864. POW at Salem Church, 5/20/64 (Old Capitol Prison, Ft. Delaware). Exchanged 2/27/65. Gen. Hosp. #9, Richmond, 3/2/65. No further record. d. mid-Sept., 1906.

SHEARER, WILLIAM CHIPLEY: b. 8/23/33. Merchant. enl. 4/18/61 at Charles Town in Co. G as Sgt. Shown as Lt. 4/30-10/31 1862. To Capt. May/June 1863, to rank as such from 9/17/62. Wded. at 2nd Manassas, date not specific. Present again by 10/31/62 muster. Absent with leave, Jan./Feb. 1864. Present again March/April 1864. Wded. at Cedar Creek, 10/19/64. Paroled 5/25/65 at Charles Town. d. 8/13/73. bur. Zion Episcopal Cem., Charles Town, W.Va.

SHEETZ, DANIEL H.: b. 1843? 5' 6", fair complexion, dark eyes, dark hair. drafted at Rude's Hill in Co. K as Sgt. POW at Spotsylvania, 5/12/64 (Pt. Lookout, Elmira). Exchanged 10/11/64. No further record. Paroled 4/29/65 at Winchester.

SHEETZ, DANIEL W.: drafted 4/14/62 at Rude's Hill in Co. K as Pvt. Absent sick and sent to hosp., 8/11/62. Still absent sick in hosp., May/June 1863. Listed as AWOL, July/Aug. 1863. Last official entry still shows him AWOL, March/April 1864. No further record.

SHEETZ, GEORGE W.: 5' 6", dark complexion, blue eyes, dark hair. Residence Woodstock. drafted 4/16/62 at Rude's Hill in Co. K as Pvt. Absent sick and sent to hosp., 12/23/62. Chimborazo #1, 2/17-4/16 1863; typhoid fever. POW at Spotsylvania, 5/12/64 (Pt. Lookout, Elmira). Oath of Allegiance to U.S., 6/27/65.

SHEETZ, JOSEPH L.: b. 1819? 5' 10", dark complexion, dark eyes, dark hair. Millwright. enl. 4/16/62 at Rude's Hill in Co. B as Pvt. AWOL 8/1-8/20 1862. Absent sick before 10/31/62-Nov./Dec. 1862. Present again Jan./Feb. 1863. Discharged 4/8/63, overage.

SHEETZ, SAMUEL W.: enl. 4/15/62 at Rude's Hill in Co. G as Pvt. Wded. severely at Gaines's Mill, 6/27/62. Shown as absent from wound through March/April 1863. AWOL 4/30-9/14 1863. Sentenced by court-martial to have all clothing allowances deducted for time of absence. POW at Spotsylvania, 5/12/64 (Pt. Lookout, Elmira). d. 3/1/65 at Elmira, congestion of lungs. bur. Woodlawn Nat. Cem., Elmira, N.Y., grave #224.

SHEETZ, WILLIAM L.: drafted 4/14/62 at Rude's Hill in Co. K as Pvt. Absent sick 5/2/62-4/5/63. POW at Spotsylvania, 5/12/64 (Pt. Lookout, Elmira). d. 2/12/65 at Elmira; chronic diarrhea. bur. Woodlawn Nat. Cem., Elmira N.Y., grave #2018.

SHEETZ, WILLIAM W.: enl. 4/8/62 at Rude's Hill in Co. G as Pvt. Deserted from Winchester 5/24/62. Recovered from desertion 9/8/63. Sentenced by court-martial to 1 year's hard labor. Sentence remitted by order of Gen. Lee. Last official entry shows him present, 4/30-10/31 1864. Surrendered at Appomattox.

SHEFFLER, JEREMIAH B.: b. 1832? Coach maker. enl. 4/18/61 at Halltown in Co. B as Pvt. To Corp. 12/1/62. POW while on furlough, March/April 1862. Exchanged 8/5/62. Gen. Hosp. Charlottesville, 6/8/64; wounded arm. Furloughed 7/29/64. No further record.

SHEIG, GEORGE: b. 5/11/38. Shoemaker. enl. 4/18/61 at Martinsburg in Co. D as Pvt. Last official entry shows him present, Nov./Dec. 1861. d. 11/14/20. bur. Greenhill Cem., Martinsburg, W.Va.

SHEPHERD, ABRAHAM S.: b. 3/21/36. Farmer. enl. 5/22/61 at Camp Jackson in Co. A. Discharged 6/6/61 "on account of being a captain in the 55th Regiment militia in Jefferson County and being ordered on duty by Col. John T. Gibson, commanding said regiment of militia." Unofficial source shows him also in Co. F, 17th Va. Cav. Wded. at 3rd Winchester, 9/19/64. d. 11/5/07. bur. Elmwood Cem., Shepherdstown, W.Va.

SHEPHERD, ALEXANDER H.: b. 1831. Farmer. enl. 4/18/61 at Duffields in Co. H as Pvt. d. 9/25 or 9/26 1861 at hosp. at Camp Harman; typhoid fever. bur. Shepherd Burial Ground, Shepherdstown, W.Va.

SHEPHERD, DECATUR J.: b. 11/15/32. enl. 8/6/61 at Camp Harman in Co. I as Pvt. To Sgt., date not given. Wded. at Cedar Run, 8/9/62. Gen. Hosp. Charlottesville, 8/11/62. Furloughed 9/18/62. Absent on detached service with Capt. William Nelson, conscript officer, Valley District, May/June-Sept./Oct. 1863. Absent on detached service, Nov./Dec. 1863-March/April 1864; duty not stated. No further record. d. 8/19/05. bur. Mt. Hebron Cem., Winchester.

SHEPHERD, EDWARD CLARENCE: b. 1836? 5'8", light complexion, blue eyes, light hair. grad. V.M.I. enl. 10/22/61 at Centerville as Pvt. Elected Lt. 4/18/62. Court-martialed for cowardice at 2nd Manassas, 10/28/62, and cashiered from the service. Went home to Jefferson Co. after the sentence. When Confederates approached his home in June 1863, he went to Baltimore. Arrested at Baltimore, 6/29/63 (Ft. McHenry, Ft. Delaware, Johnson's Island). Oath of Allegiance to U.S., 5/19/65. Postwar, mathematics professor at Frederick, Md. College. d. 8/29/07 at Frederick, Md.

SHEPHERD, FRANKLIN R.: b. 1844? 5'8", light complexion, gray eyes, brown hair. enl. 3/17/62 near Cedar Creek in Co. I as Pvt. POW at Gettysburg, 7/4/63 (Ft. McHenry, Ft. Delaware, Pt. Lookout). Exchanged 2/18/65. Paroled 4/24/65 at Winchester.

SHEPHERD, H. SMITH: b. 1838? Clerk. enl. 6/18/61 at Winchester in Co. B as Pvt. Detailed to attend to sick in hosp. at Gettysburg, 7/4/63. POW at Gettysburg, 7/3/63 (sic) (U.S. Gen. Hosp., West Buildings, Baltimore; debility). Oath of Allegiance to U.S., 3/16/65.

SHEPHERD, JAMES W.: b. 1842. Farmer. enl. 6/9/61 at Harpers Ferry in Co. A as Pvt. AWOL 12/26-12/30 1861. Re-enlisted in Cav. sometime before 10/31/62. Unofficial source says he served in Co. F, 17th Va. Cav. Wded. at 3rd Winchester, 9/19/64. d. 1/26/94. bur. Edge Hill Cem., Charles Town, W.Va.

SHEPHERD, ROBERT: enl. 2/15/62 at Winchester in Co. H as Pvt. d. 5/4/62 in hosp. at Lynchburg; pneumonia.

SHEPHERD, WILLIAM C.: b. 1842? Farmer. enl. 4/18/61 at Berryville in Co. I as Pvt. To Corp. 8/13/61. POW at Kernstown, 3/23/62 (Ft. Delaware). Exchanged 8/5/62. Wded. at Cedar Run, 8/9/62. Last official entry shows him still absent from wounds received at Cedar Run, Nov. 1862. No further record.

SHEPHERD, WILLIAM H.: b. 1829? 5'8", fair complexion, hazel eyes, brown hair. enl. 6/20/61 at Harpers Ferry in Co. H as Pvt. Farmer. Residence Berkeley Co. POW at Ft. Steadman near Petersburg, 3/25/65 (City Point, Pt. Lookout). Oath of Allegiance to U.S., 6/20/65.

SHEPPARD, H.: Residence Henrico Co. Only record is a parole statement that lists him in Co. A as Pvt. Paroled 4/24/65 at Ashland.

SHERRARD, JOSEPH HOLMES, JR.: b. 11/15/35 in Winchester. 5' 10½", florid complexion, blue eyes, light hair. m. 1) Rachael Primrose Cameron. 2) Miss Cochran of Staunton. Prewar, attd. Judge Brockenbrough's Law School in Lexington, 1860-1861. Lawyer. enl. 6/15/61 at Winchester in Co. F as Pvt. Wded. slightly at 1st Manassas, 7/21/61. Last official entry shows him absent sick, Nov./Dec. 1861. Discharged 2/10/62, reason not stated. Unofficial source says he became a clerk for C. S. government in Staunton and Richmond. enl. in Co. H, 11th Va. Cav. and was promoted Lt., 9/24/62. In command of this Co., Jan./Feb. 1863. Wded. June 1863. Gen. Hosp. Charlottesville, 6/15-8/5 1863. Gen. Hosp. Lexington, 4/1/64. POW at Saylor's Creek, 4/6/65 (Old Capitol Prison, Johnson's Island). Oath of Allegiance to U.S., 5/30/65. d. 11/20/06.

SHEWBRIDGE, JOHN H.: b. 1831. Blacksmith. enl. 6/18/61 at Winchester in Co. I as Pvt. Absent sick at 6/30/61 muster. Present again July/Aug. 1861. AWOL 12/27-12/30 1861. AWOL 9/25/62. No further record. Appears on rolls of Co. D, 12th Va. Cav. d. 1/27/03. bur. Greenhill Cem., Berryville.

SHIERY, GIDEON: b. 1841? Printer. enl. 5/15/61 at Harpers Ferry in Co. H as Pvt. Discharged 5/23/62, reason not given.

SHIFLET, P.: enl. 4/16/62 at Rude's Hill in Co. F as Pvt. Deserted 4/28/62 from Rude's Hill.

SHIPE, BENJAMIN: enl. 3/17/62 near Cedar Creek in Co. I as Pvt. Absent sick at 10/31/62 muster. AWOL since 11/22/62. No further record.

SHIPE, JOHN R.: b. 1833? Boatman. enl. 6/19/61 near Winchester in Co. I as Pvt. AWOL 8/25/61. Fined $11.00 for absence by court-martial. Present again Sept./Oct. 1861. POW at Ashby's Gap, 7/21/63 (Pt. Lookout). Exchanged 3/3/64. Present again 4/30-10/31 1864. Last official entry shows him present at 12/31/64 muster. Surrendered at Appomattox.

SHIPE, WILLIAM G.: b. 11/27/30. 5'4½", dark complexion, brown eyes, black hair. Residence Frederick Co. enl. 5/11/61 at Harpers Ferry in Co. C as Pvt. Absent on detail as nurse at Chimborazo #4, 12/12/62. Remained on this detail until he deserted 12/6/64. POW (Rebel deserter) who came into Federal lines at Williamsburg, date not specific (Ft. Monroe). Oath of Allegiance to U.S., 12/30/64. d. 6/24/97. bur. Pine Grove Cem., near Siler, Frederick Co., Va.

SHIRLEY, JOHN J.: b. 2/1/31. Laborer. enl. 4/21/61 at Duffields in Co. H as Pvt. AWOL 7/3-10/15 1861. Last official entry shows him present, Nov./Dec. 1861. d. 7/24/96. bur. Uvilla Methodist Cem., Uvilla, W.Va.

SHOBER, CHARLES: 5'6", dark complexion, blue eyes, dark hair. Residence Martinsburg. enl. 4/4/62 at Winchester in Co. D as Pvt. POW at Rockville, Md., 7/14/64 (Old Capitol Prison, Elmira). Oath of Allegiance to U.S., 6/30/65.

SHORES, JOHN T.: b. 1835? Cooper. enl. 6/19/61 near Winchester in Co. I as Pvt. Deserted 7/3/61.

SHORT, B. F.: enl. 4/9/62 at Winchester in Co. E as Pvt. Assigned and never reported.

SHOULTZ, _____. enl. 5/1/62 near Port Republic in Co. I as Pvt. Deserted 6/1/62.

SHOVER, JACOB: drafted 4/14/62 at Rude's Hill in Co. K as Pvt. MWIA in back at 2nd Manassas, 8/28/62. d. at hosp. at Aldie, no date given.

SHROUDD, KILLIAN: enl. 3/1/62 at Winchester in Co. G as Pvt. Chimborazo #3, 5/5-9/16 1864; chronic diarrhea and rheumatism. Also shown as detailed to Chimborazo #3 as ward master. Last official entry shows him still absent on detail in Richmond hosp., Sept./Oct. 1864.

SHROUDD, SHADRACH: enl. 3/6/62 in Co. G as Pvt. Last official entry shows him present, Nov./Dec. 1862.

SHRUM, MARTIN L.: 5'7", fair complexion, gray eyes, dark hair. drafted 4/6/62 at Rude's Hill in Co. C as Pvt. Absent sick 6/30-10/31 1862. Returned to regt. 11/1/62. Absent on detached service, Jan./Feb.-3/25 1863; duty not stated. Wded. at Chancellorsville, 5/3/63. Returned to regt. from hosp., 7/25/63. Wded. in head at Spotsylvania, 5/12/64. POW at Spotsylvania, 5/12/64 (Old Capitol Prison, Ft. Delaware). Paroled 4/25/65 in Rockingham Co.

SHRYOCK, JACOB: b. 10/27/28. drafted 11/1/62 at Opequon in Co. F as Pvt. Trans. to Co. D, 48th Va. Inf., March/April 1863. Deserted about 7/14/63. d. 3/21/92. bur. Greenhill Cem., Stephens City.

SHUMATE, CUMBERLAND G.: enl. 4/18/61 in Co. I. Detailed to special duty in telegraph office at Harpers Ferry, 4/18-6/30 1861. Left the Co. when relieved from this duty sometime before 6/30/61. No further record.

SHUTTERS, AARON: b. 1826? in Shenandoah Co. 5'10½", florid complexion, gray eyes, dark hair. enl. 4/18/62 at Rude's Hill in Co. B as Corp. To Pvt., date not given. AWOL 5/25/62-2/13/63. Discharged March/April 1863, reason not stated.

SIBERT, JOSEPH W.: Unofficial source lists him in Co. B Still living in Edinburg in June 1901.

SIBERT, ONESINUS: enl. 4/16/62 at Rude's Hill in Co. F as Pvt. In Cav. without proper authority, 4/30-10/31 1862. Recovered from desertion 2/1/63. Gen. Hosp. Staunton, 4/13/63; typhoid fever. Present again May/June 1863. MWIA at Gettysburg, 7/3/63. d. 7/9/63 at U.S. Gen. Hosp. at Gettysburg.

SILER, JOHN W.: enl. 8/30/61 at Camp Harman in Co. D as Pvt. POW at Kernstown, 3/23/62 (Ft. Delaware). Exchanged 8/5/62. Present again by 10/31/62. Deserted 7/26/63.

SIMMONS, JOSEPH C.: b. 1838? Clerk. enl. 5/6/61 at Harpers Ferry in Co. D as Pvt. Wded. severely in thigh at 1st Manassas, 7/21/61. Gen. Hosp. Charlottesville, 7/24-8/5 1861. Discharged 12/27/61, reason not stated.

SIMPSON, FRANK A.: b. 10/26/41. enl. 7/17/61 in Co. A as Pvt., location not stated. To Corp. 8/1/61. Wded. at Port Republic, 6/9/62. Present before 10/31/62 muster. Absent on detached service, 1/1-March/April 1863; duty not stated. Present again May/June 1863. Last official entry shows him present, March/April 1864. No further record. d. 9/18/71. bur. Elmwood Cem., Shepherdstown, W.Va.

SIMPSON, WILLIAM S.: b. 1839? Clerk. enl. 4/18/61 at Winchester in Co. F as Pvt. To Corp. 8/1/61. Absent sick since 10/15/61. Last official entry shows him present again, Nov./Dec. 1861.

SINGLETON, A. CALDWELL: b. 1838? enl. 5/1/61 at Winchester in Co. F as Pvt. AWOL since 8/25/61. Present again Sept./Oct. 1861. Last official entry shows him present, Nov./Dec. 1861.

SINGLETON, ODEDIAH W.: enl. 3/6/62 in Co. F as Pvt. To Corp., date not given. Mt. Jackson Hosp., June 1862; bilious fever. Present by 10/31/62 muster. Gen. Hosp. #1, Richmond, 5/4/63; bronchitis. Trans. to private quarters, 5/14/63. Returned to regt. 8/15/63. POW at Spotsylvania, 5/12/64 (Pt. Lookout, Elmira). d. 12/26/64 at Elmira; gangrene of the lungs. bur. Woodlawn Nat. Cem., Elmira, N.Y.; grave #1207.

SKINNER, WILLIS: b. 1843? Laborer. enl. 4/20/61 at Harpers Ferry in Co. K as Pvt. To Corp., date not given. Absent sick at hosp. at Camp Harman, July/Aug. 1861. Present again Sept./Oct. 1861. KIA at Chancellorsville, 5/3/63.

SLAUGHTERY, JOHN: b. 1840? Laborer. enl. 4/20/61 at Harpers Ferry in Co. K as Pvt. Deserted 8/8/61 from Camp Harman.

SLIFER, GEORGE W.: drafted 12/4/62 at Guinea's Station in Co. G as Pvt. Last official entry shows him present, 4/30-10/31 1864. No further record.

SLOAN, LAUGHLIN: b. 1842? Laborer. enl. 4/20/61 in Co. K as Pvt. To Sgt., date not given. POW at Strasburg, 6/4/62 (Ft. Delaware). Oath of Allegiance to U.S., date not given.

SLOAT, WALTER D.: b. 1846. drafted 11/1/62 at Camp Bitzer in Co. C as Pvt. Deserted 11/24/62 on march from Winchester to Fredericksburg. d. 1913. bur. Mt. Hebron Cem., Winchester.

SLUSSER, WILLIAM S.: 6'0", muddy complexion, dark eyes, dark hair. Residence Rockingham Co. enl 4/16/62 at Rude's Hill in Co. E as Pvt. AWOL 11/27/62-5/27/63. POW at Waynesboro, 3/2/65 (Ft. Delaware). Oath of Allegiance to U.S., 6/15/65.

SMALL, J.: enl. 10/1/62 at Bunker Hill in Co. B as Pvt. AWOL since 10/9/62 and dropped from the roll Nov./Dec. 1862. "Supposed to be in Berkeley Co." No further record.

SMALL, JAMES M. (or N.): b. 1844? 5'4½", dark complexion, gray eyes, dark hair. enl. 9/16/61 at Charles Town in Co. A as Pvt. POW at Newtown, 7/28/63 (Ft. Delaware). Exchanged 3/10/65. Paroled 4/18/65 at Charles Town.

SMALL, JOHN D.: enl. 10/1/62 at Bunker Hill in Co. H as Pvt. AWOL since 10/4/62. No further record.

SMALL, JOHN M.: b. 6/29/39. enl. 3/26/62 at Camp Buchanan in Co. E as Pvt. Absent on detail as teamster, May/June 1863-March/April 1864. Last official entry shows him still absent on detail as teamster, 4/30-10/31 1864. Surrendered at Appomattox. d. 4/17/09. bur. Greenhill Cem., Martinsburg, W.Va.

SMALL, REUBEN W.: b. 9/1/36. enl. 3/4/62 at Winchester in Co. E as Pvt. To Musician, Nov./Dec. 1863. Absent on detail to 2nd Regt. band, Jan./Feb.-March/April 1864. Last official entry shows him present again, 4/30-10/31 1864. Surrendered at Appomattox. d. 5/4/13 at Martinsburg. bur. Greenhill Cem., Martinsburg, W.Va.

SMALLWOOD, SKIPTON: enl. 10/3/62 at Bunker Hill in Co. G as Pvt. Deserted 10/16/62 from Bunker Hill.

SMELTER, CHARLES: enl. 7/16/61 at Winchester in Co. D as Pvt. POW, date and location not stated. Exchanged 8/5/62. Absent on detail as Ord. driver, 11/13/62. Present again Jan./Feb. 1863. Deserted 7/26/63.

SMITH, ABRAHAM: b. 1832? in Sharpsburg, Md. 5' 8", light complexion, blue eyes, brown hair. enl. 5/17/61 at Harpers Ferry in Co. B as Pvt. Absent sick at Shepherdstown, Sept./Oct. 1861-Jan. 1862. Surgeon's discharge, 2/2 or 2/28 1862; disability.

SMITH, CONRAD C.: b. 4/5/?9. Unofficial source lists him in Co. B. d. 3/14/86. bur. Elmwood Cem., Shepherdstown, W.Va.

SMITH, DANIEL C. (or L.): b. 1836. Carpenter. enl. 4/20/61 at Harpers Ferry in Co. K as Pvt. To Sgt. 3/1/64. Last official entry shows him present, March/April 1864. No further record. d. 2/24/80. bur. Edge Hill Cem., Charles Town, W.Va.

SMITH, EDWARD C.: b. 6/3/16. enl. 8/1/61 at Camp near Manassas in Co. I as Pvt. AWOL since 11/9/61. No further record. d. 5/22/80. bur. Grace Episcopal Church, Berryville.

SMITH, GEORGE W.: b. 3/16/33. enl. 11/1/62 at Camp Allen in Co. A as Pvt. Deserted 6/22/62. POW (Rebel deserter), 7/31/63; location of capture not stated. Oath of Allegiance to U.S., date not given. d. 4/12/04. bur. Episcopal and Masonic Cem., Middleway, W.Va.

SMITH, JOHN S.: b. 1836? Cabinet maker. enl. 4/18/61 at Martinsburg in Co. D as Pvt. Deserted 7/5/61.

SMITH, JOHN WILLIAM: b. 1842? Student. enl. 5/29/61 at Camp Johnston. Absent sick 8/8-10/5 1861. Last official entry shows him present, Nov./Dec. 1861.

SMITH, L. W.: drafted 11/1/62 at Camp Bitzer in Co. C as Pvt. Deserted 11/24/62 on march from Winchester to Fredericksburg.

SMITH, ROBERT GORDON: b. 1/19/39 at Dunkeld, Perthshire, Scotland. 5' 10", gray eyes, dark hair. m. Anna Rose Brown. enl. 4/18/61 at Winchester in Co. F as Sgt. Last official entry shows him present, Nov./Dec. 1861. Trans. 4/14/62 at New Market to Co. F, 12th Va. Cav. POW near Martinsburg, 10/15/63 (Ft. McHenry, Pt. Lookout). Exchanged 12/25/63. Paroled 4/17/65. d. 9/19/02 at Winchester.

SMITH, THOMAS: Unofficial source shows him in Co. H.

SMITH, W. CAREY: b. 1836. enl. 7/7/61 at Bunker Hill in Co. C as Pvt. Absent sick 10/10-Nov./Dec. 1861. Discharged 10/1/62, reason not stated. A later record shows him in Gen. Hosp. #9, Richmond, 3/23/65. No further record. d. 12/13/91.

SMITH, WILLIAM: Listed in Co. K as Pvt. Deserted 6/2/62, and "supposed to be in Blackford's Cavalry." No further record.

SMITH, WILLIAM C.: Listed in Co. G as Pvt., but was never mustered being "permanently sick and absent." Another source says he served in Co. D, 33rd Va. Inf. d. Feb. 1902.

SMITH, WILLIAM M.: b. 1840. Laborer. enl. 4/22/61 at Harpers Ferry in Co. D as Pvt. Deserted 5/20/61. d. 1911. bur. Greenhill Cem., Martinsburg, W.Va.

SMITH, WILLIAM R.: enl. 12/10/64 at Staunton in Co. H as Pvt. No further record.

SMOKE, DAVID L.: b. 1839. Tobacconist. enl. 4/18/61 at Winchester in Co. F as Pvt. Absent sick March/April 1863. Absent on detail as ambulance driver, May/June 1863-Jan./Feb. 1864. Present again March/April 1864. POW at North Anna, 5/24/64 (Pt. Lookout, Elmira). Exchanged 3/2/65. Chimborazo #2, 3/7/65; pleurisy. Furloughed 3/16/65 for 60 days. Paroled 4/20/65 at Winchester. Postwar, moved to Greenville, Tennessee in 1885. d. 8/16/01 at Greenville, Tennessee. bur. at Greenville, Tennessee.

SMOOT, JAMES WILLIAM: b. 1831 near Woodstock. Lawyer. enl. 4/8/62 at Rude's Hill in Co. G as Pvt. Detailed as teamster in QM's Dept., 4/12/62. Absent on this detail through May/June 1863. Listed as deserter July/Aug. 1863. Postwar, farmer; served in Va. legislature. d. 1891 near Woodstock.

SMOOT, JOHN W.: drafted 4/16/62 at Rude's Hill in Co. K as Pvt. Absent on special duty at 10/31/62 muster; duty not stated. AWOL Nov./Dec. 1862. Present again Jan./Feb. 1863. Wded. in left leg at Payne's Farm, 11/27/63. Chimborazo #3, 11/29-12/9 1863. Present again by 12/31/63. Last official entry shows him present, March/April 1864. No further record.

SMOOT, SAMUEL J.: enl. 4/8/62 at Rude's Hill in Co. G as Pvt. Absent sick at 10/31/62 muster. AWOL 11/1/62-1/29/63. Chimborazo #1, 5/12-7/10 1863; continuous fever. Listed as absent sick through Nov./Dec. 1863. Shown as deserter, Jan./Feb. 1864.

SNAPP, MARCUS JACKSON: b. 7/25/28. m. Zora Gray. A member of Winchester Riflemen but not able to join Confederate service due to poor eyesight. In foundry business at Frederick, Md. during the war. d. 7/25/06. bur. Mt. Hebron Cem., Winchester.

SNAPP, WILLIAM H.: drafted 10/3/62 at Bunker Hill in Co. F as Pvt. AWOL since 12/13/62. No further record. Appears on rolls of Co. K, 12th Va. Cav.

SNARR, DAVID: b. 9/25/20. drafted 4/16/62 at Rude's Hill in Co. K as Pvt. No record until Jan./Feb. 1863 when he is shown as present. Fined 7 month's pay by court-martial for being AWOL 6 months, Jan./Feb. 1863. Discharged 5/1/63, reason not stated. d. 2/11/67. bur. Old Keller Cem., Shenandoah Co.

SNODGRASS, ISAAC B.: b. 1842? Farmer. enl. 6/6/61 at Harpers Ferry in Co. D as Pvt. Absent sick Sept./Oct. 1861. Last official entry shows him present again, Nov./Dec. 1861.

SNODGRASS, A. PORTERFIELD: b. 2/22/46. 5' 10", light complexion, gray eyes, light hair. enl. 7/15/63 at Darkesville in Co. E as Pvt. Wded. in leg at Payne's Farm, 11/27/63. Gen. Hosp. #9, Richmond, 11/28/63. To Staunton, 12/13/63. Present again Jan./Feb. 1864. Last official entry shows him present, 8/31-12/31 1864. Gen. Hosp. Farmville, 2/25/65; wound in right leg. Paroled 5/8/65 at Winchester. d. 12/9/95. bur. Greenhill Cem., Martinsburg, W.Va.

SNYDER, EMANUEL: enl. 4/9/62 at Winchester in Co. E as Pvt. Assigned but never reported to Co.

SNYDER, HENRY M.: b. 6/7/36. Farmer. enl. 5/11/61 at Harpers Ferry in Co. H as Pvt. Wded. in thigh at 1st Manassas, 7/21/61. Last official entry shows him still absent from wound, Nov./Dec. 1861. d. 11/11/64. bur. Elmwood Cem., Shepherdstown, W.Va.

SNYDER, JOHN: b. 1822. enl. 10/1/62 at Bunker Hill in Co. H as Pvt. Absent sick at home since 11/6/62. Remained absent sick until 11/10/63 when he is listed as AWOL. Next record shows him wded. in right testicle and thigh at Spotsylvania, 5/12/64. POW at Spotsylvania, 5/12/64 (U.S. Gen. Hosp., Alexandria; wounded). d. 5/1 or 6/1 1864 at U.S. Gen. Hosp., Alexandria; from wounds. bur. Elmwood Cem., Shepherdstown, W.Va.

SNYDER, JOHN W.: b. 1841? Miller. enl. 10/23/61 at Centerville in Co. H as Corp. Appears on rolls of Co. B, Sept./Oct. 1861. Absent sick at hosp., Jan./Feb. 1864. Present again March/April 1864. No further record.

SOLOMON, A. G.: enl. 4/16/62 at Winchester in Co. E as Pvt. AWOL 5/31/62-12/21/62 and sentenced to forfeit all pay for period 5/31/62-3/1/63. Discharged 3/12/63, overage.

SOUNDERS, FAYETTE B.: b. 1838? Carpenter. Residence Charles Town. enl. 4/18/61 at Harpers Ferry in Co. A as Corp. To Pvt., July/Aug. 1861. POW at Spotsylvania, 5/12/64 (Pt. Lookout, Elmira). Released 5/14/65.

SOURS, SIMEON: enl. 4/9/62 at Winchester in Co. E as Pvt. AWOL 5/21/62 and listed as a deserter, Sept./Oct. 1862. No further record.

SOURS, WILLIAM: drafted 4/9/62 at Rude's Hill in Co. E as Pvt. AWOL 11/20/62 at New Market. Listed as AWOL through May/June 1863. Reported in Cav. without proper authority, July/Aug. 1863. Deserted 10/15/63.

SOUTHWELL, H. M.: enl. 12/6/64 at Richmond in Co. C as Pvt. POW at Ft. Steadman near Petersburg, 3/25/65 (Washington, D. C.; Pt. Lookout). Oath of Allegiance to U.S., 4/26/65; "transportation furnished to Chicago."

SOWERS, JOHN W.: b. 1834. Farmer. enl. 6/20/61 at Winchester in Co. C as Pvt. AWOL 4/17/62; joined the Cav. No further record.

SOWERS, JUSTIN O. F.: b. 1843? Farmer. enl. 4/18/61 at Berryville in Co. I as Sgt. Absent sick Sept./Oct.-Nov./Dec. 1861. Trans. to Cav., 3/17/62.

SOWERS, NATHANIEL O.: b. 11/27/42. Farmer. enl. 4/18/61 at Berryville in Co. I as Sgt. POW at Kernstown, 3/23/62 (Ft. Delaware). Exchanged 8/5/62. Present again by 10/31/62. Wded. in left arm at Payne's Farm, 11/27/63. Gen. Hosp. Danville, 6/16/64; wounded arm. No further record. d. 4/27/26. bur. Berryville Baptist Cem., Berryville.

SOWERS, WILLIAM D.: b. 1844? Farmer. enl. 4/18/61 at Berryville in Co. I as Pvt. Trans. to Cav., 10/6/61.

SOWERS, WILLIAM M.: b. 1831. Farmer. enl. 4/18/61 at Millwood in Co. I as Pvt. Absent sick July/Aug. 1861. Present again Sept./Oct. 1861. Absent on detail in QM's Dept., 11/25/61. Absent on detail as waggoner for QM, 1/1/-Nov./Dec. 1862. Next official record says he trans. 4/22/63 to Co. B, 12th Va. Cav. d. 5/16/63. bur. Old Bethel Church Cem., end of Rt. 625, Clarke Co.

SPAID (SPARDS), JOHN W.: b. 11/7/40. m. Margaret Brill. drafted 11/1/62 at Opequon in Co. F as Pvt. AWOL since 7/24/63. No further record. d. 4/9/07. bur. Shiloh Church Cem., Lehew, Hampshire Co., W.Va.

SPATES, CHARLES W.: b. 1837? Tailor. enl. 4/18/61 at Charles Town in Co. A as Corp. To Sgt. 11/25/61. To Pvt. 6/14/62. Absent sick at Leesburg since 9/20/61. Present again Nov./Dec. 1861. Absent sick in Staunton hosp., 6/8/63-Jan./Feb. 1864. Listed as deserter at 4/30/64 muster. No further record.

SPENCER, JOHN T.: enl. 6/21/61 at Wythesville. Only record says he temporarily trans. 10/31/61 to Co. H, 2nd Va. Inf. from 8th Va. Cav.

SPEROW, GEORGE T.: b. 9/17/42. Plasterer. enl. 4/19/61 at Hedgesville in Co. E as Pvt. To Corp., date not given. Deserted 7/18/63. d. 2/29/04. bur. Elmwood Cem., Shepherdstown, W.Va.

SPRIGGLE, P.: enl. 4/16/62 at Rude's Hill in Co. C as Pvt. First official entry shows him returning from AWOL, Jan./Feb. 1863. Wded. in right hand at Payne's Farm, 11/27/63. Chimborazo #4, 11/29/63. To Staunton, 12/7/63. Gen. Hosp. #9, Richmond, 5/21/64. Chimborazo #1, debility. To Gen. Hosp. Farmville, 6/2-7/12 1864. Last official entry shows him still absent from wound, 8/31-12/31 1864. No further record.

SPRIGGLE, SAMUEL: drafted 4/16/62 at Rude's Hill in Co. C as Pvt. First official entry shows him returning from AWOL, Jan./Feb. 1863. Gen. Hosp. Staunton, 5/1/63; diarrhea. Gen. Hosp. Staunton, 5/24/63; scorbutus. Returned to regt. from illness, 12/3/63. POW at Spotsylvania, 5/12/64 (Pt. Lookout, Elmira). Exchanged 10/29/64. POW 4/9/65, location not stated. No further record.

SPITZER (SPITSER), JACOB: enl. 3/1/62 at Winchester in Co. H as Pvt. Only official record lists him as POW 4/9/65, location not stated.

SPITZER, JOHN: Listed in Co. E as Pvt. MWIA at Gaines's Mill or Malvern Hill, 6/27 or 7/1 1862. d. 7/4/62. Widow Diana Spitzer.

SPITZER, JOSEPH E.: 5' 5½", florid complexion, blue eyes, auburn hair. Residence Winchester. drafted 4/16/62 at Rude's Hill in Co. C as Pvt. To Sgt. Nov. 1862. Absent sick 11/19/62-May/June 1863. Present again July/Aug. 1863. POW at Spotsylvania, 5/12/64 (Pt. Lookout, Elmira). Oath of Allegiance to U.S., 6/23/65.

SPOTTS, JOSEPH B.: b. 1843? Student. enl. 4/18/61 at Charles Town in Co. A as Pvt. To Corp. Aug. 1861. To Pvt. 11/25/61 for "bad conduct." Detailed in QM's Dept., 7/1/62. Present again Jan./Feb. 1863. POW at Spotsylvania, 5/12/64 (Pt. Lookout). d. 6/4/64 at Pt. Lookout, cause not stated.

SPRIGGS, RICHARD L.: b. 1840? Clerk. enl. 5/29/61 at Camp Johnston in Co. G as Pvt. Discharged 5/21/62, reason not stated.

SPRINT, JOHN WILLIAM: b. 6/26/29 at Millwood. Wheelwright. enl. 4/18/61 at Millwood in Co. C as Pvt. Absent sick at 6/30/61 muster. AWOL July/Aug.-Nov./Dec. 1861. No further record. Postwar, resumed hotel business. d. 10/9/17 at Millwood. bur. Greenhill Cem., Berryville.

STAUB, JOHN F.: enl. 7/2/61 in Berkeley Co. in Co. D as Pvt. Deserted 7/19/61.

STAUB, RICHARD P. H.: b. 1834? Lawyer. enl. 4/18/61 at Martinsburg in Co. D as Pvt. Discharged 5/12/61, reason not stated.

STEELE, JOHN W.: b. 1827. enl. 3/6/62 at Winchester in Co. F as Pvt. To Corp. Jan./Feb. 1863. Nov./Dec. 1862 muster lists him as a POW who was recovered from imprisonment 10/11/62. Says he was reported AWOL by mistake. AWOL since 7/16/63. POW (Rebel deserter) at Winchester, 7/27/63. Sent to Washington, D.C. Oath of Allegiance to U.S., date not given. d. 3/8/01 at Waynesboro, Pa. bur. Greenhill Cem., Berryville.

STEELE, G. W.: b. 1837? Unofficial source shows him in Co. C. d. 6/2/62. bur. Thornrose Cem., Staunton.

STEELE, PETER G.: drafted 4/14/62 at Rude's Hill in Co. K as Pvt. Discharged 7/22/62, reason not stated.

STEELE, STEPHEN M.: b. 1820. Coach trimmer. enl. 4/18/61 at Winchester in Co. F as Pvt. Absent sick Nov./Dec. 1861. Nov./Dec. muster lists him as a POW who was recovered from imprisonment 10/11/62. Says he was reported AWOL by mistake. KIA at Payne's Farm, 11/27/63. bur. Stonewall Cem., Winchester.

STEWART, CHARLES: enl. 12/11/61. Trans. to Co. D as Pvt. from Lt. Gen. Polk's Corps, Jan./Feb. 1864. POW near

133

Harpers Ferry, 7/16/64 (Old Capitol Prison, Elmira). Released 8/26/63 (sic) and remained in Washington, D.C.

STEWART, CHARLES H.: b. 1832? Clerk. enl. 4/20/61 at Harpers Ferry in Co. K as Lt. To Capt. 4/20/62. To Maj. 4/21/64. Signs rolls as commanding the regt. Nov./Dec. 1863-March/April 1864. Paroled 4/19/65 at Mt. Jackson. d. 10/18/66. bur. Edge Hill Cem., Charles Town, W.Va.

STEWART, JOSEPH: b. 1837? 5' 9½", dark complexion, blue eyes, brown hair. Manufacturer. enl. 4/18/61 at Martinsburg in Co. D as Pvt. Deserted 7/26/63. POW (Rebel deserter) sent to Ft. Mifflin, Pa. Oath of Allegiance to U.S., 10/8/63.

STICKLE (STICKLES), SIMON P.: b. 4/5/41. Laborer. enl. 6/19/61 near Winchester in Co. I as Pvt. AWOL 10/15-10/26 1861. AWOL 12/27-12/30 1861. Wded. at Port Republic, 6/9/62. Lovingston Hosp. Winchester, 7/8/62. Absent due to wound through Nov./Dec. 1863. AWOL Jan./Feb. 1864. No further record. d. 12/21/24. bur. Edge Hill Cem., Charles Town, W.Va.

STINE, ADAM RIGHT: Unofficial source says he served in Co. B. bur. Elmwood Cem., Shepherdstown, W.Va.

STONE, WILLIAM: b. 1837? 5' 11", dark complexion, dark eyes, dark hair. Farmer. Listed in Co. K as Pvt. POW (Rebel deserter) at Charleston, W.Va., March 1865. Oath of Allegiance to U.S., 3/7/65 "and sent north."

STONEBRAKER, A. S.: Apptd. 6/19/61 Regt. QM. Last official entry shows him present, Nov./Dec. 1861. Next official record says he was reassigned, 9/15/64; nature of reassignment not stated. No further record.

STONESTREET, JOHN: drafted 12/1/62 at Guinea's Station in Co. C as Pvt. Deserted 12/20/62 from camp near Moss Neck.

STOUT, _____. enl. 4/16/62 near Mt. Jackson in Co. I as Pvt. Discharged 5/1/62 after furnishing a substitute.

STOVER, C. G.: Listed in Co. D. Only record says he was wded. at Port Republic, 6/9/62.

STOVER, DANIEL T.: enl. 4/9/62 at Rude's Hill in Co. E as Pvt. Wded. at 2nd Manassas, 8/30/62. Absent at hosp. Nov./Dec. 1862. No further record.

STOVER, JACOB: drafted 4/14/62 at Rude's Hill in Co. K as Pvt. Discharged 7/22/62.

STOVER, S. D.: enl. 4/16/62 at Rude's Hill in Co. D as Pvt. Absent sick at hosp. 6/30-10/31 1862. Deserted and joined Imboden's Cav., Nov./Dec. 1862. No further record.

STOVER, WILLIAM HENRY: b. 2/26/39. enl. 4/16/62 at Rude's Hill in Co. F as Pvt. Deserted 4/18/62 from Rude's Hill. d. 3/31/18. bur. St. Peter's Union Church Cem., Elkton.

STRAITH, JOHN ALEXANDER: b. 1/26/35. Physician. Apptd. Asst. Surg., 2nd Va. Inf., 5/17/61. Last official entry shows him present, Nov./Dec. 1861. No further record. d. 1/4/72. bur. Zion Episcopal Cem., Charles Town, W.Va.

STRALEY, ROBERT S.: Listed in Co. F. Deserted about 6/15/61.

STRIDER, JOHN S.: b. 1837? Farmer. enl. 4/20/61 at Harpers Ferry in Co. K as Pvt. Absent sick July/Aug. 1861. Present again Sept./Oct. 1861. d. 12/18/61, cause not stated.

STRUTTER, A.: enl. 4/18/62 at Rude's Hill in Co. B as Pvt. AWOL since 5/25/62 and dropped from the roll, Nov./Dec. 1862.

STUART, BENJAMIN F.: enl. 4/16/62 near Mt. Jackson in Co. I as Corp. Discharged 5/2/62 after furnishing. F. Salmes as substitute.

STUCKEY, JOHN W.: enl. 4/24/62 at Swift Run Gap in Co. E as Pvt. KIA at 2nd Manassas, 8/29/62.

STUCKEY, SAMUEL A.: b. 1843? 5' 7", dark complexion, dark eyes, dark hair. Farmer. enl. 4/24/62 at Swift Run Gap in Co. E as Pvt. Wded. at Fredericksburg, 12/13/62. Winder Div. 5 Hosp., Richmond, 12/17/62. To Staunton, 1/11/63. Present again March/April 1863. Absent sick March/April 1864. POW at Back Creek, 7/12/64 (Wheeling, Camp Chase). Exchanged 3/7/65. No further record.

STUMP, C. M.: 5' 5", light complexion, dark eyes, dark hair. Residence Martinsburg. enl. 10/15/64 at Richmond in Co. C as Pvt. Wded. in left arm at Ft. Steadman near Petersburg, 3/25/65. Gen. Hosp. #9, Richmond, 3/25/65. To Chimborazo #5, 3/26/65. To Chimborazo #3, April 1865. POW at Richmond Hosp., 4/3/65 (Jackson Hosp., Libby Prison, Newport News). Oath of Allegiance to U.S., 6/16/65.

STURDY, JOHN W.: b. 1840? Armorer. enl. 4/20/61 at Harpers Ferry in Co. K as Pvt. Discharged 8/14/61 and detailed to C. S. Carbine Factory in Richmond to make arms. POW 5/6/65 at Athens, Georgia. Paroled 5/25/65 at Harpers Ferry.

STYNE, JONATHAN: 5' 10", light complexion, blue eyes, dark hair. Residence Berkeley Co. enl. 12/11/62 at Guinea's Station in Co. D as Pvt. Absent on detail as Ord. driver, 12/11/62-Jan./Feb. 1864. Last official entry shows him still absent on detail as Ord. driver, March/April 1864. POW at Waynesboro, 3/2/65 (Ft. Delaware). Oath of Allegiance to U.S., 6/21/65.

SUDDESH, ARTHUR J.: b. 1830? 6' 0", florid complexion, dark eyes, dark hair. Carpenter and farmer. enl. 4/18/61 at Martinsburg in Co. D as Pvt. Absent on detail in hosp. at Winchester at 10/31/62 muster. POW at Winchester, 12/5/62 (Wheeling, Camp Chase). Exchanged 3/28/63. Remaining entries list him as a hosp. steward at Richmond through final entry in March/April 1864. No further record.

SUDDITH, GEORGE E.: b. 1841? Machinist. enl. 4/18/61 at Charles Town in Co. A as Pvt. Last official entry shows him present, Nov./Dec. 1861.

SUITER, CHARLES M.: b. 1840? Laborer. enl. 4/22/61 at Martinsburg in Co. D as Pvt. AWOL 5/8/61. Arrested 6/6/61. Absent sick July/Aug.-Sept./Oct. 1861. Discharged Nov. 1861, reason not stated.

SULLIVAN, DANIEL F.: b. 11/17/42. 5' 10", dark complexion, blue eyes, brown hair. enl. 9/6/61 at Camp Harman in Co. D as Pvt. Deserted 7/26/63. POW near Chambersburg, Pa., 7/28/63 (Ft. Mifflin). Released 10/8/63. d. 1/27/27. bur. St. Joseph's Cem., Martinsburg, W.Va.

SUTTON, CHARLES H.: b. 1838? Carpenter. enl. 4/19/61 at Hedgesville in Co. E as Pvt. Deserted 7/14/61.

SWARTZ, CHARLES: b. 1843? Laborer. enl. 4/18/61 at Charles Town in Co. A as Pvt. Absent sick at home, July/Aug. 1861. Present again Sept./Oct. 1861. Gen. Hosp. Charlottesville, 5/13-5/20 1862; parotitis. Present 6/30-10/31 1862. Deserted 11/20/62.

SWARTZ, H.: Listed in Co. C as Pvt. Deserted 10/13/62 from Bunker Hill.

SWEENEY, JOHN E.: b. 1838? Laborer. enl. 4/20/61 at Harpers Ferry in Co. K as Pvt. Deserted 5/13/61.

SWEENEY, JOSEPH W.: 5′ 9″, fair complexion, blue eyes, light hair. Residence Henrico Co. Listed in Co. G as Pvt. Only record is a POW statement. POW at New Kent Co., 1/27/65 (Pt. Lookout). Oath of Allegiance to U.S., 6/20/65.

SWIMLEY, DAVID: 5′ 11″, fair complexion, blue eyes, light hair. Residence Martinsburg. enl. 12/4/62 at Guinea's Station in Co. D as Pvt. POW at Spotsylvania, 5/12/64 (Pt. Lookout, Elmira). Oath of Allegiance to U.S., 5/15/65.

SWITZER, ANDREW: enl. 4/15/65 at Rude's Hill in Co. A as Pvt. Discharged 7/31/62, reason not stated.

SWITZER, JACOB: b. 2/7/36. 5′ 4 ¾, light complexion, hazel eyes, dark brown hair. Residence Augusta Co. Wded. in back at 2nd Manassas, 8/28/62. Returned from sick leave, 3/6/63. Sent to hosp. sick, 4/27/63. Chimborazo #1, 5/2-7/6 1863; pneumonia. Returned to regt. from sick leave, 10/1/63. POW at Monocacy, 7/10/64 (U.S. Gen. Hosp., West Buildings, Baltimore; Pt. Lookout). Oath of Allegiance to U.S., 6/29/65. d. 12/4/91.

TABB, CHARLES W.: b. in Berkeley Co. enl. 5/28/62 at Winchester in Co. G as Pvt. Wded. at Fredericksburg, 12/13/62. Present at 12/31/62 muster. MWIA in thigh at Payne's Farm, 11/27/63. d. 2/15/64 in hosp. at Gordonsville.

TABLER, ADAM M.: b. 1843? Farmer. enl. ?/20/61 at Camp Lee in Co. E as Pvt. Deserted out of state before 6/30/61 muster.

TABLER, EPHRAIM G.: b. 7/17/16. Farmer. enl. 4/18/61 at Martinsburg in Co. D as Musician. Last official entry shows him present, Nov./Dec. 1861. d. 10/29/92. bur. Christian Tabler Cem., north of Martinsburg, W.Va.

TALBOTT (TALBOT), JOHN: b. 12/22/31. enl. 11/2/62 at Millwood in Co. D as Pvt. Deserted 6/26/63. d. 8/06/03. bur. Christ Church Cem., Bunker Hill, W.Va.

TALLEY, JAMES: enl. 3/16/62 at Winchester in Co. I as Pvt. AWOL since 5/25/62 and dropped from the roll, Nov./Dec. 1862. No further record.

TANSILL, JOHN: b. 1831? Laborer. enl. 6/22/61 at Winchester in Co. C as Pvt. Absent sick 8/3/61. Present again Sept./Oct. 1861. Absent sick at 10/31/62 muster. Returned from hosp., 11/22/62. Wded. at Gettysburg, 7/3/63. Remained absent from wound through final entry, 8/31-12/31 1864. No further record.

TANSILL, WILLIAM: b. 1829? in Jefferson Co. 5′ 10″, fair complexion, gray eyes, dark hair. Laborer and carpenter. enl. 6/22/61 at Winchester in Co. C as Pvt. AWOL since 12/2/61. Absent sick at 10/31/62 muster. Returned from hosp., 12/8/62. Discharged 12/27/62, suffering from chronic bronchial infection.

TAPPY, SIMON: enl. 4/14/62 at Rude's Hill in Co. B as Pvt. d. 10/28/62 at home from disease.

TAPSCOTT, JOSEPH B.: 5′ 4″, light complexion, gray eyes, brown hair. Residence Clarke Co. enl. 9/25/62 at Bunker Hill in Co. I as Pvt. Absent sick at hosp., May/June 1863. POW at Brandy Station, 8/1/63 (Old Capitol Prison, Pt. Lookout, Elmira). Oath of Allegiance to U.S., 8/7/65.

TAPSCOTT, SAMUEL B.: b. 1837? 5′ 7″, dark complexion, black eyes, black hair, brown whiskers. Clerk. enl. 4/30/61 at Harpers Ferry in Co. B as Pvt. AWOL May/June-July/Aug. 1861. Present again Sept./Oct. 1861. Absent sick March/April 1862. Gen. Hosp. Charlottesville, 9/4-9/16 1862; wounded (probably wded. at 2nd Manassas, although his entries state he was AWOL since 7/1/62, so there is a possiblity that he was wded. at Malvern Hill and turned up missing as a result). POW at Strasburg, 2/13/63 (Wheeling, Camp Chase). Exchanged 3/28/63. Present again March/April 1863. Gen. Hosp. #13, Richmond, 6/16/63; acute diarrhea. Gen. Hosp. Charlottesville, 7/24-8/4 1863; debility. POW at Spotsylvania, 5/12/64 (Pt. Lookout, Elmira). Exchanged 10/29/64. No further record.

TASSING, GIDEON P.: b. 1819 in Shenandoah Co. 5′ 9″, dark complexion, dark eyes, dark hair. enl. 4/8/62 at Rude's Hill in Co. G as Pvt. AWOL 7/1/62-2/1/63. Discharged 4/10/63, reason not stated.

TAYLOR, JOHN: enl. 10/1/62 at Bunker Hill in Co. C as Pvt. Trans. to Co. F about 10/26/62. No other records except one that reports him MIA at Gettysburg.

TAYLOR, JOHN: b. 3/7/41. m. 1) Evelyn Shade; 2) Anna Eliza Adams. Farmer. enl. 4/18/61 at Winchester in Co. F as Pvt. Last official entry shows him present, Nov./Dec. 1861. Postwar, member of Turner Ashby Camp #22, Winchester. d. 3/6/12. bur. Mt. Hebron Cem., Winchester.

TAYLOR, JOHN W.: b. 3/31/42. 5′ 5 ½″, light complexion, blue eyes, light hair. Residence Jefferson Co. enl. 11/22/61 at Camp Stephenson in Co. B as Pvt. To Corp. 4/18/62. To Sgt. 8/1/62. Absent on furlough, Jan./Feb. 1862. Absent sick March/April 1862. Present again 4/30-10/31 1862. Gen. Hosp. Danville, June 1864; wounded neck. Gen. Hosp. Charlottesville, 9/26/64; wounded neck. To Lynchburg, 9/28/64. Last official entry shows him present again by 10/31/64 muster. POW at Ft. Steadman near Petersburg, 3/25/65 (Pt. Lookout). Oath of Allegiance to U.S., 6/11/65. d. 12/11/05. bur. Elmwood Cem., Shepherdstown, W.Va.

TAYLOR, JOHN W.: b. 10/28/35. enl. 4/16/62 at Rude's Hill in Co. F as Pvt. Deserted from near Port Republic, 6/15/62. Recovered from desertion, 3/8/63. Detailed to work in iron foundry, March/April 1863. Last official entry shows him still absent on detail in iron foundry, March/April 1864. d. 11/22/22. bur. Lacy Springs Cem., Rockingham Co.

TAYLOR, JOSEPH F.: b. 4/1/36. enl. 4/16/62 at Rude's Hill in Co. F as Pvt. Deserted from Port Republic, 6/15/62. Returned from desertion, Jan./Feb. 1863. Detailed to work in iron foundry, March/April 1863. Last official entry shows him still absent on detail in iron foundry, March/April 1864. d. 6/3/82. bur. St. Paul's Lutheran Cem., Strasburg.

TAYLOR, LEMUEL T.: b. 1825? Wagon maker. enl. 4/18/61 at Halltown in Co. B as Corp. To Sgt. 8/17/61. POW at Kernstown, 3/23/62 (Ft. Delaware). Exchanged 8/5/62. AWOL since 8/5/62 and dropped from the roll, Nov./Dec. 1862. No further record until 10/3/64 when he is shown in Gen. Hosp. #9, Richmond. To Gen. Hosp. #5, Richmond, 10/8/64; chronic diarrhea. d. 11/2/64 at Gen. Hosp. #5, Richmond.

TAYLOR, WILLIAM G.: b. 6/30/27. Listed in Co. I. "Marched with company and served to 5/13/61, when discharged for disability." d. 12/4/91. bur. Grace Episcopal Church, Berryville.

TEAFORD, MARTIN L.: b. 1840. enl. 4/16/62 at Rude's Hill in Co. D as Pvt. Absent on detail as wagon driver, Nov./Dec. 1862. Present again Jan./Feb. 1863. Absent on detail as teamster, May/June-Nov./Dec. 1863. Deserted 1/25/64. d. 10/20/70.

TERRELL (TERRILL), JOHN URIEL: b. 8/23/43. Student. enl. 6/10/61 at Camp Jackson on Bolivar Heights in Co. G as Pvt. Last official entry shows him present, Nov./Dec. 1861. Appears on rolls of Co. B, 12th Va. Cav. d. 11/15/78. bur. Zion Episcopal Cem., Charles Town, W.Va.

THACKER, JAMES: enl. 4/16/62 at Rude's Hill in Co. E as Pvt. Absent sick at hosp. since 10/15/62. Present again May/June 1863. Absent with leave, Nov./Dec. 1863. Present again Jan./Feb. 1864. Deserted 3/14/65, and listed as living in Page Co. No further record.

THATCHER, THOMAS T.: b. 1831? 5' 10", fair complexion, gray eyes, light hair. Farmer. Residence Clarke Co. enl. 6/21/61 at Camp Myers in Co. I as Pvt. POW at Berryville, 6/14/62. Exchanged June 1862 at Winchester. POW at Harpers Ferry, 7/25/63 (Ft. McHenry, Ft. Delaware). Oath of Allegiance to U.S., April 1865.

THOMAS, JAMES H.: b. 1836? Teacher. enl. 4/18/61 at Charles Town in Co. G as Pvt. Absent on special duty, July/Aug.-Nov./Dec. 1861; nature of detail not stated. No further record.

THOMAS, M.: Listed in Co. K as Pvt. Only record lists him AWOL, Nov./Dec. 1862.

THOMAS, ROBERT: 5' 1", brown eyes, dark hair. Residence Rockingham Co. enl. 4/18/62 at Rude's Hill in Co. B as Pvt. AWOL 4/18/62-4/9/63. Court-martialed, sentence not stated. Chimborazo #5, 11/28-12/15 1863; debility. POW at Waynesboro, 3/2/65 (Ft. Delaware). Oath of Allegiance to U.S., 6/21/65.

THOMPSON, ABRAHAM: b. 1842? Laborer. enl. 6/23/61 at Camp Myers in Co. D as Pvt. Last official entry shows him present, Nov./Dec. 1861.

THOMPSON, ADAM F.: b. 11/18/26. Farmer. enl. 4/18/61 at Millwood in Co. C as Pvt. Wded. in the back at 1st Manassas, 7/21/61. Still absent wded., 6/30-10/31 1862. No further record. d. 5/18/10. bur. Old Chapel Cem., Millwood.

THOMPSON, ALBERT: b. 1839? Laborer. enl. 6/19/61 at Winchester in Co. I as Pvt. AWOL 7/27-8/4 1861. AWOL 10/7-10/26 1862. AWOL 1/15-9/25 1862. Deserted 1/29/64.

THOMPSON, BENJAMIN F. b. 1837? Overseer. enl. 4/18/61 at Berryville in Co. I as Pvt. Wded. in left side at Payne's Farm, 11/27/63. Gen. Hosp. Charlottesville, 12/1/63. Furloughed 1/9/64 for 30 days. Next official record shows him as a POW at Berryville, 8/17/64 (Ft. Delaware, Old Capitol Prison, Elmira). Exchanged 2/25/65. Paroled 4/21/65 at Winchester.

THOMPSON, CHARLES E.: b. 1840? Clerk. enl. 4/18/61 at Charles Town in Co. A as Pvt. Chimborazo #1, 10/17-10/28 1861; intermittent fever. AWOL Nov./Dec. 1861. POW at Kernstown, 3/23/62 (Ft. Delaware). Exchanged 8/5/62. Final entry states he reenlisted in Capt. Glenn's Cav. sometime before 10/31/62.

THOMPSON, CHARLES W.: enl. 6/1/62 at Bath in Co. E as Pvt. Only record lists him as a deserter, Sept./Oct. 1862.

THOMPSON, ISAAC: enl. 10/8/62 at Bunker Hill in Co. A as Pvt. AWOL since 7/22/63 and dropped as a deserter. No further record.

THOMPSON, JOHN: enl. 12/4/62 at Guinea's Station in Co. D as Pvt. Deserted 6/9/63.

THOMPSON, JOSEPH: enl. 12/4/62 at Guinea's Station in Co. D as Pvt. Deserted 7/26/63.

THOMPSON, ROBERT W.: b. 1836? Farmer. enl. 4/18/61 at Duffields in Co. H as Pvt. To Corp. 11/22/61. To Lt. 4/20/62. Wded. in thigh at 2nd Manassas, 8/28/62. Absent at home due to wound, Nov./Dec. 1862-Nov./Dec. 1863. Last official entry shows him present again, Jan./Feb. 1864. POW at Winchester, 12/2/64. Paroled at Winchester, 12/4/64. No further record.

THOMPSON, SAMUEL J.: b. 6/21/31. enl. 12/4/62 at Guinea's Station in Co. D as Pvt. Deserted 12/17/62. d. 4/8/14. bur. Old Norborne Cem., Martinsburg, W.Va.

THOMPSON, SMITH W.: enl. 4/9/62 at Winchester in Co. E as Pvt. Soldiers' Home Hosp., Richmond, 6/30-8/29 1862. Listed as AWOL, March/April 1863. No further record.

THOMPSON, WILLIAM H.: b. 1838? Farmer. enl. 4/18/61 at Millwood in Co. C as Pvt. To QM Sgt., 6/14/62. Detailed as wagoner, 10/16/61. Absent wded., May/June 1863 (probably wded. at Chancellorsville). Present again July/Aug. 1863. Last official entry shows him absent on temporary detail with Capt. Stonebraker, Reserve Ord., 4/30-10/31 1864. Surrendered at Appomattox.

THOMSON, WILLIAM S.: b. 4/12/43 in Jefferson Co. Farmer. enl. 5/29/61 at Camp Johnston in Co. G as Pvt. Last official entry shows him present, Nov./Dec. 1861. Appears on rolls of Co. B, 12th Va. Cav. Postwar, lawyer. Alive in 1898.

THORTON, JACOB P.: b. 1839? 6' 3", light complexion, blue eyes, light hair. drafted 4/16/62 at Rude's Hill in Co. K as Pvt. Detailed to work in Staunton, 9/25/62-4/1/64; duty not stated. Last official entry shows him present at 4/30/64 muster. Paroled 5/15/65 at Staunton.

THRUSH, JOHN M.: b. 1820? Coach maker. enl. 4/18/61 at Martinsburg in Co. D as Pvt. AWOL 7/2/62, "and left the state." No further record.

TIMBERLAKE, BENJAMIN T.: b. 1839? Farmer. enl. 4/18/61 at Charles Town in Co. G as Pvt. Absent sick 8/8-9/2 1861. POW at Salem Church, 5/20/64 (Pt. Lookout, Elmira). Exchanged 2/9/65. Paroled at Harpers Ferry, 3/24/65 (sic).

TIMBERLAKE, DAVID WILLIAM: b. 6/11/35 at White Hall in Frederick Co. 5' 11", fair complexion, blue eyes, light hair. Farmer. enl. 6/19/61 at Winchester in Co. G as Pvt. To Sgt., date not given. To Pvt., 10/13/63. Wded. in right arm at Kernstown, 3/23/62. Returned to duty from sick leave, 10/15/62. Wded. in face and right arm at Payne's Farm, 11/27/63. Gen. Hosp. #9, Richmond, 11/29/63. Chimborazo #5, 11/30/63. Furloughed 2/25/64 for 40 days. Surgeon's discharge, 2/24/65; "gun shot wound in right arm fracturing both the radius and ulna causing almost total uselessness." d. 12/30/16 at Clarksburg, W.Va. bur. Mt. Hebron Cem., Winchester.

TIMBERLAKE, GEORGE A.: b. 1841? Farmer. enl. 6/9/61 at Camp Jackson on Bolivar Heights in Co. G as Pvt. Last official entry shows him present, Nov./Dec. 1861. Appears on rolls of Co. B, 12th Va. Cav.

TIMBERLAKE, JAMES H.: b. 8/4/44. Farmer. enl. 6/9/61 at Camp Jackson in Co. G as Pvt. Last official entry shows him present, Nov./Dec. 1861. Appears on rolls of Co. B, 12th Va. Cav. d. 10/2/78. bur. Episcopal and Masonic Cem., Middleway, W.Va.

TIMBERLAKE, JOSEPH E.: enl. 7/10/61 at Darkesville in Co. G as Pvt. Absent on detail in Valley on special service, Jan./Feb. 1863; duty not stated. Absent on conscript duty, March/April-6/30 1863. Wded. at Payne's Farm, 11/27/63. Chimborazo #1, 2/21/64. Wded. 8/17/64. Last official entry shows him still absent from wound, Sept./Oct. 1864. Paroled 5/2/65 at Winchester.

TIMBERLAKE, SETH M.: b. 1833? Farmer. enl. 6/19/61 at Winchester in Co. G as Pvt. Wded. in both legs at 1st Manassas, 7/21/61. Returned to regt. from sick leave, 10/12/61. Last official entry shows him absent sick, Nov./Dec. 1861. Later appears on rolls of Co. B, 12th Va. Cav. Postwar, went to New York in 1866 and was employed in mercantile business in Brooklyn; then returned to Charles Town; then moved to Staunton where he served as a Steward of Western Hosp. d. 12/18/07 in Brooklyn, N.Y. bur. Tinkling Spring Church Cem., Fisherville, Va.

TIMBERLAKE, THOMAS WILLIAM: b. 10/7/42. enl. 3/4/62 in Co. G as Pvt. Wded. in face and neck at 2nd Manassas, 8/28/62. Present again Nov./Dec. 1862. Gen. Hosp. Charlottesville, 3/19-4/28 1863; continued fever. Wded. in right arm at Payne's Farm, 11/27/63. Gen. Hosp. #9, Richmond, 11/29/63. To Chimborazo #3, 11/30/63. Furloughed 1/7/64 for 35 days. Next official record shows him in Gen. Hosp. Charlottesville, 5/6-8/10 1864; wounded. No further record. Postwar, farmer at Milldale, Warren Co. d. 9/19/64. bur. Episcopal and Masonic Cem., Middleway, W.Va.

TOBIN, EDWARD: b. 1838? Stone mason. enl. 5/5/61 at Harpers Ferry in Co. E as Pvt. Deserted 7/31/61.

TOWBERMAN, GEORGE: b. 9/8/20. enl. 4/16/62 near Mt. Jackson in Co. I as Corp. Discharged Aug. 1862, overage. d. 11/8/81.

TOWNER, JAMES L.: b. 1828? Postmaster. enl. 4/18/61 at Halltown in Co. B as Pvt. Absent on recruiting service, July/Aug. 1861. Present again Sept./Oct. 1861. Absent sick Jan./Feb. 1862. Absent sick behind enemy lines, March/April 1862. No further record.

TOWNER, THOMAS HARRIS: b. 1822? Served 20 months during Mexican War. Lawyer. enl. 4/18/61 at Halltown in Co. B as Pvt. To Sgt. 8/14/61. MWIA at Kernstown, 3/23/62. d. 3/26/62 at Winchester.

TRAIL, CHARLES H.: b. 1843. Armorer. enl. 4/20/61 at Harpers Ferry in Co. K as Pvt. Deserted 6/14/61. d. 1899. bur. Harpers Cem., Harpers Ferry, W.Va.

TRAINOR, BERNARD: b. 1832? in Frederick Co., Md. 5' 9", light complexion, blue eyes, sandy hair. Moulder. enl. 4/20/61 at Harpers Ferry in Co. K as Pvt. AWOL from Camp Harman, 8/30/61. Discharged 10/21/61, reason not stated.

TRENARY, BENJAMIN F.: b. 10/27/36. Laborer. enl. 4/18/61 at Millwood in Co. C as Pvt. Absent sick 11/25/61. Last official entry shows him present, 6/30-10/31 1862. No further record. d. 3/26/03. bur. on farm near Waterloo, Clarke Co.

TRIBBY, JAMES: b. 1841? Laborer. enl. 4/19/61 at Duffields in Co. H as Pvt. Last official entry shows him present, Nov./Dec. 1861.

TRICEY, JOHN: enl. 9/12/62 at Martinsburg in Co. E as Pvt.; "known to be from Maryland." Deserted 12/20/62.

TRIGGS, HARRISON P.: drafted 9/4/62 near Guinea's Station in Co. E as Pvt. Deserted 7/18/63.

TRIPLETT, JAMES W.: b. 1835? Wheelwright. enl. 4/18/61 at Charles Town in Co. A as Pvt. Wded., thumb shot off, at 1st Manassas, 7/21/61. Absent sick at home in Charles Town, Sept./Oct. 1861. Absent on detail as wagon maker for govt., 12/28/61. Did not reenlist and is subject to conscription, 6/30-10/31 1862. No further record until parole statement, 4/19/65 at Charles Town.

TROY, LAWRENCE: b. 1816? Laborer. enl. 4/20/61 at Harpers Ferry in Co. K as Pvt. Discharged 4/25/62.

TRUSSELL, CHARLES W.: b. 1834. Merchant. enl. 4/18/61 at Charles Town in Co. A as Pvt. To Sgt. 8/2/61. Last official entry shows him present, Nov./Dec. 1861.

TRUSSELL, EDWARD C.: b. 1834? Merchant. enl. 6/14/61 at Charles Town in Co. A as Pvt. Last official entry shows him present, Nov./Dec. 1861. Appears on rolls of Co. B, 12th Va. Cav.

TRUSSELL, JAMES M.: b. 1840? Farmer. enl. 6/17/61 at Charles Town in Co. H as Pvt. Wded., leg broken, at 1st Manassas, 7/21/61. Absent sick through Nov./Dec. 1861. Absent sick 6/30-10/31 1862 through Sept./Oct. 1863. AWOL since 11/10/63. No further record.

TRUSSELL, JAMES TEMPLE: b.2/4/30 in Loudoun Co. Moved to Jefferson Co. in 1844. Farmer. enl. 6/14/61 at Charles Town in Co. A as Pvt. Absent sick at home since 10/4/61. Last official entry shows him present, Nov./Dec. 1861. Appears on rolls of Co. B, 12th Va. Cav. Postwar, farmer. d. 1/1/09. bur. Edge Hill Cem., Charles Town, W.Va.

TUCKWILLER, WILLIAM: Residence Page Co. enl. 4/9/62 at Rude's Hill in Co. E as Pvt. Wded. at 1st Winchester, 5/25/62. Present Sept./Oct. 1862. AWOL July/Aug.-Sept./Oct. 1863. Present again Nov./Dec. 1863. Gen. Hosp. Charlottesville, 6/11/64; wounded left shoulder. Furloughed 7/5/64. No further record.

TURNER, B. R.: Unofficial source says he enl. in 1861 in Co. F.

TURNER, GEORGE W.: enl. 8/15/61 at Camp Harman in Co. C as Pvt. Absent sick since 10/4/61. Wded. at Kernstown, 3/23/62. Absent from wounds until 3/15/63. Gen. Hosp. #1, Richmond, 5/4/63; continuous fever. To Staunton, 5/10/63. Present again May/June 1863. Trans. to Co. D, 6th Va. Cav., Sept./Oct. 1863.

TURNER, THOMAS H.: Unofficial source lists him in Co. B.

TURNER, WILLIAM R.: b. 5/2/24. enl. 10/4/62 at Bunker Hill in Co. E as Pvt. AWOL 11/21/62-2/15/63. Last official entry shows him present, 8/31-12/31 1864. Surrendered at Appomattox. d. 11/16/95. bur. Elmwood Cem., Shepherdstown, W.Va.

TURPIN, GEORGE WASHINGTON: Unofficial source lists him in Co. C or G. d. 9/15/63 at Ft. Delaware. bur. Finn's Pt. Nat. Cem., Ft. Delaware.

TUTWILER, JACOB O.: b. 2/14/30. enl. 10/8/62 at Bunker Hill in Co. A as Pvt. Surrendered at Appomattox. d. 8/12/13. bur. Edge Hill Cem., Charles Town, W.Va.

UMLENHOUR, JACOB: drafted 10/3/62 at Bunker Hill in Co. F as Pvt. To Corp. 1/1/63. Absent sick May/June 1863. Present again July/Aug. 1863. Absent Sept./Oct. 1863. AWOL since 11/12/63. No further record.

UNSELD, JOHN G.: b. 1838. Painter. enl. 4/18/61 at Halltown in Co. B as Pvt. To Sgt. 4/18/62. Wded. in leg, hand and thigh at 2nd Manassas, 8/28/62. Absent from wound through July/Aug. 1863. Chimborazo #3, 8/3-9/23 1863; old wound of leg. Present again in regt. by 10/31/63. Last official entry shows him absent on detail in Richmond, March/April 1864; "examining passports." No further record. d. 1906. bur. Elmwood Cem., Shepherdstown, W.Va.

VAN ARSDALE, J.: Listed in Co. D as Pvt. Only record shows him AWOL since 10/15/62.

VAN METER, JOSEPH B.: b. 2/8/40. enl. 10/1/62 at Bunker Hill in Co. H as Pvt. Only official record shows him AWOL at Bunker Hill since 10/4/62. Appears later on rolls of Co. F, 1st Va. Cav. d. 9/19/19. bur. Elmwood Cem., Shepherdstown, W.Va.

VAN METER, A. MORGAN: b. 2/17/36. enl. 10/1/62 at Bunker Hill in Co. H as Pvt. Only official record shows him AWOL since 10/4/62. Appears later on rolls of Co. F, 1st Va. Cav. d. 8/15/09. bur. Greenhill Cem., Martinsburg, W.Va.

VANPELT, WILLIAM H.: b. 1817? in Rockingham Co. 5' 9", fair complexion, gray eyes, light hair. House carpenter. drafted 4/14/62 at Rude's Hill in Co. C as Pvt. Discharged 3/23/62, overage. No further record.

VANVACTER, JOSEPH E.: b. 1842? Farmer. enl. 4/18/61 at Charles Town in Co. A as Pvt. Deserted 8/1/62.

VAUGHN, OLIVER H.: b. 1827? Clock maker. enl. 4/18/61 at Winchester in Co. F as Sgt. To Pvt. by 8/31/61. AWOL since 8/28/61. Present again Sept./Oct. 1861. Last official entry shows him in Cav. without transfer, 4/30-10/31 1862. No further record.

VAUGHN, J. D.: Only record is a POW statement that lists him as a Pvt. POW at Webster, Kentucky, 9/1/62. Sent to Vicksburg for exchange.

VETSWORTH, _____. Only record is a POW statement that lists him in Co. E as Pvt. POW near Lexington, 6/11/64 (Wheeling). No further record.

VETTERS, WILLIAM: drafted 4/14/62 at Rude's Hill in Co. K as Pvt. Deserted 6/27/63 at Chambersburg, Pa.

VOGLE, JOHN ADAM: 5′ 6½″, dark complexion, brown eyes, light hair. drafted 4/14/62 at Rude's Hill in Co. K as Pvt. Taken POW in Md. and paroled, 6/20/63. Present again at 6/30/63 muster. Last official entry shows him present, March/April 1864. Next record shows him taking the Oath of Allegiance to U.S., 10/30/64 from Ft. Delaware.

VON STEINECKER, HENRY: enl. 5/15/63 at Camp Paxton in Co. K as Pvt. Detailed in Engineer Corps, May/June 1863. Later became chief engineer on Gen. Edward Johnson's staff. Engaged in entrenching at Buckner's Neck at Hamilton's Crossing, 5/19-6/6 1863. Remained on this detail in Engineer Corps through last official entry, March/April 1864. Deserted 6/6/64. Turned himself in to Federals at Martinsburg, 6/13/64 (Old Capitol Prison). Apparently testified before the commission trying the Booth conspirators; "his testimony is important and seems to have been given with entire faithfulness." Released from Old Capitol Prison by Sec. of War Edwin Stanton, 5/18/65.

VOORHEES, ABRAHAM: b. 10/13/46. 5′ 10″, light complexion, hazel eyes, light hair. enl. 3/16/62 at Martinsburg in Co. D Pvt. POW at Spotsylvania, 5/12/64 (Pt. Lookout, Elmira). Exchanged 10/29/64. Paroled 4/16/65 at Winchester. d. 9/27/24. bur. Hedgesville Cem., Hedgesville, W.Va.

VOORHEES, GEORGE F.: 5′ 10″, dark complexion, gray eyes, dark hair. enl. 7/16/61 at Winchester in Co. D as Pvt. To Sgt. 12/17/62. Last official entry shows him present, March/April 1864. Chimborazo #3, 5/15/64; wounded right leg. To Danville, 5/20/64. Furloughed 7/13/64. Gen. Hosp. Charlottesville, 9/8/64; wounded forearm and elbow. Furloughed 9/8/64. Paroled 4/23/65 at Winchester.

VOORHEES, JACOB F.: b. 1840? Laborer. enl. 4/18/61 at Halltown in Co. B as Pvt. Absent sick July/Aug. 1861. Present again Sept./Oct. 1861. POW at Kernstown, 3/23/62 (Ft. Delaware). Exchanged 8/5/62. Wded. at Chancellorsville, 5/3/63. Last official entry shows him still absent from wound, March/April 1864. No further record.

WALKER, L. H.: Unofficial source lists him as a Pvt. in this regt.

WALKER, WILLIAM WELFORD: b. 2/20/37. Unofficial source shows him in this regt. bur. University of Va. Postwar, exhumed and moved to Old Chapel Cem., Millwood.

WALTERS, EDWARD: enl. 10/1/62 at Bunker Hill in Co. H as Pvt. AWOL since 11/4/62. No further record.

WALTERS, JOHN W.: b. 1831? Laborer. enl. 4/18/61 at Halltown in Co. B as Corp. Elected Lt. 9/24/62. Wded. in ankle at 2nd Manassas, date not specific. Absent on detail "after absentees," at 10/31/62 muster. Present again Nov./Dec. 1862. Signs roll as commanding Co., July/Aug. 1863. Last official entry shows him present, March/April 1864.

WALTERS, JOSEPH W.: b. 9/8/34. Laborer. Residence Augusta Co. enl. 4/18/61 at Halltown in Co. B as Pvt. Absent sick since 6/24/63. Detailed to wait on sick at Gettysburg. POW at Gettysburg, 7/3/63 (Ft. McHenry, Ft. Delaware, Pt. Lookout). Exchanged 9/30/64. Furloughed from Chimborazo #1, 10/10/64, length of furlough not stated. No further record. d. 11/23/68. bur. Elmwood Cem., Shepherdstown, W.Va.

WALTHER, FREDERICK: Only record is a POW statement that lists him in Co. D as Pvt. POW (Rebel deserter) at Hamilton, 10/26/64 (Ft. Monroe). Oath of Allegiance to U.S., date not stated.

WANDLING, ALLEN: b. 5/7/36. Miller. enl. 4/19/61 at Hedgesville in Co. E as Sgt. Deserted 7/18/61. d. 3/20/11. bur. Hedgesville Cem., Hedgesville, W.Va.

WASHINGTON, BUSHROD CORBIN: b. 1831. Farmer. enl. 4/18/61 at Charles Town in Co. G as Corp. POW at Kernstown, 3/23/62 (Ft. Delaware). Exchanged 8/5/62. Trans. to Co. B, 12th Va. Cav., 8/23/62. d. 1919. bur. Zion Episcopal Cem., Charles Town, W.Va.

WASHINGTON, GEORGE: b. 2/22/42. Student. enl. 4/18/61 at Charles Town in Co. G as Pvt. Elected Sgt., 6/10/61. Absent sick since 10/5/61. Discharged 8/31/62, reason not stated. Later appears on rolls of Co. B, 12th Va. Cav.

WASHINGTON, RICHARD BLACKBURN: b. 11/12/22. Attd. V.M.I., 1843. Farmer. enl. 4/18/61 at Charles Town in Co. G as Pvt. Absent sick since 8/20/61. Discharged 10/14/61, reason not stated. Postwar, farmer at Charles Town. d. 10/15/10. bur. Zion Episcopal Cem., Charles Town, W.Va.

WATSON, EPHRAIM C.: Unofficial source shows him in this regt. Also appears on rolls of Co. D, 12th Va. Cav. d. 6/14/21 at Leetown, W.Va.

WATSON, J. BART: Unofficial source shows him in this regt. Also appears on rolls of Co. D, 12th Va. Cav. d. 1921 at Middleway, W.Va.

WATSON, SAMUEL: b. 1839? Weaver. enl. 4/18/61 at Charles Town in Co. G as Pvt. Absent on 30-day detail for manufacturing duty, 10/13/61. Absent on special duty, Nov./Dec. 1861; "time unlimited." Type of duty not specified. No further record.

WATSON, WILLIAM: b. 1842? Weaver. enl. 4/18/61 at Charles Town in Co. G as Pvt. Absent on 30-day detail for manufacturing duty, 10/13/61. Absent on special duty, Nov./Dec. 1861; "time unlimited." Type of duty not specified. No further record.

WEAVER, CHARLES: drafted 12/14/62 at Morton's Ford in Co. E as Pvt. AWOL March/April 1863. No further record.

WEAVER, JOHN: enl. 12/22/62 at Guinea's Station in Co. D as Pvt. MWIA at Gettysburg, date not specific. Left in hosp. at Martinsburg. d. in hosp. at Martinsburg, no date given.

WEAVER, JOHN: drafted 4/13/63 at Camp Winder in Co. K as Pvt. Deserted 5/16/63.

WEAVER, MICHAEL: b. 1822? 5′ 4½″, dark complexion, gray eyes, dark hair. enl. 4/14/62 at New Market in Co. H as Pvt. Absent sick at hosp. since 5/7/62. Present again Jan./Feb. 1863. Chimborazo #1, 5/2/63; phthisis pul. Furloughed 6/5/63 for 50 days. Wded. in hand at Payne's Farm, 11/27/63. Gen. Hosp. Charlottesville, 12/11/63. Deserted 2/20/64.

138

WEAVER, WILLIAM: drafted 4/14/62 at Rude's Hill in Co. K. Only record lists him AWOL, 6/30-10/31 1862. No further record.

WEAVER, WILLIAM H.: b. 1839? in Augusta Co. 5'5". Listed in Co. H. Prewar, Capt. in Co. A, 93rd Va. Militia. Deprived of rank by Va. legislature in 1862 and drafted into the 2nd Va. Inf. Deserted April 1862. Turned himself over to Gen. Fremont's forces, June 1862. Then went into Md. and Pa.

WEBB, ISAAC: enl. 4/7/62 at Rude's Hill in Co. E as Pvt. KIA at Gaines's Mill or Malvern Hill, 6/27 or 7/1/1862.

WEBSTER, JOHN FRANK: enl. 2/24/62 at Winchester in Co. A as Pvt. Gen. Hosp. Staunton, 3/22/63; fever. Present again May/June 1863. Charged $1.00 for wasting 20 rounds of ammunition, Jan./Feb. 1864. Detailed as musician, 3/1/64. Last official entry shows him present, 4/30-10/31 1864. Surrendered at Appomattox.

WEBSTER, RICHARD A.: b. Feb. 1816. Smith. enl. 4/21/61 at Harpers Ferry in Co. D as Pvt. Discharged 5/22/61, overage. d. 8/16/74. bur. Greenhill Cem., Martinsburg, W.Va.

WEDDLE, GEORGE W.: b. in Berkeley Co. 5'6", fair complexion, gray eyes, brown hair. enl. 3/4/62 at Winchester in Co. E as Pvt. Wded. in hip at Port Republic, 6/9/62. Gen. Hosp. Charlottesville, 6/20-7/24 1862. Surrendered at Appomattox.

WEIR, JOHN ELLIOTT: b. 1843. Miner. enl. 4/18/61 at Millwood in Co. C as Pvt. To Sgt. 11/11/62. Wded. in left arm at 1st Manassas, 7/21/61. Absent wded. through Nov./Dec. 1861. Wded. at 2nd Manassas, 8/28/62. Returned from hosp. 12/8/62. POW at Spotsylvania, 5/12/64 (Pt. Lookout, Elmira). Exchanged 3/2/65. No further record. d. 3/15/13. bur. Stonewall Cem., Winchester.

WEISE, JAMES E.: b. 1827? enl. 7/31/64 at Winchester as chief musician of regt. Only official entry shows him present, 4/30-10/31 1864. d. 4/9/01. bur. Greenhill Cem., Martinsburg, W.Va.

WELCH, CHARLES A.: b. 1833? Printer. enl. 4/21/61 at Harpers Ferry in Co. D as Sgt. Surgeon's discharge, 4/27/61; reason not stated.

WELCH, JOHN: b. 1833? Laborer. enl. 5/11/61 at Harpers Ferry in Co. C as Pvt. Wded. in left breast at 1st Manassas, 7/21/61. Present again Sept./Oct. 1861. POW 6/10/62. No further record.

WELLARD, JOSEPH: b. 3/29/27. enl. 4/16/62 at Rude's Hill in Co. F as Pvt. AWOL 6/1/62-2/1/63. AWOL since 7/24/63. No further record. d. 5/26/99. bur. Solomon's Lutheran Church Cem., Shenandoah Co.

WELLARD, WILLIAM H.: b. 1/5/23. enl. 4/16/62 at Rude's Hill in Co. F as Pvt. AWOL 5/20/62-3/6/62. MWIA at Chancellorsville, 5/3/63. d. 5/19/63. bur. Little Brick Union Church Cem., Shenandoah Co.

WELLER, WILLIAM M.: enl. 10/8/62 at Bunker Hill in Co. A as Pvt. Absent sick in hosp. 6/4-Sept./Oct. 1863. Present again Nov./Dec. 1863. Last official entry shows him present, 4/30-10/31 1864 and on detail as an ambulance driver. Surrendered at Appomattox.

WERLINGIN, J.: b. 1831? 5'8". Only record is a paroled POW statement that lists him in Co. I and says he was paroled at Winchester, June 1862.

WEST, CHARLES: b. 1837? Laborer. enl. 4/25/61 at Harpers Ferry in Co. D as Pvt. Deserted 6/6/61.

WETHERHOLT, BENJAMIN: Residence Luray. enl. 4/9/62 at Rude's Hill in Co. E as Pvt. Wded. in leg at Chancellorsville, 5/3/63. Gen. Hosp. #1, Richmond, 5/11/63; dysentery and gangrene. Last official entry shows him still absent wded., March/April 1864. No further record.

WEVER, CHARLES J.: b. 1837. Farmer. enl. 4/18/61 at Martinsburg in Co. D as Pvt. Shot by accident 6/28/61. Still absent from accidental wound, Nov./Dec. 1861. No further record. d. 1878.

WEVER, DAVID J.: b. 1833? Carpenter. enl. 4/18/61 at Martinsburg in Co. D as Pvt. Deserted 6/4/61. Arrested 6/6/61. Deserted again 6/6/61.

WHARTON, WILLIAM: b. 1831? Saddler. enl. 4/18/61 at Millwood in Co. C as Sgt. Absent sick since 8/20/61. Present again Sept./Oct. 1861. Last official entry shows him present, Nov./Dec. 1861.

WHEELER, GEORGE W.: b. in Ireland. enl. 6/1/62 near Woodstock in Co. I as Pvt. MWIA in left thigh at Payne's Farm, 11/27/63. Chimborazo #5, 11/30/63. d. 12/31/63 at Chimborazo #5.

WHITE, BENJAMIN S.: b. 9/28/42. Student. enl. 4/26/61 at Harpers Ferry in Co. G as Pvt. To Sgt., date not given. Absent sick 10/28-10/31 1862. KIA at Chancellorsville, 5/3/63. bur. Zion Episcopal Cem., Charles Town, W.Va.

WHITE, JOHN W.: b. 7/24/24. Only record shows him on a list of POW's sent from Forrest Hall Prison to Ft. Delaware. d. 10/3/64 at Ft. Delaware.

WHITE, MICHAEL: b. 1832? Carpenter. enl. 4/19/61 at Hedgesville in Co. E as Pvt. Deserted 7/14/61.

WHITE, WILLIAM: b. 4/15/32. drafted 10/3/62 at Bunker Hill in Co. F as Pvt. Deserted before the enemy, 12/13/62. d. 3/21/09 at Welltown, Va. bur. Mt. Hebron Cem., Winchester.

WHITESELL, DAVID A.: enl. 4/15/62 at Rude's Hill in Co. A as Pvt. Absent on detail as teamster in QM's Dept., 4/27/62-Nov./Dec. 1863. Listed as a deserter, Jan./Feb. 1864. No further record.

WHITESELL, JOHN J.: enl. 4/15/62 at Rude's Hill in Co. A as Pvt. Discharged 7/31/62, reason not stated.

WHITESELL, SIMON: enl. 4/18/62 at Rude's Hill in Co. B as Pvt. POW at Mt. Jackson, 6/4/62. Exchanged 8/5/62. No record again until 3/26/64 when he returned to regt. from hosp. Present at 4/30/64 muster. No further record.

WHITING, CARLISLE FAIRFAX: b. 1843? Student. enl. 4/18/61 at Millwood in Co. C as Pvt. Wded. in left arm and stomach at 1st Manassas, 7/21/61. Absent from wound until 11/25/61. Last official entry shows him present, Nov./Dec. 1861. d. 11/31/64. bur. Old Chapel Cem., Millwood.

WHITING, FRANCIS BEVERLY: b. 10/27/26. Gentleman. enl. 4/18/61 at Millwood in Co. C as Pvt. To Corp., Nov. 1862. AWOL 8/16-10/5 1861. Absent sick since 12/10/61. Present again 6/30-10/31 1862. Wded. at Gettysburg, 7/3/63. Gen. Hosp. Charlottesville, 8/1-9/1 1863. Returned to regt. from hosp., 9/5/63. Wded. at Spotsylvania, 5/12/64. Still absent from wounds, 8/31-12/31 1864. No further record. d. 8/18/07. bur. Old Chapel Cem., Millwood.

WHITMORE, JOHN G.: b. 2/21/40. 5'7", light complexion, blue eyes, dark hair. Residence Rockingham Co. enl. 4/16/62 at Rude's Hill in Co. E as Pvt. Absent on detail as teamster in Ord. train, 6/18/62-Jan. 1864. Rebel deserter, date of desertion not given. Oath of Allegiance to U.S., 1/15/64; "sent north." d. 6/7/06. bur. Falling Water Cem., Spring Mills, W.Va.

WHITSON, GEORGE D.: b. 6/10/38. Carpenter. Residence Martinsburg. enl. 4/25/61 at Harpers Ferry in Co. D as Pvt. and Musician. Wded. in thigh at 1st Manassas, 7/21/61. Gen. Hosp. Charlottesville, 7/22/61. Furloughed 20 days. Present again Sept./Oct. 1861. Absent sick at hosp., Nov./Dec. 1862. Present again Jan./Feb. 1863. Gen. Hosp. Charlottesville, 1/24-1/25 1863; debility. POW at Strasburg, 10/19/64 (Pt. Lookout). Released 5/14/65. d. 8/18/09. bur. Old Norborne Cem., Martinsburg, W.Va.

WHITTAKER, FREDERICK B.: b. 1831? Clerk. enl. 4/18/61 at Charles Town in Co. A as Pvt. Last official entry shows him present, Nov./Dec. 1861.

WHITTER, GEORGE F.: b. 1839? Cabinet maker. enl. 5/7/61 at Harpers Ferry in Co. C as Pvt. KIA at 1st Manassas, 7/21/61.

WHITTINGTON, CORNELIUS: b. 1838? 5' 10", light complexion, blue eyes, light hair. Laborer. enl. 4/21/61 at Duffields in Co. H as Pvt. Absent on detached service under Asst. QM, July/Aug. 1863-March/April 1864. Last official entry shows him present, 4/30-12/31 1864. Paroled 4/21/65 at Winchester.

WHITTINGTON, CHARLES R.: b. 1845. drafted 10/29/62 at Camp Allen in Co. C as Pvt. Discharged at camp near Middletown, 11/22/62; reason not stated. bur. Greenhill Cem., Martinsburg.

WHITTINGTON, GEORGE W.: b. 1843? Blacksmith. enl. 4/18/61 at Berryville in Co. I as Pvt. Absent sick in hosp., July/Aug. 1861. Present again Sept./Oct. 1861. AWOL since 12/27/61. AWOL since 5/30/62, and dropped from the roll. No further record. d. 1/1/24 in Clarke Co.

WHITTINGTON, JAMES: b. 1843? Laborer. enl. 5/14/61 at Harpers Ferry in Co. H as Pvt. AWOL 31 days, July/Aug. 1861, and fined $11.00 for absence by court-martial. No further record. Later appears on rolls of Co. B, 12th Va. Cav. d. 10/28/01. bur. Edge Hill Cem., Charles Town, W.Va.

WHITTINGTON, JAMES W.: b. 4/16/39. Blacksmith. enl. 4/18/61 at Berryville in Co. I as Pvt. AWOL 8/4-8/12 1861. Fined $11.00 for absence by court-martial. AWOL since 6/1/62 and dropped from the roll, Nov./Dec. 1862. Later appears on the rolls of Co. A, 12th Va. Cav. d. 3/11/93. bur. Smoketown Cem., north of Martinsburg, W.Va.

WHITTINGTON, JOHN: enl. 9/1/62 near Manassas in Co. I as Pvt. Substitute for James E. Bonham. Deserted 10/1/62.

WHITTINGTON, JOHN N.: b. 1840? Painter. Residence Jefferson Co. enl. 4/18/61 at Charles Town in Co. A as Pvt. To Corp. 9/1/62. To Sgt. 10/31/63. POW at Woodstock, 6/2/62. Exchanged 8/5/62. POW at Fisher's Hill, 9/22/64 (Pt. Lookout). Oath of Allegiance to U.S., 5/14/65. bur. Edge Hill Cem., Charles Town, W.Va.

WILHITE, ALBERT: enl. 4/15/62 at Rude's Hill in Co. A as Pvt. AWOL 4/15/62-2/15/63. Sentenced by court-martial to have 1 month's pay deducted for absence. Discharged March/April 1863, reason not stated.

WILKENS, JONATHAN: enl. 8/10/62 at Orange Court House in Co. H as Pvt. AWOL since 12/23/62. No further record.

WILLIAMS, E.: b. 1844? 5' 8", light complexion, gray eyes, brown hair. Farmer. Only record is a parole statement that lists him in Co. F. POW in Cabell Co., 12/2/62 (Camp Douglas). Exchanged 4/4/63. No further record.

WILLIAMS, J. J.: Only record is a POW statement that lists him in Co. G as Pvt. POW at Luray, 9/24/64 (Pt. Lookout). No further record.

WILLIAMS, SAM: Only record is a POW statement that lists him in Co. E as Pvt. POW at Williamsport, Md., 9/30/62 (Ft. McHenry). Exchanged 10/27/62. No further record.

WILLINGHAM, GEORGE FRANK: b. 4/22/38. drafted 10/3/62 at Bunker Hill in Co. F as Pvt. Absent sick May/June 1863-Jan./Feb. 1864. No further record. d. 1/14/12. bur. Greenhill Cem., Berryville.

WILLINGHAM, GEORGE W.: b. 1838? 5' 9¾", dark complexion, hazel eyes, dark brown hair. Carpenter. Residence Jefferson Co. enl. 6/16/61 at Winchester in Co. I as Pvt. AWOL 8/4-8/13 1861. Fined $5.00 for absence by court-martial. Absent sick Sept./Oct.-Nov./Dec. 1861. AWOL 3/17-5/28 1862. POW at High Bridge, 4/6/65 (City Point). Oath of Allegiance to U.S., 6/22/65.

WILLINGHAM, JAMES W.: enl. 10/4/62 at Bunker Hill in Co. B as Pvt. Last official entry shows him present, March/April 1864. No further record.

WILLINGHAM, JAMES W.: b. 1836. 5' 11½", fair complexion, blue eyes, light hair. Carpenter. Residence Winchester. enl. 4/18/61 at Berryville in Co. I as Pvt. To Corp. 8/13/61. To Sgt. 6/1/63. Gen. Hosp. Charlottesville, 6/25-7/21 1862; paralysis. POW at Spotsylvania, 5/12/64 (Pt. Lookout, Elmira). Oath of Allegiance to U.S., 6/23/65. d. 1898. bur. Edge Hill Cem., Charles Town, W.Va.

WILLINGHAM, JOHN K.: b. 1840? Drover. enl. 6/17/61 at Winchester in Co. I as Pvt. AWOL 12/25-12/30 1861. KIA at Kernstown, 3/23/62.

WILLIS, WILLIAM B.: b. 1837? Farmer. enl. 4/23/61 at Harpers Ferry in Co. G as Pvt. Trans. 8/12/62 at Harrisonburg into Co. B, 12th Va. Cav.

WILLSON, BENJAMIN: b. 1835? Laborer. enl. 4/25/61 at Millwood in Co. C as Pvt. KIA at 1st Manassas, 7/21/61.

WILSON, ABRAHAM: enl. 3/8/62 at Winchester in Co. I as Pvt. AWOL since 5/25/62 and dropped from the roll, Nov./Dec. 1862. No further record.

WILSON, BENJAMIN F.: enl. 7/7/61 at Winchester in Co. I as Pvt. AWOL 7/27-8/4 1861. AWOL 11/10-12/30 1861. AWOL since 3/4/62 and dropped as a deserter. No further record.

WILSON, CHARLES: Only record lists him in Co. B as Pvt. and says he was wded. at Dinwiddie Court House, 3/31/65.

WILSON, FRANK C.: b. 1841. Unofficial source shows him in this regt. Postwar, physician. Alive in Louisville, Kentucky, 1907.

WILSON, JOHN C.: Only record is his parole statement that lists him as a Pvt. Paroled 4/25/65 at Lewisburg.

WILSON, J. W.: Unofficial source shows him in this regt. d. 3/23/62. bur. Stonewall Cem.

WILSON, JEREMIAH: b. 1826? Farmhand. enl. 5/21/61 at Lemon's Ferry in Co. I as Pvt. AWOL 7/27-7/31 1861. AWOL 8/23/61. AWOL 9/25-10/22 1861. Fined $11.00 for absence by court-martial. AWOL 12/25-12/30 1861. AWOL since 5/26/62 and dropped as a deserter. No further record.

WILSON, J. J.: Listed in Co. E as Pvt. Only record shows him as a deserter, Sept./Oct. 1862.

WILSON, JOSEPH H.: b. 1836? Miller. enl. 4/18/61 at Berryville in Co. I as Pvt. Shown as Corp. at 10/31/62 muster. To Pvt. 1/7/63. AWOL 11/19-11/21 1861. AWOL 12/25-12/31 1861. Deserted 7/16/63.

140

WILSON, LANCELOT: b. 1835? Workman. enl. 6/15/61 at Winchester in Co. F as Pvt. Under arrest awaiting trial, July/Aug. 1861; reason not stated. Absent sick Sept./Oct. 1861. Present again Nov./Dec. 1861. Listed as a deserter 4/30-10/31 1862. Next record, however, shows him as a POW at Paris, 5/16/63 (Ft. McHenry). Exchanged 5/20/63. No further record.

WILSON, ROBERT N.: b. 1839? Farmhand. enl. 4/18/61 at Berryville in Co. I as Pvt. AWOL 7/27-7/31 1861. AWOL 8/25/61. AWOL 10/18-10/26 1861. Fined $11.00 for absence by court-martial, Sept./Oct. 1861. AWOL 11/23-11/28 1861. AWOL since 12/27/61. Deserted 7/16/63. POW (Rebel deserter) at Sharpsburg, Md., 8/3/63 (Ft. McHenry). Oath of Allegiance to U.S., 3/24/64.

WILSON, VALERIUS W.: b. 1839? Farmer. enl. 4/22/61 at Harpers Ferry in Co. E as Pvt. Absent sick Sept./Oct. 1861. Present again Nov./Dec. 1861. Last official entry for Sept./Oct. 1862 says he trans. to Cav., date not given.

WILSON, WALKER B.: b. 1833? Millwright. enl. 6/21/61 at Camp Myers in Co. I as Pvt. AWOL 7/18-8/9 1861. AWOL 9/28/61. AWOL 11/21-11/28 1861. AWOL 12/25/61-1/1/62. Absent on detached service to repair a mill, Nov./Dec. 1862-March/April 1863. Deserted 5/1/63.

WILSON, WILLIAM: 5'8", fair complexion, gray eyes, brown hair. Residence Clarke Co. enl. 3/10/62 at Winchester in Co. I as Pvt. Absent sick March/April-May/June 1863. No further record.

WILT, GEORGE W.: b. 1846. enl. 9/9/61 at Charles Town in Co. K as Pvt. Last official entry shows him present, Nov./Dec. 1861. d. 3/24/07. bur. Wilt Place, Rt. 340 and Cherry Hill Rd., Jefferson Co., W.Va.

WILTSHIRE, CHARLES B.: b. 11/26/41. Farmer. enl. 6/15/61 at Charles Town in Co. G as Pvt. Absent sick Nov./Dec. 1861. No further record. Later appears on rolls of Co. A, 12th Va. Cav. d. 4/4/65. bur. Edge Hill Cem., Charles Town, W.Va.

WILTSHIRE, JAMES B.: b. 1842? Farmer. enl. 6/12/61 at Camp Jackson on Bolivar Heights in Co. G as Pvt. Absent sick, Nov./Dec. 1861. No further record.

WINDLE, GEORGE: drafted 4/16/62 at Rude's Hill in Co. C as Pvt. First official entry says he returned from desertion, 4/18/63; time of desertion not stated. AWOL 7/20-10/25 1863. d. 2/19/64 at Orange Court House; dysentery.

WINDLE, JOSEPH: drafted 4/16/62 at Rude's Hill in Co. C as Pvt. Only record shows him absent at 12/31/64 muster from wound received at Cedar Creek, 10/19/64.

WINSTON, W. H.: Residence Hanover Co. Only record is parole statement that lists him as a Pvt. Paroled 4/25/65 at Ashland.

WINTERMOYER, JACOB: b. 10/28/31. Painter. enl. 4/18/61 at Halltown in Co. B as Pvt. Absent sick 6/18/63-Jan. 1864. Deserted 2/1/64. d. 8/27/09. bur. Elmwood Cem., Shepherdstown, W.Va.

WINTERMOYER, JOHN: b. 1827? Laborer. enl. 4/21/61 at Duffields in Co. H as Pvt. Last official entry shows him present, Nov./Dec. 1861. Exchanged POW, 8/5/62. Where and when captured not stated. No further record. d. 2/28/09. bur. Elmwood Cem., Shepherdstown, W.Va.

WINTERMOYER, THOMAS H.: b. 1834? 5'8", light complexion, gray eyes, dark hair. Shoemaker. enl. 4/23/61 at Harpers Ferry in Co. B as Pvt. To Sgt. 12/1/62. Exchanged POW, 8/5/62. Where and when captured not stated. POW at Spotsylvania, 5/12/64 (Pt. Lookout, Elmira). Exchanged 10/29/64. Next record shows him in hosp. in Macon, Georgia, 11/15/64; diarrhea. Paroled 4/21/65 at Winchester.

WINTERMOYER, WILLIAM: b. 1829? Weaver. enl. 4/18/61 at Halltown in Co. B as Pvt. AWOL since 5/1/62 and dropped from the roll, 12/22/62. No further record. Appears on rolls of Co. D, 12th Va. Cav.

WINTERS, HARRY: Unofficial source shows him in Co. F.

WINTERS, SAMUEL: b. 1842? Laborer. enl. 5/29/61 at Camp Lee in Co. H as Pvt. Deserted 6/10/61.

WISE, JAMES E.: enl. 11/4/62 at camp near White Post in Co. B as Pvt. Detailed as fifer for regt., 11/14/62. Deserted 6/21/63.

WISEMAN, WILLIAM: b. 1836? 5'10", fair complexion, brown eyes, dark hair. Residence Augusta Co. drafted 4/14/62 at Rude's Hill in Co. K as Pvt. Wded. at 1st Winchester, 5/25/62. Returned to regt. after recovering from wound, 2/20/63. Detailed as guard to Ord. train, 5/20/63. POW at Beverly, 10/18/64 (Clarksburg, W.Va.). No further record.

WOLF, WILLIAM: enl. 4/16/62 at Rude's Hill in Co. F as Pvt. AWOL 5/20/62-3/6/63. Absent sick May/June-Sept./Oct. 1863. AWOL since 11/1/63. No further record.

WOLFF, BERNARD LIKENS: b. 1838? m. Eliza Preston Benton McDowell. Clerk. enl. 4/21/61 at Harpers Ferry in Co. D as Pvt. Detailed in QM Dept., July/Aug. 1861. Trans. from Co. by promotion, 10/12/61; new assignment not stated. Unofficial source says he later became a major in the Stonewall Brigade and served on the staff of Gen. William Nelson Pendleton. d. 1870.

WOLFF, WILLIAM: drafted 12/24/62 near Rappahannock Academy in Co. E as Pvt. Absent sick, Jan. 1863. d. 1/30/63 at Gordonsville, typhoid fever.

WOOD, F. J.: 5'6", dark complexion, dark eyes, dark hair. Residence Amherst. Only record is his Oath of Allegiance to U.S. which lists him as Pvt. Oath of Allegiance to U.S. at Ft. Delaware, 6/21/65.

WOOD, LEWIS H.: enl. 9/10/61 at Camp Harman in Co. C as Pvt. AWOL 12/24/61. Present again 6/30-10/31 1862. AWOL since 6/15/63. Deserted 9/1/63.

WOODCOCK, G.: Unofficial source shows him in Co. A. bur. Stonewall Cem., Winchester.

WOODDEY, PARKINSON S. C.: enl. 3/10/62 at Winchester in Co. A as Pvt. POW at Kernstown, 3/23/62 (Ft. Delaware). Exchanged 8/5/62. Last official entry for 10/31/62 says he "enlisted without consent of parents and was taken away by father." No further record.

WOODWARD, WILLIAM: b. 1846? Unofficial source shows him in this regt. d. 5/26/62. bur. Thornrose Cem., Staunton.

WOOLEY, DANIEL: Only record is a parole statement that shows him in Co. G. Paroled 4/22/65 at Winchester.

WRIGHT, DANIEL: b. 1840? 5'6", fair complexion, gray eyes, black hair. drafted 4/16/62 at Rude's Hill in Co. C as Pvt. To Corp. 11/1/62. To Sgt. date not given. Discharged 1/5/63 after furnishing substitute. Paroled 5/20/65 at Staunton.

WRIGHT, JAMES: enl. 4/9/62 at Rude's Hill in Co. E as Pvt. AWOL since 6/8/62. No further record. Appears on rolls of Co. D, 12th Va. Cav.

141

WRIGHT, JOHN: b. 1811? Laborer. enl. 4/18/61 at Halltown in Co. B as Pvt. Absent sick, 4/18-6/30 through July/Aug. 1861. Present again Sept./Oct. 1861. Discharged 11/9/61 at Centerville, reason not stated.

WRIGHT, SAMUEL S.: b. 11/4/32. Farmer. enl. 4/18/61 at Charles Town in Co. G as Pvt. Last official entry shows him present, Nov./Dec. 1861. Appears on rolls of Co. B, 12th Va. Cav. KIA in battle near Moorefield, Hardy Co., W.Va., 1/30/64. bur. Edge Hill Cem., Charles Town, W.Va.

WRITT, GEORGE W.: b. 11/25/41. Farmhand. enl. 4/29/61 at Harpers Ferry in Co. I as Pvt. AWOL 7/27-7/31 1861. AWOL 11/25-11/30 1861. Deserted 1/24/64. d. 2/21/01 at Rippon, W.Va. bur. Edge Hill Cem., Charles Town, W.Va.

WRITT, ISAAC: drafted 10/3/62 at Bunker Hill in Co. G as Pvt. AWOL in Capt. Wein's Cav., Nov./Dec. 1862-Jan./Feb. 1863. Trans. to Capt. Wein's Cav., March/April 1863.

WYNDHAM, THOMAS C.: Harness maker. enl. 5/25/61 at Lemon's Ferry in Co. I as Pvt. AWOL since 11/9/61. No further record. Unofficial source says he trans. to Co. D, 6th Va. Cav. d. 6/4/21 at his home in Brazil, Indiana. bur. Brazil, Indiana.

WYNDHAM, THORTON O.: b. 1/17/27. Unofficial source says he served in Co. C. d. Sept. 1924. bur. Mt. Hebron Cem., Winchester.

YONTZ, GEORGE W.: b. 1842? Shoemaker. enl. 4/20/61 at Harpers Ferry in Co. B as Pvt. To Corp. 8/1/62. Wded. at 2nd Manassas, date not specific. Present at 10/31/62 muster. Detailed in band, 6/20/63. Trans. to 2nd Regt. Band, Jan./Feb. 1864. Last official entry shows him present, 4/30-10/31 1864. Surrendered at Appomattox.

YONTZ, JOSEPH E.: enl. 2/18/62 at Winchester in Co. B as Pvt. To Corp. 10/1/64. Surrendered at Appomattox. bur. Elmwood Cem., Shepherdstown, W.Va.

YOUELL, ISAAC: enl. 4/9/62 at Rude's Hill in Co. E as Pvt. Only record in Sept./Oct. 1862 shows him as a deserter.

YOUNG, THOMAS B.: b. 3/5/38. Butcher. enl. 4/18/61 at Charles Town in Co. A as Pvt. To Sgt. 7/1/62. To Pvt. 10/31/63. Fined $11.00 for AWOL by court-martial, July/Aug. 1861. Absent on detached service in Valley of Virginia, 1/1/63; duty not stated. Present again May/June 1863. Charged $.50 for wasting 10 rounds of ammunition, Jan./Feb. 1864. POW at Spotsylvania, 5/12/64 (Pt. Lookout, Elmira). Exchanged 3/2/65. Jackson Hosp., Richmond, 3/7/65; debility. Furloughed 3/8/65 for 30 days. No further record. d. 11/13/90. bur. Edge Hill Cem., Charles Town, W.Va.

YOUNG, WILLIAM H.: b. 1831? Workman. enl. 6/24/61 at Winchester in Co. F as Pvt. KIA at 1st Manassas, 7/21/61. bur. Stonewall Cem., Winchester.

ZANE, NOAH: b. 1842? Gentleman. enl. 4/20/61 at Harpers Ferry in Co. K as Pvt. To Corp. 8/12/61. Last official entry shows him present, Nov./Dec. 1861. Next record states he enl. 8/22/62 in Co. A, 35th Va. Cav. Battalion.

ZEN, PHILLIP H.: drafted 4/14/62 at Rude's Hill in Co. K as Pvt. Gen. Hosp. Charlottesville, 5/13-6/7 1862; debility. Discharged sometime before 10/31/62, overage.

ZIMMERMAN, WILLIAM: drafted 4/14/62 at Rude's Hill in Co. K as Pvt. Discharged 7/22/62, reason not stated.

ZIRKLE, JOSEPH: b. 1847? 5'6", fair complexion, green eyes, fair hair. Only record is a parole statement that shows him in Co. K. Paroled 5/3/65 at Mt. Jackson.

ZIRKLE, WILLIAM S.: Unofficial source shows him in Co. F. m. Martha Rebecca Miller.

ZITTLE, JOHN H.: b. 1835? Printer. enl. 4/18/61 at Halltown in Co. B as Lt. Last official entry shows him present, Jan./Feb. 1862. Dropped from the Register of Commissioned Officers, 5/18/62; reason not stated.

BIBLIOGRAPHY

Manuscripts

Adjutant and Inspector General's Office, C.S.A. Inspection Reports and Related Records Received by the Inspection Branch in the Confederate A & IGO Office. National Archives.

Berger, Christine Blackwell. Miscellaneous Historical Records. Berkeley County Court House.

Botts, Lawson. Papers. Virginia Military Institute.

Boteler, Alexander Robinson. Papers. Duke University.

Compiled Service Records of the officers and men belonging to the Second Virginia Infantry. National Archives.

Confederate Service Records of Virginia Soldiers. Virginia State Library.

French, S. Bassett. Biographical Sketches. Virginia State Library.

Historical Records Book 18: W. P. A. Cemetery Lists. Berkeley County Court House.

Hollywood Cemetery Burial Records. Hollywood Cemetery, Richmond.

Hooke, Robert W. Papers. Duke University.

Krick, Robert K. Obituary Index of Confederate Veterans from Richmond newspapers, 1895-1925. Robert Krick collection, Fredericksburg.

Muster Rolls of Clarke County, 1861-1865. Clarke County Court House.

Nadenbousch, John Quincy Adams. Papers. Duke University.

Ritter, Ben. Miscellaneous Notes in Four Notebooks. Handley Library Archives, Winchester.

Second Virginia Statistical Summaries and Casualty Returns, compiled by the author from service records in the National Archives.

Sheetz, Daniel H. Letters to family members and friends, 1862-1864. In collection of Ronald Sheetz, Harpers Ferry Center, National Park Service.

United Daughters of the Confederacy alphabetic card file. National UDC Headquarters, Richmond.

United Daughters of the Confederacy application forms. Virginia Division, UDC, Richmond.

Virginia Military Institute Alumni records.

Newspapers

Philadelphia *Times.*
The Evening Star. Winchester.
The Shepherdstown *Register.*
The Spirit of Jefferson-Farmers' Advocate. Charles Town.
The Star. Winchester.
The Virginia Free Press. Charles Town.

Winchester *Evening Star.*
Winchester *News.*
Winchester *Republican.*
Winchester *Times.*
Winchester *Virginian.*

Published Primary Sources

Barry, Joseph. *The Strange Story of Harpers Ferry.* 1903; rpt. Shepherdstown, West Virginia: The Shepherdstown *Register,* Inc., 1974.

Baylor, George. *Bull Run to Bull Run.* Richmond: B. F. Johnson Publishing
Co., 1900.

Confederate States of America. War Department. *General Orders from
the Adjutant and Inspector General's Office, Confederate States
Army, for the Year 1863.* Richmond: A. Morris, 1864.

Confederate Veteran. 40 vols. Nashville, 1893-1932.

Douglas, Henry Kyd. *I Rode With Stonewall.* Chapel Hill: The University
of North Carolina Press, 1940.

Gold, Thomas D. *History of Clarke County, Virginia, and its Connection
with the War Between the States.* Berryville, Virginia: Thomas D.
Gold, 1914.

Hendricks, James Madison. "Jackson's March to Rear of Pope's Army."
Confederate Veteran, 17, No. 11 (November, 1909), 549-550.

Humphreys, David. *Heroes and Spies of the Civil War.* New York: The
Neale Publishing Co., 1903.

Johnson, Robert Underwood and Clarence C. Buel, eds. *Battles and
Leaders of the Civil War.* 4 vols. New York: The Century Company,
1887.

Jones, J. William. *Christ in the Camp or Religion in Lee's Army.* Richmond: B. F. Johnson & Co., 1888.

McDonald, William Naylor. *A History of the Laurel Brigade.* 1907; rpt. Arlington, Virginia: R. W. Beatty, Ltd., 1969.

Moore, Edward A. The Story of a Cannoneer Under Stonewall Jackson.
New York: The Neale Publishing Co., 1907.

Nelson, William N. "Annals of War: Before Fighting Began." The Philadelphia *Times,* 4 (January 1, 1881), 159-162.

Southern Historical Society Papers. 50 vols. Richmond, 1876-1953.

Strother, David Hunter. *Porte Crayon Sampler.* rpt. Richmond, West
Virginia: Jim Comstock, 1974.

U.S. War Department. *The War of the Rebellion: A Compilation of the
Official Records of the Union and Confederate Armies.* 128 vols.
Government Printing Office, 1880-1901.

Other Sources

Aler, F. Vernon. *Aler's History of Martinsburg and Berkeley County, West Virginia.* Hagerstown, Maryland: The Mail Publishing Co., 1888.

Bearss, Edwin C. "Troop Movement Maps: Battle of First Manassas." (Unpublished paper).

Bee Line Chapter, National Society of Daughters of the American Revolution. *Tombstone Inscriptions in Jefferson County, West Virginia.* Missouri: Walsworth Publishing Company, 1981.

Boatner, Mark Mayo, III. *The Civil War Dictionary.* New York: David McKay Company, Inc., 1959.

Bruce, Philip A. *A History of Virginia.* 6 vols. Chicago, 1924.

Bushong, Dean M. and Millard K. *Fightin' Tom Rosser, C.S.A.* Shippensburg, Pennsylvania: Beidel Printing House, Inc., 1983.

_____, Millard K. *General Turner Ashby and Stonewall's Valley Campaign.* Verona, Virginia: McClure Printing Company, Inc., 1980.

_____. *Historic Jefferson County.* Boyce, Virginia: Carr Publishing Co., Inc., 1972.

Confederate Memorial Institute. *The Returned Battleflags of the Virginia Regiments in the War Between the States.* Richmond: privately printed, n.d.

Esposito, Vincent J. ed. *The West Point Atlas of American Wars: 1689-1900.* New York: Frederick A. Praeger, 1959.

Evans, Clement A., ed. *Confederate Military History.* 12 vols (expanded editions). Atlanta: Confederate Publishing Co., 1899.

Evans, Willis F. *History of Berkeley County, West Virginia.* Martinsburg, West Virginia: Willis F. Evans, 1928.

Freeman, Douglas Southall. *Lee's Lieutenants: A Study in Command.* 3 vols. New York: Charles Scribner's Sons, 1942-44.

Gardiner, M. H. and A. M. *Chronicles of Old Berkeley: A Narrative History of a Virginia County from its Beginnings to 1926.* Durham, North Carolina: The Seeman Press, 1938.

Jefferson County Camp, United Confederate Veterans. *Military Operations in Jefferson County Virginia and West Virginia, 1861-1865.* Charles Town, West Virginia: Farmers Advocate Print, 1911.

Johnson, Rev. John Lipscomb. *The University Memorial: Biographical Sketches of the Alumni of the University of Virginia Who Fell in the Confederate War.* Baltimore: Turnbull Brothers, 1871.

Kelly, Dennis P. "Location and Significance of the Action at Brawner's Farm, August 28, 1862." (Unpublished paper).

Krick, Robert K. *Lee's Colonels: A Biographical Register of the Field Officers of the Army of Northern Virginia.* Dayton, Ohio: Press of Morningside Bookshop, 1979.

145

Magazine of the Jefferson County Historical Society. 49 vols. 1934-1983.

Mickle, William E. *Well Known Confederate Veterans and Their War Records.* New Orleans: William E. Mickle, 1907.

Morton, Frederic. *The Story of Winchester in Virginia.* Strasburg, Virginia: Shenandoah Publishing House, 1925.

Musser, Clifford S. *Two Hundred Years' History of Shepherdstown.* Shepherdstown, West Virginia: The Independent, 1931.

Sigaud, Louis A. *Belle Boyd: Confederate Spy.* Richmond: The Dietz Press, Inc., 1944.

Tanner, Robert G. *Stonewall in the Valley: Thomas J. "Stonewall" Jackson's Valley Campaign, Spring 1862.* Garden City, New York: Doubleday and Co., Inc., 1976.

Trapnell, Frederica H. "Colonel Lawson Botts, C.S.A.," *The Magazine of the Jefferson County Historical Society,* 49 (December, 1983), 27-34.

Tyler, Lyon Gardiner. *Encyclopedia of Virginia Biography.* 5 vols. New York: Lewis Historical Publishing Co., 1915.

V.M.I. Register of Former Cadets. Lexington, Virginia: Virginia Military Institute, 1957.

Walker, Charles D. *Memorial, Virginia Military Institute.* Philadelphia: J. B. Lippincott & Co., 1875.

Wallace, Lee A., Jr. *A Guide to Virginia Military Organizations, 1861-1865. Richmond: Virginia Civil War Commission, 1964.*

Warner, Ezra J. *Generals in Gray: Lives of the Confederate Commanders.* Baton Rouge: Louisiana State University Press, 1959.

_____. *Generals in Blue: Lives of the Union Commanders.* Baton Louisiana State University Press, 1964.

Wayland, John W. *Twenty-five Chapters on the Shenandoah Valley.* Strasburg, Virginia: The Shenandoah Valley Publishing House, Inc., 1957.

2nd EDITION ADDENDUM

ARGENBRIGHT, JAMES M.: b. Augusta County. Postwar, tinner residing in Middlebrook; member Stonewall Camp #25 at Staunton. Alive in 1916.

BAKER, HENRY M.: b. Feb. 1825.

BARR, MARTIN LUTHER: b. Winchester. m. Carrie Parker.

BEAVERS, J. BARTON: b. 12/28/34. d. 8/27/13. bur. Mt. Hebron Cem., Winchester.

BELL, CHARLES E.: b. July 1843. Groceryman.

BUCHANAN (BUCHANNON), THOMAS E.: d. 12/19/88.

CHAMBERS, ROBERT D. One of the first of eight Confederates imprisoned at Ft. Delaware in July, 1861. Exchanged in the fall of 1861.

ENGLEMAN, WILLIAM D.: Postwar, member of Stonewall Jackson Camp #25 at Staunton.

GRANGER, JACOB F.: b. Wertenberg, Germany. Postwar, farmer residing in Augusta Co.; member Stonewall Jackson Camp #25 at Staunton. Alive in 1899.

HENSELL, E. L.: b. Shepherdstown. Unofficial source says he served in Co. B and then trans. to Co. F, 1st Va. Cav. Postwar, farmer near Mint Springs; member Stonewall Jackson Camp #25 at Staunton. d. 3/21/13.

HICKS, JOSEPH DORSEN: b. Albemarle Co. Postwar, farmer near Stuart's Draft; member Stonewall Jackson Camp #25 at Staunton. Alive in 1896.

HISEY, JOSEPH: b. 10/4/27 on Narrow Passage Creek in Shenandoah Co. Stonemason. Unofficial source list him in Co. E. Same source says KIA at Gaines's Mill, 6/27/62.

HOLLIS, THOMAS W.: One of the first of eight Confederates imprisoned at Ft. Delaware in July, 1861; exchanged in the fall of 1861.

HULL, GEORGE M.: b. 1/7/38. d. 3/21/09. bur. Elmwood Cem., Mexico, Missouri.

McGUIRE, HUNTER HOLMES: Postwar, member Stonewall Jackson Camp #25 at Staunton.

O'BANNON, JAMES H.: d. 8/15/05 in Richmond.

RANSON, THOMAS DAVIS: Postwar, member of Stonewall Jackson Camp #25 at Staunton. d. 7/21/18.

RITEHOUR (RITENOUR), NOAH D.: b. 1845. d. Sept. 1913 at Alexandria.

RUTHERFORD, JOHN A.: b. Jefferson Co. Trans. to Co. E, 11th Va. Cav. Postwar, farmer; member of Stonewall Jackson Camp #25 at Staunton. Alive in 1907.

SOWERS, JOHN W.: d. 1889 at Stone Bridge, Clarke Co. bur. Bethel Church.

TAYLOR, JOSEPH F.: (correction) b. 1840. d. 1924. bur. Methodist Cem., Shenandoah, Page Co.

TIMBERLAKE, SETH M.: Postwar, member of Stonewall Jackson Camp #25 at Staunton.

WILLINGHAM, GEORGE FRANKLIN: Farmer. m. Hannah Elizabeth Maddox. d. 11/14/12.

VOORHEES, JACOB F.: Postwar, member of Stonewall Jackson Camp #25 at Staunton. d. 2/23/20.

Lt. Richard Henry Lee
Company G

Pvt. Carter M. Louthan
Company I

Pvt. Joseph Hisey
Company E

2nd Infantry
4th Edition

ALLEN, JAMES M.: 5'10", fair complexion, dark eyes, dark hair. enl. 7/18/63 at Harrisonburg in Co. D of 12th Va. Cav. as Corp. Present Sept./Oct. 1863-July/Aug. 1864. No further record. Paroled at Mt. Jackson, 4/18/65. Postwar, resident of Summit Point, W.Va.

ALLEN, JOHN W.: 6'0", fair complexion, hazel eyes, dark hair. enl. 7/18/62 at Harrisonburg in Co. D of 12th Va. Cav. as Sgt. On detached duty at horse hospital, Sept./Oct-Nov./Dec. 1863. Present Jan./Feb.-July/Aug. 1864. No further record. Paroled at Mt. Jackson, 4/18/65. d. by 1907.

BACKUS, GEORGE H. C.: enl. 7/27/63 at Shepherdstown in Co. D of 12th Va. Cav. as Pvt. AWOL Sept./Oct. 1863. Present Nov./ Dec. 1863-March/April 1864.

BAKER, WILLIAM H.: 5'10", fair complexion, blue eyes, brown hair. enl. 4/17/62 at Conrad's Store in Co. B of 12th Va. Cav. as Pvt. Present Nov./Dec. 1863-Jan./Feb. 1864. March 31, 1864 roll reports him absent sick since 3/14/64. Present at 4/30/64 muster. No further record. Paroled at Winchester, 4/20/65. d. by 1900.

BARRINGER, JAMES N.: 6'0", dark complexion, blue eyes, brown hair. enl. 4/17/62 at Conrad's Store in Co. B of 12th Va. Cav. as Pvt. POW 10/16/62 near Charles Town. Paroled at Ft. McHenry, 10/25/62. Present Nov./Dec. 1863. AWOL Jan./ Feb. 1864. POW at Halltown, W.Va., 8/24/64 (Old Capitol Prison, 8/25/64; Ft. Delaware, 9/20/64). Oath of Allegiance to U.S. at Ft. Delaware, 6/7/65. d. by 1900.

BAYLOR, GEORGE: Appointed 3rd Lt. in Co. B, 12th Va. Cav., 3/1/62. Horse KIA near Halltown, 11/1/62; Baylor slightly wded. In the calf of leg. Captured by 14th Pa. Cav. near Summit Point, 2/12/63 (Ft. McHenry, 2/13/63; Ft. Delaware, 2/26/63; Old Capitol Prison, April 1863). Delivered to City Point for exchange, 4/6/63. Wded. in left shoulder in charge on enemy's wagon train at Medley near New Creek, W.Va., 1/30/64. Wound dressed at home of Mr. McMechen in Moorefield, W.Va., 1/31/64; then to Harrisonburg for two weeks; then to Gen. Hosp. at Staunton until 5/1/64. Brown horse "Bonaparte" appraised at $2000 MWIA at Sappony Church, 6/29/64. Elected Capt. of Co. H, 43rd Va. Cav. (Mosby's command), 4/5/65 at North Fork Church in Loudoun Co. Paroled at Winchester, 5/8/65.

BERRY, CHARLES JAMES: enl. 10/1/62 at Charles Town in Co. B of 12th Va. Cav. as Pvt. Present Nov./Dec. 1863. Absent wded., Jan./Feb. 1864; date and battle not stated. Sent to hosp., 3/31/64. Unofficial source (Baylor and VSL) state wded. at Todd's Tavern, 5/5/64. No further record.

BILLINGS, HENRY MARTIN: enl. in Co. B of 12th Va. Cav. as Pvt. (date and location not stated). POW at Smithfield, Jefferson Co., W.Va., 9/15/63 (Ft. McHenry, 9/17/63). Later POW rolls at Ft. McHenry state "absent and unaccounted for." No further record.

BONHAM, JAMES EDWARD: 5'10½", light complexion, blue eyes, light hair. enl. 4/1/63 at Mt. Jackson in Co. B of 12th Va. Cav. as Pvt. POW at Smithfield, Jefferson Co., W.Va., 9/16/63 (Ft. McHenry, 9/17/63; Pt. Lookout, 11/2/63). Exchanged 11/1/64. POW in Clarke Co., 2/7/65 (Ft. McHenry, 2/11/65). Oath of Allegiance to U.S. at Ft. McHenry, 5/1/65. d. by 1900.

BRATNER, GEORGE WARREN: 5'10", dark complexion, gray eyes, brown hair. enl. 9/28/62 at Shepherdstown in Co. D of 12th Va. Cav. as Pvt. POW at Beverly Ford, 6/9/63 (Old Capitol Prison). Paroled 6/25/63. Present Sept./Oct. 1863-July/Aug. 1864. No further record. Paroled at Mt. Jackson, 4/18/65. m. Blanche Ann Hendricks.

BUCHANAN, THOMAS E.: enl. 2/20/62 at Martinsburg in Co. F of 12th Va. Cav. as Pvt. POW 10/20/62; location not stated (Old Capitol Prison, 10/21/62). Exchanged 5/12/63 (Ft. McHenry, 5/17/63). Paroled 5/17/63 and sent to Ft. Monroe for exchange. Present July/Aug. 1863. AWOL in Madison Co. since 9/18/63. Not present again until April, 1864. Wded. 5/5/64 at Todd's Tavern. Trans. to Gilmor's 2nd Md. Cav., 8/13/64.

BUZZARD, ALBERT: enl. 5/26/62 in Co. A of 12th Va. Cav. as Pvt. Sept./Oct. 1863 roll reports him AWOL since 9/8/63 and supposedly deserted. No further record.

CARNIGHAN, CHARLES H.: Absent at Newtown, Nov. 1862. Present July/Aug. 1863.

CHAMBERS, JOHN M.: 5'8", fair complexion, brown eyes, brown hair. enl. 9/29/62 at Shepherdstown in Co. D of 12th Va. Cav. as Pvt. Wded. at Brandy Station, 6/9/63. Present Sept./Oct. 1863-July/Aug. 1864. No further record. Paroled at Mt. Jackson, 4/18/65.

COLBERT, JOHN JAMES: enl. 4/25/62 at Charles Town in Co. A of 12th Va. Cav. as Corp. KIA at Poolesville, Md., 9/8/62.

COLBERT, RICHARD W.: POW record in 12th Va. Cav. file shows him as a Pvt. in Co. D. Rebel deserter at Harpers Ferry, 7/16/63. Confined at Ft. McHenry, 7/31/63; then to Ft. Delaware, Aug. 1863. Joined U.S. 3rd Md. Cav. at Ft. Delaware, 9/22/63.

CONRAD, ALEXANDER N.: b. 2/14/42 in Jefferson Co. 5'11", light complexion, blue eyes, light hair. enl. 8/14/62 at Orange Court House in Co. D of 12th Va. Cav. as Pvt. Present Sept./Oct. 1863. POW at Upperville, 12/20/63 (Old Capitol Prison, 1/1/64; Pt. Lookout, 2/4/64). Exchanged 2/10/65. Admitted to Chimborazo #3, 2/15/65; debility. Furloughed 2/22/65 for 40 days. Paroled at Winchester, 4/14/65. Postwar, worked for the Baltimore & Ohio Railroad. Residing in Harrisonburg in 1907. d. 10/21/12 at Harrisonburg. bur. Woodbine Cem., Harrisonburg.

CONRAD, JAMES M. M.: enl. 2/4/63 at Mt. Jackson in Co. B of 12th Va. Cav. as Pvt. Nov./Dec. 1863-March/April 1864 rolls report him absent sick since 12/16/63. No further record. Paroled at Winchester, 4/22/65. Postwar, merchant in Baltimore, Md. Residence in 1894 at 837 N. Fulton Ave., Baltimore, Md. Alive in 1900.

COOKE, BUSHROD W.: enl. 11/1/62 at Charles Town in Co. B of 12th Va. Cav. as Pvt. Shown as 4th Corp. at 2/9/64 muster. Began service as acting commissary officer, 6/1/64. Recommended for Assistant Commissary, 8/5/64, and rank of Capt. Present Nov./Dec. 1863-March/April 1864. No further record. Surrendered at Appomattox, 4/9/65. Postwar, teacher at Trimble, Kentucky. Alive in 1900.

COPELAND, PHILIP D.: 5'7½", light complexion, hazel eyes, dark hair. enl. in Co. B of 12th Va. Cav. as Pvt. (date and location not stated). Wded. 6/21/63 at Upperville. POW at Smithfield, Jefferson Co., W.Va., 9/15/63 (Ft. McHenry, 9/18/63; Pt. Lookout, 11/2/63). Exchanged 3/3/64. Still absent at 4/30/64 muster. Unofficial source (Baylor) says wded. at Todd's Tavern, 5/5/64. No further record. Postwar, builder in Baltimore. Residence 29 Loudoun Ave., Baltimore, Md. Alive in 1900.

149

CRANE, JOSEPH: 5'7", fair complexion, blue eyes, light hair. enl. 12/1/62 at Charles Town in Co. B of 12th Va. Cav. as Pvt. Present Nov./Dec. 1863. Absent sick Jan./Feb. 1864. Still absent sick 3/25/64. Entry on 4/30/64 muster shows him absent sick at hosp. since 4/5/64. Paid Nov. 1864. No further record. Paroled at Winchester, 4/19/65. Postwar, resident of Charles Town, W.Va. d. 7/18/04 at Charles Town. bur. Zion Episcopal Cem., Charles Town, W.Va.

CURRIE (CURRY), CHARLES W.: b. 1838. 5'3", dark complexion, hazel eyes, dark hair. enl. 12/6/62 at Shepherdstown in Co. D of 12th Va. Cav. as Pvt. Present Sept./Oct. 1863-July/Aug. 1864. Admitted to Chimborazo #1, 8/20/64; debility. Discharged from hosp., 8/27/64. No further record. Paroled at Winchester, 4/21/65. d. Dec. 1879 at Martinsburg, W.Va.

DECK, EDWARD: 5'10", fair complexion, dark eyes, dark hair. enl. 4/19/62 at Shepherdstown in Co. D of 12th Va. Cav. as Corp. Present Sept./Oct. 1863-July/Aug. 1864. No further record. Paroled at Mt. Jackson, 4/18/65.

DUGAN, JAMES F.: enl. 5/1/62 at Edinburg in Co. F of 12th Va. Cav. as Sgt. Present July/Aug. 1863-July/Aug. 1864. No further record. Paroled at Staunton, 5/15/65.

ESTERDAY, JOHN S.: 5'9", light complexion, blue eyes, light hair. Residence Charles Town. enl. 7/15/62 at Harrisonburg in Co. B of 12th Va. Cav. as Pvt. POW at Smithfield, Jefferson Co., W.Va., 9/15/63 (Ft. McHenry, 9/18/63; Pt. Lookout, 11/1/63). Exchanged 2/18/65. Deserted 3/19/65. No further record.

GALLAGHER, JAMES N.: 6'1", fair complexion, black eyes, red hair. enl. 10/22/62 at Charles Town in Co. B of 12th Va. Cav. as Pvt. Present Nov./Dec. 1863. AWOL Jan./Feb. 1864. Furloughed 30 days, 3/1/64. Present April, 1864. Unofficial source (Baylor) says he participated in the attack on Charles Town, W.Va., on 3/13/65. No further record. Paroled at Winchester, 4/19/65.

GINN, CHARLES L.: enl. 8/13/62 at Orange Court House in Co. C of 12th Va. Cav. as Pvt. Last entry for March/April, 1864 shows him AWOL since 10/1/63 and dropped from the rolls. No further record. Postwar, lawyer in Frederick Co., Md., 1865-1869. d. 7/6/07 at Hampton, Va. bur. Mt. Hebron Cem., Winchester.

HEFFLEBOWER, EDWARD L.: b. 4/17/45. 6'½", fair complexion, blue eyes, dark hair. Residence Markham Station. enl. 4/25/62 at Hainesville in Co. I of 12th Va. Cav. as Pvt. Wded. 10/11/63 near Brandy Station. Unofficial source (VSL) says he was Color Sgt. at this time. Absent wded., Oct. 1863-March/April 1864. Admitted Gen. Hosp. Charlottesville, 8/15/64; acute dysentery. Furloughed 30 days beginning 9/7/64. No further record until POW at Fairfax Court House, 4/10/65 (Old Capitol Prison; Elmira, 5/2/65; U.S. Gen. Hosp. Elmira, 7/13/65). Oath of Allegiance to U.S. at Elmira, 7/19/65. d. 8/3/13. bur. Rockland Cem. near Front Royal.

HESS, CHARLES WILLIAM: enl. 4/19/62 at Shepherdstown in Co. D of 12th Va. Cav. as Pvt. Wded. at Brandy Station, 6/19/63. Absent sick, Sept./Oct. 1863. bur. St. James Lutheran Cem., Uvilla, Jefferson Co., W.Va.

HEWITT, REZIN D.: Re-enlisted in Co. B of 12th Va. Cav. as Pvt. (date and location of enl. not stated). Unofficial source (Baylor) says KIA at Millwood, 2/6/63.

HIGGINS, ANDREW J.: enl. 4/19/62 at Shepherdstown in Co. D of 12th Va. Cav. as Pvt. Unofficial source (McDonald) shows him as a 5th Sgt. POW near Berryville, 4/21/63 (Ft. McHenry, 4/28/63). Paroled 4/28/63. Bay horse appraised at $592 KIA 6/13/63. Present Sept./Oct. 1863-July/Aug. 1864. No further record. d. by 1907.

HILBERT, JOHN E.: 5'10", fair complexion, blue eyes, auburn hair. Date and location of enl. not stated. First record shows him as Co. blacksmith, 2/1/64. Next record lists him as POW captured at Berryville by 12th Pa. Cav., 1/29/65 (Old Capitol Prison, 2/3/65; Elmira, 3/3/65). Oath of Allegiance to U.S. at Elmira, 6/30/65. Postwar, resident of Washington, D.C.

HUNTER, HENRY CLAY: enl. 11/25/62 at Charles Town in Co. B of 12th Va. Cav. as Pvt. Present Nov.Dec. 1863-March/April 1864. No further record. Surrendered at Appomattox, 4/9/65.

HURST, JOHN HARRY: Listed as 2nd Lt. in Co. F of 12th Va. Cav. (date and location of enl. not stated). Absent sick, Nov. 1862. POW at Beverly Ford, 6/9/63 (Old Capitol Prison, July, 1863; to Johnson's Island, 8/8/63). To Ft. Monroe for exchange, 9/16/64. Admitted Gen. Hosp. #4, Richmond, 9/23/64; chronic diarrhea and emaciation. Furloughed 40 days. No further record.

ISLER, CHARLES H.: enl. in Co. B of 12th Va. Cav. as Pvt. (date and location of enl. not stated). Unofficial source (Baylor) says POW at McGaheysville, 4/27/62. Baylor also says wded. just east of Charles Town in early Dec. 1862. Only official record is MWIA at St. James Church, Brandy Station, 6/9/63.

KEPHART, JACOB M.: enl. 4/19/62 at Shepherdstown in Co. D of 12th Va. Cav. as Pvt. Absent on special duty with Gen. Stuart, Sept./Oct. 1862. Nature of duty not stated. Present Sept./Oct. 1863. d. 12/20/63; typhoid fever.

LEGG, JOHN W.: 5'8", dark complexion, gray eyes, brown hair. enl. 7/1/63 at Orange Court House in Co. F of 12th Va. Cav. as Pvt. Present July/Aug. 1863. Present Nov./Dec. 1863. Absent on horse detail beginning 3/31/64, but present at 4/30/64 muster. Present July/Aug. 1864. No further record. Paroled at Winchester, 4/19/65. d. 2/15/74.

LUCAS, BENJAMIN F.: enl. 4/19/62 at Shepherdstown in Co. D of 12th Va. Cav. Elected Lt., 3/1/63. Present Sept./Oct. 1863-Jan./Feb. 1864. KIA at Sycamore Church, 9/15/64.

MAKIN (MACKIN), PATRICK: b. 1842. 5'3", fair complexion, blue eyes, light hair. Machinist at Harpers Ferry Armory. POW records list him in Co. D as Pvt. POW captured by 1st N.Y. Cav. in Clarke Co., 12/27/62 (Camp Chase, 11/3/62). Trans. to City Point for exchange, 3/28/63. POW at Halltown, Jefferson Co., W.Va., 7/15/63 (Pt. Lookout, 8/17/63). Exchanged 12/25/63. POW captured by 21st N.Y. Cav. in Jefferson Co., W.Va., 4/26/64 (Camp Chase, 12/15/64). Final parole at Harrisonburg, 5/8/65. Postwar, entered Soldier's Home at Richmond, 7/30/94. Dismissed from Soldier's Home at Richmond, 6/16/98.

MANNING, CHARLES JAMES: b. at Charles Town. 5'11", light complexion, blue eyes, brown hair. enl. 4/1/62 at Woodstock in Co. B of 12th Va. Cav. as a Pvt. Present Nov./Dec. 1863. AWOL Jan./Feb. 1864. Present March, 1864. Absent on furlough of indulgence at 4/30/64 muster. No further record. Paroled at Charles Town, W.Va., 5/5/65. Postwar, agent and salesman of farming implements at Bridgewater. Resident of Bridgewater. d. at Bridgewater.

MANNING, GEORGE UPSHAW: Date and location of enl. in Co. B of 12th Va. Cav. not stated. Unofficial source says captured near Summit Point, 2/12/63. No Federal POW records confirm.

MANNING, WILLIAM PRICE: 5'7", light complexion, blue eyes, dark hair. enl. 6/26/62 at Harrisonburg in Co. B of 12th Va. Cav. as Pvt. POW near Sharpsburg, Md., 9/28 or 9/30/62 (Ft. McHenry, 2/13/63). To Ft. Monroe for exchange, 2/14/63. Admitted Gen. Hosp. Petersburg, 2/18/63; debilitas. Released from hosp. 2/24/63. POW at Pommelsville, 6/2/63 (Ft. McHenry, 6/12/63). To Ft. Monroe for exchange, 6/26/63. Present Nov./Dec. 1863. Absent sick, Jan./Feb. 1864. Present March/April 1864. No further record. Paroled at Charles Town, W.Va., 5/5/65. d. 2/11/01 at Washington, D.C.

MARSHALL, ALFRED C.: 6'0", light complexion, gray eyes, dark hair. enl. 7/27 (year not stated) at Culpeper Court House in Co. E of 12th Va. Cav. as Pvt. Present Sept./Oct. 1863-July/Aug. 1864. No further record. Paroled at Millwood, 4/20/65.

MAURY, MAGRUDER: Present in Rockbridge Artillery, July/Aug.-Sept./Oct. 1861. Present Jan./Feb. 1862. Trans. to 12th Va. Cav. in April, 1862. Appointed chaplain of 12th Va. Cav., 10/20/62. Relieved of this duty by Gen. Lee and ordered to report to Gen. Elzey, 8/10/63. Resigned 11/7/64, having been called to the charge of a church in Fredericksburg where there was no minister.

McCLEARY, CHARLES F. M.: 5'10", dark complexion, blue eyes, light hair. enl. 2/20/62 at Martinsburg in Co. F of 12th Va. Cav. as Pvt. POW 10/19/62, location of capture not stated (Old Capitol Prison, 10/21/62). Sent to Ft. Monroe for exchange, 10/31/62. To Camp Chase, 1/3/63. To City Point for exchange, 3/28/63. POW at Greenspring, 8/2/63 (Ft. McHenry, 8/25/63; Pt. Lookout, 9/16/63. To City Point for exchange, 3/16/64. Admitted to Chimborazo #3, 5/1/64; gunshot wound in chest and head. Furloughed 60 days beginning 5/6/64. POW at Mt. Crawford 3/1/65 or Mt. Jackson, 3/5/65 (Ft. Delaware, 3/12/65). Oath of Allegiance to U.S. at Ft. Delaware, 6/10/65.

McDONOUGH, CHARLES T.: Listed in Co. B of 12th Va. Cav. as Pvt. (date and location of enl. not stated). POW captured by 1st N.Y. Cav. near Charles Town, 12/26/62 (Camp Chase, 1/3/63). To City Point for exchange, 3/28/63. No further record.

McMULLEN, LAMBERT G.: 5'9", light complexion, gray eyes, brown hair. enl. 3/8/62 at Winchester in Co. F of 12th Va. Cav. as Pvt. POW captured by 12th Illinois Cav. at Bunker Hill, 9/5/62 (Camp Chase, 9/15/62). Trans. to Cairo, Illinois, for exchange, 9/29/62. POW at Shepherdstown, W.Va., 7/13/63 (Baltimore; then to Pt. Lookout, 8/21/63). Exchanged 12/25/63. Absent at Staunton hosp. beginning 3/20/64. Trans. to Md. Line (probably 2nd Md. Cav. Battalion, CSA), 4/29/64.

MOLER, RALEIGH V.: enl. 12/11/62 at Shepherdstown in Co. D of 12th Va. Cav. as Pvt. Only entry shows him AWOL, Sept./Oct. 1863. No further record. Unofficial source (Shepherdstown *Register* obituary, 10/25/17) says Moler captured and sent to Ft. Delaware, where he was kept in confinement for some time. Finally, with several other Confederate prisoners, he accepted an offer of freedom from the Union authorities with the provisio that he go west for garrison duty at Ft. Laramie, Wyoming. The Confederates agreed to this condition, hoping to escape on their way west or at Ft. Laramie. Their scheme proved futile, however, as there was no opportunity for escape en route, and once in Wyoming, the hostile Indians were so numerous that it was suicidal to run the gauntlet. Therefore, Moler served in the U.S. Army until the end of the war, fighting Indians on the Great Plains. Postwar, farmer at Uvilla, Jefferson Co., W.Va. m. Lydia E. Engle, 1/5/69. bur. Elmwood Cem., Shepherdstown, W.Va.

MOORE, ALBERT L.: 5'9", dark complexion, hazel eyes, dark hair. enl. 4/19/62 at Charles Town in Co. A of 12th Va. Cav. as Pvt. Present at 12/31/62 muster. Paid $281.73 for service 6/30-12/31/63. Roll for Nov./Dec. 1863 reports him AWOL since 12/18/63. Present Jan./Feb.-July/Aug. 1864. No further record. Paroled at Charles Town, W.Va., 4/22/65. Postwar, resident of Charles Town, W.Va.

MOORE, FONROSE M.: enl. 6/30/63 at Charles Town in Co. B of 12th Va. Cav. as Pvt. Admitted Gen. Hosp. Staunton, 11/17/63; syphillis. Present at 12/31/63 muster. AWOL Jan./Feb. 1864. Absent on horse detail at 3/31/64 muster. Present at 4/30/64 muster. No further record. Unofficial source (VSL) says KIA, date and battle not stated.

MOORE, VINCENT G.: enl. 5/16/62 at Charles Town in Co. A of 12th Va. Cav. as Pvt. Present at 12/31/62 muster. Present Nov./Dec. 1863. Absent Jan./Feb. 1864. Present March/April-July/Aug. 1864. POW at Ashby's Gap, 12/26/64 (Pt. Lookout). Oath of Allegiance to U.S. at Pt. Lookout, 6/6/65. Postwar, resident of Kearneysville, W.Va.

NICELY, CHARLES A.: 5'8½", florid complexion, gray eyes, light hair. Residence Jefferson Co. enl. 9/25/62 at Charles Town in Co. B of 12th Va. Cav. as Pvt. POW at Front Royal, 10/27/63 (Camp Chase, 10/31/63; Rock Island, Illinois, 12/4/64). Oath of Allegiance to U.S., 1/17/65.

O'BANNON, WILLIAM A.: 5'6", dark complexion, brown eyes, dark hair. POW at Charles Town, 11/10/62 (Ft. McHenry). Paroled 11/12/62.

OSBOURN, ALEXANDER LINK: 5'8", dark complexion, gray eyes, dark hair. enl. 4/19/62 at Shepherdstown in Co. D of 12th Va. Cav. as Pvt. Shown as 4th Corp. on Jan./Feb. 1864 roll. Present Sept./Oct. 1863-March/April 1864. POW at New Market, 10/9/64 (Pt. Lookout, 10/20/64). Oath of Allegiance to U.S. at Pt. Lookout, 6/15/65. Postwar, resident of Shenandoah Junction, Jefferson Co., W.Va. Furnished rosters of Co. A and Co. D for William N. McDonald's *Laurel Brigade* book.

PETTIT, ALLEN O.: Prewar residence, corner of Howard and Conway Streets, Baltimore, Md. enl. 4/1/62 at New Market in Co. F of 12th Va. Cav. as Pvt. Absent at Luray, Nov. 1862. Present July/Aug. 1863. Roll for Sept./Oct. 1863 shows him AWOL since 9/22/63. Roll for Nov./Dec. 1863 lists him as under arrest since 11/29/63. Still under arrest, March/April-July/Aug. 1864. No further record. Paroled at Winchester, 5/31/65.

PRATHER, DENTON: b. 1844? 5'8", florid complexion, brown eyes, brown hair. April 18, 1865 parole record in 12th Va. Cav. file shows him in Co. D as Pvt. Alive at Leetown, W.Va., in 1907.

RANSON, THOMAS DAVIS: 5'11", fair complexion, light blue eyes, brown hair. After recovering from Cross Keys wound, enl. 11/25/62 at Charles Town in Co. B of 12th Va. Cav. Served as scout for this Co. and for Gen. Stuart and Gen. Lee. POW at Tom's Brook, 10/9/64 (Pt. Lookout, 10/20/64). Oath of Allegiance to U.S. at Pt. Lookout, 6/17/65. bur. Thornrose Cem., Staunton.

SADLER, LEONARD L.: enl. in Co. B of 12th Va. Cav. (date and location of not stated) as Pvt. No other information.

SHANER, ALEXANDER J.: 5'7¾", fair complexion, gray eyes, brown hair. enl. 3/9/62 at Winchester in Co. F of 12th Va. Cav. as Corp. Present July/Aug. 1863. Roll for Sept./Oct. 1863 reports him AWOL since 9/18/63 in Madison Co. FOW captured by 12th Pa. Cav. at Cedar Creek, 11/16/63 (Camp Chase, 12/8/63; Ft. Delaware, 3/4/64). Oath of Allegiance to U.S. at Ft. Delaware, 6/19/65.

SHEPHERD, JAMES W.: enl. 8/12/62 at Charles Town in Co. A of 12th Va. Cav. as Pvt. Present at 12/31/62 muster. Present Sept./Oct.-Nov./Dec. 1863. Absent sick at Gen. Hosp. Staunton, Jan./Feb.-March/April 1864. Present July/Aug. 1864. No further record.

SHEWBRIDGE, JOHN H.: enl. 10/16/62 at Shepherdstown in Co. D of 12th Va. Cav. as Pvt. On detail as blacksmith, Nov. 1862. Regt. blacksmith, Sept./Oct. 1863. Chief Regt. blacksmith, Nov./Dec. 1863-July/Aug. 1864. No further record. Surrendered at Appomattox, 4/9/65.

SIMPSON, FRANK A.: 5'8", fair complexion, blue eyes, dark hair. April 18, 1865 parole at Winchester lists him as a 2nd Lt. in Co. D of the 12th Va. Cav.

SMITH, JOHN WILLIAM: enl. 4/1/62 at Woodstock in Co. B of 12th Va. Cav. Absent on detail at Q.M. Dept., Sept.-Nov. 1862. On detail at Brigade H.Q., Nov./Dec. 1863. Chief clerk at Brigade H.Q., March/April 1864. KIA at Todd's Tavern, 5/5/64.

SMITH, ROBERT GORDON: Absent Nov. 1862. Present July/Aug. 1863. AWOL in Madison Co. 9/28/63. Roll for March 31, 1864 reports him absent on horse detail beginning 3/31/64. Present at 4/30/64 muster. No further record. Paroled at Winchester, 4/17/65. Postwar, gardner at Winchester. Member Turner Ashby Confederate Veteran Camp #22 at Winchester.

SNAPP, WILLIAM HARRISON: b. 7/13/39. Residence Shenandoah Co. enl. 9/11/63 at New Market in Co. K of 12th Va. Cav. as Pvt. Present Nov./Dec. 1863-March/April 1864. Absent on horse detail, July/Aug. 1864. No further record until POW at Edinburg, 2/16/65 (Ft. McHenry, 2/22/65). Oath of Allegiance to U.S. at Ft. McHenry, 5/1/65. Postwar, post office at New Market. d. 10/14/19. bur. Lutheran Reformation Church Cem., New Market.

TERRELL (TERRILL), JOHN URIEL: 5'6", fair complexion, gray eyes, brown hair. Residence Jefferson Co. enl. 3/1/62 at Woodstock in Co. B of 12th Va. Cav. as Pvt. On detail as courier to Maj. Thomas B. Massie, 12th Va. Cav., Sept. 1862. Present Nov./Dec. 1863-Jan./Feb. 1864. AWOL March/April 1864. No further record. Paroled at Winchester, 4/18/65.

THOMPSON, CHARLES E.: enl. 8/14/62 at Charles Town in Co. A of 12th Va. Cav. as Pvt. Present at 12/31/62 muster. POW at Purcellville, 5/12/62 (Ft. McHenry). To Ft. Monroe for exchange, 5/20/63. POW at Middleburg, 5/27/63 (Ft. McHenry, 6/12/63). To Ft. Monroe for exchange, 6/26/63. POW at Purcellville, 7/17/63 (Pt. Lookout, 7/31/63). Joined U.S. Service, 2/23/64, as Pvt. in Co. F of 1st U.S. Vol. Inf. Trans. to Co. I, 1st U.S. Vol. Inf., 6/6/64. Deserted 8/1/64 in Pasuotank Co., North Carolina. d. by 1907.

THOMPSON, WILLIAM S.: 5'8", fair complexion, dark eyes, dark hair enl. 12/22/62 at Charles Town in Co. B of 12th Va. Cav. as Pvt. POW at Harpers Ferry, 4/29/63 (Ft. McHenry). Paroled 5/2/63 and sent to City Point for exchange. Wded. in the leg near Upperville, 6/21/63. Present Nov./Dec. 1863. Gray horse appraised at $650 KIA at Parker's Store, 11/29/63. Trans. to J. W. Carter's Battery Va. Horse Artillery, 4/20/64. Present 4/30-8/31/64. Bay horse appraised at $3000 KIA at Tom's Brook, 10/8/64. No further record. Postwar, moved to Marietta, Georgia, in 1865. Moved to Atlanta, Georgia, in Jan. 1871. Worked in Atlanta as lawyer. m. Nena Danner. Alive in 1900.

TIMBERLAKE, GEORGE A.: 5'7½", fair complexion, brown eyes, dark hair. enl. 4/17/62 at Conrad's Store in Co. B of 12th Va. Cav. as Pvt. Unofficial source (Baylor) says wded. slightly at Front Royal, 8/11/62. Absent wded. Sept.-Nov. 1862. POW captured by 1st N.Y. Cav. in Clarke Co., 2/6/63 (Camp Chase, 2/13/63). To City Point for exchange, 3/28/63. POW at Parker's Store, 11/29/63 (Old Capitol Prison, 12/5/63; Pt. Lookout, 2/4/64). To Aiken's Landing for exchange, 9/18/64. Admitted Chimborazo #4, 9/22/64; chronic diarrhea. Furloughed 9/24/64 for 60 days. No further record. Paroled at Winchester, 4/22/65. Postwar, farmer with post office at Clearbrook in Frederick Co., Va. Member of Turner Ashby Confederate Veteran Camp #22 at Winchester. d. 2/13/13. bur. Stonewall Cem., Winchester.

TIMBERLAKE, JAMES H.: enl. 4/27/62 at Conrad's Store in Co. B of 12th Va. Cav. as Pvt. Absent on scout, Nov./Dec. 1863. Present Jan./Feb.-March/April 1864. Unofficial source (VSL) says wded. (date and location of battle not stated). No further record. Final parole at Greensboro, North Carolina, 4/26/65.

TIMBERLAKE, SETH MASON: enl. 4/17/62 at Conrad's Store in Co. B of 12th Va. Cav. as Sgt. Nicknamed the "fighting sergeant" and "Uncle Seth." Unofficial source (Baylor) says horse KIA at Front Royal, 8/11/62. Unofficial source (Baylor) says wded. east of Charles Town in early Dec. 1862. Absent on horse detail, Nov./Dec. 1863. Present Jan./Feb.-March/April 1864. No further record. Paroled at Greensboro, North Carolina, 4/26/65.

TRUSSELL, CHARLES WILLIAM: 5'11", fair complexion, blue eyes, dark hair. enl. 4/17/62 at Conrad's Store in Co. B of 12th Va. Cav. as Sgt. POW at Charles Town, 9/20/62. No Federal records confirm his capture. Present Nov./Dec. 1863. Absent sick, Jan./Feb. 1864. Absent on provost guard beginning 3/30/64. Present at 4/30/64 muster. No further record. Paroled at Winchester, 4/19/65. d. 1888. bur. Edge Hill Cem., Charles Town, W.Va.

TRUSSELL, EDWARD C.: 5'8", fair complexion, blue eyes, dark hair. enl. 4/17/62 at Conrad's Store in Co. B of 12th Va. Cav. as Pvt. Iron gray mare appraised at $620 KIA at Warrenton Springs, 10/12/63. Present Nov./Dec. 1863. Absent with leave, Jan./Feb. 1864. Present March/April 1864. No further record. Paroled at Winchester, 4/24/65. d. by 1900.

TRUSSELL, JAMES TEMPLE: 5'9", fair complexion, blue eyes, dark hair. enl. 4/17/62 at Conrad's Store in Co. B of 12th Va. Cav. as Pvt. Present Nov./Dec. 1863-March/April 1864. No further record. Paroled at Winchester, 4/24/65. Postwar, farmer at Kearneysville, W.Va.

VAUGHN, OLIVER H.: Nov. 1862 roll for the 12th Va. Cav. shows him in Co. F and absent in Rockingham Co. No further record.

WASHINGTON, BUSHROD CORBIN: 5'8½", light complexion, gray eyes, light hair. Trans. 8/23/62 to Co. B of 12th Va. Cav. as Pvt. Recommended to fill the 2nd Lt. vacancy of Co. B. Gen. J.E.B. Stuart's endorsement stated: "His escape from the enemy on the night of the 11th Oct. was made under the most difficult circumstances and exhibited a remarkable degree of coolness, skill, and courage." Appointed 2nd Lt., 12/3/63. Present Nov./Dec. 1863. Signs roll as commanding Co. B, March, 1864. Unofficial source (Baylor) says wded. at Todd's Tavern, 5/6/64. Issued clothing, 9/12/64. No further record. Paroled at Winchester, 5/4/65. Postwar, editor of William Naylor McDonald's *A History of the Laurel Brigade*. d. 2/24/19 at the home of his son Nathaniel in Spokane, Washington.

WASHINGTON, GEORGE: Unofficial source (VSL) says he served in Co. B of 12th Va. Cav. VSL also says KIA (location and date of battle not stated). d. 6/30/63. bur. Zion Episcopal Church, Charles Town, W.Va.

WHITTINGTON, JAMES W.: enl. 3/1/62 at Woodstock in Co. B of 12th Va. Cav. as Pvt. On detail as Co. blacksmith, Sept.-Nov. 1862. Present Nov./Dec. 1863. AWOL Jan./Feb. 1864. No further record.

WILLIS, WILLIAM BEALE: Trans. 8/12/62 at Harrisonburg into Co. B of 12th Va. Cav. as Pvt. POW near Winchester, 6/2/63 (Ft. McHenry, 6/12/63). To Ft. Monroe for exchange, 6/26/63. Absent on scout, Nov./Dec. 1863. Absent with leave, Jan./Feb. 1864. Roll for March 31, 1864 reports him absent with leave beginning 3/28/64. Present 4/30/64 muster. No further record. d. 1920 or 1921 in Waco, Texas.

WILT, GEORGE W.: enl. 7/1/63 at Charles Town in Co. A of 12th Va. Cav. as Pvt. Sept./Oct. 1863 roll reports him AWOL since 7/9/63. Still AWOL Jan./Feb.-March/April 1864. No further record.

WILTSHIRE, CHARLES B.: enl. 5/15/62 at Charles Town in Co. A of 12th Va. Cav. as Sgt. Present at 12/31/62 muster. Present Sept./Oct.-Nov./Dec. 1862. Unofficial source (Baylor) says wded. on New Creek Grade, about five miles above Williamsport, W.Va., 1/30/64. Official records show him wded. 2/28/64, location of battle not stated. Absent wded., Jan./Feb.-July/Aug. 1864. Document signed by surgeon of 30th Mass. Inf. says Wiltshire wded. in the right lung at Opequon Crossing, 3/29/65 — "The ball entered the upper lobe of the lung and did not make its exit." d. 4/4/65.

WILTSHIRE, JAMES B.: enl. 4/17/62 at Conrad's Store in Co. B of 12th Va. Cav. as Pvt. POW at Winchester, 10/13/63 (Ft. McHenry; Pt. Lookout, 11/2/63). d. 7/11/64 at Pt. Lookout; cause not stated.

WINTERMOYER, WILLIAM H.: 5'6", florid complexion, gray eyes, dark hair. enl. 4/19/62 at Shepherdstown in Co. D of 12th Va. Cav. as Pvt. Absent sick, Sept./Oct.-Nov./Dec. 1863. Disability Certificate at Gen. Hosp. Harrisonburg, 1/29/64 — "tertiary syphillis from which he has been suffering for 18 months." Discharged 2/23/64. Paroled at Mt. Jackson, 4/18/65. d. by 1907.

WRIGHT, SAMUEL S.: enl. 4/17/62 at Conrad's Store in Co. B of 12th Va. Cav. as Pvt. Present Nov./Dec. 1863. KIA in fight on New Creek Grade about five miles above Williamsport, W.Va., 1/30/64.